FIGHTING SUICIDE BOMBING

FIGHTING SUICIDE BOMBING

A Worldwide Campaign for Life

I. W. Charny

PRAEGER SECURITY INTERNATIONAL
Westport, Connecticut • London

Library of Congress Cataloging-in-Publication Data

Charny, Israel W.
  Fighting suicide bombing : a worldwide campaign for life / I. W. Charny.
    p.   cm.
  Includes bibliographical references and index.
  ISBN 0–275–99336–1 (alk. paper)
  1. Suicide bombers—Psychology.   2. Suicide bombings—Prevention.   3. Terrorism—
  Prevention.   4. Terrorism—Religious aspects—Islam.   5. Martyrdom—Islam.
  6. Suicide—Religious aspects—Islam.   I. Title.
  HV6431.C454   2007
  363.325′17—dc22   2006025924

British Library Cataloguing in Publication Data is available.

Library of Congress Catalog Card Number: 2006025924
ISBN: 0–275–99336–1

First published in 2007

Praeger Security International, 88 Post Road West, Westport, CT 06881
An imprint of Greenwood Publishing Group, Inc.
www.praeger.com

Printed in the United States of America

The paper used in this book complies with the
Permanent Paper Standard issued by the National
Information Standards Organization (Z39.48–1984).

10 9 8 7 6 5 4 3 2 1

PRIMO LEVI writes that
Evil is contagious and the inhuman being robs others of all human feeling. Evil procreates itself. It multiplies, corrupts the conscience of others and surrounds itself with collaborators . . . because of fear or because of some form of temptation.[1]

To **LIFE,**
In its sacredness,
To be protected in as many ways possible,
For the greatest possible number of human beings on our
planet!

and, more personally:
To dearest Judy, always,
and to all our family.

I. W. Charny
Jerusalem
August 2006

Contents

Selected Woldwide Case Incidents

IRAQ: WHERE U.S. TROOPS AND IRAQIS SET OUT TO REBUILD A POST-SADDAM COUNTRY

January 19, 2004. A suicide bomber detonated a pick-up truck laden with 500 kg of explosives at the main gate of the US headquarters in Iraq, killing at least 20 people and injuring more than 100. Most of the dead and injured were Iraqis queuing at a security cordon to enter the Republican Palace, the head of the US military and civil administration in Baghdad.

—The Guardian[1]

July 10, 2005. Suicide bombers struck Baghdad killing at least 33 people and wounding dozens more in three attacks on an army recruiting center, a police convoy and civilians.

—Moscow Times[2]

July 13, 2005. A suicide car bomber sped up to the American soldiers distributing candy to children and detonated himself. Months earlier, in September, 2004, 35 Iraqi children had been killed by a string of bombs as American troops were handing out candies at a government celebration of a new sewage plant, but many of the families blamed the Americans because their presence had attracted the insurgents to the ceremony.

—Jerusalem Post[3]

July 15, 2005. An "all-day suicide bomb blitz" claimed 22 lives in Baghdad. There were "at least" eight suicide car bombs on this day. One of the bombers blew up his vehicle on a bridge near the home of President Jalal Talabani, killing at least two presidential guards and wounding several others. "The string of attacks, which began at 8 a.m. and ended more than 12 hours later, traumatized the capital on a day [Friday] that is normally reserved for prayer and family."

—*New York Times*[4]

July 17, 2005. 99 people were killed and more than 180 injured in suicide bombings over the past two days in Iraq, including an attack which exploded a fuel tanker parked in the center of Musayyib, about 45 miles south of Baghdad in which the death toll was at least 90. The tanker entered Musayyib after being searched at the city's entrance. The bomber who was strapped with an explosive vest approached the tanker and detonated.

—*CNN*[5]

Unheard of only a few decades ago, suicide bombings have rapidly evolved into perhaps the most common method of terrorism in the world . . . The numbers in Iraq alone are breathtaking: about 400 suicide bombings have shaken Iraq since the U.S. invasion in 2003, and suicide now plays a role in two out of every three insurgent bombings. In May, an estimated 90 suicide bombings were carried out in the war-torn country—nearly as many as the Israeli government has documented in the conflict with Palestinians since 1993.

—*Washington Post*[6]

AN EXTRAORDINARY WAVE OF ATTACKS—INCLUDING THE WORST DEATH TOLL IN BAGHDAD IN A SINGLE DAY[7]

September 14, 2005. A suicide car bomber ripped through a gathering of day laborers waiting for work at 6:50 a.m. at Aruba Square in the Khadamiya district of northern Baghdad, one of Baghdad's largest Shi'ite districts, where large numbers of laborers typically gather in the morning in hopes of being hired for the day. At least 75 people were killed and another 162 were wounded. The bomber used a new tactic: luring dozens of day laborers to a van with promises of work and then blowing it up.

More bombings and attacks followed throughout the day with several each hour, as police cars careened wildly through the city struggling to restore order and hospitals overflowed with wounded people. There were at least fourteen bombings on this Wednesday that left much of the capital city paralyzed. The death toll of 167 was the worst in a single day in Baghdad since U.S. troops overthrew Saddam two-and-a-half years ago.

September 15, 2005. The following day, a second day of suicide bombings killed at least twenty people and wounded at least thirty-one.

September 17, 2005. Over four days after Al-Qaeda in Iraq declared all-out war on the Shiite majority, more than 250 people have been killed. At least fifty-two more people were killed or found dead throughout the country on September 17.

BESLAN, RUSSIA: A FIRST DAY IN SCHOOL WHERE BOMBS AND BULLETS REPLACE TRADITIONAL FLOWERS

September 1, 2004. Muslim Chechen terrorists took hundreds of schoolchildren and adults hostage on September 1 at School Number One in Beslan. In the Russian Federation, "First September" of every year is a holiday known as the "Day of Knowledge," when children are accompanied to school by their parents and other family members dressed in their best clothes. After listening to speeches, the First Graders give a flower to the Last Graders, and the Last Graders then take the First Graders to their first class.

On September 3, a chaotic battle broke out between the terrorists and Russian security forces. There are conflicting versions of what happened. One is that the terrorists set off bombs, killing children and themselves. When Russian Special Forces stormed the school, the hostage-takers set off more large explosions, totally destroying the gymnasium and setting much of the building on fire, while special forces commandos blew holes in walls to allow hostages to escape. The television broadcast chilling images of heavily armed hooded assailants among the hundreds of women, children, and men. The TV pictures showed hundreds of people crowded into the gym beneath a string of explosives dangling from a basketball hoop. By the time the event had concluded, 344 civilians were killed, at least 172 of them children, and 727 were wounded.

The attack on the Beslan school came a day after a suicide bombing in Moscow killed ten people, and just over a week after two Russian passenger planes crashed following explosions and killed all ninety people aboard. Beslan residents left teddy bears and flowers at the gutted school as a tribute to those killed.

—Compiled from *Wikipedia Encyclopedia* and the *Associated Press*[8]

A Muslim Web site in the United Kingdom, YusufIslam, commented: "Nothing is more precious to a parent than the love of their offspring, but for the parents of Beslan we can only share the tears and convey our deepest sympathies, though no words or effort could ever bring those children back . . . The fact that the hostage takers were reportedly Muslim makes it difficult for some to avoid the conclusion that the religion of Islam must be the cause of this demented act . . . The religious premise of the oft-repeated accusation disappears when you look closer at the facts: how opposed to the teaching of Islam this kind of act is. Even the most unlearned of Muslims know that the Prophet of Islam was always so merciful to children and their mothers . . . Crimes against innocent bystanders taken hostage in any circumstances have no foundation whatsoever in the life of Islam and the model example of Prophet Muhammad, peace be upon him . . ."

—YusufIslam.org.uk[9]

BEERSHEVA, ISRAEL: RETURNING WITH BOMBS FOR A FOLLOW-UP VISIT TO A HOSPITAL WHERE ONE HAS BEEN TREATED KINDLY

In December 2004, Wafa Samir Bas, a 21-year-old Palestinian woman, came to Soroka Hospital in Beer Sheva in Israel after suffering burns to many parts of her body when a gas canister exploded in her home. She received a number of blood transfusions in the course of the doctors saving her life. When she recovered, one of the doctors joked with her about her having "Jewish blood flowing in her arteries." Her family subsequently sends a letter of appreciation to the hospital.

In June 2004, six months later, Wafa comes back to the hospital as a suicide bomber to blow up the very hospital in which she had previously received dedicated treatment. In order to gain clearance to enter the hospital grounds, she used the medical follow-up form which called for her to come back to the hospital for an examination. Fortunately, she was apprehended in time by security people and the tragedy was averted.[10]

Wafa was a student at Al-Quds Open University whose president, Sari Nusseibah, is a well-known Palestinian leader for nonviolence. Wafa said she did not want to detonate herself at Soroka because many Arabs are treated there and was interested in another hospital in central Israel, but she agreed to a request by Al-Aksa brigades to take advantage of her access to Soroka Hospital.

There have been numerous attempts to send suicide bombers into Israel disguising themselves as patients asking for entry on humanitarian grounds to seek medical treatment. "A senior Israeli security official pointed out that human rights groups have often harshly criticized Israel in the past, for carrying out inspections on sick Palestinians requiring medical treatment in Israel. "Our dilemma is how to differentiate between those who really seek treatment and sometimes those who may suffer from terminal illnesses and figure they have nothing to lose by agreeing to carry out a suicide attack."" Earlier in 2005, a Hamas operative who planned to launch a suicide bomb attack in Israel succeeded in entering the Jewish-occupied West Bank on the basis of his being a possible kidney donor.[11]

After being apprehended, Wafa said: "It didn't bother me at all if children and women were killed by my suicide bomb. You have killed children too. You think that you are innocent and that only we are terrorists?" But then Wafa also added the telltale information: "Even when I was a little girl, I dreamt of dying as a *shahid* (martyr) for Allah. I am prepared to sacrifice myself a thousand times."[12]

—*Yediot Achronot* (Hebrew daily newspaper) and the *Jerusalem Post*.

Preface

This may be a politically incorrect book, but it is unshakable in supporting life for all people.

We are in the process of an historical war between the World of Arrogance [i.e. the West] and the Islamic world, and this war has been going on for hundreds of years . . . Is it possible for us to witness a world without America and Zionism? You had best know that this slogan and this goal are attainable, and surely can be achieved. —Iranian President Mahmoud Ahmadinejad speaking at the "World without Zionism" conference in Teheran[1]

Too many Muslims are being killed . . . The suicide attacks are turning many Muslims against the jihadis altogether . . . [However] the alternatives these critics recommend are no less violent . . . Many . . . suggest that jihadis diminish their efforts in Iraq and revert to spectacular attacks in the West. —*New York Times*[2]

For a long time it has seemed that suicide bombings and other megaterrorist events occur only in selected places on earth, so that one might get along fairly safely by staying out of the bad neighborhoods—like we used to do in New York City, for example.

Although it has long been known that many groups and political movements engage in terrorist murders of a wide variety of victims, in recent years there has been an increasing awareness of Islam as a major and growing source of terror. But here again many people in the West are drawn into the illusion that maybe the core of Islamic terror is their hatred of Israel and their wish to destroy that country and its people, so again the thought appears that perhaps there are ways of staying out of the bad neighborhood, or at least working at solving that basic problem and thereby putting an end to growing Islamic terror.

Slowly but surely, it has become clear that the facts don't fit. Suicide bombings and other terrorist actions have flourished in such diverse and far-off places as Sri Lanka, India, Chechnya, Russia, Turkey, Saudi Arabia and more that bear little to no relationship to the Israel-Palestinian conflict. Still, it is hard to shake off the illusion that the one issue keeping terrorism going is that Israeli-Palestinian conflict, and indeed much of Arab rhetoric keeps up a steady pounding of accursed Israel and the damned Jews.

As this book goes to press, news has come of an unprecedented plot for suicide bombers to down some ten British airplanes on their way to the United States—according to some reports the explosions were to be done over major U.S. cities so as to cause further enormous destruction. The deputy commissioner of London's Metropolitan Police was quoted as saying that the aim of the plot was "mass murder on an unimaginable scale."[3]

The plotters, who were identified mainly as Britons of Islamic origin, many from a Pakistani background, were reported to have planned to use liquids that would be smuggled into the airplanes in their hand luggage to create devastating explosions. According to the *New York Times*, a warning issued to air security officials noted that "plotters working to down trans-Atlantic airplanes might have used the most ordinary of household items and chose peroxide." The *Times* story noted further that, "The use of such compounds as a main charge was popularized in suicide bombings by Palestinian terrorist groups," and that in general "only tiny amounts of liquid materials were needed to bring down a plane."[4]

Peroxide had been used in the July 7, 2005, London mass transit attacks in which 66 died and over 700 were wounded.

One of the thousands of passengers who were stranded by canceled flights was heard saying on CNN that he had always planned his travels to stay away from the trouble spots in the world, but that there no longer was safety anywhere in the world, and we had reached a point where we were all at risk.

The *Pakistan Times* reported that, "Draconian hand luggage restrictions similar to those imposed by London and Washington were introduced in Australia, Canada, Ghana, Kenya, Hungary, Italy and Switzerland. Other countries affected included Belgium, Denmark, the Czech Republic, Russia, Sweden, Thailand and Spain, where 191 people died in an extremist attack in 2004."[5]

In a major speech to the World Affairs Council in Los Angeles, the United Kingdom's prime minister, Tony Blair, called for a radical rethink of foreign policy to combat "reactionary Islam" with an "arc of moderation" across the Middle East. The prime minister said that "the battle against global extremism will not be won unless a moderate, mainstream Islam is empowered."[6]

United States' President George W. Bush was quoted as saying that the United States was "at war with Islamic fascists who will use any means to destroy those of us who love freedom."[7] But clearly it is not only the United States that is at war. In the largest sense, the civilization that promotes life for human beings is at war with a counter-civilization that espouses, promotes, and announces proudly that it literally "loves death" (explicit quotations from Al-Qaeda to this effect will be reported later).

The latest Harry Potter book, *Harry Potter and the Half-Prince,* published in 2005, opens where the evil of Voldermort and his Death Eaters has grown so strong that they are spilling over into the Muggle world of real people.

Now try writing Osama bin Laden, Al-Qaeda, and the suicide bombers in a rewrite of the above. In our very real world, the four suicide bombings in London on July 7, 2005, and the failed attempts to replicate the bombings two weeks later on July 21 have now joined the terror bombings in Madrid (which were not suicide bombings) on March 11, 2004 (known to many as "3/11"), and the incredible airplane suicide bombings in New York and Washington on September 11, 2001 (very much known also as "9/11"); and there is no place in the world that stands exempt today. Thus, Oriana Fallaci warned her naïve and escapist Italian compatriots that Al-Qaeda most certainly will also come to Italy.

> Will the massacre touch us too?—will it really touch us the next time? Oh, yes. I haven't the slightest doubt. I've never had the slightest doubt. I've been saying this, too, for the last four years. And I add: They have not yet attacked us [only] because of their need for a landing zone, a bridgehead, a handy outpost named "Italy." Geographically handy because it is the closest one to both the Middle East and Africa; that is, to the countries that supply the greatest number of troops. Strategically handy because we offer succor and collaboration to those troops.
>
> "It's only a question of time. Al Qaeda will strike you soon," said Al Faqih, the exiled Saudi who became friends with Bin Laden during the conflict with the Russians in Afghanistan and who according to the American secret services, is a financer of Al Qaeda, adding that the attack upon Italy is the most logical thing in the world. Is not Italy the weak link in the chain of allies in Iraq?[8]

If my publisher were to allow me, I might retitle my book, *How Can Voldermort's Suicide Bombers Do It?*

A nightmarish insecurity has enveloped U.S. troops in Iraq as well as Iraq police and troops in the newly reconstituted security forces and troops of the post-Saddam effort at government, and a nightmarish insecurity is enveloping the world because the attacks using suicide bombers are increasing in many regions and are everywhere. In Iraq on one single day in April 2005, four separate suicide bombings erupted one after another successively[9]; in July 2005, there were "at least" eight suicide bombings on a single day.[10] In a single month, the same April 2005, there was an unbelievable number of sixty-seven suicide bombings in Iraq.[11] In May 2005, there were an estimated ninety suicide bombings.[12]

Many of us will remember when we were shocked at a single suicide bombing anywhere. Who knows what the record numbers will have become by the time this book is published, and who would ever have believed we would be seeing such numbers anywhere in the world?

For the Western world at this writing, the two most prominent and symbolically impressing events of suicide bombings are those of September 11 in the

United States, and July 7 in London. In both cases, Al-Qaeda delightedly showed off its trademark of carrying out several essentially simultaneous major suicide bombings. The simultaneous attacks are acted with what one might even think of as the grace and precision of concert performers, except that theirs are concerts of hell and death. A new form of ambush warfare has come into our world. Yesteryears' feared cloaked assassins jumping out of the shadows to knife and kill one or a handful of victims have become transformed into exploding bomb carriers wearing bomb-laden belts on their persons or carrying them in their cars. The suicide explosion is a sudden moment of hell. Its deadly boom sends shudders through peoples' beings, and flying bloody body parts and stumps strike out capriciously in every direction. A new mode of killing, and along with it insane, blind terror, has taken a center stage in a more mad, uncivilized world.

The reader will find at the end of the book an assembly of representative incidents of suicide bombings which are taking place in an ever-increasing number of countries, regions, and locations in the world. As time goes by, the list could be many more pages and could fill a book of its own. To read the existing list is also an experience for the reader that challenges one's ability to maintain a sense of awe, horror, and protest at repeated incidents of injuries, gore, and death.

This is and is not an academic book. It is not written in a conventional formal style. As one reader said, it is written "in a very personal style and your humanity, concern, heartbreak, and genuine compassion resonate throughout the book." At the same time, it is a book that is well grounded in the responsible and objective reports, studies, and essays on suicide bombers that our Western world has produced thus far. The above reader also gives the manuscript high marks for its coverage, and that it is "certainly thorough in its grasp and use of the extant literature."

At the same time, the reader does not feel comfortable with the fact that I move back and forth between my personal emotions and judgments and systematic analytic scholarship, and this will also be true of many other readers who are accustomed to separate facts and rational analysis from emotional and spiritual responses. For my part, I do like combining these modes. I do appreciate that there are tensions in combining the emotional and the analytic, but I like both modes touching each other. I believe in an integration of the two with a back-and-forth commentary between them leading to a synthesis that is enriched by the contradictions between these two ways of experiencing life. I think the emotional and analytic should very much live together, check one another, and complement one another.

What I do agree with is that it is that I have a responsibility to distinguish between personal statements of my opinions and presentations of information and evidence from identified sources. I hope that the reader will find that I have done this by a combination of first-person statements in which I take responsibility for my feelings and personal judgments, along with the extensive endnotes and bibliographic references that I have provided which document clearly the many specific sources of information.

Altogether, I want to invite the reader on a journey with me in which we will explore, both intellectually and emotionally, a series of challenging questions and complexities about the suicide bombers.

A simple restaurateur in Jerusalem where I live said to me:

> It is already a World War, but the world doesn't want to recognize it. The Muslim terrorist groups are exploding everywhere—look at the map of the globe: Riyadh, Casablanca, Bali, New York, Washington, Madrid, London . . . It will take a few more years with more and more suicide bombings and other terrorist attacks, and then our world will realize that it has been led into a new kind of World War.

This was the kind of conversation that is personally satisfying to me, not only because it was with someone who agrees with my views, but because in general I am the kind of person who enjoys and respects the wisdom and common sense of what I call an "everyday person." I try to have lots of conversations like that with merchants and taxi drivers, and my impression is that the plain folk I meet—in Israel, the United States, and England, which are my most frequent hangouts—already understand that what is happening in the world is a new form of genocidal terrorism, including the awesome and frightening suicide bombers. They understand that the crazy explosions of planes, trains, buses, and crowds of people are not only instruments of the endless local conflicts our world has always seen, but a growing movement in our time of a hardcore and mainly Islamic expansionism that is seeking to dominate the world (including to regain a lost glory of Islam such as it had centuries ago)—even if not all of the Muslims doing the exploding today already know consciously that they want to take over the world. It's a new kind of World War. And it is growing on us insidiously.

People who tend to be "innocents" like to have a clear-cut old-fashioned explanation for everything that happens, in terms that are familiar to them, and especially explanations of evil as events that are based on some tangible unfairness, deprivation, humiliation, and insults to the poor hapless people who were then "forced" to commit their evil acts out of their frustration at the injustices done to them.

For innocents there is no evil that grows out of plain *e-v-i-l*—a ruthless search for power, conquest, injury, and death to others, any of which, and all of which together, are plain satisfying to the cruel instincts in the people committing these acts. So the world of the innocents remains a good one even as planes topple magnificent towers in New York, bombs explode trains in Madrid (these were terrorist attacks by explosions that were set off at the targets without suicide bombers), and suicide bombers explode underground trains and a bus in London.

The causes of it all? Listen to the periodic Al-Qaeda broadcasts, and ask academics and liberals who sympathize with the terrorists, and you'll hear the real culprits of all the killings are rotten global America, of course; also the forever turbulent Middle East, including without hesitation the archevil of imperialistic Zionism; and understandably also the revolts of impoverished peoples. No mention is made of a widespread commitment of many (I will emphasize over and over again, not all) Muslims and Islamic nations to a deadly murderous jihad against the infidels, or to a quest for world domination by the representatives of Allah.

We need to know that the gods of most peoples can turn imperialistic and genocidal. Christian gods have taken their turns in the past, like in the Crusades when Jewish and Muslim blood flowed like water at their hands. Jews too have committed genocidal murders, though admittedly on a smaller scale, so they too have shown that all of God's children can do it and that all the gods can become sponsors of murder campaigns. Right now, it is the Muslims' turn.

Liberal intellectuals can be the biggest innocents around. The funny thing for me is that, to this very day, I consider myself more of a "liberal" thinker than any other political designation I can apply to myself. But the huge difference that has developed for me is that I am a liberal who knows that there is enormous evil in this world, and that we have to fight it or perish. Sometimes I say that I am a pacifist who carries a gun for self-defense. That is what World War II was about. And the emerging World War III is no different.

Writing this book has brought me smack up against a considerable number of my friend-liberals in the academic world, including editors in the publishing world, and including the kinds of successful academics to whom publishers turn for reviews of manuscripts who, in my judgment, automatically defend anyone who looks like or sounds like a possible revolutionary or oppressed person fighting for justice and self-determination. If the killers have a just political or sound cause, they at least want to "understand" them, if not actually justify their "fight for freedom." I deeply disagree.

One liberal reader of this manuscript said most complimentarily, "This is an extremely interesting and ambitious work. The work seeks to engage a number of areas that flow from the author's analysis and experience of suicide terrorism, including: problems with western psychiatry, Islam, democracy and western models of government, and culture of life versus culture of death. The work is therefore potentially fascinating and important." This is strong lively music to an author's ears. But having said these wonderful words, this quite thoughtful reviewer proceeds to criticize the book, because "Islam is given a bad press, including the fact that 'Charny's standards for treating Islam are different from those he uses to discuss Christianity or Judaism, being more forgivable and charitable to the latter and less charitable to Islam.'"

Let me be clear on this point. I will express nothing but respect for Islamic religion and culture, but I will in no way refrain from condemning Islamic terror and killing. For the record, I have already commented that Christianity has gone through many periods of incredible genocidal killing, and not only in the Crusades that I mentioned, but also in the vicious Inquisition, and in so many of the great European wars which were essentially the work of Christian nations. I also said that I know that my own Judaism has on its hands a series of "melanoma-type" spots of having committed genocidal massacres, so that my own people's vaunted traditions of ethics and greater nonviolence are also marred by indications of our very much being members of the same human race as other peoples who have specialized more in mass murder. But the facts of *our* times are that the growing number of mega-suicide-bomber terrorists are, for the most part, from the fundamentalist interpreters of Islam as a religious-culture that is at war with the West and the rest of the world in a jihad.

The above reviewer said that I am citing questionable sources that are negative on Islam. Yes, I do quote from some writers and scholars who have become systematically identified with anti-Islamic thinking such as Oriana Fallaci, Daniel Pipes, and Bat Ye'or, but in each case I identify for the reader, and in the last two cases discuss at some length and criticize the known extreme position of the writers while still making use of their legitimate scholarship and judgments. Moreover, I cite many contemporary news reports of Islamic violence from the daily newspapers and media that give the facts about Islamic violences in a wide range of countries around the world.

At the same time, I also do quote and refer to a great many voices in the world of Islam that are committed to nonviolence and a shared peaceful existence with other religions and cultures, and I treasure these voices deeply. In fact, I build the book toward a climax of a proposal for working with the peace-living people in Islam in an effort of *all* of us together to fight the next World War not only militarily, but as a battle of a Culture of Life against a Culture of Death.

Yes, I do adopt the thesis of a "clash of civilizations," or a battle between a culture of life versus a culture of death, which in our time is represented to a large but not at all exclusive extent by Judeo-Christian values versus fundamentalist Islam. Such a battle between cultures is not new in human history at all. Over the centuries, and today as well, the creation of a culture of death has been and is the work of many and various peoples far removed from any connection to Islamic thought, including pagan peoples in the distant past who butchered much of the world, fierce indigenous native peoples who as a matter of rule slaughtered other native peoples; in modern times, Nazi Germany and its super-science-and-industry of death; also in modern times Communist utopias, such as led by Stalin in the West and by Mao tse-Tung and Pol Pot in southeastern Asia that executed astronomic numbers and proportions of nations—and no less their own people; or blood-curdling rampages of death against one's own neighbors if not against one's own family in Rwanda and several other countries on the African continent.

The human species—our species—is expert at splitting into cultures which are deeply devoted to killing and death, even as the generic human experiences of savoring life—eating, procreating, and bringing up new generations—somehow remain the predominant mode of life, even for many of the most dedicated killers when they return to their abodes from their killing work.

Right now, it is Islam's turn to be at the center of the culture of death in our world and the rest of us who believe in life need to fight them, but without a holier-than-thou denial of how our various nations, ethnicities, religion and such have been there and done that killing in other eras.

Nonetheless, according to my above liberal critic, you can't predict a war between the civilizations is unfolding, or you are Muslim-bashing, and of course thereby you are very politically incorrect. The above reviewer only too gleefully notes that the United States has also violated the rules of the Geneva Convention, and that democratic cultures and governments also violate life and decency frequently enough, so why do I get up such a lather about current predominance of Muslim people in setting off waves of terrorist death all around the globe? He writes:

> I find it difficult to credit the rosy view that things are so right with democracies. Charny's instantations of what he means by culture of death are all focused on Islam, thus eviscerating his rhetorical move ... Having read bits of the Old Testament, I can attest that Islam is not unique in calling for the elimination of the unfaithful who are ipso facto enemies.[13]

I agree completely. But how much repetition and clarification does it take to get across that I am not against any specific nation, ethnicity, religion, political group, or whoever for who they are, but I am against any group that in their time takes on the role of stewarding and leading a culture of death and executing other human beings en masse. I agree that humans have always gone for the jugular of eliminating enemies. Moreover, in my judgment, virtually all religions have in them a dialectic of peace-loving, life-respecting values versus calls for death-making. Only right now it is Islam which is up to bat and, on the whole, opting for the death-making concepts that are all too available in its dogma. The need to be violent and justify violence runs deeply and naturally through many aspects of much (I will keep saying, not all) Arab culture. Thus, see the totally unexpected context of the Arab Doctors' Association in Egypt and how the association advised its doctors not to extend any help to victims of the deadly earthquake and tsunami that hit Asia in December 2004, including in Sri Lanka and in India, because the tsunami was an act of God.

> The Arab Doctors' Association secretary-general, Dr. Abd Al-Mun'im Abu Al-Futuh ... [said] that this earthquake was divine punishment because of the Muslims' oppression by the infidels, invaders and occupiers headed by the U.S., and that therefore we have no interest in what had happened![14]

Speaking of medical concepts, my critic also concludes that I am suffering from "an underlying ethnocentrism" because I also conclude that the suicide bombers are intrinsically "pathological." For me it means that they are antihuman, unhealthy, and undesirable, and certainly not deserving as being regarded as "normal people" who are "simply" suffering a political disturbance or protest. My argument is that suicide bombing is at least no less dangerous to human life than smoking, and that the Surgeon Generals of our Western world need to declare that suicide bombing, with great certainty, brings death to human beings, and therefore should be considered "sick," "abnormal," and all the other words we westerners use in our culture for differentiating between behaviors that enhance health and behaviors that kill. We shall see later that the language of our Western psychiatric classification system is ill prepared to deal with this subject as well as with a whole host of related issues of violence and evil in human life. To me this means that we in the West have our work cut out for us to revise our psychiatric classification system of human ill will and destructiveness, but not that there is anything wrong with identifying suicide bombers and other terrorists as disturbed, evil, and rotten.

So many nonpsychological or psychiatric professionals repeatedly express the truth naively that the suicide bombers must be "off their rockers;" for they are inherently violating the commonsense normality of life. Following the July 7 Al-Qaeda terrorist attack in London in which three Underground sites and a bus were exploded by four suicide bombers, an editorial in the *International Herald Tribune*, attributed to the *New York Times*, quoted author Joseph Conrad from 100 years ago "that a terrorist act is 'purely destructive,'" and continued:

> Madness alone is truly terrifying, inasmuch as you cannot placate it either by threats, persuasions or bribes . . . we still use that language—madness—because it still applies to the murder of innocent people . . . The only 'purpose' the London bombing can be said to have is to puncture the veneer of civilization, to show us what the terrorists hope is the madness that lies behind it . . . to show us how little we can rely upon the edifice of normalcy . . .[15]

As far back as 1986, I proposed in the formal mental health literature that *all* cases that are evaluated by psychiatrists and clinical psychologists should be required to include simultaneously an evaluation of whether a person is doing serious harm to their *own* life potential, along with an evaluation of whether a person is doing serious harm to the life potential of *others*. In my definitions, the "normal" and "healthy" are those who protect, enhance, love, and live life and help or allow others to do so, and the "sick" and "disturbed" are those who do harm, degrade, insult, and destroy life, whether their own or the lives of others.

It is also very important to add that just because we call someone "sick" doesn't mean they have a right to come back and demand the mercy we do offer people who are carried away by uncontrollable personal torment and tragically hurt another person. There are a certain number of cases of violence that do deserve the mercy of society such as a legal verdict of "not guilty by virtue of insanity." But mass killing is first of all criminal and most certainly calls for a response by the criminal justice system. Even if the killer is truly crazy, which is sometimes the case, the fact is that the crime is so huge that it must be punished. Mass killers deserve no mercy.

This book seeks to tell the truth about who are the main suicide bombers in our world today without fear of political incorrectness. As the previous editorial also concluded, "London has shown . . . [that] to be flung into our fears is a way of discovering who our adversaries really are—and that they are not ourselves."[16]

Moreover, this book predicts soberly, based on the facts and informed judgments of many political and security analysts, let alone common sense, that in the foreseeable future the next scenes in our lives very highly probably *will* include:

suicide bombings + *megaweapons of destruction*

Please ponder for a moment the enormity of such terrible events to come.

In making this prediction, I am not gloating nor am I a prideful predictor. I am a grieving, fearful human being who is aware that too many people and cultures in our human species make the most horrible choices to destroy and maim *millions* of fellow human beings, often including their own people. If there is anything that can be done to prevent the tragedy, or to prepare for it to minimize the destruction of lives that will ensue, and to prevent further recurrences, more than anything else I want to do these things that will save lives.

But It Is Unshakable in Supporting Life for All People

This book is not for those who need to be politically correct. Nor is it for innocents who can only see our upcoming world as one of the wholesome coexistence and mutual enrichment of different cultures, religions, and nations—that I too so deeply want and toward which I work. It is about a grim reality that is spreading insidiously.

Let it be noted again, we are not writing about something that is really new, for evil thrusts of power and murder have characterized our human race from the earliest time, wherever humans are to be found—including by Jews, Christians, Muslims, and so many other ethnicities, religions, and nationalities, and including everywhere we look, in Southeast Asia, the Indian continent, Africa, wherever. Where the next biggest destruction will come from, I don't know. I do know it will be from human beings like today's suicide bombers who set no limits on their killing.

In this book we examine through the lenses of modern psychology and psychiatry how the human mind can do these disgusting things. The book is a serious attempt to understand the suicide bombers, even respectfully in a sense, within their cultural and psychological worlds. In fact, as I wrote this book, I found myself *almost* capable of experiencing the suicide bombers' mindsets, including the sense of sacrifice and dedication of many of them, and also the incredible security of becoming part of a doctrinaire group where one gives up one's own ability to think and choose. Nonetheless, my firm conclusions are fully on the side of Western civilization's historic injunction, "Thou Shalt Not Kill."

Our understanding of the suicide bombers does not turn into acceptance or romanticization of them as underdog freedom fighters or devoted martyrs to their people. For all our efforts to understand the culture-meanings and human motivations of suicide bombers, we remain unambiguously against killing civilians and unambiguously denounce the suicide bombers.

I will be calling for a solution to the scourge of suicide bombings and terror through a combination of a resolute military battle against them, including tough preemptive legal and police means which necessarily *will* threaten to undermine our democratic civil rights, but I am willing to take the risks.

The liberals will hate the call for full force against the terrorists, and especially the approval of major preemptive measures to find the potential terrorist killers—in their mosques and community centers, when they make their purchases of explosive materials in hardware stores, through their e-mails and cellular communications, in the course of their travel to and from other countries, and so on—*before* the explosions.

On the other hand, the law-and-order people will want to destroy the terrorists and be done with them, and they are going to be impatient and totally skeptical of my further proposal that we also wage a "war" for a cultural value of respecting life over the prevailing culture of death of the suicide bombers and other terrorists. Famed psychiatrist Robert Jay Lifton has cautioned that although suicide bombing arouses our fears of "world ending or apocalyptic violence, it is tempting to plunge into combating suicide bombing in a way that resembles it and that is a great danger."[17]

This book may be politically incorrect, which means that it steps on certain toes, by calling Islamic suicide bombings and other terror a serious world threat; favoring without reservation an intelligence-police-military war against terrorism and strict intelligence-police measures to hunt down, identify, and take strong preemptive legal actions against potential suicide bombers and terrorists, notwithstanding the real threats and abuses of human rights that have to follow (and then need to be regulated and corrected by us); and daring to dream of a worldwide campaign for cultural change and evolution to greater respect and protection of human life.

Let me formulate and discuss further the three major types of political incorrectness in which this book engages:

- Political Incorrectness 1: I stand firmly against Islamic terrorism (again I emphasize not against Islam itself as a faith or culture), notwithstanding the disdain and irate criticisms of many liberals-academics who define much of the war against terror as imperialism and prejudice against Islam

There are those who don't want to talk about the facts that most—though indeed not all—of the terrorism in the world today is being executed by Muslims. Those who don't want to say so include many wonderful peace-loving people, including many academics who want to believe that if you say nice and decent things about whoever, in this case Muslims, they will come through and be decent. Oriana Fallaci describes this kind of piety as a "decadence of Westerners . . . to be identified with their illusion of being able to deal amiably with the Enemy, and even less with their fear. A fear that induces them to meekly host the enemy, to attempt to conquer him with sympathy, hoping that he will allow himself to be absorbed; while [the enemy] is the one who wants to absorb."[18]

Some highly skilled observers-researchers of Muslim terrorism have ended up being branded unjustifiably by much of the academic world as firebrand anti-Muslims, and as if have been polarized out of the intellectual establishment, so that there are respectable intellectual circles where their writings are suspect and are not at all to be cited. In fact, some of these critics of Islam really were the resolute whistle blowers who told us early on, firmly and even courageously, that a nascent worldwide movement of Islamic terror was afoot in the world, and was going to get worse and worse and worse.

Too many liberal-academic-intellectuals hate the sounds of resolute antiterrorism. They equate them with proviolence, prowar, jingoism, globalism, and imperialism. In my judgment, they are wrong. The suicide bombers and other terrorists, like the utopian visionaries of Nazism and Communism, are serious threats to the lives of decent people.

Still, there is no question that a huge number of Muslims, followers and leaders, do want peace and nonviolence, and in this book we are committed to hearing appreciatively and with a real sense of kinship many life-caring voices in Islam, and not only the hateful pronouncements of Al-Qaeda's "Death-Eaters."

- Political Incorrectness 2. If suicide bombers and other terrorists are threatening to destroy more and more lives and are aiming for world domination, we certainly need to fight them and very hard. The battle against terrorists has to be conducted with every police and military power possible, also with legal and police means to limit evil terrorists' rights and to ferret them out as early as possible.

For those who care about democracy and human rights, these tactics are very touchy and involve an inevitability of abuses of innocent people, overuse of power, and fascist violations of human rights, even if unwittingly. A liberal intellectual, like myself, is legitimately on guard against such abuses and violations of democracy, and also will oppose aspects of the battle against terrorists that are inhumane and unlawful if less violent and less invasive procedures to stop the terrorists could have been used. Yet, notwithstanding the dangers to human rights and democracy, I am firmly and fully for killing terrorists when they are ready to strike, and for heading them off as early as possible with investigative skill, courage, and preemptive power.

- Political Incorrectness 3. I also believe that if the battle against the suicide bombers and terrorists is limited to legal and police-military power, and does not extend to a major spiritual battle over values, the battle will be lost. How often now have we seen a modern military power vanquish and occupy an enemy nation and people and then fail bitterly to build a functional society? In many cases, the occupied society turns with glee on its conqueror and defeats it from within in a grueling guerrilla-revolutionary-terrorist battle for independence.

The above understanding leads many decent people to a conclusion that although a military battle against terrorists may be justified, it is largely and most often unwise. I do not agree, and thus I become politically incorrect to these lovers of peace and opponents of military actions. I am strongly in favor of President Bush and Prime Minister Blair's "war on terror." (That does not mean I agree with how we went into war in Iraq without international authorization and consensus and seriously weakened the U.N. system.) But I do believe that we also need a new kind of culture campaign to make suicide bombings and terrorism unacceptable, unattractive, even disgusting in the very cultural milieus which currently honor and sponsor such warfare.

The capstone of this book will be a proposal for a *"Worldwide Campaign for Life,"* with a large investment of international funds and energies over many years to promote new levels of caring, respect, and protection of human life in our world. The proposal very much includes working with available Islamic national, folk, and culture leaders who will be ready to join our rest of the world in a new conception of the sacredness of human life. So now I am again politically incorrect with the Bush and Rumsfeld people or the tough guys who count so much on military-police-legal power that they are uninterested and scoff at soft-hearted people who will try to talk with Islamic society and win them over.

In further fact, I am not even sure that all my academic colleagues are going to be happy about my wanting to launch a creative dialogue *with* Islamic culture, because some of them will also charge me with being an ethnocentric meddler who does not respect the rights of another culture to seek its own evolution and development from within its own self, and not from the efforts of another culture that regards itself as superior to them in seeking to influence them.

Altogether, I really have to thank my publisher for going with this book. Those who hate wars will dislike us. Mental health and other intellectuals who are convinced that mental health concepts need to be value free, and that we should not judge the values of another culture (in this case, the violence of Islam), or define suicide bombers as "pathological," will dislike us. Cultural relativists who romanticize primitive, fundamentalist cultures will hold us in low regard. Conservatives who believe only in strong actions and don't trust efforts to bring about culture change will be contemptuous of us. Is there anyone left?

The truth is that I do believe there are millions of people who are left who really want peace. I believe that even many opponents of this book will agree that it is built sensibly and with an effort at fairness on a careful and interesting assembly of information. I also believe that there will be many people who will like this book very much: first because we seek to be true to the facts of the killer suicide bombers in our world today; second because, surprisingly we are empathic to the terrorists as fellow human beings; third we stand clearly against the suicide bombers and are willing to use tough means to fight them; and fourth because, more than anything else, we are committed to a larger culture battle for a culture of life rather than a culture of death for all us human beings in all our societies.

In short, I think that many, many common sense thinkers, who care about living and letting other people live as full lives as possible, will genuinely respect and like this book.

Acknowledgments

I want to thank very deeply Pauline Cooper, my longtime colleague who serves as Office Manager of the Institute on the Holocaust and Genocide in Jerusalem, and who is also in charge of preparation of manuscripts, for her arduous and excellent work first, in assembling the research information for this work, and then for producing and maintaining the quality review of this manuscript with its demanding array of information, bibliographic references, and endnotes.

I also thank my colleague and friend of many years, Marc I. Sherman, M.L.S., Assistant Director of the Institute on the Holocaust and Genocide in Jerusalem, and Bibliographic Consultant, for his tireless professional excellence in reviewing and supervising the assembly of information for the Bibliography and endnotes as well as for his thoughtful review of the manuscript.

To Professor Alexander Alvarez, Professor of Criminal Justice at Northern Arizona University, author of the excellent book, *Governments, Citizens, and Genocide*, and Co-Editor-in-Chief of *Genocide Studies and Prevention*, the official journal of the International Association of Genocide Scholars, my warm appreciation for agreeing at a critical earlier phase to review the manuscript both for a potential publisher and for me, for his thoughtful and helpful comments and no less his serious encouragement that I continue the process of this work.

My special and unorthodox thanks also go to two very talented editors who will remain unnamed, who helped me greatly in developing this work, especially in struggling with the definitive issue of standing uncompromisingly against the new threat to the world of Islamic terrorism and identifying the actors honestly, while but remaining carefully respectful and appreciative of Islam and its millions of adherents as dear fellow human beings. One of these editors and I parted ways because she felt that I did not achieve the latter goal as fully as she believed I must. The second felt I had achieved the goal and asked his publishing house to publish the work, but for whatever reasons was not successful. In the case of both editors, I felt that I benefited from a deep, probing, and very thoughtful concern with the basic issues of this work, as well as the wonderful sound advices of accomplished literary mentors.

To my commissioning editor at Praeger Security International (Greenwood Press), Elizabeth Deemers, my warmest thanks for her unstinting acceptance of the meaningfulness and quality of this work. In this case too there is a further unorthodox twist in that Elizabeth Deemers was also my editor at her previous post at the University of Nebraska Press for my just-published, *Fascism and Democracy in the Human Mind: A Bridge between Mind and Society.* I have been given an amazing gift of seeing these two major works appear in the same year, something I could barely dream would ever happen, and the key professional person who has made this possible and who has extended to me such great respect and trust is Elizabeth.

Finally, as I say in another way in the Dedication, this book is a further expression of my lifelong quest to contribute to some measure of greater protection of our human lives on this planet. It is clear to me, including from the deeply helpful psychoanalysis I underwent many years ago, that the key personal source of my concern with protecting human life was my childhood experience of seeing my beloved mother suffer over eight years and then die from cancer. But from my personal grief and anger have come a firm conviction that the ultimate purpose of science, knowledge, and indeed all our civilization is to protect human life. For me the readiness of peoples and groups to destroy other human lives en masse is a collective malignant process, where one part of our shared humanity turns against and seeks to destroy en masse the others of us. We are nothing, and we stand a good chance of being destroyed as a species if we do not put a stop to such malignancy. I think that by the time this book will have appeared it will have become all too clear that our world is on the verge of endless threats to life everywhere on this planet, among them prominently the growing development of what I call "transnational genocidal terrorism," and that *we must fight back*!

I also want to acknowledge with thanks any number of writers and organizations who have kindly given me permission to quote from their works:

Nili Keren, Seminar Hakkibutzim [College of the Kibbutzim], Ramat Aviv, Israel, for permission to quote her citation of Primo Levi in a review article: Evil in the mirror, *Haaretz (English Edition)*, January 7, 2005.

Roger Cohen for permission to quote from his article: 10 reasons terror meets silence from Muslims. *International Herald Tribune*, October 26, 2005. Retrieved from the *New York Times*.

Khaled Abou El Fadi, Professor of Law at UCLA Law School, for permission to quote from his remarks about the concept of jihad from: Interview with Khaled Abou El Fadl, "Jihad Gone Wrong." Qantara.de, 10.27.05. Retrieved from the Web: www.scholarofthehouse.org/jgowrinwikha.html, December 20, 2005.

Robert Melson, Professor of Political Science at Purdue University, and past president of the International Association of Genocide Scholars, for permission to quote his personal communication.

Guardian Newspapers Limited for permission to quote from the article, "What does al-Qaeda really want?" by Jason Burke, March 25, 2004. With permission of Guardian/Observer Syndication.

Christian Century for permission to quote from the article, "Front Lines of Terrorism: The View from India," by Vatsala Vedantam. Copyright 2002 *Christian Century*. Reprinted by permission from the January 16–23, 2002, issue of the *Christian Century*. Subscriptions: $49/yr. from P.O. Box 378, Mt. Morris, IL 61054.

Steven Emerson, for permission to quote from his Prepared Statement before the Senate Judiciary Committee on Terrorism, Technology and Government Information: Foreign Terrorists in America. Five years after the World Trade Center bombing, February 24, 1998.

Alan Dershowitz, Professor of Law at Harvard Law School, for permission to quote from his article: Does oppression cause suicide bombing? Some overprivileged Muslims support a culture of death while impoverished Tibetans celebrate life. *Jerusalem Post Magazine*, May 21, 2004.

Daniel Ben-Simon, for permission to quote from his article: Rabbis and imams unite against religious extremism. *Haaretz* (English Edition), January 9, 2005.

Middle East Media Research Institute (MEMRI). I have drawn on the databanks of the Middle East Media Research Institute (MEMRI) many times and am pleased to express my appreciation for the thoroughness and accuracy of their data and for their standing permission to quote their materials. "The Middle East Media Research Institute (MEMRI) is an independent, non-profit organization that translates and analyzes the media of the Middle East." For further information: Middle East Media Research Institute, P.O. Box 27837, Washington, DC 20038-7837, phone 202-855-9070, fax 202-955-9077, e-mail: memri@memri.org. All citations from MEMRI have been retrieved from the Web site memri.org.

How Can They Do It?

Crowd: "Allah Akbar.Allah Akbar. Allah Akbar."
Male voice on loudspeaker: "What is your goal?"
Crowd: "Allah."
Male voice on loudspeaker: "What is your constitution?"
Crowd: "The Koran."
Male voice on loudspeaker: "Who is your leader?"
Crowd: "The Prophet Muhammad."
Male voice on loudspeaker: "What is your path?"
Crowd: "Jihad."
Male voice on loudspeaker: "What is your greatest desire?"
Crowd: "Death for the sake of Allah."   —Al-Arabiya TV, July 2005[1]

THREE SPECIFIC OPENING QUESTIONS

1. Is the suicide bomber's *suicide* crazy and immoral, or is it tragically understandable as an act of martyrdom?
2. Are the suicide bombers' *murders* of others evil or heroic?
3. Do the answers really vary only with whether you are a Muslim or a member of the victim groups?

Regrettably, it is often the major cataclysms in our human history that are needed to catalyze progress in our world. Thus, World War II made possible the emergence of the United Nations, and the incredible Holocaust by the Nazis, especially the savage organization of factories of death for the Jews and also the murders of millions of other victim peoples along with the Jews, gave rise to the *United Nations Convention on Genocide*. Today, the horrible new scourge of suicide behaviors is a remarkable opportunity for all of us to come to new grips with a number of basic aspects of human violence.

On the one hand, it is as if there may be a special moral power in the statement the suicide killers are making because they make the ultimate sacrifice by also killing themselves at the outset as their means for killing their enemy.

On the other hand, the fact that the suicide bombers blow themselves into total oblivion and nothingness shocks and horrifies normal human beings in our Western world as a violation of the most basic instinct of self-preservation. We are accustomed that even warriors normally seek to preserve some possibility of surviving for themselves.The suicide bombers' manner of death is so explosive, including eradicating any traces of their previous physical existence, that it goes against the grain of endless human stratagems not only for saving one's life if possible, but also for preserving and burying one's remains when dead with the fullest commemorative honor possible. In some cultures, the meaningfulness of preserving the body for proper burial in a sense can be even greater than the meaning of life. Thus, there is a tremendous importance in Chechen tradition of giving proper burial to the dead. In a book published in Moscow (*The Second Chechen War*), author Vtoraya Chechenskaya notes strikingly that "federal forces have been able to demand higher ransoms from Chechens for returning the dead bodies of their kidnapped relatives than for releasing them alive."[2]

The magnitude of deaths at the hands of suicide bombers so far (but who knows what is yet to come!) is generally not as great as the toll of lives taken in many shoot-out and bomb-out military events. But the nature of the suicide-killing act is so dramatic that it has galvanized worldwide attention, concern, and a desire to understand how the suicide bombers can possibly commit their acts.

The actions of the suicide bomber so contradict the survival instinct that it is hard to understand how they can do it. Suicide bombing is a strange act to the rational mind. It is an act that dramatically combines in one fell blast profound violations of two widely accepted moral standards—the prohibition against killing oneself, and the *Thou Shalt Not Kill* prohibition against taking other people's lives. Insofar as sometimes our minds can take in the possible logic or justification of either of these violences against life (e.g., suicide in great despair, or killing in revolt against a totalitarian government), the simultaneous combination of the two violations of the sacredness of life makes many of us feel perplexed if not virtually crazed. *How can they do it?* How can a behavior that is so opposed to the survival instinct become so widely practiced? How can the evil of killing and horribly injuring so many plain people going about their everyday lives become so favored?

Suicide bombing touches core issues about human violence. The suicide bomber takes us first to the very core of human sensibility and wisdom about *killing oneself*: Is it ever right to kill oneself? Is it more or less right to kill oneself than others? When is killing oneself for a cause noble and heroic? When is killing oneself cowardly and stupid? How aware and alert to one's decision to kill oneself should a person be for the decision to do so to be potentially a sane or rational choice, as opposed to decisions taken under the influence of indoctrinators, group pressures, promises of heroic status and acclaim, or other source of mind-altering states of consciousness?

The suicide bombers also take us to the very core of human sensibility and philosophy about *killing others*. Should we in the West try harder to understand, to whatever extent we can, the point of view of the suicide bombers who are so convinced of the rightness of their cause that they are willing to sacrifice their own lives? By giving up their own lives, do they perhaps, in a sense, "earn" the right to justify the deaths of their victims as well? Moreover, even if we enter their frame of thinking to an extent of understanding their grievances and devotion (but I insist without in any way approving or exonerating their terrorist acts), is it more moral or just that their victims be only the military and political leaders of their enemy? Are we justified in making a much more severe judgment of the suicide bombers when they set out to kill and maim a civilian population? When they kill civilians, does it make any difference if their victims include or are mainly children, young people, women, or old people? And does it make any moral difference where and how the suicide bombers catch their enemy's civilians: In airplanes and airports, in their homes, in public eating places and restaurants, in schools, in theaters, in shopping centers, in houses of prayer and worship?

Today's worldwide wave of suicide bombings is terrifying, it is perplexing, and it is also a new frontier for basic choices of philosophy and values in our time. Most of the West, including without hesitation myself, consider suicide bombings crazy and immoral. Besides terrorists and active supporters of terrorism whose opinions are not exactly an issue, there are a good number of cultures (mainly but not only Muslim) where many of the people consider suicide bombings heroic acts of devotion and sacrifice. Can we try to understand the spectrum of these polarized viewpoints in depth and come to reasoned conclusions about our opinions that are more than reflections of our own ethnic and national backgrounds?

THE PLAN OF THE BOOK

The following is an introductory map to what we shall attempt to understand in some depth in this book.

The Enemy Is a Culture of Death

The book assembles the various information we now have about who the suicide bombers are, describes the dynamics and meanings of their actions, locates the legitimation for suicide bombers as well as the objections to them in Islamic theology, and analyzes whether or not they are crazy in our Western frame of thinking.

It is only if we recognize an enemy for what it really is that we have a reasonable chance of combatting it. Each of the above become steps along a way that gives us some insights into the wretched phenomenon of suicide bombings. Yet each and all fall short of explaining and/or making sense out of the horror of killing oneself and killing others—let alone even happily with a satisfying sense of mission and purpose. It all doesn't make enough sense until one understands that a basic war of cultures is evolving. The suicide bombers are proud commandos of a *Culture of Death*, and they are at war with a *Culture of Life*.

This is not the first time that such a war is being waged by the idolators of death against the seekers of life. The same issue lies at the root of many of the endless wars fought in our stupid, bloody human history, including in the last century the fierce war of the West against the totalitarianism of Nazism and then the complex "cold war" of the West against the totalitarianism of communism.

Daniel Pipes, who was a member of the board of directors of the respected United States Institute of Peace, albeit a very controversial figure in the contemporary study of Islam whom we shall meet again later in this book, has written explicitly: "Militant Islam resembles fascism and communism more than any religious movement." He asserts that militant Islam "cannot be compared to Christianity, Judaism, or Hinduism" because militant Islam constitutes a totalitarian utopian ideology that seeks world domination while the other religions do not.[3] The same issues are at stake today as were in the twentieth-century battles against Nazi and communist totalitarianism: the right to live, the rights of different peoples—ethnic, national, religious—to their continued existence, and the basic freedom to think, feel, and behave within a wide range of personal choices.

How Can They Do It?

After a suicide bombing, many people cry out, "How can they do it? It's crazy. It's insane," they say.

This book sets out to answer the question as well as possible.

Most westerners react to news of major violence in our world with a kind of disbelief that life can be so unfair and dangerous to ordinary people, but at the same time also with no little understanding and acceptance that we all know this is the way our world on Planet Earth continues to be.

But when the violence makers also purposely set out to destroy their *own* lives in the process, it simply doesn't make sense to our western minds. Our thinking categories are set up to differentiate between the strong attacking person who triumphantly kills the other and the tragic weak victims of the assault, but to see the attackers obliterating themselves mixes up our mind categories of weakness *versus* power—and never were the twain to meet.

To understand the suicide bomber means first accepting that this means of warfare, which has been called "the poor man's nuclear bomb," is now in use in a growing number of countries, including, but not limited to, Iraq, Israel–Palestine, Saudi Arabia, Russia, Spain, Indonesia, and Yemen. We should not forget the United States because the horrible bizarre "successes" of September 11, 2001 were very much suicide attacks, or the United Kingdom where the multiple attackers of July 7, 2005, brought home anew that the whole world was becoming the battleground. Suicide killing already is and potentially can become an even greater worldwide problem. Moreover, the Western illusion that the supply of people waiting to be suicide bombers would be limited is just that—an illusion.

The book is a combination of an effort to understand, as I have said even respectfully, the metaphor and cognitive process of the suicide bomber and his/her suicide-bombing culture, but with a clear-cut opposition to such making of death. If we westerners are to get beyond a kind of naive shock and horror at the ugly destruction of the suicide bombers, we need to understand much more about how the suicide bombers convert images to actions which condone and elevate their actions into noble sacrifice and heroism on behalf of their religion and cause.

It is not easy to understand a way of life that one opposes and is revolted by ethically. Often people really confuse understanding with a quality of respect and acceptance. I wish to be respectful of the terrorists who are after all my fellow human beings, and who obviously are operating on some aspects of our shared human nature. Opposed as I am to what they do, I want to try to get "inside their heads" and understand how they experience their roles as suicide bombers, although obviously my larger goal is to utilize this understanding to fight them more effectively.

In this book, each well-known specific explanation of suicide bombers and bombings is tried out and acknowledged for its contributing role—including the quite considerable roles of ideology, whether religious or political, and seeking revenge. But the larger explanation proposed, which houses the above as well as other contributing dynamics and synergizes them into action, is that the execution of suicide bombings becomes possible when a person and a group have chosen a culture of death over a culture of life.

"We are not afraid of Death as you are," spokesmen of Al-Qaeda have taunted the West several times. "We love Death more than we love Life, and that is why we will win," they have said chillingly.

Suicide bombings were not always promiscuous kill-as-many-people-of-any-age-and-status as they have become in our present murderous world. There have been earlier traditions of suicide bombings that were designed to attack specifically military personnel and targets. So that the image meanings we attribute to suicide bombers today have undergone powerful changes with this shift from military targets to civilian targets.

This book attempts to take us as far inside the minds of the suicide bombers and the cultures which sponsor them as we westerners might be able to get. As I noted earlier, in the process of writing this book, I *almost* reached the point of understanding the suicide bombers—almost, but not quite; and then I came back out to renew my horror and rage, and also to my thinking about whether anything can be done about this bloody mess.

In seeking explanations of the new phenomena of suicide bombers exploding all over the world, we in the West necessarily start out with our habitual Western mode of explanation that if somebody does something bad, especially to themselves, they must be miserable, down-and-out, locked into despair, and have nothing to lose. It is then a shock to learn that the majority of suicide bombers are *not* down-and-out losers, but for the most part something quite different. This book tells us who the suicide bombers are, how their minds work in their individual framing of their decisions to be suicide bombers, what happens to them in the process of being prepared for their roles by a trainer–dispatcher and in the unfolding group process of which they become a part, and in their experience within a larger cultural milieu which raises their standing to the highest levels of approval and admiration, as well as bestows on them rewards both in this world and, they are led to believe, also in a world beyond.

Islam Is Murder or Peace Depending on the Choice

There is no doubt that it is Islam which stands at the center of much contemporary terror and suicide bombings. This book is a combination of an effort to see the dialectic of killing infidels in Islam versus seeking peace—with a clear-cut commitment to opposing the former and to respecting the latter—including warning of the dangers coming a la Samuel Huntington and Bernard Lewis of a war between civilizations.[4]

Personally, I prefer to emphasize that the war is between civilizations or cultures of death and destruction versus a culture of life; more than that there is a political war between an Islamic identity seeking to expand its rule of the world over the rule of the non-Islamic peoples, although obviously, the latter is very much involved as well.

I do know that the thesis of a war between civilizations is disliked and disputed by some scholars who see in it a kind of disentitlement of the Islamic world by the current "white rulers" of the world. I do not accept this criticism because I believe the primary question is whether there is already an actual war under way between what I can call *jihadist* Islamic peoples and the rest of the world. The number of explosions and the numbers of dead and wounded to date do convince me that a war is on, and I don't feel that I have to apologize for being either a bad scholar or a bad human being when I express a point of view like Huntington and Lewis.

The great majority, though not all, of the suicide bombings in our contemporary world are carried out by Muslims, often in the name of and certainly with the justifying rhetoric of Islam as a conquering, vengeful faith that will destroy all infidels and nonbelievers. The facts are that the prevailing motif of violence in much of the Islamic world draws on strong roots for violence that are embedded within Islamic theology and tradition. In this book, I do not refrain from engaging critically the widespread adoption of violence in many parts of Islam.

At the same time, the book maintains a basic respect and positive anticipation of Islam as a faith-culture that also has *millions of adherents who are peace-seeking*. See, for example, the beautiful Islamic legendry in the finale of the book. Fortunately, not all the Islamic world adopts a religious view that is approving of suicide bombers. As in many religions, in Islam too there are also powerful images, metaphors, and injunctions to be peaceful, kind, and protecting of the strangers and nonbelievers. Moreover, the unfolding politics of the historical narrative of Islam has led in several different cultures to beautiful voices for peace among many millions of adherents, including in countries such as Indonesia, Kazakhstan, and of course among many believers in Islam in democratic countries where inherently there is a process of acculturation to the benefits of a free life which competes with Islamic traditions of violence.

Thus, a Muslim group posted a strong apology on the Web on the occasion of the anniversary of September 11 in 2004:

> We will no longer wait for our religious leaders and "intellectuals" to do the right thing. Instead, we will start by apologizing for 9–11.
>
> What will it take for Muslims to realize that those who commit mass murder in the name of Islam are not just a few fringe elements?
>
> What will it take for Muslims to realize that we are facing a crisis that is more deadly than the AIDS epidemic?
>
> What will it take for Muslims to realize that there is a large evil movement that is turning what was a peaceful religion into a cult?
>
> Not only do Muslims need to join the war against terror, we need to take the lead in this war.
>
> We are so sorry for all the victims of suicide bombings. We are so sorry for the beheadings, abductions, rapes, violent Jihad and all the atrocities committed by Muslims round the world.[5]

In Italy a book entitled *Letter to a Suicide Bomber* has been published. It is also scheduled for publication in Spain and Germany, and its Algerian-born author, Khaled Fouad Allam, also hopes it will be published in his native Algeria as well as in an English-language edition. Allam is a sociologist, but he says he decided to write a letter rather than an academic study because "in an era of political violence, we need to reach out beyond the academic world and give different kinds of answers." *Letter to a Suicide Bomber* is a personal letter. The book is addresssed to an aspiring martyr.

"As a Muslim," Allam says, "I feel it is my historical responsibility to respond to this terrible phenomenon." He argues that the message of Islamic texts is today being distorted beyond recognition by fundamentalists. The big challenge, according to Allam, is to "define how peoples and cultures can communicate with one another," and "to offer a reading of Islam that is not about borders and violence but about openness and dialogue. I think the Muslim world is submerged in an intellectual night but it's possible to emerge from it," he says. Allam cites as an example a classic text of Islam, Ibn El-Arabi's *Illuminations of Mecca* in the twelfth century that underlined the possibility of coexistence between Islam and other faiths without involving religious wars.

Who is a shahid-martyr, according to Allam? A shahid is "a person who had been dispossessed of his own subjectivity, alienated from himself and made into a tool of destruction."[6]

In the present book, I seek to present the life-respecting trends in Islam and never to lose sight of the potential of Islam to join with other religions and peoples of the world in a better future, while looking realistically at the prevailing practice and honor of violence makers in many Islamic societies.

Are the Suicide Bombers "Crazy" or Mentally Disturbed in Western Terms?

The book also probes the question whether—admittedly from a Western point of view—suicide bombers should be considered psychiatrically disturbed. It is fascinating how with overwhelming regularity, normal lay people react to events of suicide bombing with remarks such as, "crazy," "they are out of their minds," or "you have to be psychotic to do something like that."

I believe that there is a long-standing problem in Western psychiatry which has failed to cast many problems of violence, including in a strange way even "normal" suicides, in any systematic framework of psychopathology. The emphasis in psychiatry is generally on how poorly a person has come to function, so that there are especially big problems in handling dictators, tyrants, and terrorists, including suicide bombers, who may be functioning very skillfully and having a fulfilling experience at their chosen "jobs." I will argue forcefully for a conception of mental illness that is always to be based on evaluating *simultaneously* the extent to which a person is doing harm either to *themselves* or *to other* people or to both. All wanton destruction of the deeply precious life opportunity of human beings, ourselves or others, is to be defined as disturbed.

Should There Be Free Speech for Terrorism?

We will also tackle in this book some of the thorny issues of free speech in our democracies. Americans are especially extreme about protecting free speech almost to no limit, and yet American law also includes the well-established principle that one does not have the right to yell unwarrantedly, "Fire, fire" in a crowded theater and to set off destructive pandemonium. This book argues that the imams and other institutions that openly advocate, celebrate, and educate suicide bombers need to be regulated under law, and that democracies need to make a major step forward to a new maturity where incitement to bigotry and celebration and legitimation of violence are not allowed, without damaging the wonderful principle of free speech that is so central to the maintenance of democracy.

What Will the Future Bring?

The book is hard-nosed and realistic, as well as full of hope and creative suggestions for limiting suicide bombers (and related destruction of human life). There is a byplay in the book between a dire prediction of future disasters and a war between civilizations, as well as a serious, optimistic proposal for change and improvement and reduction of risk on a global level. I am simultaneously both pessimistic and optimistic about what is coming in our future.

I am pessimistic about the growing violence in the world which I call an emerging "transnational genocidal terrorism." I sadly anticipate and fear deeply that before long there will be a use of Weapons of Mass Destruction (WMD) by terrorists, including suicide bombers, with resulting horrendous widespread deaths, agony, and breakdown of civilized life in widespread areas. However, I also envision civilization rallying against such insanity and tragedy to reorganize a more successful world government, including a world police force or international peace army, and to reconstitute a stronger culture of life.

The book proposes that the ultimate war between civilizations that has begun and is today expanding, which indeed contains within it a major conflict between much of Islam and the rest of the world, is, in fact, a war between cultures of life and death.

As I have already remarked, this is hardly the first time in the history of human civilization that the light of life values and the darkness of death values have been pitched against one another. The answer proposed to the split between the large parts of Islam as a culture that has gone down a road of approving and honoring death versus Judeo-Christian values and the interpretation of Islam that promotes life is to promote a new celebration and honor of human life, beginning with the rights of all people to enjoy maximum biological safety, and continuing with their rights to live life with dignity.

A Proposal for a "Worldwide Campaign for Life"

In addition to daring to keep a small flame of hope glowing that just *maybe* the overwhelming disasters of WMD will be averted in the coming years, this book attempts to develop thinking about how basic attitudes toward life can be changed for the better in our destruction-prone world. The book builds toward a conclusion where a major inspiring proposal for a "Worldwide Campaign for Life" is developed. This campaign is to be sponsored by the leaders of many of the world's religions and other world leaders and heroes of many different cultures. The leaders of many religions in the world will be joined by the leaders of government and the military, along with beloved folk heroes in the media, sports, music and the arts, and more to bring a message to millions of people in the world to *live and let live*. Such a campaign would utilize the tremendous impact of the new media in our world while working through the powerful archetypal influences of religious imagery on the peoples on our planet. It would seek to turn suicide bombing and terrorism into basically unattractive acts, while promoting a new worldwide consensus that the real purpose of living for all of us is to live.

If we don't head off WMD in time, at least we will have projected the direction toward which we will have to work that much harder for all of our grief *after* the disaster. And if we are amazingly lucky, a world shift toward a culture of life will take place *before* the WMD events that currently must be predicted and expected. *Inshalah.*

Suicide Bombing and Its Growing Place in the World Today

Mao Tse-tung famously remarked that, "The guerrilla must move amongst the people as a fish swims in the sea . . ." Islamic fanaticism has successfully imposed a realm of fear, on Muslim intellectuals and others. People are afraid to speak out against Islamo-terrorism for fear of being killed . . . A Muslim city councilor in Amsterdam said he often asked groups of young Dutch Muslims if they would speak out if they learned that a member of their families was preparing to plant a bomb. The response was silence and evasion.   —Roger Cohen, *New York Times*[1]

INTRODUCTION TO SUICIDE BOMBING

As a resident of Israel, I am sitting in one of the areas of the world where suicide bombings have been current and rampant, so that much of my analysis of suicide bombing has been written in real pain of seeing, hearing, even smelling various such events.[2] Of course, the horrible "art form" of suicide bombing is by no means restricted to September 11 in the United States or to the country in which I reside, Israel (the two countries of which I am also a citizen).

At the time of first writing this chapter, I was reading news reports of a Palestinian woman suicide bomber, who by profession was an apprentice attorney, who exploded herself in a jointly owned Israeli-Jewish-Arab restaurant in Haifa whose employees are both Jewish and Arab and which is frequented both by Jewish and Arab customers. There were twenty-one dead and some fifty wounded, and of course the victims were both Jewish and Arab.[3] When I went for my swimming exercise a day after, I found my chest was weighted down with a heavy load of unreleased tears for the victims of this bombing—and each such event, in turn, cannot help but rekindle the memories of so many past victims of so many past terrorist events.

This specific suicide bombing tore at my insides in a renewed way because, for me, it also ripped away at what I have always felt is a pretense of political purpose even when consciously the political cause is felt sincerely by the perpetrator. The psychologist and ethicist in me believes that, at the core, terror is intrinsically a horror of turning life into death for the *thanatonic (love of death and destruction of life) hell of it*. I do not deny that the political-ideological motives are very real for many suicide bombers, but I believe these motives also take advantage of and excite impulses to court death and destruction that are present and awaiting in all of us.

One nonpsychologist reader of the manuscript for the publisher demanded that I "prove" this point. Well, first of all, I believe that people who commit suicide generally want to die; and that people who kill and injure others generally want to do harm to others; and that intellectuals who demand proof of the existence of these motives just because there is also a political motivation to give up one's life in order to hurt the enemy are exhibiting a kind of deafness and blindness to the most obvious facts of life and death that have to be bigger than any political wishes. Certainly one must agree that there is an internal statement in the suicide bomber's mind to the effect that, "My strong political wishes (to kill the enemy) are more powerful for me than any wishes I may have to live." The proof blasts through at you.

The recruiters of suicide bombers in various cultures get to be very street-wise in picking out promising candidates. Later we shall see that these recruiters and handlers of the candidate suicide bombers play decisive roles in bringing them over the threshold to commit their acts of suicide and murder. The handlers' methods of training, indoctrination, and manipulation are intended to bring a candidate to a higher level of readiness; and the societal culture which celebrates and lionizes suicide bombers provides an overall legitimation and sense of heroism and honor.

One Palestinian who had participated in a murderous terrorist killing of an Israeli family in their home and was then captured said years later in an Israeli jail, "We Palestinians have to do a moral reckoning with ourselves. The decision that was taken in the 1970s to attack the civilian population [of Israel] was a terrible mistake. From the moment we decided to kill civilians, we gave our young people legitimation also to murder many innocent Palestinians during the *intifada*. The result has been the development in our culture of a norm of senseless, unjustified murders."[4]

In the suicide-bomber blast in Haifa, this Arab woman went to bomb a restaurant which is partly Arab-owned to kill her own fellow people along with the accursed Jews. From the accounts I have read, she did have true reason for revenge against the Jews—both her brother and a cousin had been killed by Jews, the brother perhaps even without due cause except that he was with his terrorist cousin when Israeli commandos arrived. Yet in claiming her revenge against both Jews and Arabs, this woman was saying that she didn't care much about anyone and that she was abandoning herself to kill under the umbrella of her culture's permission and approval to use this method of self-and-political-expression for revenge.

For me the truth is that the desire to kill human beings, as an intrinsically evil motivation lurking in all of us, has a horrible life of its own, and that is at the core of what suicide bombers are really expressing. For those who remember the grounded common sense of longshoreman-philosopher, Eric Hoffer, he stressed that for the "true believer," meaning someone who is committed to a cause for which he or she is willing to die unthinkingly, ideologies are amazingly interchangeable. True believers are people who are extremists, who are attracted to the mass movement that gives them reason for their self-sacrifice. Hoffer also saw how, even when they arise with a stated intention to bring a greater decency to human life, mass movements often become demonic insofar as the mass movements are rooted in extremist thinking, so Christianity became a slaughtering force in the Middle Ages which killed millions, the French Revolution turned into a tyrannical bloodbath, and the Russian Communists produced a living hell of totalitarianism and murder of tens of millions.[5]

In every generation there are extremists who are as if waiting to sign up for the contemporary forms of totalitarian and terrorist murdering of their times. Totalitarian movements influence many additional people to be inducted into their extremist way of life, so that many people who were not waiting or looking for the opportunity to be extremists end up attracted and won over by a totalitarian move-ment's calls to ideology, sacrifice, and violence. This is what I believe we have learned from the best social science thinking and scientific experiments, like those of Stanley Milgram on people giving potentially lethal shocks to another person just because they are told to do so by the experimenter; and by Philip Zimbardo on the simulation of a prison where nice, normal university students turned so sadistic in their roles as jailers that the decision was made to stop the experiment.[6] In a sense, extremism and fascist thinking are a potential state of mind in all of us humans, of course more so in those (many) specific people whose personalities are more inclined to extremism and violence, and also more so in cultures, groups, and historical contexts which encourage and celebrate extremism.

The dread and repulsive mode of suicide bombing is today a growing and spreading phenomenon in the world in which we live. One writer of an op-ed piece in the *New York Times,* who has since gone on to author a valuable book, concluded that "suicide terrorism transcends religious, ethnic, and political boundaries."[7] Surveying the last twenty-some years, he wrote: "Since the early 1980s, when the Lebanese Shia Hezbolla (with Iranian Khomeinist funds and training) and the Sri Lankan Liberation Tigers of Tamil Eelam—LTTE (Marxists/Hindus/Tamil secessionists) initiated the routine use of suicide terrorists as an instrument of war, suicide bombers have been active in Sri Lanka, Turkey, Kashmir, India, Lebanon, Israel, Russia, the U.S., and Indonesia. Failed suicide bombing attempts (including the use of aircraft) are known from France, Spain and Turkey, and successful attempts have been made elsewhere by citizens or residents of Germany, and the UK."

Moreover, so many of the conflicts all around the globe are defined along an axis of Muslims versus non-Muslims.[8] According to an increasing number of thinkers, there is an emerging possibility of a large-scale world war between Islamic and nonIslamic civilizations, Islam poised against the Judeo-Christian underpinnings of Western civilization, intertwined with a conflict between feudal-theocratic governments and democracies.[9]

Of course, suicide bombings are also employed by Muslims in their own wars among themselves, such as in the Iran-Iraq war, or in various attacks on one another by competing Sunni and Shi'ite groups, such as in the heartless crescendo of suicide murders and other terror of these groups against one another in Iraq especially since 2005. This book's analysis of suicide bombings is intended to pertain to all such acts and not only to Islamic suicide bombers against our Western world.

The underbelly or subtext of much of the pattern of conflict in our time is that it is a clash between terrorist people, movements, and governments which legitimate killing promiscuously, versus societies which are more committed to following rules of law and common sense decency against killing and for the protection of life. The former have no intention of following Geneva Conventions or, more intrinsically, listening to a universal voice that speaks against the killing of one's fellow man as a violation of common wisdom and decency as well as a violation of the value system of just about every religion.[10] The latter or more democratic cultures and governments, while themselves guilty in history of many violations of life and decency, nonetheless subscribe overall to codes of law and ethics which prohibit wanton killing, and overall hold killers and their accomplices responsible for their criminal acts.

As we shall see, according to many of its serious interpreters, Islam too is against wanton killing. On the other hand, the prevailing interpretation in a great many quarters of Islam is that it is religiously legitimate, nay it is even commanded to kill the infidel. Terrorists are highly respected in many, perhaps most Islamic communities in the world. Terrorists in general, and the suicide bombers in particular as a prime elite-priesthood of terrorism, are today like the Death Head squads of the Nazi SS were in their time, a kind of archangels of Death. They are the proponents of a cult-religion that celebrates killing and martyrdom. Thus, Osama bin Laden has said:

> In compliance with God's order, we issue the following fatwa to all Muslims: The ruling to kill the Americans and their allies—civilians and military—is an individual duty for every Muslim who can do it in any country in which it is possible to do it . . . We—with God's help—call on every Muslim who believes in God and wishes to be rewarded to comply with God's order to kill the Americans and plunder their money wherever and whenever they find it. We also call on Muslim ulema [Muslim scholars or men of authority in religion and law], leaders, youths, and soldiers to launch the raid on Satan's U.S. troops and the devil's supporters allying with them, and to displace those who are behind them so that they may learn a lesson.[11]

Of course, we have to acknowledge again and again that Western civilization, including its Judeo-Christian roots, engages in plenty of warmaking and genocide of its own, but theoretically and in its prevailing culture norms, it purports to treasure life much more as God-given, and secular people too are expected to regard life as basically sacred and inviolate. From the point of view of established Western values, the combination of suicide of oneself along with homicidal mass killing of others constitutes a violation of the basic values of life and civilization. In the popular Western mind, the behavior of the suicide bomber intrinsically is both abnormal and immoral. For Western civilization, suicide bombing violates every code of lawful, rational, sane, and acceptable behavior.

I have written elsewhere about fascist versus democratic mindsets in everyday life and behavior, such as when people demand of themselves or of others, such as their children, absolute success and no failure.[12] Suicide bombing is much more serious. There couldn't be a more pure form of what I call "Fascist Mind" than suicide bombing. It is fascism at work in its familiar deadly killing in the name of its cause. It involves simultaneously the use of the deadliest forms of violence both against oneself and against others in demands to achieve a given absolute goal. The absolute goal is held sacrosanct and overrides any possible valuing of life for oneself or for others. On the other hand, "Democratic Mind," intuitively and naturally, is opposed to the horrors of gruesome mass murder including even a degree of caring about the perpetrator who is committing suicide along with all the other victims.

In addition to the moral dimension, there is also room to pose the question whether suicide bombings are acts of mental disturbance. To engage this question, unfortunately we have to be diverted, if only briefly, by some intellectual problems in contemporary Western psychiatry. At least three things have impeded contemporary psychiatry from being able to assert the obvious existential truth that people who go around killing themselves and others are not in good mental shape (almost a bad joke when you think about it in everyday plain language).

The first problem is that in recent years psychiatry has been involved in a massive biologicizing of emotional and mental disorders. In its escape from focusing on the meanings of human behavior, contemporary Western psychiatry has worked itself into a hole about the specific subject of suicide bombers and terrorism in general as well as many other forms of violence. You would think that the obviously paranoid thinking of suicide bombers ("the infidels are against us, and so they deserve to die") would be picked up unambivalently by psychiatric thinkers as fitting the most old-fashioned rules for defining craziness, so that contemporary Western psychiatry would be saying, unequivocally, that suicide bombers are crazy. But to a large extent, Western psychiatry plays possum and leaves these dramatic events of our time to themselves as "political events" rather than as subjects for mental health judgment.

The second complication is that a person committing a terrorist act, just as the person committing violence in a family, is put on the mental examination table as if for an examination of all *other* aspects of their personality; and if in all these other respects there are no signs of traditional mental disturbance, the absurd conclusion is reached that the behavior of destroying others was not done by an evidently disturbed person! The fact that a murder of normality is staring at us right in the face in the very acts of hurting other people hasn't been allowed to enter into this silly system, even as it as if puts a stethoscope to the person to see if they are still breathing normally, while ignoring the fact that they have been spitting blood all over the place.

The third problem that has developed in Western psychiatry and civilization is that if crazy thinking or behavior is defined as a *political* statement, then all considerations of the irrationality and madness of the thinking or behavior are deferred and even wiped out so as not to intrude on people's heavenly political rights to fight for their conceptions of what is right and just.

Suicide bombing in many cases *is* very much a political statement. Much as I abhor suicide killings, and notwithstanding my basic conception that there is much pure love of killing in many of these acts, I also acknowledge that often enough suicide bombings flow from a legitimate and understandable cry of personal and/or collective revenge, and/or from legitimate political aspirations (whether or not I agree with them). Yet I believe that none of these motivations, in themselves, justify the suicide killings, certainly not of innocent civilians, and personally I think not even of many military foes.

The last problem of treating political behaviors as exempt from any psychiatric evaluation is connected with another value that has gone wrong somewhere down the line in Western society, which is a mistaken notion that free speech has no boundaries whatsoever. The cardinal rule of free speech, which is at the core of the wondrous democratic way of life that we treasure, is taken to mean that people can say *anything* they believe in without being responsible for the likely outcomes of their words leading to violence and death. Thus, an examination of the history of Islamic suicide bombers, including the infamous hijacker suicide murderers of September 11, found that many of them had worshipped regularly at mosques in democratic countries like the United Kingdom and Germany where imams regularly preached violent destruction of the infidel West.[13]

Suicide bombing and other types of suicide killings have an interesting history—"interesting" is what it is, it is not approval. I want to present some of the facts about how many peoples in the past and present engage in suicide bombings, and I even want to reach out to understand in a way that is *almost* respectful and empathetic to the disturbed and unbearable mindsets of the suicide bombers—the individuals and the cultures which support them collectively. I hate to face it, but what are for us repulsive, frighteningly evil, and insane acts of suicide bombing are for them effective acts of warfare against an enemy, self-sacrifice, heroism, and martyrdom.

At the same time, I want to unravel convincingly an analysis and my conclusions that even when motivated by a cause, suicide bombers inherently are promoters of a fascist philosophy and methodology of dispensing death to themselves and to others; that their very actions translate existentially into betrayals and disturbances of all that is alive and normal; that whatever power they use fighting at times for just causes and to achieve what may be desirable political changes, they represent the darkest forces of death masquerading as a legitimate way for solving the problems of the living.

Death is the suicide bombers' way of life, as it were; and we must mobilize the forces of life and democracy to overcome them.

Were the dark forces of fascist-minded suicide bombers ever to win out, the irrational—including a flight from knowledge and science, and the triumph of the cruel, violent, and homicidal—would prevail.

Even if a majority of a people democratically choose a know-nothing, fundamentalist, suppressive, cruel regime that crushes opposition, no true proponent of democracy can agree to such governance. For democracy is not only the rule of a majority, but first of all a rallying behind a principle of freedom that is never to be abandoned even by a majority vote, if only because once a society is run by fascists and suicide bombers, there is never again an opportunity to oppose the totalitarian way of life and return to peace-caring values.

A Christian-Arab, Habib Malik, speaking as president of the American-based Council for Christian Colleges and Universities, believes in a universality of moral values, by which he means—for me very touchingly and hopefully—that "the human mind and the human conscience will respond to the beckoning of moral universals and of natural laws any time and anywhere regardless of context."[14] Malik notes that in certain societal settings, of which the Islamic world is one, "the rate of receptivity to universal values by the receiving culture" is slower or seriously impeded, but that does not mean that there is no echoing of the universal values deep within the minds of people in that culture as well.

I would like to suggest that our mental health culture, deep within our Western society, has worked itself into a temporary time warp where, in respect of not labeling many incidents of violence as clearly disturbed behaviors, it doesn't see the obvious about psychological normality and abnormality. People who overcome despair in their lives by living lovingly and constructively as much as possible, and who help other people to live safe and good quality lives, are the psychologically healthy specimens that our clinical mental health professions should hold up as models to be respected and emulated; while the killers and destroyers of life represent ways of thinking and behaving that we need to define as clearly disturbed and pathological.

SOME HISTORY OF SUICIDE BOMBING AND ITS WIDESPREAD PLACE IN OUR WORLD TODAY

For those like myself who are deeply concerned with the current wave of suicide bombings in many places in the world, and who see suicide bombing as a true antithesis of the Judeo-Christian tradition, it will be something of an amusing paradox, and perhaps also appropriately humbling, to know that when Judea was occupied by the Romans, ancient Jewish sects of Zealots and Cicarri were among the early practitioners of a suicide killing form of attack. They would stab individual Roman soldiers in markets and alleys—even when their own capture and death were inevitable. They were suicide killers.

Other earlier practitioners of suicide killing included the Islamic Order of Assassins during the early Crusader times. There are fascinating historical legends around the "assassins." The widespread accepted story is that they were a Persian sect led by al-Hassan ibn-al-Salbah in the early eleventh century, who used hashish to drug young men in order to enlist them in his private army of assassins, and that the name "assassin" derives from "hashshashin" or hashish user. The group seized a castle of Alamut in a mountainous region south of the Caspian Sea, and from this center al-Hassan became an evil celebrity to his enemies, such as the Crusaders, who came to fear him very much as "the old man of the mountains."

The story of the recruitment of assassins is very reminiscent of the mythology offered gullible suicide bombers of today. The Old Man would give young boys hashish, and then while asleep they were carried into a garden where he had them awakened to discover they were in a Paradise, with beautiful naked women who would revel them in songs and give them everything they asked for. The assassins were later told when they were sent on their terrorist missions of political killings that if they died in the process they would be returning to the paradise they had tasted, which became a great motivator of their legendary cunning and fearlessness.

However, there are a variety of scholars who dispute any number of elements in the story beginning with questioning the derivation of the word assassin from the Arabic word for hashish users, and continuing with questioning the use of hashish which might have inclined the assassins more toward being pacifists than murderers.

A different explanation given for the name assassins is that they were followers of al-Hassan. Different explanations given for the courageous ferocity and devotion of the assassins include their taking some psychedelic substance other than hashish, such as alcohol, or more simply that the assassins were high on fanaticism itself. Says one commentator: "Our modern experience of terrorism does not suggest that its perpetrators require any narcotic stronger than fanaticism itself."[15]

Edward Luttwak, at the Center for Strategic and International Studies in the United States, places suicide bombers in the context of what he calls "asymmetric war." He notes: "Even in the best days of the empire, the Romans suffered defeats at the hands of much less accomplished enemies who lacked their costly equipment and elaborate training."[16]

Hardly very differently, Khaled Meshal, head of the Hamas' political wing, who is a top leader of the movement (who will be remembered by many as the object of a failed attempt to poison him by the Israeli Mossad in Amman, Jordan in 1997), calls Palestinian bombings "sacrifice actions." Danny Rubinstein, a top *Haaretz* reporter explains, "According to Meshal, the Israeli and Palestinian forces are so unequally matched that they [the Palestinians] have no other way of injuring the enemy."[17]

In the twentieth century, the Japanese *kamikaze* ("divine wind") made suicide terrorism famous, beginning with the battle of the Philippines in November 1944, when Japanese pilots, who of course were well-educated officers, crashed their planes into U.S. naval ships. According to one interpretation, "Few believed they were dying for the Emperor as a war leader or for military purposes. Rather, the state was apparently able to manipulate a deep intellectual and aesthetic tradition of painful beauty to convince the pilots that it was their honor to 'die like beautiful falling cherry petals' for their real and fictive families, including parents, fellow pilots, and the Emperor and people of Japan."[18] "In the battle of Okinawa (April 1945), some 2,000 *kamikaze* rammed fully fuelled fighter planes into more than 300 ships, killing 5,000 Americans in the most costly naval battle in U.S. history,"[19] and one interpretation given is that it was "because of such losses, there was support for using the atomic bomb" later to end the war.[20]

On the European front of World War II, heroic Russians would hurl themselves with Molotov cocktails underneath German tanks in what are generally considered in our West heroic acts; and of course there are many instances of soldiers who have given their all in a suicidal heroism for which they are honored posthumously.

In the war in Vietnam, U.S. troops were attacked by children and elderly people booby trapped with explosives, and this was one of the rational explanations for the Mai Lai-type cruelty of American forces subsequently wiping out villagers of all ages indiscriminately.

In still more recent times, one sees suicidal fighting practiced extensively by Iran sending waves of children into Iraqi minefields, which some consider as the opening wave of the current era of suicidal killing.[21] Many sources "credit" the suicide bombing of the Iraqi Embassy in Beirut in December 1981 with being the first major contemporary suicide bombing attack. In October 1983, a suicide truck bomb killed nearly 300 American and French servicemen and led America and France to abandon the multinational force they had placed in Lebanon. In Israel-Palestine, suicide terrorism began in 1992.

Suicide bombers are active in our times in a worldwide variety of places. The following are examples:

- Dar Es Salaam, Tanzania—in 1998 a suicide bomber attack against the U.S. embassy took place almost simultaneously with an attack in Nairobi;
- Yemen—in October 2000, when an explosives-laden boat smashed into the USSS Cole in a suicide bombing that is credited to Al-Qaeda;
- Kenya—the site of suicide bombings against the United States in 1998 in Nairobi, and then in 2002 at a resort which catered to Israeli vacationers (along with a simultaneous failed attempt to fire rockets at an Israeli aircraft departing Nairobi);
- Turkey—sixteen suicide attacks (plus other foiled attempts) by the Kurdish PKK during the period 1996–1999. These came to an end when Turkey captured the PKK leader, Ocalan, sentenced him to death, but changed his sentence to imprisonment in return for a cessation of PKK attacks.[22] As

we shall otherwise see, suicide bombings then return to Turkey thanks to Al-Qaeda.

- Pakistan—for example in 2002 a suicide bomber attacked near the U.S. consulate in Karachi; and in 2003 a crowded Shi'ite mosque in the city of Quetta was attacked by Taliban Islamic fundamentalists believed to be associated with Al-Qaeda.
- Jakarta, Indonesia—in 2003 where a suicide bomber detonated a bomb in a van outside the Marriott Hotel, also in 2003 at a nightclub frequented by many Australians;
- Kashmir, India—one report had the terrorist organizations in the Kashmir Valley conducting a recruitment drive among senior citizens to be the *fidayeen* suicide bombers;[23]
- Morocco—in May 2003 a suicide bombing in Casablanca left forty-four dead including twelve suicide bombers;
- Chechnya—where the Chechans have used suicide bombers both in their home area as well as deep in the heartland of Russia, such as in Moscow residential centers and places of entertainment, for example in June 2003, suicide bombers killed fourteen at a Moscow rock festival;
- Saudi Arabia—with an Al-Qaeda attack against a Western housing compound outside of Riyadh in 2003;
- Sri Lanka—where there have been hundreds of suicide bombings to which we will refer in somewhat greater detail shortly;
- United States—of course, lest one forget that these were suicide bombings, the incredibly coordinated four hijacked aircraft attacks on September 11, 2001;
- In post-Saddam Iraq, a series of suicide bombings ensued both against American troops and officials and against Iraqi institutions such as the police that resumed functioning in cooperation with the Americans and progressively swelled into an unbelievably endless stream of almost nonstop suicide bombings and other terror attacks.[24]

In Sri Lanka, beginning in July 1987, the Tamil Liberation Black Tigers became "the world's foremost suicide bombers, sending out about 220 attackers in all," according to a *New York Times* report in 2003.[25] An American official is quoted as saying that prior to September 11, 2001, "they were the deadliest terror organization in the world." The suicide bombers in Sri Lanka killed one Sri Lankan president, a former Indian prime minister, several Sri Lankan ministers, mayors, and moderate Tamil leaders, "decimating the country's political and intellectual leadership." They destroyed naval ships, attacked the airport, the capital, a religious shrine, and a trade center, and killed hundreds and possibly more civilians. A third or more of Tamil suicide bombers were women.

Most telling is that the Tigers promoted successfully *an ideology of self-sacrifice*. They literally advertised for volunteers and used the media to give instruction in how to be a suicide bomber, for example, how women are to play dead until enemy soldiers approach, and then blow up as many people as possible. The rhetoric of identifying mass killing of oneself and others as a desirable and decent sacrifice of oneself for a greater good apparently is an accurate description of the trance that many suicide bombers and other genocidal killers work themselves into. Obviously, many of our weak human minds can be falsely programmed by a fascist concept that making death is *humanitarian*. The Tigers' guiding concept was that suicide bombing is a gift of self—"the person gives him or herself in full." Almost comically, a Tamil spokesperson has rejected any comparison with Palestinian suicide bombers, who she suggested are more often dejected. "People dejected in life won't be able to go as Black Tigers," she said. "There must be a clear conception of why and for what we are fighting. A deep humanitarianism is very necessary—a love of others, for the people."[26]

Suicide bombing has gotten to be so "in" that at one point was even an instance of speculation in Israel that local Mafia rivals, who were engaged in assassinations of one another, might hire Palestinian suicide bombers to do the job of wiping out rival Mafia leaders.[27]

Suicide Killing Is Also to Be Found in OUR Western World

In ensuing chapters we will be looking at many kinds of information about how the suicide bombers can do what they do, when in most of our Western minds such behaviors are barbaric, stupid, heartless, and largely inconceivable to us. When we bring up the subject of how the suicide bombers are able to do what they do, our Western minds understandably quickly conjure up Arabic-featured men and women (also children who are exploited in the Arab world to carry bombs and mines into enemy land); and we as if hear them invoking their battle cries of *Allah Akbar* as they pull the strings of death against themselves and their victims. As we seek to recover from the shock of suicide bombings having become a regular repeated event in our lives over the last years, the first line of defense for many of us is to explain to ourselves that the suicide bombings are largely done by Muslims (which is true at this time, but even now there are others too). We then comfort ourselves by explaining to ourselves that *they*, after all, are different from us.

It is characteristic of us westerners that we always need "explanations" of events. Having an explanation that seems to make sense, even if it is based quite a lot on prejudiced thinking about a people whose culture is different than ours, gives us a false courage to go on.

They love to kill.
They believe in killing for their cause.
They are "crazy" in their overdevotion to religious rituals; they are especially "crazy" in their devotion to their ideologies and don't seem to mind having dictators at the head of their states.
They are devoted to violence.

They come from a long tradition of assassins who easily slit the throats of
others.

They don't feel the loss of life the way we do, and are utterly devoid of sentiments
of human connection and sympathy.

They feel the honor of participating in their cause as being of greater importance
than life itself.

Life for them is an axiomatic allegiance to whatever the cause they are fighting,
for they treasure their cause and group ideology more than they care about
human lives.

For we westerners in search of some kind of rational explanation of the suicide
bombers, these thoughts of *how they are different from us* helps us to recover
at least somewhat from our shock and horror at the suicide bombings. When
the July 7, 2005 suicide bombings in London brought Britons to the realization
that they too had devastating enemies planted inside their community, they were
"certain" at first that the bombers had come into Britain from an Arab country;
then as facts pointed more to people who came from within, the British press
became "sure" that the bombers came from Muslim families that were relatively
recent immigrants to the United Kingdom, only finally to learn in shock that
the suicide bombers were native British-born and bred sons of Pakistani-English
families.

What we don't realize and understand and is basically missing from our
explanation is that although we in the West *are* different from Muslims in the
value emphasis we place on fulfilling our own lives more than the value we
attribute to our collective causes, *we* too can and do talk ourselves into many
forms of suicide-murder. Brits, Yankee Americans, and whoever the sons and
daughters of Western Judaeo-Christian lineage, we too are not immune to killing
others and ourselves.

In general, we westerners obviously have done and continue to do enormous
amounts of killing, so that there is a good deal of fairness in saying to the Western
world's lamenting and complaining about the suicide bombers, "Look first at what
crazy killers you (we) westerners are!"

It also has to be obvious that a great many of our killings also contain built-in
suicidal meanings. Thus, the almost forgotten trench battles of World War I where
the military meaninglessly doomed waves of attackers from both sides who were
sent out to kill and be killed.

On a larger plane, many historical incidents of massive destruction of others in our Western world, such as in the Christian crusades, London blitzes,
Dresden fireballs, and certainly Auschwitzs and Hiroshimas would appear to convey metaphorically a suicide of our as if human civilization, let alone that such
incidents by definition set the stage of history for actual retaliations against the
perpetrators in the future. Thus, once you have used nuclear weapons for whatever
reasons you sincerely believe are just, you have opened the door to nuclear as well
as other weapons of mass destruction in the future, including their being aimed at

you in the future. In fact, even more broadly, what was always a spiritual truth also has become a looming planetary physical-engineering fear in the eyes of many serious observers that man may be destroying the very ecology of his existence. Certainly spiritually it is hardly ambiguous for many of us: The human species cannot engage in massive events of death making and continue to live.

There are also the too little known facts that the demonic "great" leaders of nations that embarked on genocidal campaigns to murder *other people*, for example the murders of Jews by the Germans, were also committing the suicide of their own people. First, as just suggested, to commit genocide is, with fair probability, to invite—even more to compel—retaliation, if not immediately by the weak victim people themselves (for genocide to begin with is undertaken against a people who are weaker than the perpetrators and therefore available to be victims), then by other nations who will not be able to stand by and allow the unlimited expansion of deadly killing and power, or more rarely in our still cynical world will be unable to tolerate the moral abomination of genocide. There are also startling compelling evidences that some of the "great" genociders were in fact actually heading toward killing even their own people even immediately, if not at a later date. Thus, we have literal examples of genocidal rulers who turned on their own people from the outset, and it is their very own people who were their victims. Two examples are Pol Pot and Mao Tse-tung, both of whom were very busy murdering millions of their own respective Cambodian and Chinese peoples.

Because of slavish concern with definitions, let alone the longstanding resistance of human society to recognize and confront genocide, Pol Pot's murdering two-and-a half to three million of his own people left the U.N. Human Rights Commission postponing its recognition of the killing because the dead victims were also Cambodians, and then the Commission haltingly coined a new word they themselves didn't believe in, "autogenocide."[28] In the case of Mao, the incredible murders of many millions of Chinese never even came before an international tribunal. These victims were Mao's very own people.[29] Some crimes really do pay! It can be argued that Pol Pot and Mao were executing on a collective level national suicide-murder (and that it is only regrettable that in these cases the bloodthirsty arch murderer-leaders were not killing themselves too as a full-blown suicide bomber does).

Amazingly, even in the case of the Nazis who murdered 20 million people, including the 6 million Jewish victims of the Holocaust, not only did a large number of Germans meet their deaths under this ghastly regime (Erich Boehm says the number exceeds 500,000[30]), but it has even been said that toward the end of his life Hitler had "decided also to destroy the German people, just as he had decided to deal with the Jews."[31] This concept is put into Hitler's mouth in a movie by filmmaker, Bernd Eichinger (who earlier produced "The Name of the Rose"), in a film, "Downfall."[32] In this film, Hitler is portrayed as speaking with his Minister of Industry, Albert Speer, and military leaders. It is late in the war, and he says that all good Germans have already died and only the inferior are left, and he implies that he wants to get rid of these inferiors. The film is accompanied throughout by a musical track of a requiem that conveys an impending tragic decline of the Third Reich.

Granted, some of the above comparisons between our Western ways of killing and being killed and today's suicide bombers were abstract and metaphorical, some were speculative, and some were linked directly to the madness of specific rulers. However, they are, overall, cases of a person or people killing themselves along with others, and that is the essential feature of suicide killing. We need to know that we non-Muslims also have our suicide killers.

We also have them in more concrete and specific senses. In the United States, but not only, a certain kind of public mayhem mass murder suicide killing has been elevated to a new archetypal standing in American folklore. First, over many years came a kind of choreography of killing blindly anyone and everyone who was in reach in a public setting such as on a college campus, in a McDonald's restaurant, or at a shopping center, killing and in turn being killed. A kind of choreography that is a variation on this theme that also "took off" was for a disgruntled employee, often after being fired, to return to his place of employment and kill blindly in bitter protest and revenge. To kill and to be killed has been elevated to a status of a kind of folk habit that has become a familiar feature of what can be called the folklore of American life.

In more recent years, even teenagers and even pre-teenagers have gotten further into the act in school-setting shootings and suicide killings. For their few moments of a horrible glory, the children killers are omnipotent. They control and dispense life and death for all to see them; even as some of them know that in a very short time, they too will be killed—either by the police or by their own selves. Thus, the blind murders of fellow students followed by suicides of the killers at the high school in Columbine, Colorado, have left us with an as if generic term for such suicide killings in schools: "*Columbine!*" There have been a good number of such "Columbines" in the United States, and no few in other countries too, such as in Erfurt, Germany; Dunblane, United Kingdom; Tokyo, Japan; Ruzhou, China; and more.

When reconstructed it becomes clear that many of these school killings have involved the children expecting or even planning in advance to kill themselves. However, one should note that not all of the school suicide killings show a clear or even indirect planning of suicide along with the killings. There are some incidents where the child reports he "just felt like it"—in revenge, bravado, or even in what the child calls "fun" or the excitement of the action. Of course, even if the children do not intend consciously to kill themselves, it is far-fetched to assume that unconsciously they do not know they are putting an end to their own lives by the act they are committing of killing others.

This kind of murder-suicide thinking is also likely to reflect a serious psychological problem in a given child; but more often than not it also reflects—perhaps more importantly than personal problems—a larger cultural setting in our West that has failed grievously to teach the children a basic respect for life. I suggest that what in the West may be excitement-seeking events of an aimless violence that reflects a larger culture's failure to hold life sacred can be considered the Western version of the suicide murders we see derive from Islamic ideological thinking.

Granted, in the American-Western mode of suicide killings, the paradigmatic sequence is the reverse of the sequence of the suicide bomber. In the Western mode, one first kills and then reaches one's own death. It is different, yet the same; in both cases there is an act that combines taking the lives of other people and one's own life in a mode of glorious power, revenge, and display.

To conclude this line of thought, even as we owe it to ourselves to state the true facts of how Muslims are the predominant suicide killers of our time, we in the West need to know how similar we are to these Muslim suicide killers—in our different ways. In this respect, both cultures of death making are horrible and disgusting, and both need to be fought.

Jessica Stern, the author of *Terror in the Name of God: Why Religious Militants Kill,* identifies terrorism "as a kind of virus, which spreads as a result of risk factors at various levels: global, interstate, national and personal." She also quotes Mao Tse-tung that "terrorists swim in a sea of ordinary people who are their supporters and provide logistic support."[33] However much we need to and will study Muslim thought and contemporary Muslim societies as the nexus of today's suicide bombings in the world, our own Western hands haven't been clean for ages, and the problem ultimately is another variant of the universal problem for our species, which is that too many of us are eager to kill and kill.

Contradictory Image Meanings of Suicide Bombings

This action [bin Laden's action] is not permitted according to the Shari'a, since Islam is very strict regarding the sanctity of human life, [and states that] human life is inviolable both in times of peace and [in times of] war ... The Muslim people condemn these actions, but do not say that he is not a Muslim or that he is an unbeliever, no. This issue is dangerous ... [it] is the basis of extremism. We do not want to be like bin Laden and his associates [in accusing others of unbelief]. —Sheikh Yousef Al-Qaradhawi, September, 2005. (The headline for this story is: Muslem cleric is against bin Laden's actions but cannot declare him an unbeliever.)[1]

The concept of Jihad is very much different [than it is used in] today's suicide bombings. Jihad also differs from the holy war in the Crusade period ... [where] murder is regarded as a mechanism to approach God and war is regarded as sacred ... On the contrary, Jihad always relies on the power of da'wah (missionary endeavour) and the absence of vengeance feeling. In Jihad, you should not assume yourself to be a killer, nor should you sacrifice the enemy because it is God's will. In the concept of Jihad, war is always regarded as something bad ('syarr) ... War is only permitted to liberate Muslims from tyranny or to defend them from attacks. That is the concept of Jihad. —Khaled Abou El Fadl[2]

THE OPPOSING IMAGE MEANINGS OF SUICIDE BOMBINGS

There are some people who argue that suicide bombing is not at all different from any other military weapon. In fact, it is a tool with several tactical advantages, such as it is relatively "simple" to execute, is inexpensive, requires no escape planning or rescue operations for the perpetrators, has no risk of the bomber being interrogated after the attack, allows the suicide bomber to choose the time, location, and circumstances of attack with a high degree of specificity, can promise extensive casualties, and sows terror in the hearts of the victims.[3]

Hezbollah leader, Ayatollah Fadlallah, offered a justification for suicide bombing notwithstanding the fact that suicide is strictly prohibited by the Koran. In an important work on "political paranoia," Robert Robins and Jerrold Post explain, "Fadlallah asserted that killing oneself as a means of killing an enemy 'differs little from that of a soldier who fights and knows that in the end he will be killed.'"[4]

There are many others, including noteworthy Arab (both Christian and Muslim) theologians and leaders who very much oppose suicide bombing. Thus, according to *Al-Aharam*, the late Edward Said [took] "every conceivable opportunity to denounce suicide attacks as both immoral and counter-productive."[5]

Unfortunately, Said's welcome opposition is not that simple. While he does get credit for opposing the suicide bombings, he also "understood" them in Israel-Palestine as a local phenomenon in response to what he saw as the abject persecution of the Palestinians by the Israelis. Said is quoted as saying in *The Politics of Anti-Semitism*, "Suicide bombing is reprehensible but it is a direct and, in my opinion, a consciously programmed result of years of abuse, powerlessness and despair. It has as little to do with the Arab or Muslim supposed propensity for violence as the man in the moon."[6]

Because suicide bombers in our time are in particular a worldwide phenomenon of the Islamic world, it is important to recognize that there are also many significant voices in the Islamic world who *do* oppose suicide bombing, albeit overall it appears they lack sufficient influence and success to stem the tide of an overwhelming readiness to carry out suicide bombings in many places in the world. At one point, it had seemed in our Western imagination quite impossible that the Islamic world would be able to supply sufficient personnel to carry out the threats it was making, but in one venue after another, the supply of suicide bombers appears to have proven endless. Moreover, insofar as formal and journalistic reports of public opinion are available, it appears that suicide bombers are largely popular and approved by the majority of many Muslim populations.

The following information about the cultural foundations of the suicide bombers in Islam has been assembled from the Information Service of the Library of the Israeli Knesset.[7]

Shahid means in Arabic "martyr," and its language meaning is "witness," which is the meaning of the word in the Koran. The *shahid* is to give testimony, and God and his angels are the witnesses to the *shahid*'s pure and true motives. There is also another linguistic interpretation that the word's post-Koran meaning as martyr is translated from a Greek word. In any case, the reward of those who fall in the service of the Lord is explicitly stated in the Koran: They are to live again, and to receive their recompense from their God, and they shall know no fear or pain.

In Islam there are three categories of fighters. The first goes to battle neither to kill nor to be killed. The second goes to battle to kill and not to be killed. The third goes to battle to kill and be killed. The rewards are greatest for the third category of fighter. He will meet Allah and will be welcome to reside in the Garden of Eden wherever his heart desires.

Islamic doctrine also seeks to help warriors to overcome the primordial fear of death. To do so, the doctrine seeks to teach the warrior to believe their deaths will be worthwhile. The basis for this belief is the Koranic verse that the martyr will live again. According to one school of thought, both his body and soul will return to life. According to another school, only his soul will return to life.

The Prophet Mohammed declared that the *shahid* earns three rewards: absolution for all his sins from the very moment his first drop of blood is spilled, a beautiful woman who will be the first to wipe the dirt from his brow, and entry into the Garden of Eden.

To qualify as a shahid, one must go to battle with true faith. It is also a requirement that death be caused by the warrior's battle wounds.

THE MORAL AND THEOLOGICAL LEGITIMACY OF SUICIDE BOMBINGS IN ISLAM

Notwithstanding all of the above, there are also powerful messages of peace in Islamic doctrine, and many people in the Muslim world devotedly adopt these expressions as their view of the real and true meaning of their Islamic faith.

How one views the overall legitimacy or illegitimacy of suicide bombing in Islam is very much in the eyes of the beholder!

An Islamic site on the Internet sums up the theological-moral position of Islam thus:

> The predominant theme in the Qur'an is forgiveness and peace. Allah (God) is merciful and Forgiving, and seeks that in His followers. Indeed, most people who spend time on a personal level with ordinary Muslims have found them to be peaceful, honest, hard working, civic minded people.
>
> Harming innocent bystanders, even in times of war was forbidden by the Prophet Muhammad (peace be upon him). This includes women, children, non-combatant bystanders, and even trees and crops. **Nothing** is to be harmed unless the person or thing is actively engaged in an assault against Muslims.[8]

It is noted that admonitions are not lacking in the Koran:

> ... And fight in the way of Allah those who fight you. But do not transgress limits. Truly Allah loves not the transgressors. (Surah al-Baqarah 2:190)
>
> ... Nor take life—which Allah has made sacred—except for just cause ... (17:33)

... Oh ye who believe who believe! Remain steadfast for Allah, bearing witness to justice. Do not allow your hatred for others make you swerve to wrongdoing and turn you away from justice. Be just; that is closer to true piety ... (Surah al-Maidah, 5:8)

Peace-loving people have a very strong case for claiming that Islamic scriptures are, intrinsically and essentially, peace-seeking, that life has been declared sacred by the Prophet, and certainly that noncombatants and innocent bystanders need to be protected.

The fact that Islamic violences are proliferating in recent years and have grown far beyond being specific incidents into constituting a major trend problem for our world civilization brings great grief to many adherents of Islam who care about peace, and are humiliated by the association of their beloved faith with rampant cruelty and murder.

The former deputy prime minister of Malaysia, Anwar Ibrahim, was kept in jail for six years on what many considered trumped-up charges. When released in September 2004, he pledged to resume his political leadership for tolerance and democracy in Malaysia. For Muslim leaders he had harsh criticism: "The single biggest failure of Muslims at present," he said is that "you don't have credible leaders, you don't have a real voice of conscience" ... Muslims never blame themselves for their problems, he said. "It's the Americans and the Jews and the Christians. We are still in a state of denial."[9]

Another Muslim, Nassrine Azimi, who serves the international community as director of the Hiroshima Office for Asia and the Pacific of the United Nations Institute for Training and Research wrote the following after the incomparable tragedy in Beslan in southern Russia, where Chechen suicide-bomb terrorists held 1,200 hostages—the majority of them children—in a school for two days; by the time the incident was concluded there were 326 dead (including about twenty of the thirty attacking suicide bombers) and 727 wounded. Azimi said in grief:

> Muslim countries must start questioning why so many of their sons and daughters go about claiming an Islamic inspiration for murderous acts. Who are those who perpetrated the Beslan tragedy in the name of Islam and where, pray, are Muslim politicians and commentators to condemn, unequivocally, their cruelty? ... Where, I ask my fellow Muslims, do we turn when so many atrocities are committed daily under the banner of our faith? I continue to believe that at its heart, as in other great faiths, there is a kernel of timeless beauty and humanity in Islam.[10]

On the other hand, violent religious zealots and terrorists filled with a love of killing who seek legitimation of their violence in their religious culture have all the desired "holy outs" or justifications to seize on in their texts: *Fight those who fight you; don't take life—except for just cause.* Now the message to be taken by the true believer is that one is justified in fighting one's opponents, and it is simply a matter of defining who constitute one's enemies. And, of course, there is never a shortage of passionate zealots who are ready to brand whichever nonbelievers as deserving of being crushed.

THE DIALECTICAL TENSION BETWEEN PEACE AND DEATH IN ISLAM

The seesaw of contradictory meanings about taking life are not unique to Islam. First of all, beyond the actual texts of various religions, it needs to be clear to us that the zealots of any and all religious faiths, as well as of other "faiths" such as diehard believers in political worldviews, have always been capable of radical interpretations that the nonbelievers are enemies of God, life, truth or justice, and deserve to, nay must be extinguished.

But also on the level of the texts of many religious faiths, there are frequent alternations between contradictory positions, say of respecting the lives of strangers in one's community or of conquered enemies, and taking their lives. The dialectical tension between seeking peace and calls to make death in Islam is not entirely different from similar dialectical tensions in many other religions, certainly including both Judaism and Christianity. At the same time, there are differences in the weights assigned to each side of the dialectic in different religions; and far more important, the societal-historical tradition and the political processes in each religious community end up assigning a predominant power more to one imago or the other.

Islam is, it will be seen, in the eyes of the beholder:

- a worldwide faith of tens of millions of people, the number of whom is growing steadily, including their becoming a sizable major population group in many Western, historically non-Muslim countries
- a religious culture that is devoted to a saga through the centuries of heroic mythologies, especially of great and wise leaders who teach people to live with self-discipline a life of faith, good order, and restraint of instincts
- a religious culture that seeks peaceful coexistence and respectful harmony with other religions and cultures, and a renewal of centuries-old traditions of contributing to human thought, mathematics, and esthetics
- a worldwide faith whose historical memory and collective ambition is to recover its position in the world as a major respected force
- a religious tradition of demanding infidels to convert to the only true faith on pain of suffering death; a culture that idolizes power and retaliation in the name of its Allah, that seeks to vanquish the populations of competing cultures and enslave them, including holding women in subjugated positions to serve men as their slaves, and trains many of its adherents to slit with ease and gloating pleasure the throats (and also in no few cases other organs too) of its opponents.
- a worldwide faith that seeks to become, as it once was, the dominant force in the world, if not the ruler of the world in its entirety

So many arguments in Western culture over Islam are based on which aspects of Islam are selected for discussion. To the best of my knowledge, each and all of the above conceptualizations of Islam have much truth in them. You get what you take. If you need to have a one-sided position in whichever direction, you avoid contradictions and dilemmas by ignoring the other sides of the picture.

Ask an average westerner today about Islam, and the majority are likely to associate to Islam's murderous terrorists and suicide killers. They are right; yet they are also wrong in omitting millions of Islamic believers who are committed through their religious faith to decency and nonviolence.

Ask among well-intending advocates of ecumenism, and they will tell you about millions of Islamic believers and about outstanding imams who decry violence. They are right; yet they are also wrong in omitting millions of Islamic believers, say in the Wahhabi tradition of Islam of murderous violence, whether inside the Muslim world in deadly massacres and wars between Sunni and Shi'ite believers, or in violences against outsider infidels—note the latter are variously defined as Americans, Israelis, Jews, or even "Zionist British" (that's what the English were called by Al-Qaeda after the attacks in London on July 7, 2005), or secular Muslims, for the tradition of murdering finds its victims in different locales and political scenarios and defines them as deserving to be killed so very easily.

Then there is the problem of political correctness in Western intellectual circles. Were I to have placed a description of a murderous Islam too much on its own anywhere in this book, the outcry would have been devastating that I am clearly a bigoted Jewish-Israeli and a deeply prejudiced and hostile person, without tolerance for differences in other cultures and respect for other peoples.

But this book is dedicated unambiguously precisely to such a vision of our world as a multicultural society of multiple peoples, ethnicities, religions, and cultures living together respectfully, even more living appreciatively and certainly nonviolently with one another. However, my idealistic vision, toward which I also make a major proposal in the concluding chapter, is linked to and based on seeing the *facts* of life empirically and honestly, and not on the basis of people's ideas and demands of political correctness.

Right now much of Islamic culture is the source of a worldwide genocidal terrorist movement that already has launched the opening of a new kind of World War III against the West. If you have any doubts, ask the dead people at the World Trade Center in New York or the London Underground.

In many, though not all, centers of Islamic life today, the prevailing motif that makes hearts beat in joy of being one with one's faith and people is a call to violence on behalf of the faith. Whether this is the real statistical majority of the world's Muslim population, I do not know for sure. It may or may not be. In some cases, there have been reports of a burgeoning critique and resistance to violence in Muslim populations. Thus, in a survey conducted by the Pew Global Attitudes Project among 17,000 people from late April to early June 2005, before the July 7 bombings in London, a growing number of Muslims said that violence against civilian targets is never justified. That figure was highest in Morocco, followed by Indonesia, and Turkey, countries that themselves are not at the center of major conflicts and that have also been hit by high-profile suicide bombings; here big majorities rejected suicide bombing as an acceptable means of defending Islam. At the same time, roughly, half of the Muslims questioned in Jordan, Lebanon, and Morocco said that in Iraq, suicide bombings against Americans and other Westerners could be justified.[11]

We also know that in the many regions where suicide bombers operate, there seem to be few instances when the ideologists of murder have complained of a shortage of willing recruits to be suicide bombers. On the contrary. And even when we look at critiques of violence that have arisen in some Arab countries, there are rarely statements of the sacredness of human life. For example, there are instances of dissatisfaction with violence in one's own country, such as in Saudi Arabia, which resents the suicide attacks against its kingdom, but hardly in impassioned protests of suicide bombings as insulting to basic values. (Thus, in many ways Saudi Arabia is considered a culture training ground and source of financial support for many terrorist groups elsewhere outside of its own kingdom.)

There are some voices of criticism of killing civilians in the Muslim world, and we will quote some of them in this book, and some of these deserve to be seen as thoroughly genuine, but overall we need to know that there are still high levels of confidence in Osama bin Laden in Muslim countries. There is also near universal anti-Semitism—thus, the Pew survey found 99 percent antipathy to Jews in Lebanon, and 100 percent in Jordan.[12]

As the violence of genocidal terrorism grows around the world, will there be any backlash of protest and condemnation by Muslims themselves? Perhaps. We hope so. But for now, with tongue in cheek, we conclude that there is first much to be done to promote democracy and nonviolence in Muslim cultures and nations.

We know that in many Muslim countries the political-sociological power of the call to destroy the infidel is stronger than the call for peace. Even if in these countries, too, there are many more Muslims who yearn for and believe in peace, they do not have and do not exercise a strong public voice. We also know that in some Muslim countries the peace-loving person has reason to be afraid for his own life were he to speak up against violence and terrorism.

To me the larger and most important consideration about violence by Islam is that it is not only a reflection and outgrowth of those basic sources in Islamic scripture that do condone and foster violence, but of a larger cultural commitment to and celebration of death and violence. This way of life, which I am calling a "Culture of Death," includes considerable education for and honor of primitive cruelty and killing, including celebrations of degradation in the killings. It is also linked to political systems that eschew democratic elections, deny free speech and public criticism, and tolerate and even cultivate fantasy, illusion, and lies as an accepted mode of discourse. Many of these Islamic regimes also have traditions of insatiable economic corruption that runs unchecked in the absence of democratic checks and balances.

On the level of religious thought, the culture of death is associated with the growth of fundamentalist Islamic thinking, such as the Wahhabi version from Saudi Arabia that demands the practice of a severe and ferocious literal interpretation of ancient Islamic practices of deadly punishments of offenders and suppression of the rights of women. This Islamic fundamentalism also embraces a vision of an Islam restored to rule the world. Thus, Sheikh Yousef al-Qaradhawi, whom we saw at the opening of this chapter as *opposed* to bin Laden's actions but whom we shall meet later again as head of the European Council for Fatwa and Research, whose sermons we learn often contain fiery threats and prayers ("O God, destroy the Zionist, American and British aggressors. O God, shake the ground under them"[13]) define Muslims' destiny of supremacy:

> The general overall goal is to preserve the identity of the Islamic nation and its essential entity—to protect it against the attacks that seek to tear it from its roots and change the identity of the [Islamic] nation and turn it into a different nation with a different philosophy that will make it merely a tail, while Allah has created it to be the head; make it a nation in vassalage to others, while [its destiny] is to be followed by others.[14]

It is fascinating to see the tension at play between peace-seeking leaders in the Arab world and those, like al-Qaradhawi, who press for Muslim supremacy and espouse violence as the legitimate means for achieving supremacy. King Abdullah II of Jordan is a leader representing the quest for peace. An intriguing description is given, no less than by the father of the *Wall Street Journal* reporter, Daniel Pearl who was captured and beheaded by Al-Qaeda in Pakistan in 2002, of a conference convened in Amman, Jordan, which is King Abdullah's home court so to speak, where this tension came to the fore.

Attending the conference were 170 Muslim scholars from forty countries who came to define "The Reality of Islam and Its Role in the Contemporary Society." The king himself took the position that, "The acts of violence and terrorism carried out by certain extremist groups in the name of Islam are utterly contradictory to the principles and ideology of Islam." However, at the same conference, Sheik Yousef al-Qaradhawi blamed "injustices done to Muslims by the West" as reasons for Muslim extremism, and the final communiqué of the conference obviously failed to take a stand against terror and killing: "It is not possible to declare as apostates any group of Muslims who believes in Allah the Mighty and Sublime and His Messenger (may Peace and Blessings be upon him) and the pillars of faith, and respects the pillars of Islam and does not deny any necessary article of religion."[15]

Judea Pearl concludes,

> In other words, belief in basic tenets of faith provides an immutable protection from charges of apostasy; anti-Islamic behavior, including the advocacy of mass murder in the name of religion, cannot remove that protection. Bin Laden, Abu Musab al-Zarqawi and the murderers of Daniel Pearl and Nick Berg will remain bona fide members of the Muslim faith, as long as they do not explicitly renounce it.

In the world of scholars of Islamic thought, there are also clear-cut differences between some totally categorical critics of Islam as pro-violence, and other categorical defenders of Islam as an exquisite faith and poetry of life, as well as many other scholars who see a wide continuum between the two poles, among them a small number who are able to see Islam as *both* fiercely warmaking and genuinely seeking to respect human life and do not need to settle on a one-sided definition.

Bat Ye'or is a world-renowned scholar of Islam who exemplifies the first position. She has concluded unrelentingly and uncompromisingly that Islamic *doctrine* as well as *practice* is inexorably committed to violence. The basic point of departure in much of her scholarship is the policy and attitudes of Islam toward the stranger in their midst, the *dhimmi*.[16] Bat Ye'or's unforgiving interpretation is that, at best, the stranger is tolerated temporarily and ambiguously, but basically all non-Muslims are destined for a status of a subjugated people who must convert to Islam or face a dangerous future.

> The aim of *jihad* is to subjugate the peoples of the world to the law of Allah, decreed by his prophet Muhammad. Mankind is divided into two groups, Muslims and non-Muslims ... Non-Muslims are destined to come under Islamic jurisdiction, either by war *(harb),* or by the conversion of their inhabitants ... The property of non-Muslims must revert legitimately to the sole followers of the true religion (Islam). Consequently, the jihad is the means whereby possessions considered illegally usurped by non-Muslims are restored to Muslims.[17]

Jihad, for Bat Ye'or "is a permanent war, it excludes the idea of peace but authorizes temporary truces related to the political situation *(muhadana)*. These truces must not last for more than ten years at most and can be unilaterally denounced by the imam, after notifying the adversary."[18]

Bat Ye'or is convinced that Islamic doctrine compares unfavorably in the above even to Christianity. Writing a Foreword to one of her books, Jacques Ellul very much agrees:

> It will probably be said that every religion in its expanding phase carries the risk of war, that history records hundreds of religious wars and it is now a commonplace to make this connection. Hence, religious passion is sometimes expressed in this manner. But it is, in fact, "passion"—it concerns mainly a fact which it would be easy to demonstrate does not correspond to the fundamental message of the religion. This disjuncture is obvious for Christianity. In Islam, however, *jihad* is a religious obligation. It forms part of the duties that the believer must fulfill; it is Islam's *normal* path to expansion. And this is found repeatedly dozens of times in the Koran.[19]

My personal reading of Bat Ye'or's work, which has been published extensively and respectfully by important academic presses, and who is invited to lecture at responsible and conservative academic centers, is that she apparently has pulled together a legitimate picture of all in Islam that is indeed on the aggressive march to conquest of other peoples. At the same time, it is clear to me that she avoids and passes by all the voices in Islam that speak otherwise, and they are many, and they are not only on the fringes of the Muslim world.[20]

Steven Emerson, whom we have seen as warning American society early on about the serious changes of Islamic terrorism, nonetheless testified to a Senate committee on terrorism, "The vast majority of Muslims do not support in any way the politics of the extremists. Nevertheless, to deny the existence of radical Islam—as some groups have aggressively asserted . . . or to pretend it does not exist is tantamount to defending the militants as one and the same with peace-seeking moderates . . . For the militants . . . the deliberate blurring of the distinction between militant and moderate Islam is designed to hide under the protection of mainstream Islam."[21]

So many bona fide leaders of Islam argue and insist that their faith is *not* one of an aggressive ideology. Dr. Abd Al-Hamid Al-Ansari, former dean of the Faculty of Islamic Law at the University of Qatar, stated in an article in the London Arabic-language daily, *Al-Shaq Al-Awsat,* that modern Islamic fatwas distort the meaning of jihad to justify an aggressive ideology.

Jihad, in its true sense as defined in the Koran and as implemented by the Prophet [Muhammad] and his noble companions, is a means of defending differences, pluralism, and diversity. That is, it is [a means] of defending freedom of choice [as is written in the Koran] "There is no coercion in Islam" . . . [2:256] From the beginning, jihad has been defined by two goals: The first was a response to aggression and oppression [as told in the Koran 22:39]: "To those against whom war is made, permission is given (to fight), because they are wronged; and verily, Allah is most powerful in assisting." The second [goal] is the liberation of the persecuted peoples from tyrannical regimes, as happened to the Persian and Byzantine peoples . . . The truth is that there is no explanation for the distortion of the concept of jihad, except for the fact that there is an aggressive ideology embedded in the hearts of some people. [22]

Al-Ansari believes the term jihad is widely misunderstood by many Islamist clerics, and that "the Muslim public has been deceived."[23] However, he is not trying to whitewash Islam and deny the terror Islam has wrought. He acknowledges unhappily that the result of the deceptions of the Muslim public has been a malignant one, so that even many Muslims who ostensibly condemn terrorism celebrated September 11. "The shows of rejoicing were universal . . . that America deserved what happened to it."[24] In Palestine, as in several Muslim countries, there were open celebrations of September 11. Similarly, public opinion polls in Palestine show "substantial support for suicide bombings" which is celebrated as "the nuclear bomb of the poor and oppressed, to which Israel has no answer."[25]

Education for cruelty is widespread in many parts of the Muslim culture. A report of an Al-Qaeda terrorist attack in Saudi Arabia, whose not-sufficiently-Islamic regime Al-Qaeda is sworn to topple, described the killings of infidels in terms like the following:

> We entered one of the companies' [offices], and found there an American infidel who looked like a director of one of the companies. I went into his office and called him. When he turned to me, I shot him in the head, and his head exploded. We entered another office and found one infidel from South Africa, and our brother Hussein slit his throat. We asked Allah to accept [these acts of devotion] from us ... We ... found a restaurant where we ate breakfast and rested a while. Then we went up to the next floor, found several Hindu dogs, and cut their throats.[26]

However, as noted Saudi Arabia itself has also supported many violences. Although Al-Qaeda finds major fault with Saudi Arabia for not being Islamic through-and-through, Saudi Arabia itself is also a major player in disseminating violence, and fostering what even one Saudi critic characterized as a "culture of death."[27]

The culture of death is described by a Western columnist as a "death cult that is thriving at the fringes of the Muslim world. This is the cult of people who are proud to declare, 'You love life, but we love death' ... This cult attaches itself to a political cause but parasitically strangles it ... But that's the idea. Because the death cult is not really about the cause it purports to serve. It's about the sheer pleasure of killing and dying."[28]

Muslim society has a lot of violence to answer for. A senior Lebanese journalist wrote in *The Daily Star,* which is published in Beirut:

> If the Arabs really want to be able to deal with the post-Sept. 11 era, they need to ask themselves some painfully candid questions. What are the reasons that prompted 19 Arabs to blow themselves up in the United States? Who is to blame for that? What role did Arab societies play in spawning such people? Is there a problem with the Arab media, and with Arab cultural and religious discourse? Are the education systems at fault? Is there a crisis in a society that rejects the idea of tolerance and coexistence with others?
>
> There is no substitute for a shared language that refuses to justify terror in any form, whether in the name of religions, race, or anything else.[29]

Nonetheless, we return once again to note that there are many exponents of peaceful Islam and many peace activists, including those who stand courageously in Muslim societies for peace at some risk to themselves. It is very important for us to recognize and honor the various initiatives for peace in the Muslim world. Thus, on June 21, 2002 a group of fifty-five Palestinian intellectuals published an advertisement in an Arabic-language newspaper, *Al Quds,* calling for a halt to attacks on Israeli civilians.

We urge those behind military attacks against civilians inside Israel to reconsider their positions and to stop pushing our youth to carry out these attacks, which only result in deepening hatred between the two peoples.[30]

After a series of suicide bombings of British targets in Istanbul in November 2003 which were attributed to local Islamic groups believed to be linked to the Al-Qaeda network, Turkish Prime Minister, Tayyip Erdogan, whose political party represents conservative Muslims, said true Islam has nothing to do with terrorism.

It seems to me that those who link our holy beliefs to terrorism are gaining ground even among our people, very slowly and gradually, like water drops making a hole in stone . . . This bothers me . . . I cannot stand it when I hear the phrase Islamic terrorism.

The news account added that under government instructions, sermons in mosques around the country carried an antiterrorism message in their sermons.[31]

Shortly before the above attacks on the British targets, Istanbul had been rocked by two coordinated suicide bomb attacks against two synagogues, killing twenty-three people. London daily newspaper *Al Quds Al-Arabi* received a statement claiming Al-Qaeda was proudly responsible. A Muslim shopkeeper whose shop is near one of the synagogues said, "I thought it was doomsday. No religion can accept this. We are all children of the same God."[32]

An American-Muslim, who is director of international studies at a Michigan college and is associated with the "Association of Muslim Social Scientists, Center for the Study of Islam and Democracy," writes in colloquial "Americanese" in an open letter to Osama bin Laden, "I would rather live in America under Ashcroft and Bush at their worst, than in any 'Islamic state' established by ignorant and murderous punks like you and Mullah Omar." The writer, Muqtedar Khan, notes more summarily, "There are Muslims in America and the world who despise and condemn extremists and have nothing to do with bin Laden and those like him for whom *killing constitutes worship* (my italics)."[33]

Abdurrahaman Wahid is an excellent example of an Islamic clerical leader who devotedly seeks peace. Wahid is no less than a former president of Indonesia, teaches religious law, and is a strong advocate of moderate Islam. According to Wahid, the radicals "are trying to impose a new and distorted interpretation of Islam."[34] Wahid, who maintains active ties with Israel, was one of the framers of the "Pancasila," which means five principles of law, which declares a belief in one God, but avoids according supremacy or a preference to any specific religion. The Muslim organization headed by Wahid has 35 million members, and is the largest Muslim organization in Indonesia and possibly in the Muslim world! In itself, this one Islamic group is a huge constituency for peace.

On the other hand, we are again to remind ourselves that notwithstanding such clear-cut theology of peace loving, any number of Islamic clerics have interpreted the Koran's writings and/or have adopted overriding rulings to justify suicide bombers, and obviously the political positions of these clerics are the ones that prevail in very large swaths of the Muslim world today.

Were Wahid's conception to be accepted by all Muslims in Indonesia, there would not be Islamic suicide bombings in his country. Tragically, this is not the case. We have already referred to at least two such events of suicide bombing in Jakarta, let alone other Islamic terror attacks such as the bombing of two nightclubs in Bali in 2002, which killed some 200 people.

Were the peace-respecting pro-life conception of Islam to predominate in the worldwide cultural process of Islam, it would not necessarily mean that all radical Islamic groups would cease to function and all terror would stop, but it would put Islamic terrorists on the fringes of their own people and religion, reduce the numbers of recruits to terrorism, and facilitate the antiterrorist measures of law and security forces everywhere. This is not the case, and, unfortunately, nothing could be further from likely today in many Islamic communities. As an outsider, I am reluctant to judge what may or may not be the prospects for a peace-respecting Islamic theology some day or in some cultural contexts, for example, Muslim-Americans living in the United States or the United Kingdom who are genuinely interested in becoming part of the American or English democratic ways of life.

Today, in many parts of the Islamic world, implicitly, if not manifestly and brazenly, terror in general and suicide bombing in particular are honored and admired. This also applies to the surviving family of a suicide bomber. One might wonder what some people *really* feel, but what many are reported saying, that evidently is politically correct in many Muslim communities, is that they are proud of their dead suicide bomber and feel that a great honor has been added to their family.

The parents and family of the woman apprentice attorney in the Haifa suicide bombing referred to in the previous chapter are described as reacting to her suicide bombing thus:

> There was a studied stoicism, a fragile air of calm characterized by Rahmeh Jaradat, the mother, who described the attack as "God's will"; by the father, who said the family dwelling was "not a place for condolence" but for pride and joy at their daughter having become an Islamic martyr; by wan smiles among Hanadi's brothers and sisters; and by a stream of visitors from across Jenin and other Palestinian towns eager to offer their congratulations on the "honor" bestowed on the family by Hanadi's action.

Asked if the family had any words of sorrow for the Israelis mourning their dead, anything to acknowledge that others had lost sons and daughters, and mothers and fathers in the attack, the Jaradats allowed silence to fall on the room, nobody wanting to answer for a long period. Eventually the mother spoke up. "Tell them they should think about why our daughter did this," she said. After another pause, she resumed. "In any case, she has done what she has done, thank God, and I am sure that what she has done is not a shameful thing; she has done it for the sake of her people."[35]

The father of one suicide bomber is reported to have said, "To put it simply, we love martyrdom, they love life." I believe this thematic conclusion summarizes the basic line dividing between what I call "trans-national genocidal terrorism" and a culture of death from the rest of civilization and its greater commitment to a culture of life (notwithstanding the many ugly acts of serious destruction also committed by democracies at this stage of our human evolution).

As I will develop later, the real issue in an emerging war between civilizations will not be Islam against the world, but a culture of death and killing versus a civilization that holds life as more sacred and seeks to correct its own violences, slowly but surely, by a rule of law—local, national, and international—against murder, terrorism, and genocide.

It is important to emphasize that the same justifications of killing innocent people will be found not only among Islamic killers, but among the terrorists and their devoted apologists and supporters in all peoples. Thus, Jewish-American physician, Dr Baruch Goldstein, who had immigrated to Israel and was well known among his circle of fundamentalists as a devoted physician, was responsible for a cowardly murder of twenty-nine Muslim civilians and the injury of about hundred more during Friday prayers at the Cave of the Patriarchs in Hebron, a site holy both to Muslims and Jews. Goldstein was thirty-eight and a father of four, from whom he had parted lovingly before heading out to kill, and then to be killed. The rabbi who eulogized him said Goldstein "took action for no other reason than to sanctify the holy name of God"; and supporters continued to hold celebrations at his tomb (until they were made illegal) that is inscribed to "a righteous and holy man ... [whose] hands are innocent and his heart is pure." (Despite many efforts to have the inscription removed it is reportedly still there as of 2005).[36] According to the *Boston Globe*, Goldstein's mother also said she was proud of her son.[37]

The same culture of death is at work in the Christian zealots in the Crusades or in the Inquisition, the Nazis under Hitler, the Russian Communists under Stalin, the Communists under Mao Tse-tung, the Chechnan terrorists fighting Russia, and the Al-Qaeda terrorists blowing up people at multiple locations around the world. The justification and love of bringing death to civilians are the core issues and not any questions of whether the killers at times may be fighting for perfectly understandable and perhaps justifiable political values. At any given point, a culture of death can gain the ascendancy and dominate a given group's cultural and historical process. All cultures of death have in common the legitimation of killing the infidels or nonbelievers and the identified opponents of their group. They go out on holy crusades against their enemies.

A friend of one suicide bomber in Israel-Palestine is quoted as saying, "It is an honour to be able to blow yourself up this way."[38] When a 22-year-old young man, a Jordanian who had been living on the West Bank, exploded a suicide bomb outside a Tel Aviv discotheque killing twenty young Israelis in June 2001, his father was quoted as saying to the Associated Press, "I am very happy and proud of what my son did and I hope all the men of Palestine and Jordan will do the same."[39] A photograph accompanying the AP story showed a touching picture of a grieving, sensitive-looking father holding a picture of his handsome and also sensitive-looking dead son; it is impossible not to feel a degree of human kinship with both of them. A student friend of a woman suicide bomber in Israel said,

"She made us feel proud. More important and even older people couldn't make that decision. It's courageous."[40] (Ironically, the woman speaking was a student at Al Quds Open University whose president, Sari Nusseibah, is prominently identified as the author of a heartwarming and impressive joint peace manifesto with the former head of the Israeli security organization, Ami Ayalon.)

On the other hand, there also are breakthroughs of ambivalence, certainly on an emotional level of poignant reactions to personal loss which then lead some people on to a kind of intuitive grasp of the fundamental immorality of a suicide killing which has also taken from them a loved one. When the mother of a woman suicide bomber referred to earlier was asked whether her daughter's action was right or wrong, she said: "I don't know. I can't tell. I'm sure she believed in what she did." She then added, as if speaking to her dead daughter, that had she known what she was going to do, "I would have tied you up with a rope."[41] Some newspaper reporters have suggested that although it is common and publicly expected of families of Palestinian suicide bombers to thank God for their child's heroic death and achievement of the status of *shahid*, increasingly there are subtexts of mourning, regret, and criticisms by some parents of the heads of Palestinian society, including Arafat before his death, for sending their children to death. Such protests are the more likely from the women and mothers in Palestinian society, but not only.[42]

Returning once again to the woman lawyer suicide bomber, another report quotes the father and each of two cousins thus:

> *The father of Hanadi*: My daughter's action reflected the anger that every Palestinian feels at the occupation. The occupation did not have mercy on my son Fadi, her brother. They killed him even though he was not a wanted person, they murdered him in cold blood before Hanadi's eyes … I will accept only congratulations for what she did. This was a gift she gave me, the homeland and the Palestinian people. Therefore, I am not crying for her.[43]
>
> *One cousin of Hanadi*: I understand her. I understand what pushed her to that place. I understand the moment when she couldn't take it any more.
>
> *Another cousin of Hanadi*: It's something lunatics do, a moment of craziness. [The cousin is described by the reporter as shaking his head from side to side as though in disbelief.] They used her, they took advantage of her pain, they pushed her into the craziness. It's not normal. It's impossible to understand a thing like that.[44]

The second cousin raises a consideration we will be looking at shortly that there were self-interested political figures who were out to take cynical advantage of Hanadi's grief and rage, but also goes further to make a point that I will be making very strongly from my Western point of view that taking life—one's own and others—is, quite simply or ultimately, an act of madness. One implication of such reports is that, to quote Habib Malik again, there are the same "universal values deep within the minds of people," and perhaps some day there can be more of a shared language of people on Earth that killing and premature deaths are tragically wrong.[45]

The reader should note that I am very aware that some suicides under grave conditions, such as soldiers bravely giving their lives to save others, and terminally ill people who decide to end their misery, are not at all cases of "madness," even though after we discuss this issue soon at length, my reasoned conclusion will be that laymen are correct when they say, spontaneously and naively, that most suicide bombers do have to be thought of by us as disturbed.

MUSLIMS WHO LIVE IN DEMOCRATIC COUNTRIES

The language of the second cousin also brings us once again to the particularly fascinating and perhaps also practically quite important question as to what is going to happen to Muslims who live in democratic countries? Will the prevailing democratic ethos, say of the United States, United Kingdom, or Australia, win over a majority of Muslims to reject terrorism? For Muslims everywhere, there is a profound tension between identification with one's own people and the longstanding traditions of violence and terrorism in Islamic culture, versus being a loyal American or Briton, let alone a tension on practical levels that approving terrorism can be bad for one's employment or even against the law in democratic countries. It is not surprising to learn of situations where Muslim communities in democratic countries overall may disapprove of a suicide bomber, and yet also experience understanding and respect for the act.

When two Muslim British citizens were identified as the suicide bombers in April 2003 in a Tel Aviv nightclub, *Mike's Place*, a jazz bar next door to the American Embassy that is popular with U.S. and British tourists as well as Israelis, there was consternation in many quarters. For British who take pride and believe in the capacity of their democratic way of life to win over people from other cultures such as the large Muslim population that has made its home in England, it was a shock to find that a Muslim child from a Westernized family could embrace political terrorism. One of the suicide bombers, for example, was from a relatively wealthy Westernized family who lived in an English Midlands town, had been educated at a private school, and went to a university in London. Still, a spokesman for an Islamic group that has been prominent in celebrating the attacks of September 11, Al Muhajiroun, was quoted as saying to BBC, "The feeling for jihad at the current time of Iraq and Afghanistan and the continuing intifada in Palestine is very hot in the Muslim community."[46] Muslim neighbors in the town of Derby from which the suicide bomber came, condemned the suicide bomber, but a *New York Times* reporter observed, "Scratch beneath the surface in Derby and one finds a good deal of empathy for the motivation." One young man in the town explained, "Killing people is wrong, obviously, but if he was doing it for God himself—then fair enough. You have to be pretty brave to do something like that to hold a bomb in your hand and blow yourself up."[47]

The suicide bombings in London on July 7, 2005 of three Underground stations and one bus, with 56 dead, over 700 wounded, and thousands more traumatized by vicious experiences of being trapped underground rocked the English on more than the level of the tragic number of dead and wounded. The *New York Times* reported about the perpetrators of the July 7 bombings that three of the four men were British nationals raised in the United Kingdom, while the fourth was born in Jamaica and had spent much of his life in the Caribbean as well as six years as a youth in Cleveland in the United States.[48] Roger Cohen wrote in the *International Herald Tribune* after July 7, "Put the video images of the four London suicide bombers side by side with that of Mohamed Atta entering the airport at Portland, Main, on September 11, 2001, and the resulting collage could not be more banal. The Leeds killers with their caps and backpacks and sneakers are just another bunch of lads dressed in the garb America offers the world."[49] Two of the suspected suicide bombers, Shehzad Tanweer, 22, and Hasib Hussain, 19, were described as "British to the core." Tanweer was a university-educated cricket fanatic who also excelled in soccer and whose father ran a profitable fish-and-chips shop. Hussain was a bright student who graduated from Matthew Murray vocational school in 2003. In recent months, both began to shake off Western habits. "This is a shock to the Muslim community here," said a Pakistani woman who said she was too fearful to give her name. "He looked respectful. He looked educated. His father had a business," she said of Tanweer. "You can't explain it. It's not right what happened."[50]

An older man who was close to one of the bombers, who regularly called him, "Uncle," couldn't believe his beloved "nephew" was identified as a terrorist. "He's a quiet youth who loves to play cricket ... He's a good boy. He goes to several mosques ... I can't believe he would get himself into such a mess ... We don't believe this was done for the people of Islam."[51]

Germaine Lindsay, the 19-year-old man suspected of blowing up an Underground train at Russell Square, took hold of Islam four years ago zealously. He had been a natural athlete who played soccer, ran, was a regular at the gym, and took up boxing. "He was a very happy person," said a schoolmate. But after his conversion, he changed strikingly. He rejected some of his old friends and stopped smoking, listening to music, and playing soccer. He "shut himself away," she said. His wife who was eight months pregnant said she didn't believe it.[52]

The worst fear of the British intelligence services had come to life: The suicide bombers were native Britons. "Security sources in Britain now must confront something they feared for a long time ... suicide bombers who were born in England. What worries the security service is that the four responsible for the suicide bombings in London went through the radicalizing processes of becoming extremists in Britain and did not undergo brainwashing in training camps in Afghanistan or the Middle East."[53]

MUSLIM REACTIONS TO LONDON JULY 7

In response to July 7, the reactions of Arab leaders and the Arab press around the world included many statements of condemnation. Syrian President Bashar al-Assad, Palestinian President Mahmoud Abbas (Abu Mazen), and Prime

Minister Ahmad Qurei (Abu Alaa), and other leaders sent clear messages, some presumably letter-perfect politically correct, but some of which also conveyed what may be a genuine thoughtful engagement with the horror of such actions. Thus, Palestinian Prime Minister, Abu Alaa said: "It is inconceivable that there [would be] a logical justification that the human mind can accept for the harming of innocent civilians."[54] However, there were also many statements that were lukewarm condemnations and were accompanied by immediate statements of understanding and even justification of the suicide bombers. Others added no less immediate repetitions of tough anti-Americanism, anti-Britishism, and anti-Israelism/anti-Semitism hardly ways of confirming sympathies for the British victims. Of course, some of these added demurrers such as, "We are not justifying [the attack]; rather we are interpreting and analyzing it."[55] And they emphasized their genuine feelings for the victims: "We completely identify with the victims of the explosions in London ... But—and there is no escape from this 'but' ..."[56]

Similarly from religious leaders in Islam. Some famous imams, like one who will emerge as our favorite "poster-sheikh" in this book, Sheikh Tantawi of Cairo, really laid on the condemnation, and that "those responsible for London attacks are criminals who do not represent Islam or even truly understand (its message)," and then with subtle malevolence condemned the killing of civilians, including women and children, "without differentiating between combatants and non-combatants." In other words, suicide bombings against the combatants, oh great sheikh of war and killing, remains kosher, and we know exactly against whom because you have told us so! As a grieving Londoner, wouldn't you love to have a comforting spiritual visitor like that to help you in your sorrow?

Still others who did the right thing to stand up against the terrorism in London really made it all alright by beginning a wonderful trail of conspiracy thinking that no doubt will yet evolve to bigger and better fantasies (comparable to the nonsense of who is said to have been the real perpetrator of September 11). Thus, a columnist in Saudi Arabia said poetically already the day after July 7: " ... We are a nation [that is sitting] on the defendant's bench ... [But] I can almost smell the scent of conspiracy in the affair."[57]

Outdoing him, the chairman of the Saudi Association for Aviation and Space Sciences already put the conspiracy all together: Al-Qaeda had nothing to gain ... The British would now have justification for staying in Iraq ... Israel's Minister of the Treasury, Benjamin Netanyahu, was in London and was warned not to go out before the attacks by Scotland Yard.[58]

Other Islamic leaders put their condemnation of the bombings to immediate work as incitements and evocations of more hate—and no less than calls for death to the accursed Americans and Israelis. Great condemnations of terror these are. A Teheran Ayatollah protested the bombings thus:

> The entire Iranian people condemn this. Massacring women, children, old and young is entirely inappropriate for a human being, and cannot be accepted by anyone with a conscience.

The same report continues that the Ayatollah said further that Al-Qaeda is the illegitimate son of the United States and Israel:

> Have you forgotten who the mother and father of Al-Qa'ida are? America is its father, and Israel its mother. It is the illegitimate child of these powers.

And then the crowd responded by chanting:

> Allah Akbar. Allah Akbar. Allah Akbar . . . Death to those who reject the rule of the jurisprudent. Death to America. Death to England. Death to the hypocrites (Mojahedin-e Khalq) . . . Death to Israel. [59]

Thus spoke an erstwhile regret and condemnation, unabashedly inspiring yet more killing.

As I brought up earlier, in the long run there remains an especially crucial question of whether Muslims in a democratic country will be loyal as citizens of their country and to Western culture's prevailing values opposing terrorism, or will they generate disproportionate numbers of dissidents, spies, and saboteurs against their country's democratic ethos? One thing that is clear about our human minds is that we can be exposed to the values of another culture, its language and even speech quite meaningfully, BUT in many cases people hold on to their original cultural values and rationalize away altogether easily any conflicts between the two in favor of their default value system.

A well-educated Iraqi engineer who teaches in Qatar has a sense that he himself does not want to be a person who seeks to or approves murders of non-Muslims, but this is how he explained to a companion in a taxi crossing Iraq to Jordan what it was that bin Laden intended when he blew up the towers in New York:

> He *only* (my italics) wanted to get the Americans out of Saudi Arabia and the Israelis out of Palestine. He saw how the West is taking over and wanted to help. Fortunately, he had enough money to establish the resistance movement, al-Qaida. No Arab country, no Islamic body, has helped Islam like bin Laden. I don't say that one has to kill. I'd be happy if the Jew or the Christian would listen to me and see how I, not only personally but Muslims in general, want peace. But they don't listen and therefore they have to learn the hard way, and they'll learn.[60]

Little did the engineer know that his companion in the taxi was an Israeli newspaperman.

Earlier we "met" Sheikh Yousef al-Qaradhawi, a Sunni Islamic cleric who heads the European Council for Fatwa and Research. The Council meets two or three times a year in a European city with the express purpose of evaluating discrimination against Muslims in Western countries and issuing fatwas to protect Muslim communities. In a conference in Stockholm in July 2003 entitled "Jihad and Denying its Connection to Terror," the Council approved the employment of suicide bombers on three fronts: Palestine, Kashmir, and Iraq. Sheikh al-Qaradhawi rejected the notion that martyrs are committing suicide. Suicide is an act of people who fail in business, love, and so on, he said, but suicide bombers "give themselves to Allah in order to receive paradise in exchange." As for the legitimacy of the weapon, "What weapon can harm our enemy, can prevent from sleeping, and strip off a sense of security and stability, except for these human bombs? ... It is a unique weapon that Allah has placed only in the hands of the men of belief. It is a type of divine justice on earth, the weapon of the wretched weak against the powerful tyrant." The Sheikh also clarified that it is also permissible to kill Muslims when an enemy that is attacking Muslims hides behind Muslims.[61]

Thomas Friedman has observed that the spread of suicide bombing threatens to become a built-in given of reality in our world society. Following a suicide bombing in Tel Aviv, Friedman wrote, "Suicide bombing is becoming so routine that it risks becoming embedded in contemporary culture." He warned at the time that the process of acclimatization and as-if acceptance of suicide bombing in the Middle East must be stopped, including from the point of view of America's own self-interest. "Otherwise, this suicide madness will spread, and it will be Americans who will have to learn how to live with it."[62] Since then American troops indeed have been faced with more and more suicide bombings in Iraq, let alone one should not forget that the awesome airplane attacks of September 11 earlier were ultimate forms of suicide killings.

THE MEANING OF SUICIDE BOMBING IS IN THE EYES OF THE BEHOLDER

Clearly, the meaning of suicide bombing is in the eyes of the beholder. The act of suicide bombing means whatever the theological, political, and psychological definitions imposed on the act. We each choose what suicide bombings are to mean.

- Suicide bombing is heroic, and the perpetrator is a loyal son or daughter of his or her religion and a person deserving praise and gratitude!
- Suicide bombing is a depth of evil, cowardice, and madness that violates every standard of human decency, and the suicide bomber deserves severe condemnation!

Even when a religious code provides an obviously explicit text for condemning suicide bombings, in the case of Islam on the basis both of suicide being deemed a violation of Mohammed's will and on the further basis that killing innocent people is a violation of the Prophet's will, our human minds are never at a loss as to how to retranslate a text to bring it in line with whichever policy we want to adopt. If it's suicide bombings we want, it is child's play to "prove" that it is Allah's will!

(Of course, this is not unique to Islam. The dialectic of peace-seeking and death-making referred to earlier as present in most religions means that there is some degree of duplicity in each of these religions, so the proper texts for legitimating violence are always there waiting to be coopted and exploited sanctimoniously by the violent zealots of each faith.)

The same terrifying principle that the meaning of it all is in the eyes of the beholder is true not only in societal-political thought, but in the minds of each of the specific individuals who make up their decisions whether or not to be suicide bombers. Since it is, first of all, all in the mind, can this also mean that people or cultures or both conceivably can change their minds? In individuals, we have occasional testimonies of a person changing their mind.[63] It is encouraging to think of how a friend or a loved one might intervene in time, to change a suicide bomber's mind, and maybe better yet to imagine an imam who would intervene just in time with the message that Allah does not want a person to bring death to innocent people. For a culture as a whole, dare we imagine what could develop if imams together with other respected leaders of the community would call for protecting life? We will return to these fantasies before we complete this work.[64]

Let it be entirely clear that none of the observations I make of the amazing relativity of the meanings of suicide bombers mean that I do not believe completely firmly in the rightness of protecting life and the wrongness of destroying life. What my efforts to understand different images and meanings do imply is that in order to fight against suicide bombings, we need to understand what these acts mean to the tens of thousands of people who are prepared to give their lives and to take the lives of others.

Personally, I do not believe that the heroic meanings assigned to suicide bombings even by a whole culture, nor other understandable and not-illegitimate motivations of fighting back against humiliation, or taking revenge for bitter personal losses, however important at one quite real level of the mind, in themselves *really* explain the act. At the core, I think many of us human beings are prepared to take advantage of excuses and seeming justifications for acting on the powerful attractions of suicide and murder, and the even more irresistible attractions of the two combined in suicide-murder.

The story of man's romances with death of course has produced a huge and in a sense endless literature. There is a profound psychology of man's attraction to the safety and fatalism of nothingness and the consummate finality of death. Here I would restrict myself to a deeply respectful reference to the creative thrust of Sigmund Freud in his identification of *thanatos* or an inherent drive toward or in the direction of death as a goal of life and thereby as a central force in man's psyche. I don't think Freud developed the understanding of thanatos as deeply as it warranted—perhaps for him too, in his time, even in his greatness, it was bigger than he could handle.

For those who insist, cogently in my opinion, that there are very powerful ideological reasons for suicide bombings (such as in Islam identification with a theological "jihadist" point of view or a philosophy of killing the infidel as enemy); and for others who insist, again cogently in my opinion, that political motivations are strongly at work in motivating suicide bombers, turning to a psychology of desires to kill and die and as if embrace death can seem trivial and sissy. After all the former conceptions are rooted in concrete hard facts that have been available to research, while the "psychobabble" of unconscious motives is hardly subject to most direct interviews, questionnaires, or opinion polls.

Academic thinkers so often get locked into their one explanation, whatever it is, that one almost loses academic popularity by not taking a strong-minded single-dimensional position so that so-and-so researcher can be identified with that one idea and not with a confusing combination medley of ideas.[65] So that there already have appeared students of suicide bombings who insist so strongly on an explanation of religious ideology that they virtually exclude political motivations—which I think is dead wrong; and others who insist on the political motivations and adamantly minimize religious ideology as a prime mover—which again I think is dead wrong.

Some reviewers of manuscripts such as this on suicide bombings and terrorism hate any psychological explanations. Politics, ideology, strategy, historical imperatives—fine, but there is no place for the vagaries of the human mind, spirit, and soul.

Again, I appeal to the common sense of most people:

Think of committing suicide for a cause you care about very deeply.
Think of killing many civilians by your suicide for the advance of your cause.
Do you sense that part of you could consider such steps?
Do you sense that the ideas of suicide and murder touch on deeper parts of your mind, and that no matter how much you care about your cause you won't be able to do it without a major decision inside of you that you want to die and that you want to kill and injure others?

I think that psychological explanations are also vital parts of the puzzle along with ideological, political, and other causes (which we will review more systematically later).

It also should hardly be a secret that many human beings love to hunt, maim, and kill other people. So that there are some of us who will have answered the above exercise with discoveries that we don't mind dying if only we can do the killing that excites us. Moreover, others of us are on or close to an edge, and if the right leaders and movements come along, we can be pushed over the edge.

The raw aspects of our human primitivism are always waiting for various "priests of death" or con men or cult leaders or military leaders to arise to activate in many of us our fascination with and love of death over our no less basic love of life and survival.[66] There is no doubt that images and meanings laid down variously by different cultures go a long way toward contributing to each individual's ultimate personal choices; and that the quality of mind and spirit that await in each person play roles in deciding who will and who won't commit acts of spreading death.

AN EXPLOITATIVE TRANSFORMATION OF WOMEN INTO "KOSHER" SUICIDE BOMBERS FOR HAMAS IN PALESTINE

In January 2004, Reem Salah al-Raiyshi, a Palestinian woman suicide bomber exploded herself at—in fact, directly inside the Erez checkpoint from Gaza in the Palestinian territory to Israel, where thousands of Palestinian laborers eager for work in Israel undergo a security check. What was noteworthy about the bomber's technique is that she managed to talk the Israeli soldiers into letting her *into* the checkpoint through posing as a handicapped person—she feigned limping and told the soldiers she was on her way to medical treatment, and she also told them that she had a metal pin in her leg from previous surgery that would set off the metal detector. There have been many shameful incidents where Israeli soldiers have denied passage to obviously sick people or women giving birth with terrible health consequences. This time the soldiers were decent, and they paid with their lives.

What was further noteworthy about this bomber is that in the Palestinian-Israeli conflict, she was the first female suicide bomber to be sponsored by the terrorist Hamas movement which previously had insisted, even pridefully, that they would not use women as suicide bombers as other Palestinian terrorist groups had begun to do. The issue of not allowing females to be suicide bombers was even attributed quasi-religious meanings.

A year and a half earlier, in an interview with the Egyptian newspaper *Al Ahram*, then political-religious leader of Hamas, Sheikh Ahmed Yassin, had said: "We have no need for suicide operations by women now because preserving the nation's survival is more important." By that, the Hamas leader had meant that the role of women is to have children and increase the strength of the Islamic nation, while war is the job of men.

Now the Hamas appeared eager to take credit for the woman suicide bomber. After the bombing at Erez checkpoint, Yassin told the world, "It is an innovation and a change in tactics by Hamas, as for the first time, a woman is carrying out the operation." In a newspaper interview, Yassin explained: "Even though the use of women is considered unusual, jihad is an obligation of all Muslims, men and women."[67]

What made Yassin change his mind? In the final analysis, the approval of women suicide bombers by Hamas was understood by many as one of its ways of competing for greater popularity in the Palestinian community toward its ultimate bid to take over the Palestinian Authority from Arafat and his faction, the Fatah. So the change in "religious doctrine" by Hamas was in the service of an old-fashioned quest for political power which was tastier than religion or family life values.

For the longest time, women were ruled unacceptable as suicide bombers by the large Palestinian terrorist group of the Hamas under the leadership of their all-powerful if also blind and frail spiritual head, Sheikh Ahmed Yassin. While other Palestinian groups such as al-Aksa and Islamic Jihad had given the OK for women suicide bombers, and the first bombing by a woman was in January 2002, Hamas retained its opposition (although it was known to refer women who wanted to volunteer to one of the other groups). The woman's place was in the home, making and bringing up children for Islam. In January 2004, in the case we are describing of 22-year-old Reem Raiyshi, herself the mother of an 18-month-old daughter and a 3-year-old son, Hamas changed their longstanding rules and even theology and proudly accepted responsibility for the suicide bombing by a woman. Sheikh Yassin announced that Hamas would increasingly dispatch female suicide bombers in a "new beginning" for Palestinian women.

Yassin said jihad "is an obligation of all Muslims, men and women." He added that women had been excluded from carrying out suicide bombings only because there had never been a need for them. "Women were spared until the time of need arose," Yassin said. "When the brothers in the military wing saw that the time was right to carry out an operation using a woman, they sent Reem Rayshi." With that attack, the group send a clear message that women must step up and fulfill their "obligations," said Yassin.[68]

Intriguingly, Hamas' change of heart was also reported as predicated on a further definition that the woman who is to give her life is one who has "desecrated family honor," which means that she has been unfaithful. The use of the woman as a suicide bomber could now serve two functions, one of avenging the family's loss of honor by having the woman die in atonement for her infidelity—which is often enough arranged in Arab society in any case, and the second of attacking the Israelis. According to a *Washington Times* story, the Israeli newspaper, *Yediot Ahronot*, reported that Raiyshi was compelled to carry out the attack as atonement for betraying her husband, who was a Hamas operative, with another man, and that her husband urged her to carry out the suicide mission. Citing Israeli security officials, the Associated Press reported that Raiyshi was an adulterer who was forced to carry out the attack to restore her family's honor. The *Washington Times* report added: "It is not uncommon for Palestinian women accused of adultery, or of having sex before marriage, to be killed by their families trying to rid themselves of perceived disgrace." According to the Associated Press it was Raiyshi's lover who had recruited her and gave her the suicide bomb belt, while her husband actually drove her personally to Erez to carry out the attack.[69]

One group of Israeli men in a health club locker room, after getting past the inevitable grief and anger at the loss of life at the Erez crossing, began joking good-naturedly enough that the Arab men were lucky to have a way of getting rid of their unfaithful women of which they, the Jewish men, were jealous.[70]

According to an Israeli television channel, "a new theology" is emerging about female suicide bombers among some Palestinian Muslim religious leaders. Male "martyrs" who blow themselves up in suicide attacks are already promised a place in paradise alongside seventy-two dark-eyed virgins, and now, according to Arab affairs analyst Ehud Ya'ari, the women are promised to dwell forever alongside the husband or fiancé they have left behind.[71]

The progressive expansion of the clerical and public legitimation of women as suicide bombers in Islam gives a further perspective on the expansion of warring ambitions in the Islamic world. It was shocking how easily the religious attribution of holiness to women and their family-building roles could be desacrilized in order to free a large new reservoir of manpower.[72]

CHANGES IN IMAGES OF SUICIDE BOMBERS WITH THE SHIFT FROM MILITARY TARGETS TO CIVILIAN TARGETS

Table 3.1 is intended to show how the image meanings of suicide bombing have shifted for our Western world from a once-suspicious but still grudging acknowledgment of the somewhat heroic meaning of suicide bombing so long as it was a military act against a military target. Even in respect of pure military action, Judeo-Christian culture looks unsurely at the suicide component and wonders if there isn't something kinky, disturbed, deceitful, or immoral to the self-destruction, but it also recognizes the honorable, heroic, and sacrificial nobility of the warrior. But once suicide bombings shift over to being the works more of self-appointed terrorists than men on military missions, even if they are aiming at military targets, and especially once they are aimed more ruthlessly and cruelly at civilians of all ages, the image meaning of the suicide bombing shifts dramatically for our Western minds toward a combined evil, stupidity, and craziness.

From a larger point of view, the choice to be a suicide bomber is an ultimate expression of fascist thinking by the individual and the culture which sponsors it. The battle our civilization must wage to put an end to deadly suicide bombings is a battle on behalf of Democracy over Fascism.

The original form of suicide-murder attacks was much more one of military forces against military targets, where the attacks take place largely within a traditional military context. The sponsoring culture and people consider such attacks basically as acts of bravery of warriors who have gone forth in the tradition of the noble heroes to do war against the enemy, using unusual but quite legitimate powerful weapons. Intriguingly, as I noted earlier, even on the part of the victim cultures, there can be a degree of acceptance of the honor of such attacks, although it should be added that Western or Judeo-Christian communities also uneasily begin to attribute elements of cowardice to the unexpected sneak nature of the attacks that do not come in the form of traditional military actions, and there is also some distinct queasiness about the use of suicide as a weapon by the warrior. Whatever heroic meaning was present for Western or Judeo-Christian cultures then drops sharply when the attack shifts from a clear-cut military target to a somewhat but less militarily significant target.

Insofar as the destruction of civilians begins either to be allowed as an inadvertent necessity of the mission, and certainly insofar as the killing of civilians

Table 3.1 Changes in Image Meanings of Suicide Bombers from a Western Point of View with the Shift from Military Targets to Civilian Targets

Types of Suicide–Murder Attack	Predominant Image Meanings
1. "No-escape attack" or suicide bombing by a military force within traditional military role and purpose against military targets • *heroic Samson-like charge against a strong enemy encampment* • *Japanese kamikaze pilots in WWII* • *Al-Qaeda boat loaded with explosives rams USS Cole in Yemen in 2000*	1. Brave, loyal, self-sacrificing warrior in tradition of noble hero going to war against enemy with unusual but basically legitimate powerful weapon • *If attackers are a terrorist group, and especially if their identity is largely unknown and their action unexpected, some of the luster of military heroism is reduced and replaced with images of a dastardly sneak attack*
2. "No-escape attack" against militarily or politically significant target in process of which destruction of civilians is allowed or more actively sought and welcomed • *Palestinians attacking well-guarded Israeli outpost settlements in politically disputed areas* • *September 11 attack against U.S. military headquarters in Pentagon*	2. Some image elements of military heroism are retained, but overall fades into images of cowardly war crimes of murdering civilians indiscriminately • *The more repulsive and criminal the more the victims include civilians going about their normal lives (e.g., a family at a Sabbath dinner at home in an Israeli settlement), or when innocent civilians of all ages who have no connection to the military target are murdered (e.g., passengers on the airplane hijacked by Al-Qaeda for use as a bomb to explode the Pentagon)*
3. "No-escape attack" or suicide bombing which targets civilian populations in apartment or office buildings, cafes, restaurants, discos, buses, airplanes, etc. The suicide bomber explodes himself or herself with the explicit purpose of killing as many people as possible, and also wounding and maiming as many additional people as possible. • *Dr. Baruch Goldstein, an extremist Jewish settler, for all that he was a dedicated physician, goes on a murder spree against civilian Arab worshippers at a holy site in Hebron* • *September 11 attacks against World Trade Center by Al-Qaeda* • *suicide bombing by terrorists of residences and recreational centers, e.g., Chechens in Moscow, or Al-Qaeda in Saudi Arabia residential areas, and Islamic terrorists in nightclubs in Bali and Jakarta in Indonesia*	3. Evokes horror, terror, disgust, and revulsion at spree of apocalyptic murder of innocent unarmed civilians going about their lives, especially in recreational leisure settings, as well as at self-immolation by attacker

actually becomes sought after actively as a direct goal of the attackers, a full measure of condemnation of suicide bombings follows in the Western mind. The overall associational picture becomes one of cowardly war crimes involving cruel, indiscriminate killings of civilians that are entirely repulsive to the fair-play mind of the West.

Note that suicide attacks need not be always with bombs, but can also be what have been called "no-escape attacks" or attacks by an armed person with whatever weapons against a target group where it is quite clear that the attacker will die. We gave one terrifying example of such a suicide killing by an Israeli Jew, a former American, Baruch Goldstein, the physician, who for all the reports that he was continuing practicing as a devoted doctor, went on a disgusting murder spree against Arab civilian worshippers at a holy site in Hebron.

CONTRADICTORY IMAGES IN CULTURES WHICH CONDONE AND CULTURES WHICH CONDEMN THE SUICIDE KILLINGS

Table 3.2 presents a series of contrasting image meanings, where one frame contains images approving, legitimating, and celebrating suicide bombings, while the second frame presents images which seriously disapprove of the killers and their murdering, both themselves and, of course, the more so the others whose lives they entitle themselves to terminate.

For the West, terrorist bombings which specifically and purposely target innocent civilian populations, such as in residential buildings (e.g., Moscow) or office buildings (e.g., New York), cafes, restaurants and discos (e.g., Tel Aviv, Jakarta), buses (e.g., Sri Lanka, Israel, and London), subways and trains (Madrid and London), airplanes (e.g., September 11 in the United States) are attacks which evoke horror, terror, and revulsion. They are seen as murder sprees against innocent civilians going about their lives. The viler the attacks, the more are the victims blown up in settings where they are pursuing the pleasures of normal life, such as restaurants and places of recreation, and the more are young people and children the victims. Under these circumstances in particular, the lines of contradictory meanings are fully drawn between the killing cultures and those who oppose the deaths of innocents.

For the former, the perpetrators continue to be brave martyrs doing their all for their gods, leaders and people, who deserve rewards on Earth (to their families) as well as in the heavens beyond and in the historical memories of their home community and culture. For the latter, they are criminal, godless, heartless, cruel and ultimately evil, and they are in violation of normative international law. Thus, a report by Amnesty International in July 2002 concluded, "The deliberate killing of Israeli civilians by Palestinian armed groups amounts to crimes against humanity."[73] (Note that the same Amnesty report does not spare Israel from the most serious criticism for its own crimes against humanity.) Similarly, a Human Rights Watch report that covers suicide bombings against Israeli civilians in the

Table 3.2 Contrasting Image Meanings of Suicide Bombings in Cultures Which Condone and Cultures Which Condemn the Killings

Meanings to the Suicide Bombers and to the Cultures that Celebrate their Suicide Killings	Meanings to the Victims and to Western Cultures that are Revolted by and Condemn the Suicide Killing
Military attacks to kill as well as to terrorize the enemy with surprise, suddenness, totality, and the horror of being exploded, which are carried out by brave warrior patriots and freedom fighters	*A perverse apocalypse* which includes ending the world of one's own existence by surrender to suicide—often backed by whatever ridiculous illusions such as of an eternal immortality, along with despicable and immoral killing of innocent civilians and cruel wounding and maiming of others
Collective and/or personal revenge for historical losses of ethnic pride and power, e.g., Islam's loss of its past power and glory to Christianity, current battles for independence in Chechnya or Palestine, and/or revenge for personal losses of family and friends killed by the enemy	*Continuation and escalation* of cycles of deadly violence and nullification of any possible political progress and diplomacy toward a peaceful solution
Legitimate weapon of the wretched and oppressed against the high, mighty, and powerful	*A runaway evil of crimes against humanity and genocide* by cruel cowards who stand in violation of civilization's advancing laws against mass killing
Noble sacrifice and martyrdom (shahid) in fulfillment of religious command and privilege to serve the true religion gloriously against the infidels (jihad)	*Violation of universal religious value of sacredness of life*, including Islamic prohibitions of spilling innocent blood
Faith in promises of rewards of ecstasy in death and further rewards in eternity, such as seventy-two beautiful virgin maidens	*Crazy thinking, stupidity, and submission to brainwashing and lies* of religious and political leaders and the handlers they send to manipulate, hypnotize, and coerce the suicide bomber to give up his or her life and to kill the innocent
Honor and glory as an eternal hero and celebrity among one's people, as well as elevation of the status of one's family	*A twisted glory of a costly exhibitionism*, a pathological identification with a cause and readiness to adopt its goals to a point of loss of one's own identity and life
Financial rewards for one's family	*A ghastly and dishonorable way of "making a living,"* and a way of providing for one's family that is deeply marred by one's eternal absence as a real spouse and/or parent, or as a son or daughter to one's surviving parents

period between September 20, 2000, and August 30, 2002, came to the conclusion that the "leaders of Hamas and Islamic Jihad appear to be criminal offenders under international humanitarian law for having encouraged and endorsed suicide attacks against Israeli civilians."[74]

For the suicide bombers and their cultures, the entire civilian population is a target. The acts of killing *always* remain military attacks designed to terrorize an enemy who deserves nothing less than the sudden horror of being exploded by the brave patriots and freedom fighters. The attacks constitute both collective revenge and in many cases acts of personal revenge for specific losses of family and friends to the enemy. The attacks restore ethnic pride and a sense of power. They are a legitimate weapon of the wretched oppressed against the high and mighty. Religiously, the suicide bombings constitute noble sacrifices and earn martyrdom. They also earn all the celestial rewards that a religion-folklore can promise, such as the well-known current Islamic promises of a payoff of seventy-two beautiful virgin maidens.[75] Honor and glory are bestowed on the hero after his or her death, and the status of their family is significantly elevated.

From the point of view of the victims and from the point of view of Western cultures in general, the above meanings are entirely reversed. The suicide bombers are perverse, morbid practitioners of apocalypse. They themselves have stupidly surrendered the gifts of their lives to suicide and whatever illusions accompany their suicide of an eternal immortality or the pleasure of a triumphant revenge they will never live to see in this world or the next; but even more deserving of condemnation is their hateful cruelty of killing innocent civilians and injuring countless others with disfiguring wounds and painful disabilities. In Western eyes, they are pure evil. Theirs are clearly crimes against humanity and genocide, deserving of harsh prosecution under the developing codes of law for such criminal acts. On the level of universal religious values, the suicide bombers stand in utter violation of a universal sacredness of life in every extant religion, *including* Islam. Suicide bombings also contribute terribly to escalations of cycles of violence which destroy any possibilities of political progress toward negotiations of peace. Finally, the honor and celebration that the suicide bombers earn are a twisted exhibitionistic glory that is hardly worth the price of one's own life and cannot possibly justify taking the lives of others.

Robert Melson, a professor of political science and former President of the International Association of Genocide Scholars, has stated passionately:

> Suicide bombers and their ideology are pure evil and they put into practice everything we despise. They must feel empowered and so must their supporters, by the realization that they've spooked their hated and dehumanized enemies. You can't discuss their mentality without tapping into that sense of empowerment, and revenge, and twisted glory. There is [also] the cultural dimension. What kind of belief system is it that glories and feels empowered by the destruction of innocent women and children![76]

Are Suicide Bombers a Proper Subject of Psychology?

> Terrorists are not born but shaped by events, experiences, impressions, hatreds, ethnic myths, historical memories, religious fanaticism and deliberate brainwashing. —Zbigniew Brzezinski, former National Security Adviser for President Jimmy Carter[1]

> As a Jordanian I have been haunted by a gruesome, saddening portrait of humanity, with its pitfalls garishly highlighted. —Munjed Farid al-Qutob[2]

At the outset, let me help readers who may not be familiar and comfortable with essays that go through a sequence of contradictory evidence and thought (a kind of Talmudic type of exercise) with an outline of this chapter. First, I will show that the suicide bombers are not "crazy" or "disturbed" according to current Western psychiatric rules, but then I will argue that the result of leaving them and their actions defined as "normal" itself is too crazy to bear. I will therefore propose, as I did in the field of psychiatry years ago in response to the same dilemma regarding people who commit genocide, that the rules of psychiatric diagnosis have to be changed. My proposal is that in all psychiatric evaluations all people should be looked at both as to whether they are doing serious harm to THEMSELVES in their own personal lives and whether they are doing serious harm to OTHERS. I will conclude that, as most plain people conclude spontaneously from their common sense (without a Talmud in hand) that the suicide bombers are to be defined as psychologically disturbed in their viciousness to life—their own and others.

The *How Can they Do It?* and *Why Do they Do It?* questions that roar into our minds in our amazement and disbelief of the suicide bombers are based on recognizable definitions of proper and normal human experience in *our* Western world.

In our Western world, it is wrong to kill others. "Thou Shalt Not Kill" is a fundamental canon of our Western faiths. But let's not kid ourselves. Notwithstanding the canons, in many a Western city, and certainly in the virtual world of our fictional violences in Western TV and cinema, we are accustomed to police sirens blaring day after day and a deadly record of murders in our societies. There is no Western person who has not developed a measure of acceptance and indifference to homicides as a part of life—which we simply hope we and our loved ones will be statistically lucky enough to escape. Nonetheless, for most of us, basic elements of shock, horror, fear, revulsion, and moral condemnation still remain our natural responses to the murdering of others.

In our Western world it is also understood that it is weak, disturbed, and "crazy" to take one's *own* life—except for well-defined situations such as terminal illness or being subjected to insufferable torture such as by a totalitarian government. In a sense, Western life is so geared to winning and achieving, that taking one's own life is as if an obscene disavowal of the holiest Western canon of all: live in order to win and achieve. For some westerners, there is a degree of acceptance and understanding that a person can be so overcome with pain, grief, shame, or helplessness that he or she may have to take their life, but even such understanding remains secondary to a judgment that the perpetrator should have gotten to his or her psychiatrist in time, and that in hurting oneself, he or she has done something terribly wrong and virtually obscene notwithstanding the tragedy involved.

Fascinatingly, between the two—murder and suicide—the latter, suicide, is treated in Western imagoes as the crazier. Killing others at times can somehow be a fulfillment of traditional Darwinian and capitalist competitiveness. It is a lousy thing to do, but at least it's usually in the direction of trying to gain power and advantage, which is what our Western gods want us to do: *win, don't lose*. But there is simply no point to going to good schools, getting prestigious and well-paying jobs, jogging, eating and otherwise watching your health, investing profitably in the stock market, and everything else that defines success in Western life if you are going to knock yourself off. Not only is suicide prohibited by Moses, Jesus, and Mohammed, a person who commits suicide is a loser—which is perhaps the ultimate sin in our Western values.

Now combine suicide and murder, and you have an unspeakably monstrous synergy that evokes a haunting combination and amplification of the horrors that already attach to each violation of killing—murdering oneself and murdering others—that is hard to put into words, but it is experienced immediately, inchoately.

- How can they end their own lives? There is absolutely nothing left after that. They have blown life into a bottomless void of nothingness. Now there is no way for them to retrace their steps and recover from what they have done.
- How can they kill innocent teenagers and people having a bite at a pizzeria, or out at a nightspot for dancing, or simple people riding a bus in the routines

of their lives? How can they play so dirty and dishonorably, and not let the victims know they are being attacked, or give them a chance to fight back or escape?

The combination of the two—murder and suicide—brings a shudder of horror and disgust as well as pure fear and terror. It is unbearable that such a sudden, unheralded blow can catch us unexpectedly at any time.

Suicide-killing is the ultimate attack on life. Nothing survives, not oneself, nor others. The two-way act of total destruction as if makes all of life meaningless as both perpetrator and victims are sucked into a huge black hole of nonexistence.

"GOOD GUYS" AND "SUCCESSFUL WOMEN" WHO BECOME SUICIDE BOMBERS

- The headline reads, "A Shy Child's Journey to Fiery Mass Murder."[3] The story is about Mohamed Atta. The article is an attempt to piece together how Atta became an Islamic terrorist. At age 33, Atta appears to have been the central person coordinating the incredible Al-Qaeda attack on the United States on September 11, 2001, and he himself was one of the skyjacker suicidal terrorists—Atta personally commandeered Flight 11 from Logan Airport in Boston that crashed first into the World Trade Center in New York.

  Atta was born in Cairo to a family that was viewed as thoroughly modern—two other sisters became respectively a professor and a doctor. The father, an attorney, was the family disciplinarian, and would complain that his wife was raising Atta as if he were a third girl. Perhaps psycho-analytically that is also an important inroad into the labyrinth of Atta's mind, but it feels so far away from the finish line of the readiness of this once-overindulged boy to commit daring and fierce mass murder that one cannot put the information immediately to use in an effort to explain his readiness to destroy himself and so many others. "I used to tell her that she is raising him as a girl, and that I have three girls, but she never stopped pampering him," the father said on interview. Apparently Atta, the boy, also did not play much with the other boys, one of whom commented on the fact that he was focused very strongly on being excellent in his studies to become an engineer. The father described his son as beginning to be devout in prayer at around twelve or thirteen. From then on, he was a devout Muslim.

  After graduating from Cairo University's engineering department, Atta found work with a German company in Cairo, and then accepted his father's advice to go study for an advanced degree in Germany. In Hamburg, Atta was seen as he had been in Egypt—"polite, distant and neatly dressed ... He impressed his co-workers with his diligence and the careful elegance of his drafting." Atta apparently found his sense of connection in an Arab-language mosque in Hamburg where his imam would preach that America was an enemy of Islam. At some point, according to his academic supervisor at the university, he "changed somewhat" and "looked more serious, and he didn't smile as much" as he had previously, and others say that he became more brooding and more troubled. Some noted he was rude to women whom he considered insufficiently devout. In the late 1990s, Atta trained at an Al-Qaeda camp in Afghanistan. He returned to Hamburg where he defended his thesis successfully and graduated with high honors—his father says that he received a Master's degree, but the record shows in fact that he received an undergraduate degree in Germany.

The rest of the known story involves the obviously intricate and dedicated path of Atta's preparations for the dreadful history-shaking attack on the United States. Atta traveled to various places where he met with his Al-Qaeda contacts. "The awful efficiency of the attack demanded a leader with a precise and disciplined temperament, and Mr. Atta apparently filled that role."

A picture accompanying the story in the *International Herald Tribune* shows a little boy of about fourteen who is being vigorously hugged by his mother, who is looking like she is "eating him up," with a smiling handsome father standing on the other side of the boy, perhaps a little disconnected from the bountiful intimacy between his wife and son but nonetheless the father looks happy and approving.

The family of this polite student refused to believe the reports that their son had been a hijacker in the September 11 attacks.

- The headline of a *Boston Globe* story reads, "How Did a Courteous Student Turn into a Terrorist?"[4] The accompanying picture shows a handsome, tall young man, grinning from ear to ear, dressed like a young Wall Street executive on the rise in his career, standing alongside of his smiling mother in Beirut in February preceding the September 11 attacks on the United States.

Jiad Jerah, 26, was a Lebanese student. He participated in the skyjacking of United Airlines Flight 93 from Newark to San Francisco that was redirected by the suicide hijackers toward Washington, DC where its target is reputed possibly to have been the White House, but the plane crashed on the way there in western Pennsylvania, from everything we know as a result of a courageous battle of the passengers on that aircraft against the hijackers.

Jerah was known to his family and friends as moderate in religious matters, pro-American, and a young man who loved life. He apparently had led a double life as an Al-Qaeda agent for some time. An uncle in Lebanon said that whole story was "illogical," since Jerah had called them just two days before on September 9 to tell them he was coming to his cousin's wedding later in September and that he had bought a new suit for the occasion.

There is very little in the known story of Jerah's life that fits the expected profile of a radical Muslim. Jerah's father is a government worker, his mother a teacher, and the boy was sent to a series of modern Christian schools. The boy was not religious. He drank alcoholic beverages and dated girls. The uncle said, "There is no one in the family who is extreme in his religiosity." In the wake of September 11, it was Jerah's German girlfriend in Hamburg who notified the police of his being missing. In Hamburg, Jerah is remembered as "a polite and quiet person." His landlady described him as a "very lovely young man."

- Wafa Idris was "a 28 year old volunteer medic who raised doves and adored children, music and a good laugh." On January 27, 2002, Wafa Idris became the first woman suicide bomber in the bloody Palestinian-Israel conflict when she detonated a powerful bomb in the shopping district in the center of Jerusalem, as a result of which one Israeli man was killed and more than a hundred people were wounded.[5] Many people following the Israeli-Palestinian conflict were shocked that a woman could be a suicide bomber, and the incident was correctly perceived as setting a dangerous precedent for more women to follow, which in fact is precisely what has happened.[6] However, the Middle East watchers were deeply mistaken about this being an unprecedented step for women, for there have been many women suicide bombers in recent years, for example, in Sri Lanka and Chechnya.[7] The day Wafa Idris exploded the bomb, she made a point of buying some fruit juice and a bag of potato chips for a beloved niece, and then ran off to her work and suicide bombing.

  Idris had suffered a miscarriage late in a pregnancy some years ago and was told by doctors that she would be unable to have children. Her husband then wanted to take a second wife as is permitted under Islam, and when she objected, he divorced her. Idris' mother said that her daughter had recovered from the traumas in her life of the miscarriage and divorce and did not do the bombing out of desperation.

To the horror of the Western world, it is becoming clear that Islamic terrorists are also succeeding in recruiting people who have been living in and are fully vested citizens of Western countries, such as British citizens. We referred earlier to a suicide bombing in May 2003 in Tel Aviv by two British citizens of Muslim origin, which was the first known instance of British suicide bombers; and then, of course, there came the first and very major attack on British soil on July 7, 2005 by three British-born Muslims and a fourth who grew up in the United Kingdom. Reporting from London about July 7, *New York Times* correspondent Alan Cowell observed: "As on previous occasions when British Muslims were found to have been fighting for the Taliban in Afghanistan or planning alleged terrorism in

Britain, the suspected terrorists seemed to have grown up in innocuous, middle-class or blue-collar environments far from the conflicts they came to espouse as their own." One neighbor was quoted, "We just can't understand what happened . . . His whole family was fully Westernized . . . They were gentle people."[8]

The possible sacredness of the lives of people who are to be the victims seems to disappear entirely from the minds of the perpetrators who are drummed into a corps of killers for an ideological cause. Sheikh Yousef al Qaradhawi told the *Al Raya* newspaper in Qatar about suicide bombers sent by the Palestinians against Israel, "They are not suicide operations. These are heroic martyrdom operations."[9]

As if plunging deep into the psychology of suicide bombers, Sheikh Aabd Al-Solano Abu Shukheydem, Chief Mufti of the Palestinian Authority Police Force says, "From the moment the first drop of his blood is spilled, he [the suicide bomber] does not feel the pain of his wounds and he is forgiven for all his sins; he sees his seat in Paradise . . ."[10]

According to reporter Bob Woodward of the *Washington Post*, a document in Arabic that had been distributed to the several groups of terrorists who attacked the World Trade Center in New York and the Pentagon in Washington, DC on September 11 was "a cross between a chilling spiritual exhortation and an operational mission checklist, and may turn out to provide the most vivid and penetrating glimpse into their mental states." The Al-Qaeda suicide bombers who brought down the World Trade Center and a part of the Pentagon on September 11, 2001 were told as follows:

> "Purify your heart and clean it from all earthly matters. The hours left you in your life are very few. From there you will begin to live the happy life, the infinite paradise. Be optimistic. The Prophet was always optimistic."
>
> Regarding the night before, they are advised: "You must pray, you must fast. You must ask counsel from Allah, pray all night, continue to learn the Koran. Cleanse your hearts . . . Later you will begin to live the happiest life in the eternal Garden of Eden . . . The Garden of Eden has already been beautified for you and the beautiful angels who have dressed themselves in their most beautiful dresses are calling you."
>
> "When you enter the plane, pray: Oh God, you who open all doors, please open all doors for me, open all venues for me, open all avenues for me. Remove from me the burden I carry."[11]

New York Times correspondent Thomas Friedman has written about the psychology of suicide bombers that they become *people who hate life,* but even more their psychology becomes one of being *enemies of civilization* itself.

> How do you deter young people who hate America, or Israel, more than they love their own families or their own future? . . . What worries me is that . . . once people feel empowered by this sort of thing, they will turn in on their own . . . And it becomes "normal."[12]
>
> With bin Laden and Quaida, we are up against radical evil—people who not only want to destroy us but are perfectly ready to destroy themselves as well. They are not just enemies of America, *they are enemies of civilization . . .* Most of these hijackers

come from big families. They left behind parents, brothers, sisters and, in at least one case, a fiancée. They hate us more than they love their own families … they hate us more than they love life itself.[13]

There is no question that there is a profound and definite cultural-spiritual difference, to the point of a fundamental clash of values between the civilizations, between Islamic suicide bombers and Western civilization, a theme to which I will return and around which I will attempt to make a constructive proposal for combating suicide bombing before completing this book.[14]

THE PSYCHOLOGY AND SOCIOLOGY OF SUICIDE BOMBERS

Is there a psychological-psychiatric moral to the above stories?

There are many mental health professionals who will say that suicide-bomber terrorists do not deserve a mental health analysis. They are properly the subjects of sociology, political science, and military science but not of psychology, psychiatry, and psychopathology, they will argue. True, there are tens of thousands of sworn killer terrorists operating around our globe in an endless range of countries, including Ireland, Spain, Colombia, Peru, Sri Lanka, India, Russia, Pakistan, Iraq, Indonesia, and many more, and obviously they are a problem for us all in our world, but not specifically for our mental health professions to worry our pretty heads about.

According to accepted professional standards in psychiatry, the profession of terrorists, if you will, does not define a person as *ipso facto* disturbed. Explanations of this choice of profession will be found elsewhere than in concepts of emotional disturbance. Even if terrorism in the final analysis is a form of human behavior (of course), and therefore by definition the subject has to constitute part of the subject matter of psychology (the study of individual and collective human behavior), it is not a subject of the mental health or illness aspect of psychology.

It sounds logical enough, but to me it also sounds like a cowardly retreat of the mental health professions from one of the burning issues in the human behaviors of our era. There are any number of us who would like to believe that psychology and psychiatry also can be sources of wisdom and inspiration for the burning issues in our human lives. The basic issue of *a choice of death over life* sounds like it goes to the very core of the psychology of human beings.

Perhaps we can first ask ourselves what we know of the general psychology and sociology of suicide killers. The following findings are representative of reports by a good many different scholars, journalists, and observers:

- First, here are some of the sociological characteristics of the first seventy suicide bombers in Israel-Palestine during the period 1993 through 2000 following the signing of the Oslo Agreements in 1993:
- 83 percent of the suicide bombers were single; 64 percent were between the ages of 18 to 23, and most of the remainder were under 30

- 47 percent of the suicide bombers had an academic education; an additional 29 percent had a high school education; so that a total of 76 percent of the suicide bombers had a high school or further education[15]
- 76.1 percent of Palestinian adults favored suicidal attacks against Israeli civilian sites, such as a shopping mall, 12.5 percent opposed, and 11.4 percent expressed no opinion[16]
- Nasra Hassan, a Pakistani, interviewed nearly 250 Palestinian recruiters and trainers, prospective suicide bombers, failed suicide bombers, and relatives of deceased bombers between 1996 and 1999. Of the bombers who were men aged 18 to 38, she concluded: "None were uneducated, desperately poor, simple-minded, or depressed . . . They all seemed to be entirely normal members of their families . . . All were deeply religious." They believed their suicide bombings were "sanctioned by the divinely revealed religion of Islam."[17]
- Contrary to some reports and to the hopes of many westerners of finding a salacious explanation for the suicide bombers, it should be noted that apparently the majority are *not* under the influence of drugs. Yehuda Hiss, the director of Israel's Institute of Forensic Medicine, has stated: "No alcohol and no drugs are known to us," He noted that the suicide bombers on whom he conducted autopsies were fully lucid at the moment of death. "They are motivated by some psychological motive prior to the suicide attack."[18]
- Many of the suicide bombers speak of a deep need for personal revenge for family and friends who have previously been killed. Many others speak of revenge and fulfillment of their specific national political goals, e.g., an independent Palestine and the destruction of the Jewish State of Israel, or in other parts of the world conquering Kashmir from the Hindus, or destruction of the godless United States. Some speak of a sense of historical revenge for Islam having lost an earlier glory as ruler of the world. Some suicide bombers combine different levels of the above themes of personal and collective revenge.
- Suicide bombers can be obedient conformists and slavish followers of leaders, whether on the basis of a generalized readiness to follow a leader and/or the culture of an overall movement, or in specific response to the famed promises of seventy-two virgins when they reach heaven.[19]
- Let us also not forget financial rewards to many terrorists. The going price for a *shahid* or holy martyr for the Palestinians in the intifada against Israel at first was reported to be $2,000—although families would complain that the sum turned out to be less because it was minus an amount taken off the top by the local warlord who was designated by the Palestinian Authority to deliver the money to the family of the bereaved. Before his downfall, Saddam Hussein had upped the price to pay from his funds—$10,000 to each martyr's family, and later he raised the prizes again to $10,000 for shooters and $25,000 for suicide bombers.
- Now add to the above a sociology of invitation to fellowship, camaraderie, and the opportunity to play significant roles in an exciting group who plot,

train for, and carry out the mission, as well as in a larger network of a terrorist movement.

- Being a suicide bomber promises fame and honor for one's identity, and also for one's surviving family.[20] A research scholar at Delhi's Jawaharlal Nehru University in India is reported saying about suicide bombings in Sri Lanka that "the motivation for suicide attacks seems to be a kind of en masse cult hysteria that the LTTE [Tamils] consciously cultivates through rituals like Martyr's Week, promoting a cult of martyrdom, building special cemeteries, naming weapons after Black Tigers. In short, the promise of honour after death."[21]

- Add in also the power of a psychology of thrill-seeking, also the pleasures of power and violence, and the dramatic roulette-joys of pushing a plunger to its super-dramatic consequences of bringing an "end to it all"—a kind of universal and archetypal fantasy that appears in the play of children who push the button that as if destroys the world, and also appears in the fantasies of some psychotics precisely because of their fears that they might push the button (they prefer to be crazy than killers!).

- Now describe the responses of people in the politics of competition, sep-aratism, and insults between warring factions, clans, religions, ethnicities, and political groups. The rules of the game are that some people are to be defined as lowly, worthless, vile, poisoned, ugly, and dispensable—they clearly are not human beings like we are (dehumanization). At the same time, the same people are the ultimate satanic incarnations of hell, and we must get rid of them before they get us (demonization or the attribution of ultimate terror and danger to the other). *What this means is that whatever we will do to them will be experienced and defined as entirely in self-defense.*

- The single most frequently observed characteristic of the suicide bombers is that they are ideologically committed. I noted that Nasra Hassan referred to the bombers as being "deeply religious." She gives an eloquent description of one would-be suicide bomber's preparation for his mission in which he described a state of ecstasy.

  "We were in a constant state of worship," he said ... "Those were the happiest days of my life."
  "What is the attraction of martyrdom?" I asked.
  "The power of the spirit pulls us upward, while the power of material things pulls us downward," he said, "... Our planner asked, 'What if the operation fails?' We told him, 'In any case, we get to meet the Prophet and his companions, inshallah.' We were floating, swimming, in the feeling that we were about to enter eternity."[22]

Roni Shaked, an Israeli expert in terrorism, is reported as concluding: "In the end, most of the bombers don't sign up for martyrdom for the promise of unlimited sex. They join because of their absolute devotion to God and their desire to die with Jewish blood on their hands ... It's not a heroic thing, it's a holy thing."[23]

The same kind of information reaches us from other parts of the world, such as from a Muslim who was put on trial for his role in the Bali nightclub blast in October 2002. "It's a martyr's death I am looking for," he said during his trial in Denpasar, Indonesia. The same bomber turned around, smiled broadly, and turned his two thumbs up in the air when the court sentenced him to death by a firing squad. The CNN reporter who provided this description concluded, "While there are many reasons young Muslims sacrifice their lives—including the honor and money bestowed onto their families after their death—it is the martyr's afterlife that captures the imagination."[24]

The same reporter brought in additional observations of Muslim terrorists arrested in Singapore:

> Following the arrests of 31 members of the Jemaah Islamiyah (JI) terror network in Singapore, the government released a paper detailing just how such groups cultivated their mindsets. Leaders from JI, an al Qaeda-linked group seeking to set up a pan-Islamic state spanning Southeast Asia, eyed captivated students at mass gatherings. They then indoctrinated those deemed suitable into the clandestine group over 18 months. During that time they were taught "JI-speak." Those who believed in the "truth" of JI doctrine became closer to Allah. They learned the "true" JI knowledge of jihad—that innocents, both Muslim and non-Muslim, could be sacrificed. They were promised martyrdom if they died in the cause of jihad. And anyone who left the group was called an infidel ... the psychologists interviewing the detainees said many JI members turned to the leaders to find a "no-fuss" path to Heaven. They wanted to be convinced that they had found "true Islam" and free themselves from the endless searching. Especially since they believed they could not go wrong, as the JI leaders had quoted from holy texts ... The recruits became so committed to the cause they become perfect jihad machines.[25]

THE MULTIPLE PATHWAYS TO BECOMING A SUICIDE BOMBER—IN AN APPROVING CULTURE GROUP

Now I suggest we try to add up or put together many of the observations we have gathered.

If we put the many very powerful dynamics described together—not necessarily every one of them at the same time—but in different clusters of interlocking dynamics, we have the elements for springing several kinds of Frankensteins on the world. My conclusion is that an intriguing variety of configurations of human tendencies can give us the blindly robotized people who are "happy" to sacrifice their own lives and blast away the lives of many others. In other words, my conclusion is that it is an error to offer any *single* explanation of the suicide bombers.

Some want virgins. Some want fame and glory in their community. Some want money for their family. Some are good soldiers and believe suicide bombing is the best means for achieving a military target. Some want revenge for specific loved ones they have lost. Some want revenge for their nation over their loss of world power. Some want to fulfill a traditional motif in Islam to kill infidel nonbelievers. Some want to obey the calls of their leaders. Some want the excitement of their belonging to a group preparing to act dramatically. Some feel hypnotized or even coerced by the seductions and pressures of their skillful handlers whose job it is to bring the designated suicide bombers to complete their tasks. In many cases, different combinations of two and more of the different motives create the specific motivational package of any given suicide bomber.

One might also say that one thing that is held in common by most of the suicide bombers is that they submit themselves and then become captives of a compelling process which is both self-hypnotizing and group-coercive from which, after a given point, many people would find it very difficult to extricate themselves. Psychologist Ariel Merari, suggested that the key ingredient may be susceptibility to indoctrination. Merari's thought was drawn from the empirical information he was looking at in about thirty-two suicide bombers almost all of whom were young, unattached males, a cohort vulnerable to violent organizations in any society.[26] But overall, there is no question that many of the suicide bombers believe and feel ardently that they are serving the call of their religion, prophet, and God.

In other words, while the specific motivators vary for different suicide bombers, what seems to be the necessary enabling context for these various motives to work is a belief system that one is meaningfully saving one's God and/or people by being a suicide bomber. It is doubtful if any of the specific dynamics, however real they are, would result in suicide bombing were there not an overall culture of legitimation and celebration of making violent deaths.

Jason Burke, a writer for the London *Observer,* also cautions against a search for a single cause of suicide bombing. He too concludes that there is a range of different motivations for suicide bombings.

> "What do they want?" implies a Western concept of acting to achieve goals ... The answer is that, from their twisted standpoint, they believe they have no choice.
>   Islamic militants have shown many different motivations. Ramzi Yousef, who tried to destroy the World Trade Center in 1993, was driven more by a lust for notoriety than religious fervor. Mohammed Atta, the leader of the 9/11 hijackers, acted because he felt, with absolute certainty, that he had no option but ... to fulfill his religious duty. One of the men who organized the bombing of a night club in Bali in October 2002 said he had been disgusted by the "dirty adulterous behavior" of the "whites" there. Another said he was angered by the war in Afghanistan ... Recent strikes by Islamic militants in Iraq ... make a statement about the vulnerability of the West and America's inability to protect its allies.

At the same time, Burke concludes that, overall, the predominant meaning of much contemporary suicide bombing is to respond to Western humiliation and to restore the centuries-lost pride of Islam.

> This perception that a belligerent West is set on the humiliation, division and eventual conquest of the Islamic world is at the root of Muslim violence. The militants believe

they are fighting a last-ditch battle for the survival of their society, culture, religion and way of life . . . The bombs are designed to restore the pride of Muslims worldwide and, by weakening the "Crusaders" and their allies, hasten the eventual return to the golden age of a thousand years ago when the lands of Islam were the world's leading powers.[27]

While it is clear to me that overcoming humiliation is certainly a major motivation in the Muslim culture in general and in suicide bombings specifically, I think this writer too stepped somewhat into the error he himself wrote about of choosing too much one single motivation largely over others. I prefer to conclude that the widespread cultural support for suicide bombing as a noble service to the pride of Islam provides an overall climate for legitimating suicide bombings for all those who have other motivations or reasons for undertaking the suicide bombing, including many who feel humiliated, others who strive for revenge, others who seek to restore Islam's glory in the world, others who believe nonbelievers must be eliminated, and still others who joy in a jingoistic and violent interpretation of Islamic scripture, as well, of course, as those who resonate to more than one of the above.

Crazy as it seems to our Western minds, the unfortunate fact is that there has been no shortage of people who have been readily available to be suicide bombers in many countries. We need to conclude that in many cultures and times in history, many thousands of our human species can be recruited voluntarily into the ranks of suicide bombers. Obviously these are cultures which do not place life as sacred. They are part of what I call a *Culture of Death* in which there is little resembling the conscience we in our Western conception of life *want* to attribute to a normal human mind, neither about blowing themselves up, nor about blowing up other men, women, and children. The victims can be shopping in a market in Moscow, eating in a pizzeria in Jerusalem, at work in magnificent tall towers in Manhattan or in a government military building in Washington, DC, in their homes in Riyadh, in a nightclub in Bali, worshipping in synagogues or even in the "wrong" mosques in Istanbul or Kabul or Baghdad—it makes no difference whatsoever. In a culture that honors making death to oneself and others, suicide bombing becomes a rewarding single-minded goal for many, and a way of belonging loyally to one's people, tradition, and cause. Making death can become God's work, or the selfless offering of oneself to a leader or a political goal. But within a larger shared climate of the legitimacy and nobility of suicide bombings, the specific suicide bombers vary with their personal life story and their personal central motivations.

UNDERSTANDING SUICIDE IN CONTEMPORARY WESTERN PSYCHIATRY

One of the main reasons so many westerners react to suicide bombers in disbelief and with spontaneous remarks that they are "crazy," "insane," or "out of their mind" is because the killers also kill themselves. Even westerners who have been socialized to accept lots of murdering in their everyday lives in their cities are shocked by the suicide bombers taking their own lives. That is not the way it is supposed to be even for killers. The understandable purpose of the game, based on what is presumably the most powerful instinct of all in the human repertoire—our survival instinct, is to stay alive if at all possible even when taking risks of going on the attack against one's enemies.

Understanding the suicides of the suicide bombers is not exactly easy. At the outset we owe a huge caveat, that whatever we westerners may believe we understand about the choices of suicide may not be applicable to people from another culture, including certain religious cultures, where the meanings of life and death may be dramatically different than ours. On the other hand, there are also universal meanings to choices of life and death, and presumably a bedrock of instincts for life and death that is shared by all of us human beings.

Logically, one of the first places we should look to for understanding suicide should be the field of mental health. Yet one of the first things we will discover is that, strangely, in contemporary Western psychiatry, suicide is *not* included as a psychiatric condition in the formal book of diagnosis, the *DSM*.[28] The ostensible explanation and justification of the apologists for the profession is that suicide is not a condition—it is not the illness, but rather a symptom of the illness, which more often than not is depression.

Obviously, there is some truth to the argument, but only some. In medicine, coughs, convulsions, bleeding are not in their own right illnesses. And yet often there is a definite need for physicians to address management of these symptoms in their own right if they are severe even before there is an assessment of a more real or underlying illness.

In the case of suicide, the symptom itself will make any bona fide practitioner in psychiatry, or another mental health profession like clinical psychology or social work, jump to attention and activity. Suicide is among the most dramatic calls for emotional help, and if only as a major symptomatic crisis, common sense would seem to call for it to be represented and covered at length in any basic manual for mental health professionals.

In the case of suicide there is a deeper problem, for there is much to argue that a state of *suicidality* is not only a symptom of another disorder but also a psychiatric disturbance on its own. Considering suicide, attempting suicide, or committing suicide are aspects of a mentally disordered state in its own right, a condition that is rooted in an existential process of a choice of death over life. Note that even many people who suffer from a condition of depression will not consider suicide in any real way, but will seek to find other *living* solutions to their depression, for good and even for bad reasons such as undue narcissistic self-importance or self-indulgence. These depressed patients are committed to life, and will not allow a process of suicidality to take over and envelop them. So it is really the basic choice to die that is the primary psychiatric condition in suicidality.

Not surprisingly suicidality also has its diagnostic complexities. There are many different reasons for wanting to die. Suicide also has its treatment complexities as well, many of which are related to understanding the reasons for the desire to commit suicide in the first place, as well as to other considerations such as the nature of the patient's primary relationships (for example, unmarried versus married, childless, or a parent), employment (for example, unemployed or failed work versus successfully employed), choice of method of suicide ("painless" such as an overdose of medication versus assaultive such as shooting or hanging oneself), and more. But the crucial issue in just about all cases, that combines with the specific motivations of the suicider, is the individual's overarching philosophy of life and how it is that he does or does not authorize the taking of life.

On the level of an individual's personal psychological experience, suicidal thinking often takes over the mind and in effect creates a new mental state of suicidality or being obsessively concerned with the presumed and imagined rewards of suicide as well as with one's intended suicide plan. Larry Gernsbacher has written that the common characteristics that are present to some degree in all suicides are narcissism, eccentricity, compulsivity, perfectionism, and irrationality.[29] He says further that in suicide there is an unconscious element that, unbeknownst to the individual, gradually exerts control over his or her thoughts and actions. This analysis of the suicidal mind may be helpful to our understanding of the suicide of the suicide bomber. According to Gernsbacher, the suicidal mind includes an unconscious dictator, which he calls the "fantastic self," which represents all that a person believes is absolutely true. The fantastic self endorses a person with a sense of being in the right and with a feeling that he will overcome all the woes of life with a sure-fire solution. The fantastic self adopts suicide as the "mother of all solutions" to life's needs and problems.

> The "suicide" of the individual who is governed by the suicidal syndrome accepts the premise of the syndrome which is that he or she can realize the abstract absolutes that compose the fantastic self ... The only way to interrupt the suicide's inevitable progress to the logical conclusion is to make the person realize the irrationality of the pursuit to attain the absolute qualities of the imaginary fantastic self. Only when the individual has realized the impossibility of attaining the all powerful fantastic self can he or she escape its control.[30]

In respect of a suiciding individual's psychological relationship to his or her society, which obviously is of considerable if not paramount relevance in the cases of suicide bombers, the basic typology created by sociologist Emile Durkheim in 1897(!) stands as outstandingly useful to this day.[31] Durkheim's greatness lies in the fact that he raised simultaneously cultural-societal issues about the individual's relationship to others and to his society, philosophical issues about the values the suiciding person was responding to and expressing, and basic psychiatric issues of mapping the style and modus operandi of the suiciding person.

Durkheim posited three basic categories of suicide:

1. *egoistic suicide* or a person who is unable to find his place in his society;
2. *anomic suicide* or a personal loss of orientation-identification with one's society, which has become strange to a person, either because of changes in society or in the person, such as when a person is unable to continue their religious tradition, or is unable to continue their past work or economic patterns, or when a person suffers a loss of a mate or has remained unmarried and alone; and
3. *altruistic suicide*, when individuals are willing and eager to sacrifice their lives for the benefit of their group (the category which of course will be of most interest to us).

The egoistic suicider is unhappy and sees no place for himself in the world and the anomic suicider experiences a world which is meaningless for him, and both in effect are weary and depressed of living; the altruistic suicider as if disregards his individual fate and "gives" his death as a gift to the cause of his people in faith, affirmation, and even enthusiasm.

Kenneth Thompson has described how altruistic suicide is a result of *too much* integration into one's society, which is very different from the losses of connection to other people and to one's society in the other two primary types of suicide defined by Durkheim. In altruistic suicide, self-sacrifice follows being so well integrated into one's group that one loses one's individuality and is willing as if to sacrifice oneself to one's group, or perhaps to the commands the group has issued to sacrifice oneself for the interests of the group. The tradition of altruistic suicide is common in military annals also in the West where it is often encouraged and honored.

Durkheim also observed cogently that there are suicides caused by a kind of contagion. People who see others committing suicide can be more inclined to repeat their actions, and there can be a kind of "moral epidemic" of suicide in a whole group (see the famous suicidal epidemic in our times in Jonestown when several hundred followers of the Reverend Jones committed suicide together.[32])

The fascinating question remains why contemporary Western psychiatry on the one hand busies itself with healing suicidal people very actively, but doesn't give the condition reasonable coverage in its basic diagnostic bible.

Personally, I believe this amazing discrepancy follows from contemporary Western psychiatry's basic or overall escape from existential and relationship issues, as well as from moral or spiritual issues, as basic explanations of mental and emotional illnesses to an almost exclusively medical-like world and to treatments that are mainly and largely based on medications far more than psychotherapy.

In my judgment, to treat suicide effectively, one must have a conviction that life is sacred, and that the choice of suicide is also a choice of a moral position. The exercise of the choice whether to live or die is a statement of one's relationships to a wide variety of people, of course beginning with oneself, and also extending very directly to one's family, as well as to one's community in an immediate sense of one's personal circle, in addition to one's relationship to one's larger community and the world. In my own clinical experience as a practicing psychotherapist, it is the re-clarification of the essence of the suiciding person's choice within the network of their human relationships—to their own self and to others—that gives the suiciding person a chance to revise their suicidal inclination and choose life.

Treating crises of suicidality is wonderfully interesting and rewarding work, I find. It has little to nothing to do with pills, potions, electric shocks, or psychiatric hospitalization. Insofar as contemporary psychiatry favors the latter and avoids psychotherapeutic processing of existential choices, it does not really know how to talk about let alone even classify suicide. Durkheim, the sociologist of more than a hundred years ago, knew a lot more than today's medicalizing psychiatry about the relationship of the suiciding person to his or her larger social community and to his feelings about wanting and not wanting to live. I don't believe that contemporary Western psychiatry really makes it clear to itself and to its practitioners why life is to be saved and suicide prevented if possible—beyond a kind of carryover from the overall value position of medicine as a whole that death is to be fought off. To treat suicide effectively, I find one has to have a clear moral or spiritual conviction about the holiness of life; and one also has to care about the people the suiciding person will leave behind if they take their life.

The suicides of suicide bombers *might* deserve to be seen as courageous selfless contributions to a cause were it not for the facts that they bring death to so many people, and that also includes the bombers themselves, and obviously real losses to many of their families no matter how the families present themselves as proud of their martyrs, as well as a legacy encouraging further destruction to future society.

The Terrorist is a film by Indian director, Santosh Sivan, which he describes as an attempt to understand the psychology of the Tamil suicide bomber who assassinated Prime Minister Rajiv Gandhi in 1991. Malli is a beautiful female Tamil guerrilla fighter, who has never known any life outside the struggle. Her father was a famous Tamil nationalist poet; her brother a fighter who gained notoriety by swallowing cyanide to evade capture. In the opening moments of the film, she coolly executes a collaborator. She is selected for the prestigious suicide bombing of a high-ranking Indian politician. But once she reaches the Indian mainland, she begins to waiver in her convictions. One reason is that she has become pregnant after making love with a dying comrade. A second influence is the kindness of an Indian farmer she stays with as she prepares for her mission. She becomes convinced that it is better to build a normal life for her child than to sacrifice both their lives. A reviewer on a Web site entitled "Culture Wars" calls the film "an utter gem."[33] Malli in effect chooses life over the love of death that is terrorism.

Michael Radu is a specialist on terrorism for the Foreign Policy Research Institute. He is naturally very attuned to the political causes of terrorism, and in respect of the suicide bombers concludes that religion as such or religious-like thinking of a single-minded devotion to a cause and/or to a "supreme charismatic leader" are characteristic of suicide bombers all over the world, including "secular" groups like the LTTE in Sri Lanka and the PKK in Turkey. He also recognizes that some suicide bombers have personal motives such as revenge. Nonetheless, Radu concludes that suicide bombers are also products of psychological processes. First, most suicide bombers are the victims of "well planned recruitment and indoctrination schemes ... special recruiters bring the suicide [bomber-IWC] candidate together with the group." Second—and here Radu goes so far as to insist that suicide bombers are people who do not want to live—, "What they share is Roman philosopher Seneca's opinion that he who does not prize his own life threatens that of others."

Spoken like a psychologist.[34]

If I sum up what I believe we may take from Western understanding of suicide that can be helpful to our understanding of suicide bombers, it is that while people who are deeply identified with their people and their cause can consciously give up their lives for them, suicide nonetheless remains also an existential choice of death over life that becomes an irrational, compelling, and also narcissistic goal; suicide also leaves a trail of deep hurt to one's closest intimates; and certainly suicide killers impose an ugly trail of deaths and injuries on other human beings.

Are there effective antidotes to suicidality in everyday life? In my experience, when there is an opportunity for psychological treatment, very much so. In the psychological treatment of individuals that I know, the antidote is a basic revision of the choice by the individual to want to live more than to die, to believe in the dignity of human life, and to accept responsibility for not leaving behind a terrible burden to others. When family therapy is possible, which I strongly recommend be combined with the individual therapy, the antidote also includes either a message from some close relationship that there is someone who cares very much about the person and wants him or her to live; or, paradoxically, an opportunity for the intended suiciders to decide that it's *not* worth their while to kill themselves over the likes of someone who is supposed to be close to them but in fact is rejecting them and even wishing them dead—the hell with such a relative or lover or seeming friend! (The first thing I do as a therapist after someone has made a suicide attempt is convene a family therapy session for the immediate family with the suiciding person and lead a discussion of how each one feels about the possibility that their suiciding relative might not have been there anymore. The conversations never fail to be dramatically revealing.) When the causes of suicide strongly involve a large cultural group or society that obviously wants the suicide bomber to "work" for them and give his or her life for the cause, the best antidote would seem to require effecting a change in the philosophy of life and death of the society, such as giving prominence to religious leaders who seek life for all people over religious leaders who promote death. In this connection, I will be proposing a cultural "*Worldwide Campaign for Life*" later in the book that could help to reduce the attractiveness and seeming legitimacy of both suicide and murder.

THE SEARCH FOR THE PSYCHOPATHOLOGY OF SUICIDE BOMBERS

So do the suicide bombers constitute cases of psychopathology?

Needless to say, whatever our psychological-moral analysis of suicide bombers is going to be, it will be dismissed out of hand by the celebrators of the bombings. A pro-Islamic Web site comments ironically:

> While Americans ponder the roots of murderous martyrdom, searching for explanations that fit within their notions of Third World psychology and religion, the Palestinians seem less interested in spiritual inspiration than in practical military innovation.[35]

Still, arriving at a conception of whether suicide bombers should be thought of in Western psychiatry as abnormal or not is very important to us and to our way of life, and perhaps will arm us intellectually and spiritually with greater power to fight back to stop the suicide bombers.

An interesting pro-Palestinian, anti-Israel essay solved the problem of the suicide of the suicide bomber as if by removing it at all from constituting an existential fact in the suicide killing process. The writer says thus:

> I have been placing 'suicide' in 'suicide' bombings within quotes. This requires an explanation. The *Oxford English Dictionary* defines a suicide as 'one who dies by his own hand.' This definition is clearly inadequate. In the absence of a motive, we cannot distinguish between (i) a person who takes his life because he wants to die and (ii) a person who takes his life because this will save her soul—or her honor, her family, her friends, her community, or her country. The first suggests suicide; the latter is ordinarily regarded as a martyr. Judge for yourself then whether the Palestinians are suicides or martyrs.[36]

The above is almost convincing as it invokes the selfless and heroic but it is still gibberish, because it denies the realness of the suicide as death, and celebrates it as an act of dedication oblivious to the real purpose the suicide serves of killing and maiming civilians.

Surprisingly, in conventional psychiatric terms, the answer to the question of whether the suicide bomber is psychiatrically disturbed is also *no*. Here the reason for the answer is somewhat different, however. Psychiatry does not honor the martyrdom; it evades it or any other "cause" to which a person gives his life. There is no psychopathology involved because the suicide bombings are political acts, and the subject of political self-expression is simply ignored in psychiatry.

A British psychiatrist had commented: "When a central belief that life is but a temporary prelude to everlasting utopian existence is . . . [a] regulatory norm, the definition of suicide itself becomes ambiguous and the role of psychiatry as a valid therapeutic intervention is also questionable."[37]

Voila. Now you see it, now you don't. Here psychiatry contributes another way of making the phenomenon disappear. But as I wrote earlier, psychiatry has a hard time knowing how to treat suicide as a fundamental mental health problem even when no political motivations are involved. The subject goes to basic philosophical-psychological issues that psychiatry wishes would go away from all aspects of life and leave them mainly with troubles for which they can dispense pills—not wisdom.

Sociologically, there are some data we have seen that have suggested *some* clustering of suicide bombers among the younger, unmarried and unattached, and sometimes also from among the poorer and more marginal people. Regarding the latter, we also saw that these data fade into a larger picture that suicide bombers come from all socioeconomic strata, including often from the better educated. On the other hand, the former data about a predominance of unmarried among the suicide bombers does say something important about some of the suicide bombers lacking a primary attachment, which can bespeak a psychiatric finding about people who are not succeeding in creating and maintaining attachments. On the other hand, a great many of the suicide bombers also are young and simply have not reached the age where they normally would have settled down into marriage and family. Whether or not it is a bona fide psychiatric finding or indicator or a more broad socio-demographic indicator, the empirical information about unconnected people being more likely to be terrorists is useful working information for counterterrorism police and military.

Robert Robins and Jerrold Post are important students of terrorism. They suggest that, "The contented individual in a rewarding society does not tear himself from family and the nation's institutions to follow a leader attacking the society."[38] I think they are reading into the phenomena of people who join the goose-stepping arm breakers, mob-lynchers, and machine gun-toting and bomb-exploding terrorists that they must be miserable individuals to go toward such occupations of dispensing deaths to others, but I'm not sure that we see enough evidence for that. I really wish it were true as they suggest that "at the heart of the mass movement are many who are not at peace with themselves" and that "beneath the discontent with the society is discontent with the flawed self."[39] For this is the psychological culture on which I have grown up and which I love, and I have no doubt that it is true that people who hate themselves are much more likely to join the attackers and killers. But I am not at all convinced that it is not plain ordinary people who are the backbone and majority of many of the killing forces in society. See, for example, the important work of Christopher Browning on the ordinary men in the German army who made up a squad of killers of the Jews for the Nazis.[40]

When all is said and done, after we have studied the various dynamics and possible combinations of dynamics for different suicide bombers, it seems to me that the outstanding characteristic of the suicide bombers is that they are ideologically committed, whether to a religious or political ideology or both combined, and that the overall climate of their culture approving and honoring their actions is central to any understanding of their actions.

Many of the suicide bombers take on with their entire beings fervent theological and/or political goals. Additionally, a number of the suicide bombers are seeking revenge and fulfillment of a deep hatred against the enemy. Psychologically, they also are submitting themselves to the thrills of being identified with and being parts of a stirring group drama both in the immediate sense of the pressure and approval of the group to which they belong, which prepares the attack, and also in a larger more "eternal" sense of serving their people, ethos, and tradition, both of which can give very warm feelings of belonging and meaningfulness. Finally, as noted earlier, it can be surmised that the suicide bombers enter into the kind of enveloping process in which people get swept up in a sense of disconnection from everyday reality and the capacity for plain common sense choices. They become captives and victims of the dramas to which they entered.

Disturbing as it is to our Western minds, in some sense many of the suicide bombers are *happy* to do the "work" that they do. There have been several reports, from different places around the world, that some suicide bombers evidence a distinct happiness in anticipation of or at the actual time of their self-destruction and murder of others. In a television documentary originally produced by BBC and then aired around the world including PBS in the United States, an 18-year-old who did not complete his mission, "recalled feeling an emotion he rarely experienced in his young life: happiness. 'I knew I would soon become a martyr,' he said of the day he was to carry out a suicide bomb attack. 'That made me happy.' "[41] Ariel Merari, a terrorism expert whom we cited earlier, who heads the Center for Political Violence at Tel Aviv University, and is described by CBS News as having studied every suicide bombing in the Middle East since the U.S. Marine Barracks were blown up in Beirut in October 1983, is quoted that some suicide bombers are downright elated: "Ecstatic, in the last moments. You probably remember the description of the suicide guy who drove a truck into the Marine Barracks in Lebanon in October 1983. He was described by the guard at the entrance to the compound, and the guy said amazingly, 'He was smiling.' "[42]

Amira Hass, an Israeli reporter for the respected *Haaretz*, who herself has lived among the Palestinians for many years and reports on their experiences and suffering sensitively (for many readers even too much so), respectfully, and without criticism observes:

> The claim that personal despair pushes the suicide bombers arouses sharp opposition among Hamas [a leading Palestinian fundamentalist group] operatives ... The sense of national purpose, a sweeping rage [at Israel], and a patriotic wish to advance the battle for independence are the main motivations.

Hass' article in *Haaretz* is entitled, "The suicide-bomber, says the doctoral student [one of the Palestinians Hass interviewed for the article, a psychology graduate student in the Islamic university in Aza], is a happy person who loves life."[43]

To extend an earlier comment on how convincing the defense of suicide can be (while also hiding the killing, of course), some of the stories of devotion to political and religious ideological commitments of the suicide bombers appeal to some of our time-honored Western ideals of loyalty, faithfulness, and sacrifice for noble values and causes, so that at some level even a Western mind can be drawn toward honoring these aspects of the perpetrators and not think of them only as disturbed and/or evil.

Haaretz reporter Amira Hass has another intriguing article where she reports on a Palestinian, Walid Dakah, who has spent the last eighteen years in an Israeli prison, and who as a veteran prisoner has become a kind of mentor and an observer of the new Palestinian prisoners. He expressed to Hass "astonishment and grief" about the growing number of youngsters who were on their way to suicide killings, which he opposes as both immoral and harmful to the Palestinians' cause. In effect, this prisoner has been conducting a sociological study. Hass reports verbatim some of the excellent interviews Dakah has conducted in which he repeatedly finds that the stated observations and explanations of the suicide bombers are political, religious, and nationalistic.

> *Dakah questioning a prisoner:* As a religious person, are you convinced that you have the right or that you are permitted to kill women and children and civilians?
>
> *Interviewed prisoner replies:* Israel is killing elderly people, women and children. Therefore, I consider myself exempt from the duty not to kill civilians. Exempt from the prohibition . . . As long as the occupation lasts, readiness to resist will also remain . . .[44]

Much the same information reaches us from other places in the world. During a four-month period in 2003 in Russia, seven suicide attacks by Chechens took place, six of them executed by women, with a toll of 165 dead. The Russian press has dubbed the perpetrators "black widows," based on the women being prepared to die in avenging the deaths of their fathers, husbands, brothers, or sons. Many but not all were devoted to radical Islamic theology. All seemed devoted to the Chechen protest against the Russian occupation of their land.[45]

Obviously, all human actions are part and parcel of the subject matter of the science of understanding human behavior. But that doesn't mean we have made any kind of strong case for analyzing suicide-bombing behavior as belonging to the domain of psychological abnormality versus psychological normality or health. Should we not "simply" say that devotion to a cause and one's people, revenge, hatred, being caught up and losing oneself in a group process in the name of a cause, and being carried away by an hypnotic scenario are the main psychological or mind causes of the "madness" of suicide bombing? These are each, at least up to a point, emotionally normal responses to life. Our conclusion *could* be that, however undesirable and repulsive to our Western selves, the culminating behavior of suicide bombing is not ipso facto disturbed behavior.

In an interesting article in the American Psychological Association's flagship journal, Roy and Judy Eidelson put forth a series of five "dangerous ideas" that propel both individuals and collective groups toward conflict. In the following amalgam they pull together several of these dangerous ideas into a kind of manifesto that sums up and speaks for the mind(s) either of individuals or of groups that are heading out to violent action against others:

> We are a special people deserving of high stature [superiority], but we have been unjustly denied our rightful place [injustice]. Our situation is precarious; we are staggering toward an abyss [vulnerability]. Why is this the case? Because other groups have repeatedly acted against us and betrayed us [distrust]. We must pull together and take action now.[46]

Here are common sense psychological concepts that give us some understanding of the psychology of suicide bombers without our needing to dip into the specific specialties of clinical psychology and psychiatry for what become pejorative labels of the suicide bombers as *disturbed*. The suicide bombers are, like all of us, humans; they are angry as hell; they feel beleaguered by the greater power of their enemy; they want to make a statement. The fact that they terrify and horrify us doesn't mean they are necessarily crazy.

It was also noted earlier that many academics and professionals in psychology believe the subject of terrorists is so much a political one that, although obviously aspects of human behavior are involved, in their opinion the subject essentially is not a proper one for psychology or psychiatry.

Moreover, in the largely liberal corridors of academia, the seemingly humanistic viewpoint that terrorists have rights to their heartfelt political convictions and readiness to sacrifice for their causes also do not go unrepresented.[47] There are behavioral science thinkers who see terrorism "simply" as "another form of politically motivated violence that is perpetrated by *rational, lucid people who have valid motives*."[48] An article by a teacher of anthropology at an Australian university, which provides a full-blown apology-defense of suicide bombers, and was published in a bona fide professional journal published by a reputable university press, poses the question, "Are suicide bombers human beings like us?" and comments further, "Arabs are demanding to be included as part of humanity. They're claiming, 'We are not as weird as you think.' "[49]

We should also take note that there are any number of behavioral scientists who have tried to put their finger on a core psychopathology in the suicide bomber and have failed. Charles Ruby has summarized some of the arguments that "terrorists have fundamental and pathological defects in their personality structure which result from unconscious forces in the terrorists' psyche."[50] Among the various explanations of psychopathology, one finds conceptions that terrorist acts are a reflection of unconscious feelings of hostility toward parents, rebellion especially against the father, responses to poverty and other injustice, overreactions to childhood experiences of humiliation and a consequent use of terrorism to maintain one's sense of self-esteem, failure to differentiate oneself from parental objects and hence overloyalty to a cause, and more. Ruby concludes, I think correctly, that our access to terrorist behavior is so restricted that most of these speculations are unlikely ever to be tested.

It seems to me self-evident that occasionally suicide bombing can be a way out for a sad, depressed, deprived, alienated, or marginal person, and sometimes also for an evidently demented person. However, the much greater weight of evidence to date is that, in many if not most cases, the pathology of suicide killing is essentially and mainly at the level of submitting oneself fanatically to an ideology to destroy life, consuming vengeance as a total way of life (and death!), and also to the joys of being part of a group, including often vainglorious wishes to be a celebrated hero. Moreover, to me, even if present in any given case, all personal psychodynamics such as fighting for one's virility and pride are somehow trivial in the face of the enormity of the acts of exploding one's life and exploding other peoples' lives with a deadly finality.

The discussion raises another fascinating psychological and epistemological question as to whether there ever comes a point where the definiteness and conclusiveness of conscious and rational motivations are so decisive that they eliminate any need for understanding more personal motivations including unconscious motivations?

The traditional psychoanalytically oriented view, which I admit to favoring and even loving, is that when all is said and done about conscious motivations and the power of cultures that promote and encourage suicide bombings, there is also a crucial further dynamic deep in the mind-spirit-soul of a person who elects to bring death on himself or herself and so many others.

Strentz has written that one must go beyond the general social-psychological environment that engenders terrorism to see more true or deeper causes in the person. He says the terrorist's disturbance lies in his needs for himself to fulfill a certain role, rather than his genuine desire to do something for the political-social good, including people with feelings of inadequacy who must make themselves into leaders, and antisocial personalities, opportunists, and inadequate personalities who are never satisfied with the status quo and seek a reprieve in idealism.[51]

Still, with all my love for understanding the personal emotional roots and dynamics of each individual case (indeed, like many people I am continuously interested in the life stories of individual suicide bombers), it seems that we have to acknowledge first of all that there is a larger pattern of a culture of death-making that is wrong which then provides a facilitating context for individual stories, choices, and disturbances.

So is that it? Have I myself now "proven" the very thesis to which I object, that the suicide bombers are not crazy or disturbed, which indeed many and quite possibly most of them are not, according to the existing current standard diagnostic system in psychiatry?

We should also ask whether we stand to gain something worthwhile if we define suicide bombers in our Western psychology and psychiatry by any of our characterizations of *not normal, abnormal, mentally disturbed, mentally ill, crazy, or psychotic*? What will be the implications of such a diagnosis? Could a diagnosis of psychopathology help us save lives? Or will it only complicate our fight to save human lives? Are suicide bombers really within the domains of clinical psychology and psychiatry? Is it better to avoid as-if medical thinking and stay purely with issues of politics and morality?

Perhaps those who claim suicide bombings are "simply" political or religious statements are right, and the language of mental health really is not appropriate. When ideological political convictions and socio-psychological brainwashing take over, are considerations of normality and abnormality even relevant? Is it right to translate our Western Judeo-Christian value that life is sacred into a cornerstone of scientific psychology and psychiatry? Do we have a right to define normality in a broader value context as the ability to live and let live, or is normality simply an ability to go about life and execute any job that our culture assigns us effectively—including killing? Granted suicide bombers obviously are a subject of psychology, but are they really a proper subject of psychopathology?

In the next chapter, I shall try to reach the further missing element that I believe leads us to an inescapable conclusion to all these questions: if we stay committed to our Western psychology-psychiatry, there can be no doubt that, most of the time suicide-murderers are disturbed on both counts of

- taking one's own life, even in devoted battle against an enemy
- taking the lives of defenseless civilians going about their everyday lives, even in the name of an overriding political goal.

I also suggest the above is not only the best solution to the conundrum of how to regard devoted fighters for a cause; it is essential for Western civilization that the values of our mental health system be for promoting and safeguarding life and against promoting death both to oneself and to others.

The Ultimate Existential Meaning of Suicide Bombings: The Killing of Human Life

Our Jihad in Iraq is a Jihad of the [Islamic] nation, and not a regional Jihad . . .
Today we wage Jihad in Iraq, [but] tomorrow it will be in Saudi Arabia, and after
that in Morocco, as the Prophet Muhammad said: "The jihad will continue for me
and for my nation until Judgment Day."   —Al-Qaeda in Iraq[1]

. . . One on one, with the only weapon for the Palestinian people being dynamite,
then you will see all Israelis leave, because there is not even one Israeli among
them willing to don a belt of explosives.   —Adel Sadeq on Iqra Television[2]

The ideology known as Islamic radicalism, militant Jihadism, or Islamo-fascism—
different from the religion of Islam—exploits Islam to serve a violent political
vision that calls for the murder of all those who do not share it . . . Islamic Radical leaders have endless ambitions of imperial domination, and they wish to
make everyone powerless except themselves. While promising a future of justice
and holiness, the terrorists are preparing a future of oppression and misery—
banning dissent and books, brutalizing women, and controlling every aspect
of life.   —President George W. Bush[3]

President Bush said the United States and its allies have disrupted ten Al-Qaeda
terrorism plots since September 11, 2001, including three inside the United States.
The White House said Bush was referring to a 2003 plot to blow up a New York
bridge, a plot to set off a radioactive "dirty bomb," and that details of a third case
could not be revealed.[4]

If as we have learned is bitterly true that there are tens of thousands of available suicide killers in many different countries around the world, *psychological*

considerations somehow seem trivial and irrelevant in the face of the overriding reality of the awesome military-political issues of life and death.

In the face of the overriding reality issue that human lives are at very real risk, our first concern in the democratic world obviously has to be how to fight back hard in very real self-defense rather than dabbling in esoteric and impotent theories of psychological health and illness. When I think of the Nazis carrying out the Holocaust, my first concerns are with what could have been done to stop them much more than whether Hitler was crazy; or whether, although Nazi society constituted a phenomenon of a group insanity and a collective process gone bad, which psychology as a science of human behavior does need to understand, could England and the United States have fought back earlier against the Nazis? Could the Allies have bombed Auschwitz? Was there any possibility the German generals' revolt against Hitler could have been helped to be successful?

English Prime Minister Tony Blair said of the suicide killers who attacked the United States on September 11:

> The world now knows the full evil and capability of international terrorism which menaces the whole of the democratic world. The terrorists responsible have no sense of humanity, of mercy, or of justice. To commit acts of this nature requires a fanaticism and wickedness that is beyond our normal contemplation.[5]

American leaders, including Vice President Richard Cheney and other senior cabinet members,[6] have said that further terrorist attacks, including suicide-killer attacks in particular, will *inevitably* find their way once again to the shores of the United States. There are also clearly voices in the Islamic world that are calling for the victory of Islam *everywhere around the globe* and the constituting of worldwide Islamic rule. We have noted a growing expectation in the Western world that there will be (or already is under way) a war between cultures or civilizations,[7] which for me in large part means a war between cultures that are committed to the sacredness of human life versus cultures that celebrate death.

The truth of an emerging war between the West and Islam is also being brought home repeatedly by the spread of a virulent anti-Semitism and an anti-Israel rhetoric as a metaphor of a new contemporary anti-Semitism. The Western world was shocked in October 2003 when Mahathir Mohamad, known as the moderate Prime Minister of Malaysia, spoke to a summit of Islamic leaders in a blatantly anti-Semitic way:

> Jews rule the world by proxy and the world's 1.3 billion Muslims should unite for a "final victory." The Europeans killed 6 million Jews out of 12 million, but today the Jews rule the world by proxy. They get others to fight and die for them. We are up against a people who think they survived 2000 years of pogroms not by hitting back but by thinking. Jews invented socialism, communism, human rights and democracy to avoid persecution and gain control of the most powerful countries. 1.3 billion Muslims cannot be defeated by a few million Jews.

The Associated Press reported that

> The audience of sheiks, emirs, kings and presidents gave Mahathir a standing ovation after his speech. Asked their general reaction, they said they found Mahathir's analysis on target, though they did not specifically address the comments on Jews.[8]

The Western world is facing once again, as it did most recently with Nazism and Communism, threats of political and/or military conquest and domination of many of the peoples in the world. This time around the flagrantly totalitarian polity threatening the safety of millions is the radical-violent interpretation of Islam, which some scholars too are beginning to refer to as "Islamofascism."[9]

The threat to the Western world is, first of all, a military and political threat to the lives and liberty of people who are being declared legitimate targets because they are infidels and therefore inferior and unacceptable.

There is also a threat developing to the free world's concepts of free and open minds. By definition, all totalitarian governments and movements are deeply against an authentic use of mind. In totalitarian worlds, ideas and feelings must be loyal to the dictates of the prevailing political or religious leader and philosophy. There is no room for dissent, individuality, freedom, choice, questioning, or a commitment to nonviolence. These regimes will kill dissidents and opponents. The transnational genocidal terrorist movement of our times is the same old-fashioned madness we have seen before of a fascist mindset gone wild in its certainty, superiority, and violence. It is an effort at world domination that is the same old political effort at taking over the world that has been attempted and at times succeeded over the centuries by any number of empire-builders, dictators, religions, or political movements. It is a phenomenon of deep evil, which means that it brings death to many millions of people.

And yet, after the urgent real military-political issues are done, there do also remain psychological issues. The past, present, and future battles between democracies and totalitarian states are first of all over brute power and the physical survival of democratic societies, but the battles are also over the moral and psychological values of democracy in its emphasis in the sacredness of life versus the deification of death by totalitarianism. In our Western language, declarations that whoever—Jews, Serbs, Croats, Muslims, Tutsi, Hutu—should be killed, can never be accepted as normal. Killers who follow the orders of their superiors to machinegun unarmed groups of vulnerable men, women, and children can never be accepted as legitimate even if we know that they are the true "moral majority" of a given culture.

At the same time, beyond understanding what are the powerful cultural patterns that invite, justify, and honor the suicide bomber, we need to engage a more fundamental existential level of explanation of suicide bombers as well. Clearly, there are universal existential meanings in the act of suicide killing which exist in their own right, no matter what the socialization and downright brainwashing to which a suicide bomber has been exposed in his or her culture, as well as by the handlers and organizers of suicide bombers who corral them toward their missions. We need to push beyond cultures and various individuals' concrete motives to identify and encounter the *basic existential meaning* of an individual suicide murderer's choice in (i) knowingly giving up life, and (ii) knowingly killing and maiming innocent unarmed civilians.

Practitioners of health professions who by definition seek to stave off death and prolong healthy lives have to know that suicide bombing is unhealthy for one and all. Suicide bombing obviously is not a result of any mysterious biological cause of madness such as contemporary psychiatry likes to attribute to many mental illnesses. Suicide bombing is an evil psychological choice of behavior that is both self-destructive and destructive of the lives of others by an individual who is pushed, aided, and abetted by powerful cultural forces to destroy life. But beyond calling suicide murders *mad* as an affirmation of the core values of our Western science and Western civilization, we need to study and speculate about the mind processes that are at work when the suicide killer pulls the trigger of hell.

Intriguingly, as I have remarked several times, the majority of ordinary people in our Western world react spontaneously to suicide bombers that something is basically wrong with them. They say they are crazy. They also say that they are evil. "The attackers [in the terrorist attacks on the World Trade Center and the Pentagon] are popularly thought of as mentally deranged individuals who are evil," wrote Charles Ruby in a journal of the much-respected American Psychological Association's Society for the Psychological Study of Social Issues.[10] In my judgment the spontaneous remarks heard from people everywhere are correct. They are the statements of people who know in their natural selves what professionals can get all mixed up in their obsessive intellectualizations and academic politicking. This wisdom of the man in the street also fits the common sense knowledge that is at the heart of my proposal to revise *all* psychiatric diagnosis to include an evaluation of the extent that one is doing harm to life—to one's own life or to others. In the cases of suicide bombers, the harm obviously is overwhelming and irreparable simultaneously both to oneself and to others.

I want to bring together now our discussion of the question whether the suicide bombers are to be defined as disturbed:

- Traditional psychiatry basically says *No*—they are not disturbed unless their beliefs, "work," or actions get to them and they become unglued, that is, suffer nervousness, weak stomachs, shake, can't sleep, experience guilt, get delusional, or whatever from the *DSM* psychiatric manual of diagnoses.

  Personally, I can only be happy about suicide bombers who get upset with their "work" (and of course very grateful when it can lead a suicide bomber to turn back without completing their mission).

- For different reasons than traditional psychiatry, many academic and theoretical psychologists, will also say *No*—you can't judge people according to *your* values, especially if they have grown up in a society which teaches them to idealize terrorism on behalf of their faith or ideology.

Personally, I hate a cultural relativism and deconstructionism that end up understanding and accepting the normality of people who were socialized to be totalitarian killers (although I definitely acknowledge the scientific validity of the observations of the great power of any given socialization experience).

- The practitioners of mental health in totalitarian societies say that serving their regimes and natural goals by killing people constitutes personal excellence and the best mental health.

For me, practitioners of mental health who aid and abet abusive limitations of personal freedom, cruelty, torture, and murder are fascists whom I oppose in every way; plus I feel an added personal bitterness that they do such deep disrespect to the values I believe are at the core of the science and healing profession I love (just as Mengele et al. of the physicians who are masters of murder are the satanic antithesis of all that the wonderful profession of medicine stands for of saving lives and healing).

- A majority of practitioners of psychodynamic, relationship, humanistic, and existential psychotherapies basically say *Yes*, terrorists killers are people who hate life and hurt so many people that they hardly deserve medals as emotional normals who are devoted to their principles and causes.

This is my value system. I am convinced that terrorist killings of civilians is both evil and also a madness of the human spirit.

- The suicide bomber is a prime example of a person who allows meanings, goals, and absolutes to overwhelm the ultimate facts of life, which are their being alive and other people being alive. For the suicide bomber, having to reach the vaunted goal of suicide murder in their theatre of destruction is made into and becomes quite literally bigger than life itself.[11]

The notion that a cause justifies both death to oneself and the use of one's own death to destroy civilians busy at their daily lives is not acceptable to me even in a context where I believe I have to be at war.

- I also go one big if obvious step further to look at the evident psychodynamic or emotional meanings staring us in the face from the very actions of the suicide bomber. I say that killing life on the face of it is mentally sick. We don't have to strain our minds or our definitional structures to see the basic psychopathology in the suicide bomber's existential experience; it's there for us as big as the human life that is being destroyed.

The penultimate or peak in the psychopathological process of the suicide bomber is the choice to activate the choice to die and kill. It is the last choice one will ever make. It is a disastrous choice to end life irretrievably for oneself and others. The moment of the final choice to take deadly action is where the ultimate breach with reality takes place. There will be no more opportunity for choice after this. Quite obviously, the suicide bomber is presiding over a moment of infinite power that consummates the proverbial wish of "pushing one button which will destroy the world" of so many living creatures.[12] This is pure and familiar megalomaniac madness in the classic definition of a person taking life and death in their own hands in an inflated godlike way.

When a person ends his or her life, ends the lives of many others, and seeks to torture and maim horribly still many others, this is the ultimate psychopathology. These are ipso facto disturbed behaviors against life itself, and not simply a battle for a cause.

- Notwithstanding all the above, I am prepared to take the risk of agreeing that in some situations, such as when an enemy has an iron upper hand and there are no prospects for alternative methods of political and military battle against the hated enemy, and perhaps also no chance to escape with one's own life if one does nothing, suicide bombing makes a lot of sense. It also makes sense as a military strategy and technique against an enemy in war, though there are serious questions as to the extent to which a people can justify sacrificing their own people against the leaders and fighters and formal representatives of the enemy. But there is no justification possible for suicide killing of civilians or plain people. However meaningful may be reasons such as ideology, revenge, loyalty, noble sacrifice, or also fame and reward, suicide bombing as a strategy of warfare against civilians must be judged as criminally rotten and humanly insane.

Suicide bombing is apocalyptic. Ultimately it is a murderous attack on life itself. All are slated to die. Nothing of life is to survive it.[13]

MANKIND'S LOVE OF MURDER AND KILLING

There remains one more very unpleasant truth that we haven't really brought up yet in the course of analyzing the causes, motivations, and reasons for the suicide bomber. Reluctantly and fearfully, I have to say that like the endless genocides of groups in human history, some of the motivation for suicide bombing issues from a profound flaw in our human nature, which is an evident love and penchant for murder and mass murder. There are simply too many people in our species who want and like to kill for us to ignore this side of human nature. Rationalizing, explaining, and understanding the "reasons" for a deadly massacre can trap us into not seeing that mass killing is a goal in and of itself for enough members of our so-called human race who really want to destroy others, period. Thus, another of the endless examples of humans who want to kill was the leader of the Aum cult in Japan who made elaborate preparations for a sarin-gas attack in Tokyo trains. I have never heard of any "reason" attributed to his behavior or any elaboration of cause in the group ideology. Their cult goal simply was to kill nonmembers![14]

The *why* of the desire to destroy other human beings is a crucial psychological-biological-scientific issue that takes us on a long and complex path in its own right. For now let us simply recognize that we have added the motivation of a "plain desire" to kill along to the more understandable motives as we have identified such as ideology, religious belief and fervor, revenge, loyalty to one's group, and more. In my estimation it is only a few political observers and also only a few psychological observers who allow themselves to get to the point where they recognize as a driving major motivation for terrorism, war, and genocide the joy of violence in its own right. Violence is intoxicating and addictive; it sweeps up a person and a group in a powerful sense of drama; it fills a warrior's heart with pleasures of virility and power; it swells the ego with archaic competitive triumph; it whets the lust and pleasure of savoring the weakness and defeat of the other; it excites sadistic joys of another's suffering; it is a marvelous relief from the ennui, boredom, and somehow chronic disappointment that are frequent existential modes for many people.

Our human minds try to avoid recognizing these primitive and quite nasty parts of ourselves. Our minds also like to think that we have some degree of control over events and that we understand quite well the "real reasons" for the big events of suffering in our lives. Following the July 7 London suicide bombings, and especially the realization the bombers were U.K. people, a commentator observed the frustration of not understanding anything: "We crave some clue to what is about to happen and we find none. We look into those eyes and we see only blankness. We seek some sign of madness and encounter only the mundane. In short, we are frustrated in our search for meaning. What remains are questions: Who are these people who live in our midst and deceive even their own families? Who are these people dressing as we do, conversant with our habits, healthy, capable of rational thought, ready, in the name of their interpretation of Islam, to kill themselves and as many citizens of the infidel West as they can?"[15]

We in the West, and certainly in the social sciences give facile explanations for major violences, whether by individuals or groups: this one is frustrated, this one wants to be more prominent, this one wants more power, etc. Our political analysts are never at a loss to identify some of the ubiquitous tensions and issues that are central to every group's collective experience. So, it is doubly refreshing when a political commentator sees that the major motivation of some political terrorists is, plain and dirty simple, *a love of violence and the spilling of blood in their own right.* Writing his prominent column in *Newsweek* under the heading, "Cruelty is all they have left," Fareed Zakaria says:

"The purpose of terrorism," Vladimir Lenin once said, "is to terrorize." Like much of what he said, this is wrong ... With many terrorist groups ... violence has become an end in and of itself. They want a lot of people dead, period ... In the 1940s and 1950s, communist groups were popular and advanced their cause politically. By the 1960s, after revelations about Stalin's brutality ... facing irrelevance, the hard-core radicals turned to violence, hoping to gain attention and adherents by daring acts of bloodshed. Thus the proliferation of terror by groups like the Red Brigades and the Baader-Meinhof gang. Similarly, for decades Islamic fundamentalists tried to mount political opposition in Arab countries. Frustrated by failure, they have become terror machines and nothing more.[16]

Notwithstanding the considerable capacity of the human mind to kid itself, hide from itself, and delude itself, the mind must know when it is bringing on death to itself and/or others. And notwithstanding the tremendous capacity of group, cultural and ideological processes to put people into trances where consciously they do not know what they are doing, and they are caught up and swept away unconsciously by mind processes which swallow up their remaining sense of personal identity and will, people must know when they are bringing their lives and/or the lives of others to an end. Basically, the machinery of human experience *must* bring up inside the ultimate being of a person an awareness of basic realities that he or she (i) is ending his or her life, and (ii) bringing death and bitter injuries to many other living people—characteristically, to unarmed civilian men, women, and children going about their normal lives.

My readers will not be surprised that my firm conviction is that *yes, suicide bombers are disturbed*—as seriously disturbed as the behaviors they undertake of killing themselves and others imply in plain common sense.

I believe it is cowardly for Western psychiatry as well as scientifically wrong to avoid such a huge area of human behavior, to back away into any relativism about suicide killing. *Suicide killing is dead wrong.* Being a suicide bomber is a choice to kill big time. It is a disturbed choice to be evil, and an evil choice to be the worst kind of disturbed person that destroys lives.

Let's look more at how I get to the above position and how I defend it.

First, I want to argue that we must reach the above conclusion if we are to defend our Western civilization, meaning the basic ideas and values of a decent nonviolent humanity to which our finest thought and social institutions have always been dedicated.

I believe that from the point of view of a philosophy of the psychological, psychiatric, and other mental health professions, it will be ridiculous and absurd if all the ideological killers in our world no longer remain also subjects of a discourse about what is desirable and healthy mental living and what is not. Support murdering oneself as a favored routine instrument of warfare, and devoting one's death to destroying children, the aged, and others innocently going about their daily lives, and you are no longer a proponent of a civilized humanity. If you describe such killing and murdering as "normal," therefore not "abnormal," therefore somehow as belonging to the healthy and acceptable in the concepts of psychology and mental health of your society, the logical implication could be that you also need to instruct your counselors and therapists to encourage suicide bombing. If it's normal behavior, one's counselors and therapists may have to be understanding and downright supportive to people who are going to be suicide bombers, and maybe even to recommend suicide bombing to others as a way of life—forgive the expression. Obviously, for most of us, endorsing suicide bombing is hardly going to be an acceptable purpose for mental health. (Do see later in this chapter the unstinting praise by a distinguished Egyptian psychiatrist of the transcending final moments of the suicide bomber.)

Second, for our own sake, we need to find a way to define suicide bombing on the face of things as disturbed behavior. Not including killers in the world of psychopathology would mean that *abnormality* includes people who have break-downs when they are supposed to be killers but become too disturbed and can't meet the requirements of their jobs; while *normality* will include all those who are exemplary and capable in *yes* fulfilling their jobs in the death squads.[17] It hardly sounds like a psychology of which Western thinking could be proud. It is certainly not the kind of psychology I personally want to encounter in any professional ser-vices I receive for myself when I am a patient undergoing psychotherapy—no way will I learn from or be healed by a therapist who is free of values or wishy-washy on the crucial issues of human life. Nor can I myself as a practitioner offering psychotherapy to others agree to represent such a psychology that does not take clear stands about violence, terrorists, or genocide.

THE ALL TOO OBVIOUS DISTURBANCE OF SUICIDE BOMBERS AND ALL PEOPLE WHO HARM HUMAN LIFE

My basic conception of mental health is that the first test of any human behavior is whether the goal sought through the behavior and the behavioral means chosen to reach that goal do or do not advance the security, safety, and quality of life of people.

Human life is an evolutionary process, which for me means working toward extending our human longevity, not only in the face of the medical illnesses everyone seems to agree we should try to conquer, but also in the face of man's worst psychological disorder of a powerful interest in and readiness to commit mass killing. Psychological health is to know, appreciate, and commit oneself to life being sacred. In the report of a suicide bomber who turns back, which will be found later in the chapter devoted to a proposal for a *"Worldwide Campaign for Life"* by the leaders of the world's religions and other world leaders and heroes, the woman terrorist changes her mind in a moment of inspiration. She says touchingly:

> 'I look at the sky,' Ms. Ahmed recalled . . . speaking English as she described a kind of awakening. 'I look at the people.' She said she remembered a childhood belief' 'that nobody has the right to stop anybody's life.'[18]

For me, mass killing is obviously deserving of being thought of also as a health problem,[19] so that no matter how many humans have been afflicted by this disorder, mass killing of others needs to be recognized in modern psychology and psychiatry as a serious disturbance of the human mind.

As noted earlier, I have previously published in the psychiatric literature a proposal that *all* psychiatric diagnoses be based on an evaluation of the functioning of the person for his or her *own self*, and a person's impacts on the functioning of *other persons*.[20] I am happy to repeat this concept as I continue in various of my writings to promote interest in this idea and ultimately its adoption by the mental health field. I propose that the test of whether a person is doing harm *either* to one's own life *or* to other peoples' lives very much be the sine qua non for defining mental disturbance. In this conceptual frame, the bare facts that a person is killing either their own self and/or other people directly establishes that they are suffering a state of the most serious psychiatric disturbance.

I am saying that psychology has a very important something to say about suicide bombers and about all violence against human life. Once people set out to harm life (except in clear-cut self-defense), we should define them as psychologically disturbed. By this standard, the suicide killers *are* patently disturbed. The suicide killers are intrinsically deeply immoral, and in mental health terms, they are *crazily* against life. Loyalty to a cause that seeks to wipe out others because they are infidels and unworthy, and to conquer other peoples and nations, perhaps even the world, is not an admirable idealistic dedication to a cause but crazy dangerous because in truth it is inherently a dedication to killing people.

For me, a totalistic devotion of one's mind to *any* ideological movement or value goal is a priori suspect as an escape into overcertainty and a fascist system demanding total obedience and compliance.[21] The same concern and judgment would apply were the value in question devotion to our own beloved ideals of the truest mental health (a la the tried joke, *Support mental health or I'll kill you*).

Certainly, devotion to death of oneself and especially as a tool for killing unarmed people is fascist and mentally dishonorable and quite simply "disturbed." Liberal academics, beware and know that your lives have never been spared by the totalitarians of whatever era. On the contrary, often you (we—for I continue to insist I am a very wholesome member of the liberal camp) have been among the first to be executed, lest our capacity to think (sometimes our eyeglasses are the giveaways that mark us for being taken away) becomes a threat to an antidemocratic regime.

At the same time, I need to make it clear that I am not forgetting that the people who do actual violence are first of all criminally violating the law; and therefore are subject first of all to police and military operations to stop them and save their victims; and then to the legal proceedings of criminal justice systems at whatever local, national, and international levels, such as the new International Criminal Court for Crimes against Humanity and Genocide. Psychological and psychiatric definitions of abnormality should never "cover the asses" of the perpetrators of mass killing. One does not have to be a slave of logical consistency and say that our tradition of appeals for clemency and understanding, and for treatment more than punishment for mentally disturbed killers, will also apply to would-be suicide bombers and other terrorists and people who commit genocide because we define them as mentally disturbed. It is not difficult to differentiate between a genuine rush of uncontrollable passion that renders a person mentally unaware and less responsible for his or her behavior in the case of an individual homicide, versus calculated mass murders of others—no matter how these too may be driven by passions, say, such as revenge. In my opinion, any act of collective violence that targets a group of people as victims who weren't directly associated with the original hurt to the revenger should be excluded a priori from any possible consideration of an extenuating mental disability in the perpetrator. Society cannot possibly countenance or "understand" sprees of murder of collective groups; and psychology cannot be used as an extenuating explanation inviting mercy for such killers.

Granted too, all of history is filled with people and movements who seek to achieve destructive supremacy over everyone else, for example, Genghis Khan, the Crusaders, Nazis, and Communists. This overwhelming fact has led some thinkers to conclude that genocide is *normal* on the basis of the fact that it is so statistically widespread and normative that you can't call it abnormal. But I continue to say if *all* the people in town die from the Black Plague, or SARS, or Aviary Flu, the condition killing them is not therefore normal. It is a pathological Killing Condition, which is what suicide bombing is.

THE SUICIDE-BOMBING CULTURE DISPLAYS ADDITIONAL SIGNS OF IRRATIONALITY

It is interesting, and I think also not unfair circumstantial evidence, to consider that in addition to the overriding meaning of suicide bombings as destruction of life and thereby unmistakably pathological, the suicide bombers and their culture also demonstrate several other characteristics of mental disturbance. *Appeals to nonreality are intrinsic to the suicide-bomber culture.* They are victims of and spokespersons of quite irrational ideas and beliefs. Language in this culture (and in others, such as among bigots or totalitarian nations or any group that is busy defending its ugly record of cruelty and violences against others) characteristically is used in a lawless fashion, unchecked by any requirements of being matched by empirical facts. The main purpose of rhetoric is to embellish and glorify violence in defense of the fascist ideology being served.

Thus, the suicide-bombing culture is one of beliefs that September 11 was perpetrated either by Israel or even by the United States itself; a way of thinking that totally demonizes Israel and the West, especially the United States, for every conceivable cruelty and perversity. It appeals to a basic archetypal construct that jihad is justified against all infidels to restore the kingdom of Islamic rule of the entire Earth; a self-deluding reliance on the celestial rewards of seventy-two virgins, and whatever additional forms of ecstasy including the overflowing praise of all the occupants of heaven; and a culture of metaphoric exaggeration, hyperbole, and lack of responsibility for relating to objective and empirical facts, so that it is expected and legitimate to say *whatever* will serve to advance one's basic ideological agenda.

Beliefs in unproven mysterious plots such as the above are part of a genre we know of as *conspiracy theories*. Conspiracy theories enable one to reduce or remove the blame for an event that belongs to the real perpetrators, and to reassign the blame to a preferred object, that is, to one's standard and favorite enemies. This device is employed over and over again following suicide bombings and other terror attacks. Thus, just as September 11 was the work of the United States and/or Israelis-Jews. July 7 was the work of Britain itself. The suicide bombings in Taba, Egypt, in May 2004 which is immediately alongside the border with Eilat, Israel, was of course the work of the Israelis and the United States; and the suicide bombings in Sharm-el-Sheikh, Egypt, in July 2005 were again the work of the Israelis and the United States.

Here is a typical example of conspiracy theory rhetoric following the last of the above attacks:

> Dr. Abdallah Al-Ash'al, former assistant to the Egyptian foreign minister and lecturer on international law at Cairo University, was quoted on an internet site that "All of the signs indicate that Israeli hands were [behind the attacks]."[22] "It is in Israel's interest that there be an Egyptian response to what happened, since it wants Egypt to join the American campaign against terrorism . . . It is likely that Israel recruited some people in coordination with terrorist groups in order to hurt Egypt . . . Israel's goal in this operation was to bring terrorism back to Egypt . . ."[23]

In general, Islamic thought is characterized by a deep reluctance if not inability to acknowledge error. Habib Malik has commented in this respect, "There [is] an absence of any Islamic mea culpa. Islam has no regrets and may be incapable of them. In other words, mea culpa is regarded as a sign of weakness."[24]

An Egyptian progressive, Mamoun Fandy, writing in the London Arabic daily, *Al-Sharq Al-Awsat*, after the attack on Sharm-el-Sheikh writes:

> How do these people want the world to believe them when they attempt to defend the Arab truth by concocting lies and absurdities? In my opinion, there are thousands of facts which could provide the best defense of the Arab truth. Why do we forsake these facts and turn to lies instead?! What causes this disease?!

Criticizing the Arab TV networks, *Al-Arabiya* and *Al-Jazeera*, Fandy said:

> Terrorism is terrorism and the killing of peaceful vacationers is terrorism; of this there can be no doubt. Some of us call these people 'conspiracy theorists' . . . but the undisputed truth is that this is a group of people who are either paranoid or insane.[25]

A *New York Times* account of the "Tipton Taliban" or four young men who lived in a Muslim area of a small town near Birmingham, England, who left to join the Taliban in Afghanistan (three of them have since been taken prisoners by the United States and the fourth is missing), describes the religious or political indoctrination they received with no holds barred against the use of lies, distortions, and fantasy to foment a battle against non-Islamic lives.

> The goal of the radicals is to make Islam a political force. To do this, they employ a potent mix of vivid imagery, Koranic scholarship, hard facts and soft-boiled conspiracy theories: The Jews attacked the World Trade Center to discredit Osama bin Laden; the CIA did it to give America a way into Central Asia; bin Laden is a U.S. agent meant to discredit Islam.[26]

Dear reader, be careful as you read one glib conspiratorial fairy tale after another, let alone you see them repeated and they begin to acquire a sense of familiarity, that you don't lose the ability to react with shock and dismay at the systematic lies, bald prejudices, and craziness of denials of known reality. In general, the language of explanation, justification, and legitimization of suicide bombing is a bizarre and corrupt demagogic use of language that warps facts in pursuit of its destructive ideology. *Is this so different from other violations of reality by psychotics?*

In June 2003, a standing-room-only meeting took place at no less than Humboldt University of Berlin. As a *New York Times* reporter comments, although the university is "one of Germany's premier institutions of higher learning . . . a lower sort of learning was taking place." Unbelievably, more than 700 people enthusiastically joined in a series of speeches that advanced the claim that September 11 was not carried out by the nineteen perpetrators. Who then? "The answer was not clear, but the implication was: It was either allowed to happen or supported by the United States itself." The report goes on to say that "the Sept. 11 conspiracy theory mania" has grown in strength in Germany and also in France. Newspaper polls in Germany show one in five Germans agreeing that the United States itself carried out September 11![27]

The thinking-belief system of the Islamic suicide bomber as a son and daughter of Islamic culture in general is further enhanced by the kind of magical thinking that is characteristic of people who are going to commit suicide as we see them in everyday tragedies of suicidal disturbances. On a certain level of mind, they do not believe they will really be dead. There results a montage of irrationality, violation of logic, disregard of facts and evidence, and an abandonment of self to delusional thinking. The delusional process leads to and justifies the ultimate mental disturbance of ending one's own life, and the criminality and mental disturbance that is involved in taking the lives of others.

Take any nonpolitically defined behavior which is invested with the same characteristics of irrationality and delusion, and there will be no question in the minds of any psychopathologist or psychiatric observer that a person who succumbs to such thinking, even in the midst of a whole culture gone crazy, is himself or herself quite crazy. Does a political context or cause really justify recasting crazy behavior into being not-crazy?[28]

Writing in a Pakistani publication, Jonathan Eric Lewis has pointed up sharply the severe irrationality of the Arab world that *simultaneously* promotes the popular notion that Muslims were not responsible for September 11, but that the attacks on the United States were entirely justifiable.

> The simultaneous insistence on the part of the Arab Street that Arabs were not respon-
> sible for the World Trade Center attack and that the attacks were a justifiable reaction
> to American foreign policy ... [is] a retreat from historical reality and societal re-
> sponsibility and into the fundamentally anti-democratic politics of the irrational ...
> Political irrationality is a mindset that lends itself to denial of all empirical evidence
> that disproves their widely held beliefs; a virulent anger at perceived conspiracies being
> directed against the Arab world; and an intense fear of non-conformist intellectuals ...
> who critically examine the flaws of Arab society and Islamic civilization.[29]

By every Western standard, the thinking promulgated by the world of Islamic terrorism is corrupt, out of touch with reality, mad (unrelated to facts), and inciting to violence (fomenting wild murderous actions). Are individuals who adopt such thinking and join and participate in such an ideological group to be thought of as *normal*—having had the bad luck of being born into and becoming normally attracted and loyal to their crazy culture? Are the behaviors of murderous terrorists including suicide bombers simply *political* acts? Does Western psychiatry not have its right to identify suicide-murder thinking as disturbed even if it is rooted in a sponsoring culture and is adopted as a political stratagem?[30]

Any and all considerations of how pathological the suicide bombers are also runs into another prime problem that, in a larger sense, we human beings are quite defective in the workings of our minds most of the time, to a point where so many of us might be thought of to begin with as disturbed and maybe even somewhat crazy. It makes it harder to know who and when we should characterize as really crazy! Thus, so many seemingly normal people stay organized around a chronic hatred of someone or other—say one or more members of their family, or another ethnic or other group; and their hatred and prejudice obviously play a large role in organizing them and keeping them going in their otherwise seeming adjustment. Additionally, passions of taking risks, the thrills of undertaking dangerous adven-
tures, walking excitedly the tightropes of Russian roulette type threats to one's life and tightropes of criminal duels and contests with law enforcement agencies all obviously entice huge numbers of people around the world into dangerously crazy behaviors everyday. Further thrills of surprising others and overwhelming them with one's smartness, agility, tactical superiority are an endless game for millions more. For example, ever since the birth of the computer age, there is an increasing number of what may be called terrorist attacks on computer systems, which have been described as "virulent ... attacks by malicious programmers" that seek to crash computers and networks throughout the world; in 2002, a center at Carnegie Mellon University that monitors such attacks reported no less than a total of 82,094 rogue attacks.[31]

The more one accumulates information about the foibles and weaknesses of the human mind, the more we have to conclude, what I fear has been obvious for a long time, that overall our human species is more flawed than not, including our being variously ridiculous, stupid, immoral, and evil much of the time. Although a majority of us human beings are capable of zones of normal functioning, and we are generally decent and human toward one another, under circumstances such as personal upset, ideological recruitment, or false-messiahs, probably a majority of us are available to harm others. Thus, we know scientifically that *at least two thirds of us will give "Milgram electric shocks" to one another.*[32] Human beings everywhere, including the well educated, up to and including those crowned with Ph.D. or M.D. degrees, are regularly capable of every conceivable and obvious distortion of reality, blatant manipulation of facts for purposes of emotional self-protection, ugly prejudicial statements about whomever, and strategies of disinformation against rivals and enemies. In virtually every society, there seem to be few social constraints against demagoguery and even incitement to violence. So a further question is whether we have to draw a line of definition as to what is and what is not *crazy* and where to put that line? Can we simply state the truth (I believe that in many matters there *are* truths!) about all statements that are widely discrepant with the empirical facts, and identify these statements and their exponents as disturbed, no matter that at one time or another this includes most of us?

THE ULTIMATE EXISTENTIAL MEANING OF CONTEMPORARY SUICIDE BOMBINGS IS TO KILL MORE AND MORE INNOCENT PEOPLE

When all is said and done, and we will know "everything there is to know" about the suicide bombers; we will understand and even respect, first, that many of them are making a political statement of loyalty to an ideology or a personal statement of revenge that are very important and real for them, and, second, we will understand how they are variously socialized, inculcated, indoctrinated, brainwashed, coerced, manipulated, rewarded, and transported into states of altered experience, and what not. Nonetheless, there will still remain a larger existential truth:

> *There is a fundamental moment of basic human experience where the human mind is profoundly conscious of the two key choices it is making, whether to die and whether to kill.*

Suicide bombing has to be an ultimate moment of existential awareness. No other levels of meaning can erase the instinctual awareness of life versus death we all sense in ourselves and see in other living creatures.

The awareness of life versus death is the single most profound aspect of existence. The suicide bomber suspends what the philosopher Spinoza called a drive for self-maintenance against destructive forces coming from inside or outside the human organism.

It is true that the suicide bomber is transported into a dissociated state of having redefined his or her existence as secondary to being submerged in a noble sacrificial project for his or her people. Adrian Mirvish, a professor of philosophy, describes the suicide bomber as left with a shell around an empty mind:

> In the case of the suicide bomber, we are in effect dealing with a strange case of inverted solipsism. . . . The authoritarian structure of the Islamic organizations . . . molds and shapes an inverted personage, one where there is no internal life left over. In place of a private mind and ground for conscience there is instead a rigid set of prescriptions totally open to public scrutiny. Better yet, through years of the enforcement of hatred one is left with the mere shell of a complete person, one where the mind is merely a mirror, the product of absolute, authoritarian and public scrutiny.[33]

I personally believe that any act we do to damage life—our own lives and the lives of others—needs to be seen as unhealthy from the point of view of a scientific Western psychology. Whenever a given individual succumbs to unrealistic far-fetched thinking, and especially when a person succumbs to acting out actions that lead to the destruction of their own life or the lives of others, they should be defined as mentally ill. *People who kill themselves and kill other people certainly should not be thought of as mentally healthy.*

To understand suicide bombers, we need to understand several levels of dynamics in the suicide bomber's mind. This is not unusual with respect to many human behaviors many of which are multidimensional and multidetermined.

A BBC report described the suicide bombers as "likely to be motivated by religious fervour," and an NBC report described an intense period of indoctrination of the bombers: "The bombers believe they are sent on their missions by God, and by the time they are ready to be strapped with explosives . . . they have reached a hypnotic state. Their rationale: that by blowing themselves up in a crowd of Israelis, they are forging their own gateway to Heaven."[34]

People can be tricked, cheated, and led into insane behavior by selling them a bill of goods that they are doing idealistic and valuable God-or-Empire-mandated acts. Linda Skitka and Elizabeth Mullen call this "the dark side of moral conviction," and suggest that it is some part of the explanation of why people are willing to embark on "an incredibly horrific mission," such as September 11, which involves "not only a willingness to be a martyr for one's cause, but also a willingness to take the innocent lives of untold numbers of others."[35]

As we have also noted, the group process of indoctrinating suicide bombers and moving them along to completing their missions is based not only on ideology, but also on a medley of excitement, intoxication, and ecstasy, loss of self and an amazingly comforting sense of being fused into a larger identity. These dynamics too are part of the "explanations" of suicide bombers we are seeking. In fact, they add to the recognizable psychopathology of suicide bombing, insofar as being a suicide bomber involves an extreme loss and abandonment of the normal self to blending into others, and to hypnotic and orgiastic experiences that destroy the boundaries of the self and its normal preservation. The boundaries between existence and nonexistence are erased in a terrible "meltdown" of the mind's ability to recognize the legitimacy of one's own life and of the lives of other human creatures which are overridden by deadly outcomes of the death of self along with the cruelties of severe injuries and death to other living creatures.

Robins and Post engage in a kind of existential black humor when they refer to "the paradoxical solace of belonging to a paranoid group . . . We melt together in the mob, become as one, and each member suspends individual judgment. All are equal within the group. It is as if the group had a mind of its own."[36] We all have normal or milder experiences of the pleasure of being parts of groups and reassuring ourselves against the vast inner existential anxiety that is part of our human condition. Thus, we wear labels of designer clothes; we become deeply impassioned on behalf of our political parties; we clap heartily in mass approval in group events, plays, and concerts; we roar our loyalty and approval in the aggression-releasing heroic contexts of sporting events; and we rally to our countries with dedication and patriotic fervor. Suicide bombers go further. To understand them is to understand the process of being a part of a group to a point where it seems worthwhile to give up life itself for the group. To understand this dynamic, one must get into an emotional mindset and make an effort to feel something of the passion and sense of being transported to an intoxicating sense of purpose and safety by virtue of being part of a group taking dramatic action.

Le Bon, a sociologist who wrote with amazing perspicacity at the end of the nineteenth century said:

> A person is not religious solely when he worships a divinity, but when he puts all the resources of his mind, the complete submission of his will, and the whole-souled ardor of fanaticism at the service of a cause or an individual who becomes the goal and guide of his thoughts and actions.[37]

The suicide bombers also suffer another aspect of weakness of mind in that they have succumbed not only to powerful collective beliefs and identifications with one's group and ideology, but they are often also plain suckers who have fallen for the manipulation and exploitation of what can be described as "professional handlers" who cold-bloodedly employ strategies of indoctrination, coercion, hypnotic suggestibility, and the power of authority to induct the suicide bomber and make sure he or she goes the full route of their deadly mission.[38] Terrorism expert, Michael Radu, of the Foreign Policy Research Institute has concluded that the first thing he would do in order to combat suicide bombing would focus on eliminating the enablers—the recruiters and ideologists—wherever they are (mostly in London, Pakistan, and Saudi Arabia). "This must . . . be the first step in eliminating the problem."[39]

In an intriguing piece of academic research for a Ph.D. thesis, Anat Barko interviewed five handlers of suicide bombers who were caught and imprisoned in Israeli jails. She found that they had what she called a duplicitous double system of morality. On the one hand they themselves are good family people who worry and care for their families, and yet they are entirely capable of sending others to murder innocent families, including the women and children in the victim families. Barko says that the suicide bomber "is a human being in all that is connected to his own daily experience, but then ... he pulls down a veil and can do what he does ... the handler is both human and inhuman at the same time."[40]

Barko also began a fascinating research process with the senders in which she attempted to evoke more of their latent moral feelings. In the initial stages of her contacts, she presented the handlers with dilemmas that counterpointed group ideological motivations versus human considerations and concern for the victims. After completing this stage of the evaluation, Barko continued discussing the moral meanings of the suicide bombing with the senders. She reports that she was careful to reinforce their periodic statements of humanism and concern for people, and that the result was first of all a triggering of a wave of nostalgia for their families and a great longing particularly for their own mother as well as for their children and wife. At the conclusion of her interviewing sequence, Barko presented the handlers with the same dilemmas she had at the beginning with the intriguing result that a change had taken place in them in the direction of greater humanity. "They were much more human and empathic toward their terror victims and less justifying the criminal violence and terrorism that they had activated and harm they had done to people." Barko concludes that, hopefully, she succeeded in uncovering "seeds of humanity" in the handlers.[41]

A BBC documentary referred to earlier includes an interview with a handler or dispatcher. The interviewer asks him why he himself does not fulfill the holy task of becoming a martyr. The dispatcher replies in seemingly practical terms that barely conceal his self-serving: "We are the seeds so that the trees can survive. Either I will die or he (the suicide bomber) will. There is no other solution."[42] One would think the dispatchers would agree to being rotated from their jobs after some number of months to undertake a sacred suicide-bombing mission themselves.

To sharpen our sense of the transcendental experience of the suicide bomber and what I claim is a profound inner existential choice, we have the point of view by a respected, betitled mental health professional that suicide bombing is a sublime peak moment of no less than *superior* mental health! Believe it or not, an Egyptian psychiatrist has been quoted at length that the moment of execution of suicide killing of any and all civilians is a penultimate triumph of human existence. Nor is Dr. Adel Sadeq a run-of-the-mill professional. He was an honored recipient of the 1990 Egyptian State Prize, chairman of the Arab Psychiatrists Association, and head of the Department of Psychiatry at Ein Shams University in Cairo. Sadeq is an enthusiastic supporter of Palestinian suicide attacks. In an article in the Egyptian newspaper, *Hadith Al-Madina,* and in an interview on Saudi-Egyptian satellite

TV, Sadeq praises the moment of death of the suicide bomber as "the height of bliss:"

> The psychological structure [of the perpetrator of a suicide attack] is that of an individual who loves life. This may seem strange to people who see the human soul as most sublime. They are incapable of understanding [the suicide attack] because their cultural structure has no concepts such as self-sacrifice and honor. These concepts do not exist in a number of cultures, and therefore they offer stupid interpretations, attesting to ignorance. But we know this well, because our culture is one of sacrifice, loyalty, and honor. [US President] Bush was mistaken when he said that the girl was killing the future when she chose to kill herself.[43] On the contrary: She died so that others would live.
>
> When the martyr dies a martyr's death, he attains the height of bliss. As a professional psychiatrist, I say that the height of bliss comes with the end of the countdown: ten, nine, eight, seven, six, five, four, three, two, one. And then, you press the button to blow yourself up. When the martyr reaches 'one,' and then 'boom,' he explodes, and senses himself flying, because he knows for certain that he is not dead.
>
> It is a transition to another, more beautiful world, because he knows very well that within seconds he will see the light of the Creator. He will be at the closest possible point to Allah. None in the [western] world sacrifices his life for his homeland. If his homeland is drowning, he is the first to jump ship. In our culture it is different.
>
> [In the western world], they have lost the ability to understand the situation. According to my professional assessment, they have lost their faculties. They do not understand what is happening. They see [the suicide bombers] as a strange breed of people. As far as they are concerned, life is sex, love, and money. So they tell you: 'It's someone committing suicide, a drug addict, someone in despair.' This is a mistake! Someone committing suicide hates life and considers it a burden. They want to impose the term 'suicide' on them, but they are not suicides, rather 'those who sacrifice their souls'.[44]

Personally, I believe my Egyptian psychiatrist colleague is off his rocker, and that he is a cynical promoter of terrorism. I cannot think for a moment of many cases of murder-suicide in everyday life as anything but *abnormal*, and I cannot think of the great majority of political suicide bombers as anything but mentally *abnormal*. The exception I am prepared to make is when the intended victim is a known arch-killer like Hitler or Pol Pot and the murder-suicide is committed to stop the killings of other human beings. I can't make any exceptions when the victims are plain, ordinary people who have every right to live.

In everyday American life we have seen murderers who then commit suicide dead set on taking revenge against those who have humiliated and hurt them. It would be another matter if their victims were specific people who have been the sources of their humiliation and hurt, which at least makes sense; but the general case is that the victims are randomly and unfairly chosen in a public setting, such as a post office, eating place, a public school, or a university campus. The murder-suicide act is a constellation of venomous, spiteful, fierce, ugly hatred, contempt, and vengeful triumph over others. It is a dramatic triumph of an embittered beaten self as it were proving its superiority and power to hurt any other human beings at hand before it terminates itself. It is criminally sick and unforgivable.

In purely military suicide killing, such as the Russians' defense in World War II against German tanks rolling in to the USSR, when a Soviet soldier would sacrifice himself by jumping under a tank and turn himself into a bomb, or when Japanese pilots became *kamikaze* warriors against the Allies' ships, there is room to argue that they were brave soldiers who, like many soldiers, sacrificed their lives for their nations—although here too I continue to insist on differentiating between those who are fighting a war of self-defense against a killer nation versus those fighting for an aggressor nation. It gets very complicated because we know that Stalin's Soviet Union also was very much a killer nation. From a moral point of view, I hardly believe that the Soviet Union per se "deserved" to be saved in its own pure right. For many years scholars believed Stalin had murdered 20 million of his *own* people in internal genocides of different ethnic groups and of endless identified "dissidents,"[45] and more recently according to the great scholar of genocide, R.J. Rummel, the more correct number is a staggering 54 million.[46] So we get into a strange philosophical loop when we say that the Russians who were suicide bombers against the Germans deserve to be identified as brave soldiers and neither as "terrorists" on the political level nor as "disturbed" on a psychological level even though they were defending a genocider country. On the other hand, the Germans to whom the Russians were in danger of losing were certainly another kind of ultimate killer regime, they were the then-active genocider government ceaselessly transporting Jews and others to death camps, and their threat was the more immediate. The Russian troops were sincerely fighting to save their homeland against the bestial Nazi; they were not fighting *for* their regime as an active genocider. But then if we make comparisons, one might also argue that the Japanese *kamikaze* were also dying and killing out of a sincere wish to protect their land. It is enormously complicated, certainly in the case of soldiers who are bravely defending and fighting for their people and homeland in full devotion when they are suicide bombers.

Dear readers who share with me a fierce prayer and dream of a less psychotic-evil world, I leave you and me with these quite crazy conundrums; and I leave you and me with the thought that in war there are situations where brave soldiering may well include the strategic device of suicide killers. I also leave it to other times for us to work out an ethical-political decision about the justifiable extent and the conditions under which such a military tool is to be honored, as opposed to indiscriminate use of thousands of soldiers who are sacrificed willy nilly to the battle, such as in the Iran–Iraq war when Iran sent thousands of children into the mine fields as sacrificial mine detectors. Personally, I will consider blowing myself up to kill a Hitler, but I intend to desert and flee like hell if I am instructed to be a suicide bomber on a more routine military mission.

Where I am unambiguous and totally not available to further contemplation or argument is the use of suicide bombers against civilian populations. I have no room for consideration of honor and devotion when the purpose of terror is to kill and injure as many ordinary people a possible. And psychologically, I have no doubt that such offering of my life is pure suicide—which I don't feel I have to argue is disturbed behavior par excellence. I also have no doubt that killing, tearing apart, and maiming others is murder and murderous injury to others, and these also are clear-cut disturbed behaviors whether or not a ridiculous professional system (mental health) has gotten around to including them in its formal list of conditions of craziness!

CONCLUSION: NORMAL PEOPLE WANT TO LIVE

I believe we have solved most of the problem we started out with—that we do not want to leave terrorists in general and suicide bombers in particular defined as psychologically and psychiatrically *normal*. We've beaten down the threat of suicide bombers qualifying as psychologically healthy specimens because we have defined mental and emotional illness as any "killing" of the life opportunity of oneself or of another person. To me, this way of thinking makes the psychological and psychotherapeutic professions genuinely relevant to the huge issues our world faces. Personally I could never stand a psychology and psychiatry that simply help people to be good at whatever they want to do—like to be suicide killers.

I admit that suicide bombers are in many ways *normal* representatives of a culture of death. But I insist both that their culture of death itself is pathological, which means that it is deserving of the most serious criticisms from the point of view of an intellectual-moral analysis of cultures; also that individual choices to serve a culture of death deserve to be defined in Western psychiatry as pathological violations of the deepest calls of life that, normally, have the power to transcend even cultural training for death-making.

Suicide-bomber terrorists are "bloody sick bastards," because they are out to kill life itself. Almost always their choice of actions goes far beyond the possible justifications of their understandable and even legitimate political and personal issues and motives for normal human beings.[47]

Normal people want to live.

Facing the Dangerous Future of Civilization Honestly

Overcoming Knee-Jerk Fallacies of the Heroic Underdog and Conspiracy Theory Supporting Terrorism

Abd Al-Aziz Zaynab: . . . The method used in destroying the three [sic] towers was 'controlled demolition.' This is an architectural engineering theory, which was invented by the Americans. They teach it in their universities. They make movies and documentaries about it. They incorporated it in movie scenarios and then carried it out in real life . . . You could sense the [9/11] operation was pre-planned because many things were revealed in the days that followed. For example, 4,000 Jews caught influenza on that exact day. They set a timer, and all 4,000 . . .

Host: By God, you crack me up! "They all set a timer and got influenza on the same day." So the building was completely empty of Jews.   —Egyptian researcher, Zaynab Abd Al-'Aziz, interviewed on Iqra TV[1]

There are only two camps—the camp of truth and its followers, and the camp of falsehood and its Shi'ites. You must choose in which of the two trenches you lie . . . Whoever is proven to belong to the Pagan [National] Guard, to the police, or to the army, or whoever is proven to be a Crusader collaborator or spy—he shall be killed . . . This is his reward for betraying his religion and his nation, so that he shall serve as a clear lesson and a preventive warning to others.   —Abu Mus'ab Al-Zarqawi, the leader of Al-Qaeda in Iraq[2]

THE LIBERAL FALLACY OF THE HEROIC UNDERDOG SUICIDE BOMBER

There is a substantial number of westerners who so want to believe in the inherent goodness or at least reasonableness of human beings that, all-too-rapidly, they "understand" that the suicide bomber simply must be responding to real hurt, insult, and degradation.

"I do not condone suicide bombers. No one can condone them ... but I do understand why people out there become suicide bombers," a Liberal Democrat MP Jenny Tonge said in London in January 2004, stirring up a hornet's nest. She said suicide bombers were "born out of desperation," and that if she lived in Gaza and the West Bank she might consider becoming one herself. "It is out of desperation and I guess if I was in their situation, with my children and grandchildren, and I saw no hope for the future at all, I might just think about it myself."

Labour peer, Lord Janner, called the comments "disgraceful" and "wrong." "She is saying she supports people who are suicide bombers, which means murderers and terrorists," he told *Sky News*. "To say in any way that you understand it, or ... that you approve of it is totally disgraceful and wrong."[3]

Suicide bombing is, in fact, a new form of battle technique that is frequently employed in the name of an ethnic political cause that in many cases makes *some* real sense and even has its degrees of legitimacy and justification in the endless historical struggles and natural competition between different peoples. But that does not mean that the choice of *any* means of warfare whatsoever is justified. Most people in the world today oppose the use of gas or biological weapons or nuclear weapons. Now liberals need to ask themselves if they agree to suicide bombers in the name of a cause when they indeed believe the cause itself has a degree of justice to it.

The liberal reflex is also to attempt whenever possible to cast suicide bombers into individual tragic heroes and heroines who lost loved ones, saw their people's children destroyed, and/or are grieving profound insults to their people and land.

One contemporary example that is prominent today in the Western world, especially in Europe, is the Palestinian cause versus Israel. The Palestinian cause is frequently romanticized, as once upon a time heroic Zionist pioneers fighting to create a post-Holocaust haven for the Jews in Israel were celebrated by much of the world.

Shock is a theater performance by a Belgian group, "De Queeste," in which Palestinian refugees and a mother who lost her daughter as a suicide attacker tell their story. Through newspapers, witnesses, and Web sites, the show tries to understand the people behind the suicide bombers and sympathize with their motivations. Among others, a young Palestinian tells his story of anger, destroyed hope, and confusion, and finally the moment when he is forced to do something. The play starts with video material from an interview with the provocative but largely respected late Israeli philosopher, Yeshayahu Leibowitz, who argued, to my mind correctly, that occupation of another people's land destroys the moral fiber of the conqueror, but that still does not mean that suicide bombing is justified in any way whatsoever.

An explicitly pro-intifada Web site carried a review of *Shock*, which included the following quotation from a Palestinian journal:

> Suicide bombings and all these forms of violence are only the symptoms, the reaction to this chronic and systematic process of humiliating people in an effort to destroy their hope and dignity.[4]

This kind of sentimentality and idealization of the human motivations of suicide bombers puts back a sense of justice and goodness about human life into the worldview of caring and liberal people. But is suicide killing inherently a tool of justice? Were the Chechen suicide bombers who threatened to blow up hundreds of people attending a performance in a Moscow theater just fighters (meaning fighters whose honorable motivations can be understood and respected as justifying the losses of life of the theatergoers)? Were the Al-Qaeda suicide killers who blew up the World Trade Center honestly aggrieved people fighting their people's just battle?

Some suicide bombers are inducted into their roles in the honesty of their cause against an oppressor, but even then it does not mean their handlers and the overall managers of their side of the battle are anything but very dedicated terrorists who want to *kill* many people.

If traditionally the fascist motto and fallacy is "*Might Makes Right,*" the liberal fallacy might be said to be "*Suffering Makes Right.*" For caring people, human suffering inherently deserves remedies, attention, and sympathy, but it does not mean that the cause of the suffering people is inherently or automatically right. In World War II, the German people suffered extensively and seriously. One can argue that they "deserved" it because of their support of Hitler and all of his rotten policies. But even if one does not want to justify imposing suffering and death on the German populace, it is reasonable to recognize that in the battle against Nazism, which had to be fought, there were generally few alternatives to the attacks on the Germans by the Allies,[5] let alone that it was the Germans' own leaders who imprisoned, tortured, and executed many of their own people.[6] The fact that the Germans suffered did not mean their enemies, the Allies, fighting against a warped Nazi civilization of horror, brutality, and a virtual religion of killing were basically in the wrong, even if they also committed some criminal excesses in their just battle.

Of course, the Nazis were ugly exponents of an evil cause. But even when a cause is deemed to be a just one to whatever degree, such as a battle for national or ethnic independence or freedom, it also does not imply that any and all means such as suicide bombing or other deadly weapons are to be employed legitimately for that cause.

At a conference sponsored by the prime minister of Sweden on the prevention of genocide in the world today,[7] I had a confrontation with a very angry liberal: A woman, who is a former Israeli who has been honored internationally for her human rights work in Africa, said to me angrily (similarly to the British MP quoted earlier), "If I were a Palestinian, I would be a suicide bomber." For her, justice is in the cause and in the status of rights people have and has nothing to do with *how* one fights for these rights. I replied to this woman that cruel killing and injuring of civilians is hardly the way to fight for and achieve human rights and dignity. She shot back that Western concerns with lost human lives since September 11 are ridiculous, the issue really is stopping global imperialism, and that "after all, only 3000 people died at the World Trade Center, and you would think from the uproar about it that there were millions." By now, a small crowd of colleague genocide scholars and diplomats attending the conference were watching our exchange. I told her forcefully that I never agreed to any statement that "*only*" such and such number were killed about any event of violence. (The "only" argument is a favorite of deniers of genocides, for example.)

"Liberal" thinkers, of course, divide into many types. There are liberals who are totally pacifists and don't agree to killing even in self-defense. Personally, I see myself belonging to the group of liberals who oppose killing except for genuine self-defense against an objective threat to one's life—such as terrorists who come at us to kill us! Unless there is a threat to our lives, I am deeply against killing in order to "achieve democracy, justice, freedom," etc., but as I said I am entirely in favor of killing in real self-defense.

In all cases, I dislike liberals who are so angrily resolute and imperiously adamant about their truths—and this will be the case even when I agree with their position. Ours will always be a tough world of differences and conflicts between peoples, and we will always require a lot of maturity and decency for the clarification of differences. If we are ever going to make peace in some of the deadly conflicts on our planet, both committed terrorists and rabid liberal "Jacobins" as if protecting justice and democracy will have to be contained. Amazingly, both camps inspire hatred and justify violence.

There is another kind of liberals who are so genuinely sincere in their quest for peace, and conduct themselves so authentically in their personal acceptance of other people that one cannot help but respect and love them. This becomes all the more true when such caring persons volunteer themselves actively to contribute personally to bringing about peace, often enough by serving in a region of conflict that is quite dangerous, and some of these noble volunteers then pay with their lives as a result of their goodness. You can't help grieving them and respecting and loving them even more. Nonetheless, even some of these very good people may be wrong in overadopting the cause they identify with and in the blindness of their devotion to their chosen side. It happened, for example, to many a pro-Communist who refused even for years to see the incredibly extensive genocidal brutality of Stalin and his regime.

As caring people, there is almost a reflex tendency for liberals to sympathize with and identify with the smaller, weaker underdog people who are taking hard blows and losses from their stronger opponents.[8] But in some cases the truth is that it is the underdogs who are the attacking brigands and terrorizing provocateurs, and they would not be suffering the losses they were if they didn't attack and kill in the first place!

Nicholas Robins has analyzed a little-known war of Indians in Peru against their oppressor enemy, the Spaniards, in the years 1780–1782. There is no question who was the initiating force of oppression that had invaded the natural homelands of the Indians. There is no question who were the underdogs in the battle between native peoples and a more militarily advanced people with greater fire power. But Robins' point is that the underdog Indians also committed genocide against their enemy. He argues persuasively that being a victim and underdog does not provide a blanket of justice to cover truths of being murderous and genocidal.[9] Robins' point is important not only in respect of the specific case he studied, but for scholars of genocide in general, where it is emerging that there are other cases where victim peoples, at the same time as they were victimized, have committed genocide; and that perpetrators, at the same time as they were committing mass murder, were also the victims of genocidal attacks on them. In addition, there are cases where the same people have played the different roles of perpetrators and victims in different periods of time in history. Up until recently, genocide scholars too have tended to relate to different peoples as belonging only to one category or another.

If we look at the Palestinian-Israeli conflict, earlier the Jews were the survivors of the unspeakable Holocaust, its gas chamber, huge crematoria, and all the brutal murders by the superarmed Nazi-German state. The Zionists were then the brave, hardy settlers of a frontier land who needed to repeat ancient historical scenarios of protecting their new colony against attacking indigenous peoples who wanted to destroy them. By 1947, the Israelis were implementing legally the establishment of their state as authorized by the United Nations General Assembly, and were fully willing to cooperate with the establishment of a Palestinian state alongside them. It was the overwhelmingly numerous Arabs from many countries in the region, continuing a long tradition of murders of Jewish settlers from the beginning of Zionist settlements years earlier, and ancient traditions of Islamic violence, that went to war against the tiny Jewish state. The world loved the underdog Israelis.

Fifty-some years later, having grown into a brilliantly modern country with a thriving strong army, Israel—not unlike its greater protector and democratic model, the United States—has made many mistakes and committed many grievous acts against Palestinians. However, much of the reprehensible Israeli misuses and overuses of power have come in response to never-ending attacks against the Jewish state in acts of infiltration, killings, terror, including suicide bombings, and full-blown wars intending to destroy Israel. Notwithstanding Israeli hubris and arrogance, militancy, land grabs, shameful cruelty, and incivility to Arabs in occupied territories, the people of Israel overall have remained consistently committed to a readiness to adopt peaceful solutions, including the establishment of a Palestinian state. The tough Israelis really thirst for peace.

It is the Arabs who not only press as is their right for greater civility and more political freedom, but use stones, guns, lynches, bombs, and now suicide bombers. They kill not only Israeli soldiers in what might be legitimate according to time-honored rules of engagement against an occupying power, but also civilian men, women, and children, in schools, buses, restaurants, discotheques, wherever they are. In a recent terrorist attack, Palestinians shot a woman driving her family in their car, and then approached the car and shot point blank to ensure killing each of four young children, ages 11, 9, 7, and 2, who died with their mother, a social worker, who was also pregnant in her eighth month.[10]

Here is a story of a very decent peace-seeking liberal who came to Israel to identify with the underdog Palestinians: Claire Theret is a 45-year-old French woman, a language-teacher, who lives near Newcastle, with her husband and 20-year-old daughter. She traveled to Israel as a peace observer with the International Solidarity Movement. The group spent two weeks in the Aida refugee camp near Bethlehem, meeting refugees and helping distribute aid, and then found themselves caught up in a stand-off between Israeli troops and Palestinian gunmen. "We spent two weeks in the camp. I was very frightened, of course, but at the same time I was happy to be there because even just our presence helped protect the Palestinians. At one point, the medical supplies ran low and we decided to defy the curfew and go to the hospital to get medicine. If the Palestinians had gone, they would have been shot but it was less risky for us." During Claire's stay, soldiers smashed their way into the youth centre. Claire's photographs show the damage—broken camera equipment, tubes of paint squeezed all over the computers and theater props destroyed ... "Fortunately, no one was hurt but the people they targeted weren't terrorists, they were children. There's no excuse. But I think the Palestinians are very brave and they won't bow down to this sort of thing ... It's ethnic cleansing. It's genocide ... I am Jewish myself, although not practising, and I am ashamed of what the Israelis are doing. They are behaving exactly as the Nazis did against the Jews." Claire then goes on to say about the suicide bombers that she doesn't condone their killing, but she says *she can understand* how the Palestinians justify their actions. "Of course it is terrible when innocent people are killed but, when I did history at school in France, we learned about the Resistance and the acts of sabotage they carried out during the Second World War. We would never have dreamt of calling them terrorists—they were heroes—and I don't believe the suicide bombers will be known as terrorists in the Palestinian history books."[11]

Without investigating the specifics of the case, I accept at face value Claire's reports of the undue suffering of the Palestinians. As an Israeli, I am aware of many serious cruelties and injustices by Israeli troops and government edicts, just as an American, I am aware of many acts of cruelty and corrupt military actions by the United States, such as gratuitous slaughter of civilians in the Korean war; agent Orange and My Lais in Vietnam, let alone the overall choice to make war in Vietnam, years of cooperation and support of "the Cambodian Hitler," Pol Pot, and more. Democracies too make any number of terrible choices and errors. But the valid concern that plain Palestinians are suffering too much needs to be taken back to the root of the violence: the Palestinians have been sending killers against Israel. They blew up a promising peace agreement with Yitzhak Rabin's government, sending their police force which was newly armed by Israel(!) to fire on the Jews, and they blew up a potentially generous renegotiation with Ehud Barak's government. And now, in recent years, they have been sending suicide bombers.

A strategic analyst in India had this to say about the seesaw of world public opinion about Israel in the new age of suicide bombers. "When Israel retaliated with military operations to root out the menace of suicide bombings, all of a sudden the conscience of the world's human right crusaders, liberalists and the media woke up in a shrill outcry against Israel. They seemed to project a perverse argument that terrorists and suicide bombers have human rights while the innocent Israeli civilians targeted in supermarkets and cafes do not qualify for the same. Indian readers of the discerning type would be struck by the similarity of this argument with a similar campaign in the Indian media against Indian security forces engaged in combating Pakistan sponsored Islamic Jehadi terrorism in Jammu & Kashmir including suicide bombers."

The same writer also takes note of the fact that Yasser Arafat took pride in adopting underdog positions, including his signing peace agreements within a guiding conceptual framework *in his mind* of planning to abrogate and abandon any such peace as soon as he had the power to do so. Arafat was quoted as saying, "We respect agreements the way that the Prophet Muhammad and Salah-al-Din (Saladin) respected the agreements which they signed." It is well known that both the prophet and Salah-al-Din are celebrated for having employed and justified a policy of entering into truces until they were ready to overcome their enemies![12] This is a tactical or strategic model that is inconceivable to the fair-minded Western, but it is no less than real within a Salah-al-Din cultural tradition.

I believe that genuine liberalism is a life-promoting liberalism, not an underdog-liberalism. For me, the test of any liberal position is the extent to which it seeks to salvage, rescue, and protect human life—for *all* sides in the conflict.

Taking any one side in its piece of the true story of justice, and using that comprehension to "understand"—which means variously to forgive, condone, approve, encourage, assist, or perpetrate—indiscriminate violence and killing against the other side is thoroughly unacceptable to me. Killing in tangible, manifest, provable self-defense is the only killing I can justify.

Neither Jews killing Muslims nor Muslims killing Jews gives me any joy. If Jews attack Arab civilians, as some of the "Jewish right" have done, or as Israeli forces have done in several documented massacres of Arab civilians since 1948, they should be shot at, or if captured and arrested, they should be tried and punished severely.[13]

A *Wall Street Journal* article, in the wake of September 11, suggested that multiculturalism and democratic theory when taken to an extreme becomes an

ideology [that] goes way beyond preaching the tolerance that is a bedrock virtue of a pluralistic society to insisting that all cultures are equally good—regardless of whether they beat their women, practice slavery or torture political dissidents ... The moral paralysis these ideas have caused is blatantly obvious on college campuses ...

A Hamilton College philosophy professor noted that his students were reluctant to judge Hitler, apartheid, and slavery.

"Of course I dislike the Nazis," one student observed, "but who is to say they are morally wrong?"

If one can't judge Nazism morally repugnant, it's easy to ascribe to murderous terrorists understandable and even valid reasons.[14]

Suicide bombers should not be the darlings of civil rights protests as if they are courageous revolutionaries standing up heroically against a repressive power. They are not a poor man's selfless and honorable weapon against a vastly superior Goliath enemy.

They are an immoral choice of weapon—just as many of us are firmly convinced that the choices of poison gas, biological infections, chemical poisoning of crops, nuclear weapons, and other futuristic weapons of destruction are intrinsically immoral and need to be regulated by Geneva-type conventions, and their use punished most severely by courts for genocide and crimes against humanity.

We saw earlier that after studying the issue of suicide bombings against Israelis carefully, the respected human rights group, Human Rights Watch issued a carefully argued and detailed report defining suicide bombings as crimes against humanity. The 170-page report is a full-fledged examination of individual criminal responsibility for suicide bombings against civilians. Human Rights Watch said that the people responsible for planning and carrying out suicide bombings that deliberately target civilians are guilty of crimes against humanity and should be brought to justice. "The people who carry out suicide bombings are not martyrs, they're war criminals, and so are the people who help to plan such attacks," said the executive director of Human Rights Watch, Kenneth Roth. "The scale and systematic nature of these attacks sets them apart from other abuses committed in times of conflict. They clearly fall under the category of crimes against humanity."[15] Human Rights Watch also urged the Palestinian Authority to undertake a public campaign urging an end to suicide bombings and other attacks against civilians and making clear that the PA does not consider as "martyrs" people who die carrying out attacks that deliberately or indiscriminately kill or cause great suffering among civilians.

To conclude, my advice to liberals, with whom, overall, I continue very much to associate myself happily, is not to succumb to a knee-jerk sympathy for people who are suffering, as if their suffering proves the justice of their cause, and not to overlook evidence that an underdog is a full-blown perpetrator. Rather, a real liberal looks at how to bring about less suffering and to afford greater protection and more life to *all* concerned while pursuing justice as well.

Suicide bombers are nasty, cruel killers of everyone in sight.

For those who hesitate to condemn the suicide bombers fully and resolutely I would also add that informed opinions in many places in the world agree that more and more suicidal destruction is facing us everywhere. The reports literally are pouring in.

Sana, YEMEN: Eight suspected Al Qaeda members, including an Iraqi with Swiss nationality, admitted in court to planning attacks on Western embassies . . . The eight suspected Al Qaeda members told the court that they had planned to attack the British and Italian embassies and the French cultural Center in the Yemini capital, and that they were receiving money and instructions from Al Qaeda operatives in Saudi Arabia.[16]

Kabul, AFGHANISTAN: An al-Qaida booklet dating back at least to 2001 when it was found in Afghanistan lists a worldwide constellation of militant groups that are "helping Afghanistan in their fight against the infidels." The list includes the Egyptian Islamic Jihad movement; the Libyan Jihad Fighters movement; the Abu Sayyaf separatist movement from the Philippines; a group called Abu Al Hasan-Al Ansar; and what the booklet calls "Jihad militants" from Jordan, Lebanon, Turkey and Pakistan, and also unnamed "groups from Kashmir, Indonesia, Somalia, Burma, Bosnia, Uzbekistan, Turkmenistan and Tajikistan."[17]

Washington, DC, USA: A conference on al-Qaeda in Washington, DC in December 2004 produced many analysts who predicted many further terrorist events were ahead of us. Marc Sageman, a former CIA case officer and author of *Understanding Terror Networks* predicted "a succession of Madrids, Casablancas, Istanbuls," or deadly coordinated multiple attacks on smaller scales than a mega-event like 9/11. Michael Scheuer, former CIA Counterterrorism Center chief and author of a book on "why the West is losing the war on terror" expected additional catastrophic attacks on the U.S. He said, "I'm really very pessimistic about where we stand with this war."[18]

GERMANY: *Der Spiegel online*—Reporting on the 7/7 London bombings, *Der Spiegel* reported that the bombs were made out of ingredients which are available over the counter in normal pharmacies. According to BBC sources, the chemical is acetone peroxide and has been discovered at one of the bombers' homes in Leeds. Originally because of the size of the explosions, police had assumed that the bombs had been manufactured commercially or militarily. It now becomes a reality that someone can build such weapons in their home . . . The same chemical was what Richard Reid had in his shoes when he boarded a trans-Atlantic flight from Europe to America in 2001, presumably with the intention of blowing the plane up.[19]

Later we shall also be looking at dire predictions of grave new scenarios of mass killing by suicide bombers, and at predictions of the use of weapons of mass destruction by them.

The suicide bombers are hardly underdogs. It is the decent people of this world, from all faiths, and whatever we do have that deserves to be referred to as "civilization," who are much more the underdogs.

CONSPIRACY THEORY AND IRRATIONALITY—AN ESCAPE FROM REALITY IN SUPPORT OF TERRORISM

As we have seen over and over again, insane though it may be, the conspiracy theorists love to believe it is the United States that committed September 11 against itself!

Or the Israeli Mossad (virtually a modern-day bogeyman, I think).

Or both powers together, in a satanic collaboration.

In France, a book was published, which became a best-seller, *The Frightening Deception*, which claims that the Pentagon was not damaged by suicide bombers who had hijacked an airplane but by a truck bomb. The allegation is that the U.S.

government has deceived the world as part of its scheme to orchestrate the September 11 attacks in order to justify its own violences elsewhere—Afghanistan and the Middle East, for example. *Le Nouvel Observateur* said the thesis "eliminates reality"; *Liberation* called the book "a tissue of wild and irresponsible allegations, entirely without foundation."[20] But no matter that sane people react with incredulity. The believers believe, happily and adamantly.

A European colleague of mine at a genocide conference at a major university in Asia told me with absolute conviction that the photographs of the explosion at the Pentagon "prove" there was no airplane. He prodded another colleague, originally an Australian, who now teaches at another Asian university, and the latter half agreed.

The first colleague is personally a lovable and well-meaning person, but a diehard conspiracy thinker. He is a betitled and quite brilliant professor of peace studies who hates America and attributes to the United States primary if not exclusive responsibility for the hell of Cambodia (forget the Khmer Rouge and their insane killing fields!), Afghanistan (forget the primitive Taliban blasting images of Buddha, forbidding the education of women, and training Al-Qaeda terrorists and suicide bombers, including for September 11), and Iraq (forget Saddam's poison gassing of Kurds, or the mass graves for the tens of thousands Shi'ites he executed in broad-based genocidal murders, the 1991 invasion of Kuwait, and Scud missile attacks on Israel and Saudi Arabia, or threats of biological and chemical warfare, all of which simply don't count). In this learned man's thinking, America is evil incarnate, and only the United States bears responsibility for the losses of life in these countries.

I had a moment of "bad boy inspiration." In one sense, I tried to show my colleague how he lets himself get sucked into unsubstantiated conspiracy theory and accusations of the United States, Israel, the United Kingdom, and the West in general. In another sense, I wasn't able to resist teasing him as I fed him the possibility of a new conspiracy that he hadn't heard that Israel was behind the suicide bombings of two synagogues in Instanbul. I told him that I had read a report that some Islamic sources (it was the editor of *al-Akhbar* in Egypt[21]) had suggested Israel itself had committed the pair of suicide bombings against the synagogues. First, there was a wave of surprise on his face (partly, I suppose, because he didn't expect this kind of material from me, since he already knew how opposed I was to his conspiratorial way of thinking). This was followed by a wave of pleasure and then by intense concentration as I saw him figuring out just how much Israel would have to gain from such a ploy. Calculating the strategic advantages Israel *might* have gained from such an attack on Jews in the synagogues was then enough to convince my colleague that the whole idea was quite factual. Within no more than two minutes he had gone through the sequence of convincing himself that it was all very real and proven. "It's quite impossible that Jews would blow up a synagogue and kill other Jews," I then told him, "besides the fact that Israel has never engaged in suicide bombing." "No, no," he insisted with the voice and look of certainty I had come to know characteristically accompanied his accusations of evil destruction by Western imperialists. "It is obvious how much Israel had to gain. Of course, they did it." He was a happy man.

There is a convoluted logic in conspiracy arguments. It is a "blind argument" that is not based on evidence, but on rumor, fantasy, and often blind hatred. Such thinking is very different from a humanistic liberalism that is anchored in efforts at a genuinely factual map of reality in order to fight effectively against evil and totalitarianism.

As we have seen, the blind argumentation of conspiracy theorists can go so far as to take the violence done by the terrorists and, in one sense or another, attribute, assign, or blame the violence on the victims.

Conspiracy thinkers can somehow allege that the victims so benefit from and exploit the violences done to them that the implication left hovering in the air is that the victims virtually if not actually created the events of their own victimization. Thus, a respected peace researcher from Germany, speaking at an institution we otherwise can only love for its representation both of the suffering of the victims of the nuclear bombings in Japan and the grave dangers of WMD in the future, told her audience how the United States was delighted to have terrorists attack America on September 11 and give America the opportunity to "use them." She asked: "Weren't the terrorist attacks used by the U.S. as an occasion to realize its hidden agenda and to teach its allies how to use them for such a purpose?" She further concluded knowingly that, "for many people the 'war on terrorism' appears rather to be a war against Islam."[22]

For those who want to understand step-by-step how to do it, the very poor thinking and actually unacceptable logical fallacy employed is as follows:

1. *Show or prove that so-and-so gains in a substantial way from the terror attack;*
2. *Assert that you have proven that so-and-so is the* real *perpetrator of the attack;*
3. *If challenged, fall back on saying you were only showing how much so-and-so had to gain and therefore they could well be "behind" the attack, but you didn't really say they actually did it;*
4. *Once you see that your defense relieved some of the tension over your earlier aggressive violation of logic, you can add something like, "But it's very likely so-and-so organized the attack," and then add something like, "And everyone in Europe or wherever knows it."*
   You are now a qualified conspiracy spokesman.

Incredibly, conspiracy theories are widely held in the minds of millions of people. In my judgment, there are deep-seated psychological needs for conspiracy thinking, including an effort to keep up with the quite real conspiratorial truths that do attend many historical events in our scheming complicated world, but also as projections of the suspiciousness and hatreds in the human soul, as well as efforts to "know" what "really" happened as if to let us believe we have a greater sense of control over our lives than we do.[23]

It is quite proper to question the official governmental versions of many events, for governments, including those of our democracies, are notorious liars and deceivers. It is also quite legitimate and potentially quite productive to think about and to brainstorm alternative possible scenarios of historical events in the course of investigating and deciphering them. But it is another matter to conclude with certainty or to announce with assurance a conspiratorial version of what happened when there is no hard evidence for such a plot. In the long run, what matters is that we undertake sound investigative and reportorial accounts of historical events, and that fantasies, conjectures, and crackpot ideas are not elevated to consensual rumors and pseudotruths.

It is downright frightening how widespread conspiracy thinking about September 11 is. One *might* understand the high rate of acceptance of these theories in many Muslim countries (including some which are our allies), where they represent a primitive reflexive effort at self-defense against taking responsibility for the errors of one's people and its Islamic culture. At the same time, we have seen that many Islamic observers also insist that it is this kind of thinking that also holds the Islamic world back from developing. The net result is a weakening of the possible development of Islamic culture in general which, as a consequence of such irrational nonsense and antiempiricism, in too many instances remains lost to rhetoric and fantasy more than being anchored in reality.

Dr. Gamal 'Ali Zahran, head of the political science department at Suez Canal University, wrote in *Al-Ahram* shortly after September 11: "At the World Trade Center, thousands of Jews worked in the stock market, but none of them were there on the day of the incident . . . The Jews, who were huge stockholders in the insurance companies, sold their stocks at the highest possible prices some 10 days before the attacks on America. After the stock market began functioning again . . . they competed amongst themselves to buy [these] stocks at the lowest possible price."[24]

Some voices in the Arab world itself recognize the ridiculousness and the danger to Arab culture of the constant production of conspiracy myths. Youssef M. Ibrahim, Managing Director of Strategic Energy Investment Group in Dubai, wrote,

> Fear is deeply ingrained . . . in the Arab mind no matter where it lives. There is a fear to speak, write, read or even hear truth. The fear hangs in the air, blocking oxygen to the Arab mind, dominating thinking processes, surfacing in a self-censored media, nervous jokes, absurd commentary that wastes hours describing black as white.
>
> Arab media filters news through the prism of fear, disguised as political correctness, politeness and Information Ministry rules, so that facts become fairy tales.[25]

Unhappily, the September 11 conspiracy theories that reconstruct history according to fantasy, speculation, and personal political agendas also have far too much acceptance and following in non-Muslim countries as well. One-third of Germans under age 30 said "yes" when asked if the U.S. government could have itself ordered the September 11 attacks. 20 percent of Germans in all age groups held this view.[26]

In a sense, much conspiracy thinking is also as if a tacit celebration of the event. The know-it-all conspiratorial twisting of the event as if justifies the harm that happened or was done to the victims. Conspiracy theory often is just one step short of open approval of the violent event; and approval is just one step short of calls for continuation or repetition of the same or similar violences. Thus, in London, the rallies honoring the "magnificent 19" were planned by the Islamic group al-Muhajiroun. A spokesman for the group, Abu Omar, told BBC that the September 11 hijacker-suicide killers were " 'completely justified' and 'quite splendid' and that any Muslim who thought otherwise was an apostate."[27]

Conspiracy theories and theorists also like and favor one another. Start up with September 11 as the work of America, and then one can easily throw in an add-on about the assistance of the Israeli Mossad, plus-minus another crazy rumor such as the one we read that thousands of Jews were told to stay away from work at the Twin Towers on September 11 ("Didn't you know?"). Blame September 11 as the work of the United States and/or Israel, and then you can go for the craziness of attributing to Israel the suicide bombings of the two synagogues in Istanbul.

Here is another example of how conspiracy theories are created. There is a fake quatrain (verse) attributed to Nostradamus circulating on Internet, which is proposed to be an awesome prediction hundreds of years earlier of the incredible fall of the Twin Towers.

> In the City of God there will be a great thunder,
> Two brothers torn apart by Chaos,
> while the fortress endures,
> the great leader will succumb,
> The third big war will begin when the big city is burning

Presumably, the "two brothers" are the Twins. Impressive, it would seem, and mystical too! But the first problem pointed out by the Committee for the Scientific Investigation of Claims of the Paranormal (CSICOP), which has undertaken to track "misinformation and hoaxes in the wake of the terrorist attacks," is that the date of the above verse attributed to Nostradamus is close to a hundred years *after* his death. What is far more important and should quash the nonsense forever is that the quatrain actually originates from a 1990s paper written by a student from a university in Canada who concluded that "the verses demonstrate how any obscure verse can be interpreted to fit [just] about any historical event."[28]

But do you really think even such a decisive demonstration of how conspiracy theories are fabricated will deter committed conspiracy thinkers?

MOST UNFORTUNATELY, I BELIEVE WAR IS ALREADY UNDERWAY AND WORSE IS COMING

I have a great deal of joy about many of the new ideas for greater decency and the improvement of human life that have developed in our Western intellectual tradition, including in my specific field of psychology and mental health which I love; but at the same time, reluctantly, I have to voice my sense that overall a very troubled future history is coming our way, which I fear will include WMD and therefore mass deaths of civilians on a scale never before seen in our already bloody history.

If true, it is tragic.

To begin with, the balance of forces in the world today seems to me to predict the likelihood of a long-lasting and perhaps huge war between a culture of democracy and a culture of terrorism and murder.

In my opinion, the history books of the future will record that the beginning of the war dates from the suicide bombings of September 11 in New York and Washington, although there definitely were terrorist acts of war against the United States and others earlier. See at the end of the book the list of representative suicide bombings for several major events preceding September 11. In the olden days of nations, attacks on a ship or an army base by the forces of a nation with a name and territory certainly would have constituted acts of full-blown war. I suggest that September 11 was the Pearl Harbor of this War between Civilizations. The battle then continued with blood-curdling messages that the war would be brought to the homes of the West everywhere—Russia, Israel, Iraq, Saudi Arabia, Morocco, Kenya, Indonesia, Australia, and many more. Another message that has been delivered to the world is that indiscriminate suicide bombings had become a new technique of war including against civilians.[29]

The fact that a worldwide jihad is in process against all the West is slowly and surely becoming clearer as parallel, and periodically already operationally related terrorist events, literally span the globe from continent to continent. In conquered Iraq, the United States encountered almost immediately not only deadly intense local resistance, but also a phenomenon of hundreds of Islamic fighters streaming across the willing borders of Syria and Iran to fight the infidel Americans,[30] and then steadily a further proliferation of attacks by *both* Sunni and Shi'ite despite their own deadly rivalry against one another.

As was noted at the opening of the book, we are going to press with this book just as news has come of the British succeeding in stopping a plot for suicide bombers to blow up some ten trans-Atlantic airplanes on the way from the United Kingdom to the United States. We report elsewhere in the book how Britons were shocked earlier to find British-born Muslims involved in suicide bombings, first outside of the United Kingdom (in a suicide bombing in Tel Aviv), but then most shockingly in the United Kingdom itself in the July 5, 2005, attacks in the Underground in London. The initial reports in August 2006 are that the plotters who were arrested are British-born Muslims. The plot itself was not a new one and was described by authorities as resembling a 1994 plot by Al-Qaeda to blow up simultaneously several airliners over the Pacific.

Outstanding Holocaust scholar, Yehuda Bauer, generally known for his conservatism in scholarship and political opinions, has given his opinion (the same as that of Daniel Pipes at the beginning of the book) that:

> Radical Islam parallels strikingly Nazism and Communism in its intent to rule the world, its readiness to destroy political freedom, and its genocidal ideology.[31]

Bauer attributes the greater danger to the Sunni majority in the Muslim world and sees the beginning of its radical extremism in the founding of the Muslim Brotherhood (which later assassinated President Sadaat) in Egypt in 1928. He notes that recently this movement issued a call on the Internet to kill no less than 4 million Americans, of whom 2 million need to be children. "Why these numbers? Because according to their warped thinking, this is the number of Muslim children who have been killed by the West over the course of history." Bauer adds, "Whoever does not accept their rule is targeted for destruction, the Hindus in India, Jews, and first of all moderate Islamic regimes such as Turkey or Egypt or Indonesia."

Granted the war of Islam against the West is also intertwined with the battles of Muslims against their fellow Muslims—including their use of their weapon of suicide bombings against one another. bin Laden is, of course, a prime example of a terrorist who has struck on different continents both against the West and against his fellow religionists, such as in multiple suicide bombings in Saudi Arabia.

On December 31, 2003, the *New York Times* reported as follows: "Until this year most major attacks by suspected Qaeda militants in Saudi Arabia have been directed against American or other western targets. Al Qaeda militants have carried out a wave of major suicide-bomb attacks in Rayadh, killing at least 50 people in the last seven months."[32]

Al-Qaeda is emerging as a movement and/or guiding philosophy of pan-Arabist dreams of restoring Islamic honor, power, and domination of countries, regions, and perhaps latently fulfilling the dream of becoming again the predominant power in the world replacing Christianity, which defeated Islam hundreds of years ago.

Al-Qaeda is radically opposed to anything Western, and also to any form of moderation in religious-political practice within Islamic countries. In 2003, public opinion polls in many countries, including Morocco, Indonesia, Jordan, and Turkey showed greater confidence in bin Laden, who for the Western world is a proven genius of terror killing, than in U.S. President Bush. The equivalent in the language of WWII would be to trust Hitler over the U.S. president. Al-Qaeda has now emerged as an idea, and one commentator observes, "Although it is a relatively simple matter to arrest people, it's altogether another thing to arrest the spread of ideas."[33]

Perhaps it is even somewhat comforting that the forces that undertake destruction of life as their preferred modus operandi almost inevitably turn their own hateful killing methods against their own ranks too—ultimately a cancer's triumph involves killing its own self as well. After a suicide bombing in Saudi Arabia, which killed and wounded an "almost entirely Arab and Muslim population," there were reports that many Saudis for the first time were "appalled." "They are killing people with no cause ... They lost their support on the street," said one young man. A professor specializing in Bedouin poetry at King Saud University said, "It is getting so irrational that you cannot explain it, you cannot defend it, you cannot understand it. They can no longer say they are more or less raising the banner of jihad. Jihad is not against your own people."[34]

But the committed terrorists do not waiver. An Al-Qaeda representative, Mohammed al-Abla, proudly claimed responsibility for the attacks in Riyadh, and further warned that new attacks will be carried out in Japan, which had agreed to send troops to Iraq. He promised further, "The attacks against Jews and America will follow. Let America and Israel cry for their dead from today and the destruction that they will suffer."[35]

On December 22, 2003, Al Jazeera, the Arabic Television Network, broadcast a statement by the chief deputy of Osama bin Laden, Ayman al-Zawahiri: "We are still chasing the Americans and their allies everywhere, even in their homeland," he said. General Richard Myers, Chairman of the Joint Chiefs of Staff, said that such remarks were not to be taken lightly. "There is no doubt, from all the intelligence we pick up from al Qaeda, that they want to do away with our way of life," he said in an appearance on Fox News. "And if they could cause another catastrophic event, a tragedy like 9/11. If they could do that again, if they could get their hands on weapons of mass destruction and make it 10,000, not 3,000, they would do that, and not just in the United States but in any of the free world or any peoples that treasure their freedom. So we take all these intelligence tips very, very seriously."[36]

What is the ultimate terror of the future for me is precisely the likelihood of WMD appearing in the terrorists' armamentarium. The possibility has been implicit for some years ever since major terrorist events have burst on us.

When on August 7, 1998, two amazingly well-coordinated bomb attacks were carried out against two U.S. embassies separated from each other by 700 kilometers in Nairobi, Kenya, and Dar es Salaam, Tanzania (in one case the apparently would-be suicide bomber jumped out of the car loaded with explosives, threw a grenade, and escaped as the car crashed into its target, in the other the car bomber blew himself up), the ever-thoughtful *Christian Science Monitor* pondered whether a "new age" had begun in which

> secret cell groups expressing twisted ideals of hatred or revenge in pursuit of a cause can move more clandestinely, more maneuverably than the defenders of social order, sanity, indeed civilization. Thus last week's tragic, unconscionably cruel bombings of innocent East Africans and Americans have produced dire forecasts of a new age of unpredictable, strike-anywhere-anytime terrorism ...

The *Monitor* added:

> The more scholarly take their cue from Samuel Huntington's 1996 book, *The Clash of Civilizations and the Remaking of World Order*, which argued that at the end of the cold war a Pandora's box of ethnic and religious collisions would spring up to challenge world stability.[37]

The *Monitor* decided to reassure itself and its readers with a conclusion that the attacks were not unprecedented and they were not harbingers of a new age of unstoppable attacks. My perspective today is that the editors of the *Monitor* were prescient and should have stayed with their initial prediction.

Slowly the stakes rise. Scott Atran, who is identified as a research scientist at the National Center for Scientific Research in Paris and at the University of Michigan, reported that, "Charting terrorist attacks by organization and lethality, Robert Axelrod, a political scientist at the University of Michigan has noted an increasing interest in well-planned attacks intended to produce high numbers of civilian casualties. This trend also seems to point to an eventual suicide attack using chemical or nuclear weapons."[38]

Slowly and much too surely the reports are coming in on different levels. In April 2004, police in Amman, Jordan, averted a serious attack that was described as follows:

> The police in Amman, Jordan killed three people who were believed to have planned to detonate a bomb that could have flattened much of the city, the Associated Press reported ... The three were believed to have links to a terrorist group that had plotted to attack the prime minister's office and Jordan's secret service with a powerful chemical bomb ... Had the bomb exploded, it could have killed at least 20,000 people and wrecked buildings within a half-mile, government officials have said. The group is also believed to have planned to attack the U.S. Embassy and other diplomatic missions with poison gas, government officials have said ... The plots were hatched by the Jordanian militant Abu Musab al-Zarqawi, thought to be a close associate of Osama bin Laden.[39]

Back in the United States already in testimony before a Senate Subcommittee on Terrorism in 1998, Steven Emerson described how thousands might have been killed in the New York City subways:

> Last summer, two militant Palestinians were arrested in New York hours before their crudely made bombs were apparently set to be detonated in the busy underworld of the New York City subway system. Had the attack not been prevented by an informant who stepped forward, the possibility is great that thousands could have been killed. Police breathed a sigh of relief when it was determined that the two men were not part of a larger Hamas conspiracy; yet the absence of a larger conspiracy is precisely what should be so worrisome. The two men had apparently been ultra-radicalized by the Islamic fundamentalist infrastructure in the United States and became emboldened

on their own to strike a blow here on American soil. The self-activation of individual bombers and terrorists, indoctrinated in the propaganda disseminated by radical Muslim organizations, is far more difficult to prevent than organized acts of strategically premeditated terror.[40]

It is paradoxically both reassuring and disquieting that the highest officials of the United States and Europe are very much taking the threats of future WMD by terrorists seriously.

President George Bush warned that the greatest threat to the world was in terrorists and renegade countries acquiring nuclear technology on the black market. In a speech at the National Defense University, Bush proposed restricting the ability of countries to obtain reprocessing and enrichment technology for what they say are civilian uses, such as power plants. The president warned that chemical, biological radiological or nuclear weapons are becoming easier to acquire, build, hide and transport, and said, "We must confront the danger with open eyes and unbending purpose."[41]

In Europe officials were reported conducting a simulation:

Brussels: European officials have conducted a simulation showing how Al Qaeda could kill 40,000 people [with] exploding ... a crude nuclear device near NATO head-quarters ... on the outskirts of Brussels, immediately killing 40,000 people, over-whelming hospitals with hundreds of thousands of injured, spreading panic through Europe and plunging the world economy into turmoil ... "We are in a race between cooperation and catastrophe," said Sam Nunn, a former U.S. senator who helped organize the exercise, named Black Dawn.[42]

IS THE DESCRIPTION OF A LIKELY WAR BETWEEN CIVILIZATIONS EXAGGERATED AND PROVOCATIVE?

Still, in all fairness including intellectual humility, one needs to wonder and ask if we are not exaggerating? Are we succumbing to another universal folk-myth trap of predicting a too-early and too-grim end to our civilization? Human fears of death, and now the increasing actual knowledge we have that in the end of time even our planet also will die, spur on too-foreboding views of our future.

The prediction of a clash between civilizations is popularly credited to Samuel Huntington. However, according to Peter Waldman in the *Wall Street Journal*, the concept of a clash of civilizations actually was advanced earlier by Princeton University Middle East scholar, Bernard Lewis.

A central Lewis theme is that Muslims have had a chip on their shoulders since 1683, when the Ottomans failed for the second time to sack Christian Vienna. "Islam has been on the defensive" ever since, Mr. Lewis wrote in a 1990 essay called "The Roots of Muslim Rage," where he described a "clash of civilizations," a concept later popularized by Harvard political scientist Samuel Huntington. For 300 years, Mr. Lewis says, Muslims have watched in horror and humiliation as the Christian civilizations of Europe and North America have overshadowed them militarily, economically and culturally.[43]

Lewis believes the crux of Islamic terrorism is that it is a prologue to a full-scale war for rule of the world. Nothing less. To understand Islamic terrorism as a protest of a contemporary injustice or political problem is to miss the point by several hundreds of years.

"The question people are asking is why they hate us. That's the wrong question," said Mr. Lewis on C-SPAN shortly after the Sept. 11 attacks. "In a sense, they've been hating us for centuries, and it's very natural that they should. You have this millennial rivalry between two world religions, and now, from their point of view, the wrong one seems to be winning."[44]

America and much of the rest of the Western world were stunned and couldn't understand September 11 except perhaps as an extension of the Israeli–Palestinian conflict, but this explanation doesn't hold water. The Israeli–Palestinian issue has nothing to do with Al-Qaeda attacks against America going back many years such as the blasting of two separate U.S. embassies in Africa in 1998 referred to earlier, nor does it explain Al-Qaeda's repeated attacks against fellow Muslims in many Muslim countries. Lewis does understand, and does not get stuck on contemporary issues. The battle goes back centuries. It is about a long-lost Islamic glory of power.

For Osama bin Laden, 2001 marks the resumption of the war for the religious dominance of the world that began in the seventh century . . . Today, America exemplifies the civilization and embodies the leadership of the House of War, and, like Rome and Byzantium, it has become degenerate and demoralized, ready to be overthrown . . . Sooner or later, Al Qaeda and related groups will clash with the other neighbors of Islam—Russia, China, India . . . If bin Laden is correct in his calculations and succeeds in his war, then a dark future awaits the world, especially the part of it that embraces Islam.[45]

Thomas Friedman also understands. According to Friedman, "September 11 amounts to World War III—the third great totalitarian challenge to open societies in the last 100 years." Friedman also cites another specialist, "longtime Middle East analyst, Abdullah Schleiffer" as saying to him:

World War II was the Nazis, using the engine of Germany to try to impose the reign of the perfect race, the Aryan race. The cold war was the Marxists, using the engine of the Soviet Union to try to impose the reign of the perfect class, the working class.

And Sept. 11 was about religious totalitarians, Islamists, using suicide bombing to try to impose the reign of the perfect faith, political Islam.[46]

Friedman notes again the suicide bombers' devotion to death and the absence of a devotion to life:

With the Islamist militant groups, we face people who hate us more than they love life. "When you have large numbers of people ready to commit suicide, and ready to do it by making themselves into human bombs, using the most normal instruments of daily life—an airplane, a car, a garage door opener, a cellphone, fertilizer, a tennis shoe—you create a weapon that is undeterrable, undetectable and inexhaustible."[47]

How grave is the danger of Islamic terrorism?

Is it perhaps essentially westerners who are the avowed enemies targeted by the Islamic fundamentalists, or perhaps especially people of the Jewish faith because of understandable Islamic political opposition and hatred of Israel and Jews?

No matter what the evidence, the Western mind persists in efforts at "making sense" of it all with our familiar logic that there *must* be a specific political cause which the enemy is fighting. Yet we will see in the next chapter that Salman Rushdie thinks the threat of Islam is basically very much a pure deadly matter. And so we saw previously that this is the way Christian-Arab, Adam Malik, thinks. There are many others who join with them. The Web site of the *Pakistan Daily Times* ("Your right to know—A new voice for a new Pakistan") reported a month after the suicide bombing on Bali by Jemaah Islamiah (JI):

"The willingness of JI to conduct a suicide attack is a demonstration that members of Southeast Asian groups are radicalised now, and sooner or later we will witness suicide attacks in this region," said Gunaratna, author of "Inside Al Qaeda: Global Network of Terror." Police say Jemaah Islamiah is intent on building a Muslim state spanning the southern Philippines, Malaysia, Singapore, Indonesia and southern Thailand.[48]

We have also seen in opinion polls from Muslim countries that a majority of Muslims do support the attacks of suicide bombers, such as the September 11 attack on the United States. I have not succeeded in finding opinion polls in the United States and United Kingdom specifically of Muslim-Americans and Muslim-Britons, but as noted earlier my understanding from various newspaper accounts and columnists reporting from the United States and United Kingdom is that there is a widespread sense of tacit sympathy to explicit identification with the suicide bomber attackers (along with explicit condemnations of suicide bombers as well).

The texts of Al-Qaeda generally are not case-specific to a particular arena of political and social conflict and don't offer a promise that if such-and-such issue is resolved, the attacks will stop and peace will reign. Al-Qaeda does not say, for example: *Free Saudi Arabia of its pro-Western (infidel) government, and we will see to it that peace will reign everywhere else*; or *establish a Palestinian state within the borders proposed by the U.N. General Assembly in 1947 authorizing both Israel and Palestinian states, and we will bring peace and prosperity*. Al-Qaeda's message is one of unbridled hate of America, Israel, and Jews, the West, the global community, indeed anything and everything that is not their brand of Wahhabi fundamentalist Islam, so that prominent among their victims are also a great many Muslims—see Al-Qaeda operations in Turkey, Morocco, Iraq, and Saudi Arabia for example.

The message of Al-Qaeda is one of explicit love of death. It hurls itself mockingly and terrifyingly in the face of our Western sentimentality and romanticizing of life. Al-Qaeda tell us, quite clearly, that we are facing another of the endless battles throughout human history between the light that keeps human life alive and the darkness that plunges living human creatures to their destruction before they can complete their normal life opportunity.

However much our extreme liberals—adorable naifs of a wished-for-goodness-in-life—seek to find some good cause for killing in this world and try to credit terrorists, including suicide killers, with having meaningful and reasonable causes against our Western imperialism and injustices, I believe the messages of today's killing jihad is no different than the cruel Nazi and Communist efforts at world domination of the twentieth century.

I hasten to acknowledge that we of the West often *are* imperialistic, exploitative, and criminally unjust, and that our injustices should be opposed and fought against, but these do not make us deserving to die.

There is also the large danger, which history teaches us not to minimize, that Muslim communities in democratic countries may not be fully committed to democratic process and institutions; and that were the demographic realities some day to shift toward their being the majority, they might—like we once learned to be the case when democratic regimes were toppled by fascists or communists wherever in the world—establish a nondemocratic Islamic rule.

On the small level of the individual security of whoever has dared expose the dangers of terrorism in the Muslim community, Steven Emerson told the Senate Subcommittee on Terrorism in 1998 of how he had to go underground to protect himself against threats of violence:

In November 1994, I served as the executive producer and reporter for the PBS documentary "Jihad in America." The film included previously unknown videos of the clandestine activities of radical Islamic terrorist groups operating in the United States, and featured interviews with moderate Muslims and federal counter-terrorism officials speaking for the first time about the magnitude of the threat posed by militant Muslim groups on U.S. soil ... Immediately following the release of "Jihad in America," I became the target of radical fundamentalist groups throughout the United States (and internationally) who fiercely denied the existence of "Islamic extremism" and accused me of engaging in an "attack against Islam."[49]

Daniel Pipes, an arch critic of Islamic terror, opines about American Muslims:

Whatever the majority of Muslim Americans may believe, most of the organized Muslim community agrees with the Islamist goal—the goal, to say it once again, of building an Islamic state in America. To put it another way, the major Muslim organizations in this country are in the hands of extremists . . . a significant movement in this country aspires to erode its bedrock social and legal arrangements, including the separation of church and state, and has even developed a roadmap toward that end.[50]

Nonetheless, in the framework of the wonderfully strong functioning democracies we certainly have today in the United States and United Kingdom, we owe it even to ourselves to ask if there is no element of prejudice and witch-hunting of Muslims in the emphatic recognition that suicide-bombing terrorism is largely the weapon of Muslims. Thus, I am rankled and quite frightened by remarks such as we also see by Daniel Pipes that "individual Islamists may appear law-abiding and reasonable, but they are part of a totalitarian movement and as such, all must be considered potential killers."[51] Even if it is true that there are significant risks of terrorists and active accomplices being found in Muslim communities, the phrasing that "all" must be viewed and suspected as "potential killers" is totalistic, inflammatory, and inviting of serious abuses against Muslim-Americans, which both decency and the successful protection of democracy cannot possibly tolerate. That *is* Islam- and Muslim-bashing to my mind, and I am resoundingly against such.

As one deeply committed to democracy and human rights, in a tense and dangerous period of history such as we are in, I expect the police-security measures to be intensified legitimately with special awareness of the risks of terrorists in the Muslim community, but at the same time with redoubled respect and attention to the civil rights and basic dignity of every person investigated. It is a tall order, of course, and one that runs in the face of known psychological principles that excesses and abuses of power are inherent in any system to which increasing power is assigned, including in democratic societies. But that is the genuine challenge of the maintenance of democracy.

So how great are the risks, first of the spread of the emerging wave of suicide bombings against civilians in today's world; second of a proliferation of larger-scale terror attacks, including the infinite tragedy of the use of WMD; and third of the unfolding of a degree of a fully patterned world war?

My own reading is that all of the above are real risks, even more that they are quite real probabilities in the world we live in today.

Suicide bombing is amazingly widespread. Not so long ago, one could hardly believe the threats of Hamas in Palestine-Israel that they would unleash an endless supply of suicide bombers, but they have proven totally accurate. So too around the world, the hundreds of suicide bombings now taking place in the course of a year is convincing proof how many people are willing and even eager to die and kill. It is our Western spiritual and psychological views of life that will need changing to incorporate these new "facts of life" about the readiness of people to surrender their lives.

My fears and predictions are also based on the observation that human beings have long since shown that we break through all limits, in fact we seem to have a definite need to "go all the way" and try out everything possible even when we know in advance that there will be enormous destruction of life.

An intriguing thoughtful scientific aspect of my admittedly sad and scary doomsday thinking is that I believe the evidence is that too many of our human minds are not able to overcome the many forms of primitivism that are obviously present in our thinking.

Psychologist, Daniel Kahneman, who was awarded a Nobel Prize in economics for work on how people make decisions ("decision analysis") that have economic implications, has come to a pessimistic conclusion about human thinking and decision making. For example, Kahneman studies what he calls "counterfactuals," which are stories people construct about events that didn't happen. "People hold on to their counterfactuals. They hang on to their beliefs. When people are wrong these beliefs help them to feel they were almost right."[52]

Kahneman contributes to our understanding of the pitfalls of knee-jerk or extreme liberal thinking. He describes a *"Fallacy of Transparency"* as the mistaken liberal belief that, "if our intentions are good, the other side is bound to react to our good intentions."

More important is that this veteran student of human thought does not trust us. He thinks that people take many risks because they "don't know they are taking risks, they are actually engaging in delusional thinking." He believes that people are out more for their personal interests than they care about ethical values. His overall picture of our human use of mind leads to a pessimistic evaluation of what man is capable of doing, and is likely to do. Kahneman's analysis fits my conclusion that it is unlikely that either good reasoning or decency will stop many humans from suicide bombings, including the use of WMD.

> I am now a lot more pessimistic than I was ... Important decisions tend to be unique and because they are unique there is very little learning from experience ... In an idealized model of what decision making should be, we would want a dispassionate analysis ... and serious thinking about tradeoffs ... We are far from it ... It is going to be hard to avoid mistakes.[53]

Moral considerations are not a sufficient barrier for too many people. Worse, in any generation there are plenty of people who joy in taking on a clear-cut commitment to be big-time destroyers. It seems that it is a matter of time before there will be further and larger acts of terror. Since the most fierce acts obviously will be enabled by WMD, and it is known that in the long run WMD are within the reach of terrorist groups, one has serious reason to expect that some terrorist groups will be the one to commit the unthinkable.

The terrorists have the motivation. They endow themselves with the conviction that they are entitled to kill their designated enemies. Increasingly they are committed to martyrdom for themselves as suicide killers, and of course the fates of other "incidental" people who will be destroyed in the process—and the damages to planetary society and ecology—are totally irrelevant to them. On the contrary. Just as the Nazis laughed and smiled watching the Jews being humiliated and tortured in the early "street-scenes" of the Holocaust (see the photographs from the time); just as the Turks laughed as they rounded up the Armenian intelligentsia and community leaders in Istanbul in 1914 to send them off to their deaths (also to be seen in photographic evidence); so bin Laden and his cohorts laughed and whooped it up with self-congratulatory glee when they saw what they had wrought to bring the World Trade Center towers come crashing down (see the TV clips of Al-Qaeda messages following September 11). The gods of destruction become exhilarated with their omnipotence.

I am less concerned that it will be nation states that will be responsible for the next megadestruction of our world, because I believe the quid-pro-quo regulatory and retaliatory tools available to other nations and to the international community is sufficient to constitute a workable deterrence. It is our as-yet lack of cleverness and will to define creatively powerful enough deterrents against terrorists that leave us more exposed.

In my opinion, the Islamic terrorist groups constitute a nascent movement of a transnational genocidal terrorism that seeks, at this point mostly implicitly and symbolically, to defeat the West, and *may* evolve some day into an effort to take over the world, as was the case first with Nazism and then with Communism in the last century. Granted there is no single totalitarian government or movement poised literally to conquer the world and exterminate hordes of people in its path. But the rhetoric of world conquest is there, Al-Qaeda is in itself already active in an amazing and depressing number of countries, and *Al-Qaedaism* as it were is a spirit of encouragement of Islamic terrorism by others too. Indeed Islam is sprouting new terrorists groups and movements all the time in many places in the world. For the most part, each country's and region's terror is treated as if it is not related to the others and as if no parallels are to be sought in events in other regions. But I believe that in the long run these many groups are laying the foundations for a possible worldwide bid for Islamic power over the rest of the planet. Certainly many of these terrorist organizations also spring from shared ideological-cultural roots, also Islam includes a strong imago of seeking the role of prime mover in the world, so that it is not far-fetched to be concerned about their forming a coordinated web some day. Harsh, scary, and I hope I'm wrong. Paradoxically, when the terrorists movements affiliate with each other more explicitly and form regional political-geographic-national identities who define themselves as enemies of the rest of world, and especially the West, it may be easier to fight them.

The larger picture I have of the future of contemporary civilization is that there will be some sort of world war in the early twenty-first century, in which there will be a major battle between pro-Death-and-Fascism forces versus pro-Life-and-Democracy forces.

Thomas Friedman observes:

> We are seeing—from Bali to Istanbul—the birth of a virulent, nihilistic form of terrorism that seeks to kill any advocates of modernism and pluralism, be they Muslims, Christians or Jews. This started before Sept. 11, 2001, and is growing in the darkest corners of the Muslim world.[54]

I fear very much that we will yet live and die to see the use of megaweapons that employ nuclear, chemical, or biological agents. In 2005, the Department of Homeland Security identified various strike scenarios that it views as most likely and devastating, including detonation of a nuclear device in a major city, release of nerve agent sarin in office buildings, and a truck bombing of a sports arena. Other scenarios included blowing up a chlorine tank, killing 17,000 people and wounding more than 100,000; spreading pneumonic plague in the bathrooms of an airport, sports arena, and train station, killing 2,500 and sickening 8,000 worldwide; and infecting cattle with foot and mouth disease at several sites. Another scenario predicted was an aerosol anthrax attack. "The anthrax attack scenario involves terrorists filling a truck with an aerosolized version of the deadly biological agent and then driving through five cities over two weeks, spraying it into the air. Public health officials, the report predicts, would probably not know of the initial attack until a day or two after it started. By the time it was over, an estimated 350,000 people would be exposed, and about 13,500 would die, the report predicts."[55]

Sadly, it may well be that big changes for the better in our human race, including a more rational world government and an international police and military force that will respond to mass violence more readily and effectively, will only arise after a next cataclysm that brings home to all living creatures that staying alive is a task that requires commitment and actions on behalf of life.

Could we possibly create a regulatory force for our world *before* disaster strikes?

A hopeful but obviously idealistic view is that if the world generates a powerful will to gain ironclad control over WMD, mobilizes a resolve to stop all terror including suicide bombing without romanticization of any killing as a heroic fight for freedom, and inaugurates a powerful worldwide system for containing, destroying, and punishing terrorists, including insisting on extraditing them from countries which give them safe haven, the grim future might be prevented.

Otherwise, the best I can hope for is that *after* a horrible disaster such as nuclear destruction of a city, the world's international political system will be forced to make a huge step toward reorganizing and will finally create a meaningful international police-regulating force, such as the proposed *International Peace Army* I described in the *Encyclopedia of Genocide*.[56]

The proposed *International Peace Army* would include an *integrated* force of three armies: (1) *The IPA Military;* (2) *the IPA Medical and Humanitarian*

Army; (3) *the IPA for the Rebuilding of Safe and Tolerant Communities.* The *International Peace Army* would be triggered into action virtually automatically whenever masses of human lives are threatened anywhere in the world. Its most distinctive features are that it includes bringing medical-humanitarian relief to a population as an immediate goal of its military and not as a subsidiary goal or one left to other agencies; and that it includes no less than an army devoted to rebuilding a new community order that is courageously devoted to overcoming ethnic-historic enmities and hatreds. Together, this army of three coordinated armies makes a huge effort not to look like or act like a brute invader and occupier. It is an army of food and medicine, and the most thoughtful social science-communications strategies for bringing people together to share the opportunity to rebuild a caring society, together with a military force that is used to kill killers and stop killers.

THERE NEEDS TO BE A WAR NOT *AGAINST* ISLAM, BUT *FOR* LIFE AND AGAINST NEEDLESS DEATH

If there will be a growing war, which I think has already begun in several parts of the world, I want us to go further into such a war fighting *for* the value of life and for democracy and not just militarily. Standing for these ideals will give us a sense of purpose, which we soldiers of life also need. It will make us more humane in our methods of fighting, for like all fighters in history, we too will be drawn to cruel excesses. Fighting for life will lay the groundwork for a better world when we win the war for life against death.

In the controversy over whether the United States should go to war against Iraq[57], after quoting from an Al-Qaeda document, "We Love Death as Much as You Love Life, So We Will Win," Flora Lewis observed:

> Not dialogue nor reason nor compromise can restore order against the use of terror. It is crucial that the enemy not be defined as a religion or a population but a glaringly evil intent. Regretfully, arms have to be used but the purpose remains peace.[58]
>
> We must show that the action we want to offer is for life.[59]

Some westerners do not believe that overall *we* are fighting for a culture of life and democracy, and there are some in the West too who do not believe that suicide bombings are inherently wrong. William Pfaff has observed:

> People outside the United States have stopped believing the American story. They don't think terrorism is an Evil force the United States is going to defeat. They say instead that terrorism is a way people wage war when they don't have F-16's or armored divisions. They say that Chechens, Moros, Taliban, Colombian insurgents, Palestinian bombers and Iraqi enemies of the U.S. occupation do not really make up a single global phenomenon that the world must mobilize to defeat.[60]

In contrast, Condoleezza Rice, then National Security Adviser to President George W. Bush, and now Secretary of State, has said that "terrorists declared war on America and on the civilized world many years before September 11, 2001" and cites terrorist attacks since 1983 as "part of a sustained, systematic campaign to spread devastation and chaos."[61]

I believe that in the coming years we must continue—and that we will be led by events into—a larger military war against transnational genocidal terrorism.

But simultaneously I *must* believe in the human spirit and creativity. When the day comes that we will have won the military battle, I want us also to know what we were fighting *against*—contempt for and wastage of human life; and for us to know what we were fighting *for*—the protection of human life, and for us to be on the way to achieving a major evolutionary change toward a human species that is committed to a godliness of all human life.

To conclude, in democracies, it is of course blatantly illegal to be a suicide bomber or any other form of terrorist, no matter how just one's cause may be. At the same time there is a wide range of freedom (however much I deplore such positions) for citizens to approve the cause of terrorists, or at least to "understand" (and in that sense to approve)—while not assisting or inciting *acts* of terrorism. Each of us has a right to choose where we stand conceptually on terrorism, including the suicide bombers of the Chechens, Tamil, Palestinians, Al-Qaeda, and whoever.

Personally, I am dead set against the use of the weapon of suicide bombing in virtually all conflicts, no matter how just the cause may be.

Is It Right to Fear and Condemn all Muslims? *(Of course not!)*

Perhaps the reason for the intensification of terrorism in the Arab world, in the form to which we are witness today, was first and foremost the encouragement it received from Islamic legal scholars, under a mantle of religion that is in most cases false, hijacked, and defective. If the legal scholars—who have encouraged terrorism by means of these vocal religious fatwas—were acting properly, they would be issuing a fatwa calling to kill bin Laden, Ayman Al-Zawahiri, Al-Zarqawi, and all Al-Qaeda leaders everywhere.   —Shaker Al-Nabulsi, a Jordanian intellectual who is a resident of the United States, published in Kuwait[1]

"Listen!" says a rabbi to a young Jew. "We have received an order from above. We need the blood of a Christian child for the unleavened bread for the Passover feast." In the following scene, a terrified youngster is seized from the neighborhood. Then the camera zooms in on the child for a close-up of his throat being cut. The blood spurts from the wound and pours into a metal basin.   —Part of a 29-part series, Al-Shatat (Diaspora), produced by Al-Manar TV with Syrian government backing, broadcast for first time in 2003[2]

ARE WE ENGAGING IN ISLAM-BASHING?

So is it right to criticize Islam for being a haven for terrorism? In democratic terms, it sounds to many like Islam-bashing and the kind of prejudice that the best of the Western world tries to overcome.

Postmodern concepts of understanding different peoples' narratives add a considerable pressure to respecting that there are rational reasons for the other's position, and therefore, in a sense, to accepting the other's behavior or at least their motivation. This kind of thinking lays a basis for differentiating between what for some becomes "justified" terrorism versus terrorism that is rejected outright as immoral. Some observers have noted that Europe, on the whole, has sought to maintain such a differentiation between justified and unjustified terrorism, while the American conception is much more to define all terrorism as criminal. It will be interesting to see whether this difference is reduced as more Al-Qaeda attacks pound Europe. As we shall see, the July 7 and July 21 attacks on London have led to the United Kingdom undergoing major policy changes in its handling of imams' rights to preach terror, and as to the rights of people who voice approval of terrorist attacks.

Our goal in this book, of course, is very much to understand the suicide bombers, but in no way to justify them.

Before the attacks on London, one graduate student in the United Kingdom described to me how an instructor defined a given book of interviews of a convicted terrorist as "must" reading. The understanding conveyed to the students was that there is some sense to the terrorist's actions, and that there is good reason for sympathy toward the terrorist as a freedom fighter who is being held as prisoner of an exploitative global society.

The same student told me that she spoke up and said to her instructor and group: "Aren't we forgetting something? This is a convicted terrorist who killed innocent civilians." Another student promptly replied, "But we need to understand what motivated him." "He did what he did out of a sense of seeking justice," added another student. It was clear that the consensus in the group was tilted in the direction of sympathy for the freedom fighter mystique of the terrorist.

So long as much of the suicide bombing that was blasting the West seemed centered on or related to Israel as the chosen victim of Palestinians, any number of Europeans, extreme left liberals, and postmodernists were able to shake off any moral protest of the bombings because, after all, the Jews-Israelis *[now choose how to end your sentence]* make troubles, deserve what they get, are helplessly mired in an insoluble chronic conflict with the Palestinians who have so few weapons compared to them that they need to fight back in this way.[3]

However, all too steadily a spreading terrorism is moving and expanding into a worldwide web that has already included targeting so many countries, to name many of them once again: the United States, England, France, Spain, Russia, Afghanistan, Iraq, Yemen, Morocco, Egypt, India, Sri Lanka, Indonesia, Malaysia, the Philippines, and many more. Terror alerts and security processes are now a part of life just about everywhere in our world. A sense of threat and danger attends most trips for people voyaging between different cities and countries. For many people there is emerging an understanding that a new type of war has been unleashed between proponents of *widespread random death to civilians* versus those who want to maintain a framework of civilized *protection of life*.

One reviewer for my potential publisher of this book gave me hell for the above statement that "it is an empirical claim offered without empirical support of any kind." But as we have seen, I am far from alone in making such observations that a war has already begun. Here are the words of another observer who predicts more suicidal death-making is on the way. The writer is a reporter for the *Los Angeles Times* who is discussing a book about the nineteen suicide bombers of September 11: "There are more of them. Whether we are more prepared for the next strike than we were for their last . . . we cannot know, but this much is certain. It will happen."[4]

As pointed out earlier, many liberals want so much for the world to be just and intelligible that they make themselves believe that even authoritarian, totalitarian, and outright murdering regimes must be intending to create a better society. Many maintain such beliefs stubbornly even after serious contradictory information has begun to flow in, for example, the unshakable belief of many devoted Communists about Stalinist Russia for many years when it was already clear that Stalin was presiding over a deadly fascist prison society. Die-hard liberals also held out for the Cambodian Khmer Rouge even after the cruel forced transfer-expulsion of the population of Phnom Penh.[5] The want-to-be-liberal mind, who is a want-to-be-a-kind-person and a want-to-believe-in-the-good intentions-of-revolutionaries-and-freedom-fighters has the same tendency to believe in suicide bombers as bringing to their victims, and the world, a message of social protest—even if their methods of suicide and murder "leave something to be desired."

In Anglo-Saxon countries, Islam also produces phenomena of totally Western-ized and well-educated Muslims who are bigots, jingoists, and open proponents of violence but who say their thesis in the finest and most politically correct language of the contemporary academic and even liberal establishment. Thus, note even the delicately gender-correct language in the following argument that Palestinian suicide bombers are freedom fighters comparable to the heroes we would dream of having had against Hitler in order to *prevent* the Holocaust.

> Use your imagination again. Consider a different history of Germany and Europe—one without the Second World War, without the Final Solution, without Auschwitz—all because a lone Jewish 'suicide' bomber in 1938 had penetrated the inner chambers of Nazi leadership and blown them to smithereens while also killing herself. Would this 'suicide' bomber—and her likes—also be regarded as a threat to all civilization? What would Mr. Friedman say about her? (The reference is *to New York Times*' correspondent, Thomas Friedman, of course.)[6]

The argument is seductive. I would personally have prayed for someone to kill Hitler, and as I wrote earlier, I can imagine myself being a suicide killer for such a purpose. But that's where the argument ends for me. I do not believe any credit or grace should be extended to suicide killers who set out to kill innocent civilians.

In no way are the suicide bombers attacking Hitlers.

And many of the suicide bombers do not even have a sense that they are fighting tyranny.

In March 2004 Israeli soldiers discovered a bag of explosives among bags that a 10-year-old Palestinian boy was carrying through a barricade between the Palestinians and Israelis. The youngster, a fourth grader who lives in a refugee camp east of Nablus, regularly made a living by transferring bags from one side to the other.

The Fatah-affiliated Tanzim reportedly paid Abdullah Kuran a little more than one U.S. dollar to hand the bags to a woman waiting on the other side and Abdullah was unaware that one of the bags contained a 10-kilo bomb. He was stopped by Israeli soldiers who discovered it during a routine inspection. When Abdullah's dispatchers saw that he had been stopped, they attempted to detonate the bomb by cellphone, but failed.

The boy explained: "Yesterday, I came to the barricade as usual and started shouting, 'Who wants to transfer their bags to the other side?' A few people piled on their bags . . . I don't remember who put the bag with the bomb."

One Israeli doctor reacted with exasperation: "I don't believe these suicide bombings have anything to do with liberating their people! They're psychotic blowing up a 10-year-old kid. If they loved their people, they couldn't blow up a 10-year-old kid."[7]

According to Israeli security officials, up until March 26, 2004 there had been twenty-nine suicide bombers younger than eighteen who were dispatched by Palestinian terror organizations.

In another case, a 16-year-old mentally retarded boy from Nablus was recruited as a suicide bomber, but was intercepted by Israeli soldiers. The boy was caught at an Israeli Army checkpoint with an explosive vest strapped to his body. The family of the boy was furious that he had been dispatched to carry out a suicide attack, although the boy's mother said she would not have opposed the decision to send her son on the suicide mission had he been over eighteen.

We condemn those who sent the boy to blow himself up," said Abdu's uncle, Abu Muhammad. "He was an innocent and quiet boy. He was a short, naive boy who had been struck in the head when he was a child and has been suffering from an illness since then. We always kept an eye on him because we knew he was a small child. Although he's 16, he thinks like a 10-year-old. If I find out who sent him on this mission, I will not hesitate to fire two bullets at his head. I don't even mind spending the rest of my life in prison. Those who did this are criminals."

In videotape provided to journalists by the Army, the boy said he decided to blow himself up because "people do not like me." He said he learned about the pleasures of heaven from his teacher. "My teacher in school told us about it," he explained. "He told us to fast, to pray, and to do good deeds to reach paradise. He told us about the life of pleasure which is waiting for us there: a river of honey, a river of wine, and 72 beautiful girls."[8]

Photographs of the boy being arrested were widely shown in the press. The boy waited at the checkpoint near Nablus as an Israeli Army robot brought him scissors so that he could cut the straps holding his explosive vest. After his vest was on the ground, soldiers ordered him to strip to be sure he wasn't carrying any other bomb. The BBC characterized the event as a "cynical manipulation of a Palestinian youngster for propaganda purposes;" Israeli Minister, Natan Sharansky, who is famous for having survived a decade of imprisonment by the Soviet regime, fumed and sent a protest to the British news service.[9]

A few days later Palestinian militants tried to lure a 15-year-old schoolboy, Tamer Khuweir, into carrying out a suicide mission by promising him eternal paradise and cash for his family if he blew himself up. Tamer's eldest brother, Raed, said: "He was crying and shaking when he told me, 'They lured me, I was supposed to do the attack today but I decided not to. I am not going,'" the brother said after Tamer's arrest. "They later took him to see a (religious) sheikh, who sat in a dark room and told him that death was inevitable, that paradise was eternal and that if he committed the attack he would go to heaven where he would live with virgins for ever after," the brother said.[10]

According to the *Jerusalem Post,* Tamer ran home and buried his head in his mother's arms. Sobbing, he repeated over and over: "They tricked me, they tricked me ... I want to stay here with you. I want to be part of this life," the boy cried according to his brother.[11]

The *Jerusalem Post* comments:

Tamer Khawireh is the fourth boy of his age to be arrested in Nablus in recent weeks for planning to carry out a suicide attack. The militias in the city are so powerful that even their own supposed controllers say they can't rein them in. Abu Said, 30, the sturdy-looking leader of the Tanzim branch in the Balata refugee camp said that he begged the Aksa Martyrs Brigades ... to leave the kids alone. "But it is hard to approach those who are armed," he said from his office. "We just provide them with money and supplies."

Tamer's father owns a restaurant near the central market in Nablus. A group of men gathered near the restaurant around a reporter. One man swore that the Israeli secret service fabricated the stories of youths being conscripted, that "no Palestinian group would do such a thing." When asked how many of them believed that version, all the men, young and old, raised their hands.[12]

There have also been megaterrorist attacks which have brought home in a powerful way the terrorists' total indifference to those whose lives are taken—so long as blood flows and flows.

Such a memorable attack was the "3/11" of multiple bombs on commuter trains in Madrid on March 11, 2004. On another eleventh day of a month, which some in Spain began to refer to as "our country's 9/11" and to which one newspaper offered quickly the designation "3/11," no less than ten bombs were placed in three commuter train stations in Madrid during the morning rush hour and detonated within a 10-minute period. The genius of coordination was again displayed. The initial reports were of some 200 dead and 1200 injured. Al-Qaeda claimed responsibility.[13]

One reason this attack assumed a degree of memory-imprinting, legend-creating importance was the fact that such a large number of people were killed.

But more than that, the terrorists' messages were that they were reminding the entire global community, as if renewing the triumphs of their piece de resistance of September 11 in the United States, that they had the ability to extend their sphere of operation to still another continent; they were enlarging their web to include a new country which heretofore had seemed outside the range of Al-Qaeda; they were continuing their use of their hallmark technique of brilliant coordination of simultaneous multiple events; they were blasting the world with a demonstration that the world was up against a formidable opponent; and that there was to be no place that human life was to be safe anymore.

From the point of view of the concrete topic of this book about suicide bombers, it should be noted that the Madrid attack did not require the use of a suicide bomber as the attacks on September 11 had; but some weeks later when Spanish security forces came to arrest the core group of terrorists, they responded with an open shootout and then a suicide bomb. However, one hardly needs the concrete connection of this later suicide bomb to make connections between nonsuicide terrorism and suicide terrorism. The tape on Madrid left by Al-Qaeda contained a familiar text as if repeating September 11. Although there was as if an "explanation" of specific grievances against the West in Afghanistan and Iraq (in this rare case Israel was given a "day off"), the real message was the threat of endless, limitless massive death and extermination—by whatever terrorist means.

In my opinion, what we basically hear from the megamurderers of every era are their ostensible complaints and grievances even about very real injustices (which we should *not* neglect), but these are poor excuses for their true ultimate dark agenda. In truth the megakillers of every era are seeking to take over our world and to destroy as many people as they can in order to prove they are as if the gods-on-earth and masters-of-life-and-death in this universe.

This was the Al-Qaeda text:

> This is an answer to crimes which you committed in the world, notably in Iraq and Afghanistan, and there will be more, so help us God. You want life, we want death, which is an example of what the prophet Muhammad said. If you do not stop your injustices, more blood will be spilt, and these attacks are very little compared to what could happen with what you call terrorism.[14]

Am I too angry and condemning of the suicide bombers (which to my ears sounds like an oxymoron question)? One quite decent young woman was shocked at reading an earlier draft of my manuscript of this book.

> "You can't criticize all Muslims and all of Islam!" she protested. "You certainly don't mean to be engaging in Islam-bashing!"
> "No, I don't intend Islam-bashing at all," I replied. "I welcome—even treasure— any religious faith, and any person with whom I can share a heartfelt and resolute commitment to protect human life. When Islam identifies with the sacredness of human life, I am only respectful and appreciative."

My above critic was further shocked by the prediction I make of a major, even world-level war, quite possibly involving major weapons of mass destruction, between those I call transnational genocidal terrorists and the countries and cultures which will opt for a civilization that is committed to human life.

"Suicide bombers may be unacceptable to us (westerners) who don't want to see so much bloodshed, including the suicide of the bomber," opined the young woman, "but surely they are fighting for their cause, the freedom of their people and their dignity. They're not like the Nazis or the Communists who were out to take over as much of the world as possible."

"Yes they are," I replied. "Under the guise of whatever political or ideological cause, in some cases perhaps even with a considerable degree of justification, they choose a way of life that is inherently committed to destroying life. The process of becoming agents of death becomes in its own right so addictive and intoxicating that before long the terrorist movement is more committed to fomenting death far and wide than it is to its original cause."

In the case of Al-Qaeda, from the outset there has been an explicit dance and idolatry of death in their pronouncements. Thus, we saw in the materials of September 11

We love death as much as you love life, so we will win.[15]

Following the "3/11" massacre, Al-Qaeda announced:

Our brigades are getting ready now for the coming strike. Whose turn will it be next? Is it Japan, America, Italy, Britain, Saudi Arabia or Australia? The brigades of death are at your doors. They will strike "with an even hand at the right time and place."[16]

A senior advisor to the French Institute of International Relations observed: "Islamic fundamentalism is at war against democracies, irrespective of their stand toward Washington. It is liberal democracy that terrorists want to punish . . . "[17]

New York Times' Thomas Friedman was upset that the Spanish people, who were on the eve of an election when March 11 took place, responded to the terrorists by replacing their antiterrorist government with a new government that planned to pull their troops out of the Western alliance in Iraq. For him this was appeasement of evil, and he referred to the political transition in Spain as one "when the Axis of Evil intersects with the Axis of Appeasement and the Axis of Incompetence."[18] Indeed, subsequently the Spanish have arrested a ring of Al-Qaeda terrorists who, despite Spain's withdrawal from Iraq, were planning a further series of major attacks on Spain including on the Central Criminal Court—which has been fearless in indicting terrorists, and other attacks on the Real Madrid soccer stadium, the Picasso Tower skyscraper, and the Madrid Conference Center. The director of Europol, the European police coordination office, said that Spain's pullout of troops "had done nothing to lessen the threat of Islamic terrorism in Spain."[19]

In the column from which I have previously quoted which is entitled, "Cruelty is all they have left," Zakaria Fareed questioned, "Does it matter whether the carnage in Madrid ... was the act of the Basque terror organization ETA or of Al Qaeda? ... They have something in common that is revealing about the nature of terrorism ... they are increasingly defined almost exclusively by a macabre culture of violence ... With many terrorist groups—like ETA, like al Qaeda—*violence has become an end in and of itself. They want a lot of people dead, period*" (my italics).[20]

All of these observers are aware that the terrorist groups speak as if they are going about a social-political agenda of protest, but even if this was in some real part their genesis, they become cults of murder and death that feast on the horror and terror of endless deaths. An "Islamic Human Rights Commission" in the United Kingdom complained as befits a human rights watchdog group, about a BBC Channel 4 documentary about Palestinian suicide bombers. "The programme made no reference to the context in which Palestinians undertook such actions, i.e., military occupation, apartheid style conditions and legislation, systematic denial of basic civil, political, economic and social rights, etc. Instead the programme blames Palestinian TV for promoting violence."[21] I wish it would be possible to take every sanctimonious liberal apologist for terror and place him or her in the midst of the carnage of dead and painfully wounded civilians. No goal, cause or political agenda can justify these injuries to plain and simple people going about their lives.

Worldwide terrorism is growing insidiously and expanding toward

- more frequent terrorist attacks
- bigger, more devastating attacks
- coalitions of existing terrorist movements in various countries and cultures
- overthrowing vested governments and replacing them with fundamental Islamic-law governments, such as the Taliban in Afghanistan and the ayatollahs in Iran
- establishing larger regional Islamic governments

I am far from alone in predicting that suicide bombing as such is going to increase; that there will be larger and larger numbers of attacks; that the bombers will attempt to get at more and more serious political targets, such as executive, legislative, and judicial leaders of countries, also actual legislative bodies as groups, and also well-known cultural leaders and heroes; and worst of all, that the suicide bomber-terrorists will employ more and more dangerous weapons of mass destruction.

After what was in effect a suicidal attack on the Indian legislature in December 2002 that was foiled when security guards shot and killed five armed suicide bombers who were about to attack the two Indian Houses of Legislature which were in full session, with 400 members of Parliament waiting to hear an address by Prime Minister Atal Behari Vajpayee, a commentator, Vatsala Vedantam, observed:

> Security guards shot the five armed suicide bombers before they could carry out their mission. The aim of this attack was unambiguous: to wipe out the country's elected leaders. Terrorism is nothing new to India. The nation has seen two recent prime ministers assassinated. Indira Gandhi was gunned down by her own security guards, while her son, Rajiv Gandhi, was killed by a suicide bomber. Several other political leaders, including state chief ministers, have died violent deaths in similar circumstances. An estimated 55,000 men, women and children have been victims of terrorism in different parts of India. The assault on the Jammu and Kashmir Legislative Assembly in Srinagar two months ago when 38 legislators were gunned down, was the beginning of more daring attacks. The modus operandi of the suicide terrorists in both cases point to the same suspects—the dreaded Jaish-e-Muhammad (JeM) and the Lashkar-e-Taiba (LeT)—terrorist groups operating from Pakistan. *This attack shows what is in store for other countries if this kind of terrorist culture is allowed to escalate* (my italics).
>
> The world needs to realize, first and foremost, that there is no such thing as a holy war. The perpetrators of such notions are merely exploiting religion for their own ends. Whether it is the Taliban or the JeM or the LeT, each is pursuing its own agenda in the guise of religion.[22]

The terrorists in different countries did not necessarily start out as linked to one another, but what needs to be appended to this statement is that, in many cases, they share with each other key value-purposes, namely a desire for a triumph of Islamic rule through bloodshedding and murdering civilians, use of suicide bombers, and I fear deeply, what will yet emerge, a commitment to the use of any and all weapons including WMD. It is entirely natural for such groups to seek each other out and embrace one another as true brothers, slowly but surely to assist and cooperate with one another, and to launch coordinated attacks. Insofar as a worldwide terrorist movement—such as Al-Qaeda—seeks purposefully to establish itself as an international organization, it will have an ever increasing number of branches in multiple countries.

I suggested earlier that we might think of *Al-Qaedaism* as it were as a spirit of encouragement of Islamic terrorism internationally. Al-Qaeda is an actual organizational structure, but no less is also an emerging spiritual-ideological framework, almost like a new religion that is on a spree of gathering new adherents. In essence, it has declared war against the non-Islamic fundamentalist world. In political terms, this means a war especially against the United States and all the West, but also against any and all countries that cooperate with Western globalization, even such as far-off Japan, Korea, China, and Thailand. In religious terms, the war is especially against all of Judeo-Christian civilization, but it also is directed against all other faiths, in fact very much also at *Islam as an enemy wherever Islam is not practiced in a stark fundamentalist way* (see later in the chapter the section "The

Deadly Violences of Islam against Islam"). It is nothing less than a beginning of a *world* war. Thus, in an audio tape, Al-Qaeda's second-in-command, Dr. Ayman al-Zawahri, an Egyptian-born surgeon says:

> We should not wait until U.S., British, French, Jewish, South Korean, Hungarian or Polish forces enter Egypt, the Arabian Peninsula, Yemen and Algeria before we resist. The interests of the Americans, British, Australians, French, Polish, Norwegians, South Korean and Japanese are spread everywhere . . . They all took part in the invasion of Afghanistan, Iraq or Chechnya or enabled Israel to survive.[23]

The geographical, political, and religious identifiers of today's transnational genocidal terrorism are all mixed. Older conventional terms for understanding a war no longer apply. The Al-Qaeda call is, in effect, a war against anyone and everyone in the whole world who does not practice an Islamic fundamentalist way of life and/or who does not submit to Al-Qaeda Islamic power.

A *New York Times* report analyzed the larger picture of growing global co-operation between Islamic terrorists even as at the immediate time of this writing the power of Al-Qaeda as such seemed to be reduced.

> The landscape of the terrorist threat has shifted, many intelligence officials around the world say, with more than a dozen regional militant Islamic groups showing signs of growing strength and broader ambitions, even as the operational power of Al Qaeda appears diminished. Some of the militant groups, with roots from Southeast Asia, Central Asia and the Caucasus to North Africa and Europe, are believed to be loosely affiliated with Al Qaeda, the officials say. But other groups [which] follow their own agenda, merely drawing inspiration from Osama bin Laden's periodic taped messages . . . have shown resilience in resisting the efforts against terrorism led by the United States . . . by establishing terrorist training camps in Kashmir, the Philippines and West Africa, filling the void left by the destruction of Al Qaeda's camps in Afghanistan.[24]

The worst of it according to some observers is that Al-Qaeda has become a symbolic force for the regeneration of terrorist groups. The vision these local groups adopt has shifted under the inspiration and examples of Al-Qaeda to become more ambitious and extensive, so that they have become devoted to an image of Islamic power that goes beyond the original regional cause which first inspired them. "They are like little time bombs that have been sent out into the world," said an F.B.I. agent and the director of counterterrorism at Interpol's international headquarters based in Lyon, France. "You never know where it might go off . . . " Another senior intelligence official based in Europe said: "Al Qaeda's biggest threat is its ability to inspire other groups to launch attacks, usually in their own countries." A senior Australian official said, "I'm most worried about the groups that we don't know anything about. Every day around the world, we are discovering Al Qaeda members and cells previously unknown."[25]

IS IT RIGHT TO CONDEMN ALL MUSLIMS? NO, OF COURSE NOT. BUT IT IS RIGHT TO CONDEMN ALL PARTS OF ISLAM THAT CONDONE TERRORISM AND SUICIDE BOMBING

There is a natural tendency for Muslims who love and identify with their tradition at any given time to seek to present their heritage in as positive a light as possible. This is true of the members of all ethnic and religious groups, and is both natural and admirable.

At the same time, the challenge for all of us is to remain open to the truths of the serious failures of just about every one of our churches or other institutions, and to speak up honorably in criticism, both to ourselves and our own communities, and then to others. More than not, too many of us, in all faiths and all ethnic groups, do not rise to this standard. A blindly apologetic and contentiously defensive style is more characteristic of the members of most faiths and ethnic groups.

When events involve terrorist and revolutionary activities, whether in genuine or in ostensible protest against oppression or imperialism, there is no shortage of people who rush to a blind defense of the protesting group, and now there develops a chorus of loyalists that includes their natural faithful joined by passionate blind justice-seekers. I have seen this process over and over again, including the decent people seeking social justice whom we have referred to who denied to the prover-bial last minute Stalin's incredible murders of no less than millions of people; the Khmer Rouge apologists who wanted to believe that they were out to build a new and better agrarian society in Cambodia; or pro-Palestinians today who refuse to criticize the pagan orgies of violence by Palestinians or to understand the agonies of Israelis in response to suicide bombings.

John Esposito is a professor of Islamic studies at Holy Cross College "who, in books like *The Islamic Threat: Myth or Reality* and (with John O. Voll) *Islam and Democracy,* popularized Edward Said's ideas by purging them of their ... anti-Americanism." Esposito claimed that Islamic fundamentalism was a movement of democratic reform all along, and only prejudice against Islam prevented westerners from seeing this happy truth. Esposito mocked and rejected public concern about terrorism as barely disguised anti-Muslim prejudice.[26]

Sarah Lawrence professor, Fawaz Gerges, said six months before September 11 that one must be skeptical about the U.S. government's assessment of increasing terrorist threats, and that the fears of terrorism were irrational and farfetched.[27] *Hah.*

We considered earlier that Islam as a faith does have within it a dialectical strain between calling for respect for the lives of all human creatures, including those who are not Muslims, and calling for the outright elimination of the unfaithful who are deemed ipso facto the enemies of Islam.

There are large Muslim populations which live under the religious and political leadership of Islamic clerics and statesmen who devote themselves to advancing not only a humanistic peace-loving Islamic way of life, but also ecumenical respect and active cooperation with other faiths in a shared conception that all human life issues from a common God. On the other hand, there are huge Muslim populations who live under clerical and political leaderships and in societies where the prevailing public opinion is explicitly and feverishly pro-terrorism. Objectively, most of the suicide bombing in today's world is the handiwork of Muslims. Is saying so in any way in bad taste or insulting to the peace-caring people and institutions in worldwide Islam who want a safer and more decent world and are against terrorism?

The reader I spoke of who reviewed an early partial manuscript of this book and was critical that it was "Islam-bashing" really believes that if people are only treated fairly and decently, they cannot possibly be or remain violent. On the level of her everyday life, she does not know that some people are committed and addicted to evil. On the historical level, she does not recognize that there are cultures that devote themselves to violence, warmaking, terror, and genocide and will not cease until they are defeated by a stronger force.

Insofar as Muslims who love and are proud of their faith which they understand as essentially nonviolent are hurt and upset by criticisms of Islamic terror, one can only sympathetically and respectfully confirm their correct knowledge that Islam *does* speak considerably for the sacredness of life. There are deep thrusts of peace-caring in Islam. Thus, as another example, Islam has existed in Senegal for over a thousand years. By the beginning of the twentieth century, most of Senegal had been entirely Islamized. However, the style of Islam practiced in Senegal is significantly different than that found in most other Islamic countries. It is similar to the mystical Sufi tradition, which is characterized by its reverence of spiritual beings (alive or dead) who are believed to embody extraordinary amounts of *baraka* or divine grace. The Mouride brotherhood is one of the three main sects of Islam in Senegal. It was begun by Cheikh Amadou Bamba who lived from 1850–1927.[28] Bamba was a pacifist and did not wage war on pagans as many other Islamic leaders had done. A recent exhibition and lecture on Bamba at the Center for Jewish Studies at UCLA described him as a "profoundly pacifist Muslim teacher . . . whose deeds and life lessons inspire the exhibition, [who] once said that the only jihad (which means 'struggle' in Arabic, NOT 'holy war') he would engage in was with the imperfections of his own soul." The center's flyer concludes that "Bin Laden is an anomaly with Islam," and that the exhibition is an "opportunity to challenge what 'jihad' means in popular—and some scholarly— thinking in the U.S."[29]

There have always been believers and interpreters of Islam who advanced a humanistic interpretation that Islam prohibits many forms of killing. However, as is often the case, many ideological causes progressively become more and more radicalized, and the rules of theological definition and the rules of adversarial engagement with other religions and with nonbelievers tend to become more extreme. According to many observers, the overall worldwide direction of Islam today is toward greater extremism, including broader support for Islamic violence and fears of criticizing the violence even in peaceful Islamic communities; and including an emerging image or historical vision that an explosion of Islamic populations in many countries across the globe is building toward a natural possibility of restoring Islam as the world's leading power a few decades from now.[30]

It should also be noted that even some peaceful trends in Islam are contextualized more as "if ... then" commitments not to kill, such as giving potential victims the right and opportunity to convert to Islam, and if they do so their lives are spared, but if they do not do so ... Holocaust historians and survivors have long pointed out, in a sense enviously, that the Jewish victims of the Nazis had no such option, unlike the case in some Christian pogroms against Jews in earlier centuries where the option to convert was offered. In a 1996 book on jihad, Rudolph Peters, a Dutch scholar argued that the doctrine of jihad forbids the killing of noncombatants like children, women, and old people. According to Peters, no war against unbelievers may be mounted without summoning them to the opportunity to submit and embrace Islam before the attack; people must be given a chance to embrace Islam before they may be killed.[31] *(Hooray?)*

Still, there are no doubts that there are also uncompromising clear-cut protests against violence from prominent Islamic scholars who oppose killings such as September 11 that deserve to be heard unambivalently and respectfully, in a full sense of brotherhood and shared humanity.

A statement rejecting violence and terrorism issued on September 11, 2002 was signed by many prominent American Muslims, and scholars of Islam from all over the world:

> As American Muslims and scholars of Islam, we wish to restate our conviction that peace and justice constitute the basic principles of the Muslim faith. We wish again to state unequivocally that neither the al-Qaeda organization nor Usama bin Laden represents Islam or reflects Muslim beliefs and practice. Rather, groups like al-Qaeda have misused and abused Islam in order to fit their own radical and indeed anti-Islamic agenda ... We say most clearly ... that the killing of innocent civilians, whether Christian, Muslim, or Jewish, is always wrong and is forbidden in Islamic law and ethics. Illegitimate means can never be justified by a desirable or noble goal. On this first anniversary of the tragedy of September 11, we call on all people of conscience to denounce violence and to work peacefully for the creation of a better world.[32]

Beyond the understandable defensiveness and efforts at self-protection of their Muslim community, there is a ring of sincerity in many of their pronouncements of identification with nonviolence. There are many who suggest that the Muslims in the world who interpret Islam as not violent actually are the majority. In addition, there is every reason to believe the Anglo-Saxon ethos that military force is only to be applied in self-defense and defense of freedom will be incorporated into the life philosophy of many Muslims who become part of the societies of Anglo-Saxon countries or other democracies. Like the statement against violence we just read, the American Muslim Web site brings from a Muslim-American magazine published in September 2002 a wide range of Muslim antiviolence statements following September 11, including an organization of "Muslims Against Terrorism" in which there are Egyptian, Turkish, Iranian, American, British, Pakistani, and Jordanian Muslims. Many of the texts are impressive and heartwarming.[33] Thus:

- Mufti Nizamuddin Shamzai, Pakistan: It is wrong to kill innocent people. It is also wrong to praise those who kill innocent people.[34]
- King Abdullah II, Jordan: What these people [terrorists who committed 9/11] stand for is completely against all the principles that Arab Muslims believe in.[35]

On the other hand, there is also a subtle tension of the measure of untruth staring out from *some* of these sources who fail to grapple with the facts of the widespread support for terrorism in Islam, and also the possible duplicity or at least restricted application intended by some of those who protest September 11 but do not necessarily or really protest other Muslim violences such as suicide bombings against the hated Jews-Israelis. Thus, one quotation is given of an Iranian ayatollah who says that "killing of people, in any place and with any kind of weapons ... is condemned." Sounds marvelous! And the case examples he cites include Yugoslavia and even Hiroshima and Nagasaki which could place this Iranian religious leader with some leading liberals in genocide scholarship— unless his motivation really is to attack the United States more than it is to decry nuclear genocide. But then the case examples of killings that he marshals from the Middle East include several atrocities by Israelis, but not a single Palestinian killing of Israelis.[36]

Similarly, a fine condemnation of "attacking innocent people" is quoted from the Egyptian imam, Shaikh Muhammed Sayyid al-Tantawi, imam of al-Azhar mosque in Cairo who has been referred to as "the highest authority in Sunni Islam,"[37] but Tantawi has been known to move dramatically from participation in statements of nonviolent principles to outright approval of jihadic violences (in the last chapter of this book, Tantawi's flip-flopping record is discussed at length). Here let one reference to his approval of killing suffice: In April 2004 Tantawi affirmed that Palestinian resistance against the Israeli military is a form of "legitimate jihad," and not terrorism, according to Agence France-Presse reporting from Cairo. "Everything that the Palestinians do against the army of the occupiers of their country is legitimate jihad and not terrorism," he told the government newspaper, *Al-Akhbar*, and that the operations of the radical Islamist movement Hamas and other Palestinian groups against Israeli military targets were a form of self-defense.[38] An Indian news source reported that when another religious leader, the Grand Mufti of Saudi Arabia, Sheikh Abdul Aziz al-Sheinh had declared that "any act of self-killing or suicide is strictly forbidden is Islam" including one who blows himself up "in the midst of enemies," Tantawi countered saying suicide bombings were legitimate if directed against Israeli soldiers.[39]

Still, we return to the larger picture and see that as Islamic terrorism continues to spread around the world and grow over these years, many Muslim organizations and institutions take undeniably clear stands against terrorism. Do the pronounce-ments of these organizations genuinely reflect the inner hearts and minds of their constituencies? Do their pronouncements meaningfully impact on and shape the attitudes of members of their groups? One certainly hopes so, although I know from my own experiences in Jewish communal life that lofty statements about a commitment to peace in Jewish theology and tradition (which are largely true) don't mean a thing to the diehard right-wing Jewish terrorists and devotees of arms dealings, landgrabs and unabashed power among my people. Fortunately, the Jewish right-wing is a small percentage, although like all fascists they are dangerous and capable of killing innocent Palestinian civilians as well as capa-ble of assassinating an Israeli hero and prime minister (Yitzhak Rabin) who was pursuing peace with the Palestinians in a creative way.

In any case, the antiviolence and antiterrorism positions taken by many Muslim community leaders are extremely important and their pronouncements are most encouraging. Thus too:

- The Muslim Council of Britain wrote to 1,000 mosques, asking that a message of vigilance and nonviolence be part of their sermons ... the council's secretary general, Iqbal Sacranie, said that "Islam categorically forbids violence and killing of innocents, let alone indulging in violence which can cause death and mayhem." He urged Muslims to cooperate fully with the police.
- In June 2003, a council at Rome's mosque—the largest in Europe—suspended an imam after he gave a sermon praising Palestinian fighters and calling for the destruction of Islam's enemies.
- Nadeem Elyas, head of Germany's Central Council of Muslims, said that since September 11, 2001, his group has issued more than thirty statements against terror in newspaper articles, television interviews, or direct meetings with imams. "We have very clearly said that Islam rejects violence and terror, and we have asked our imams in their Friday services to condemn terrorism," Elyas said. "And we have called on them to report to authorities anything that is suspicious in their mosques, and not to allow anyone to promote anything terrorist or extremist or fanatic."[40]

Regrettably, as usual in the dialectical cauldron of violence and nonviolence, there is a *but*. For example, a Muslim official in Italy acknowledged that there is no monitoring of imams outside of Rome, and U.S. officials have called one mosque in Milan "the main Al Qaeda station house in Europe in 2001." In Spain, even after the deaths of some 200 people in the terrorists' strike in Madrid in 2004, the Union of Muslim Communities in Spain said it had no plans to urge mosques to undertake public opposition to terrorism.[41]

As I have already noted, there is a considerable sense that there are many Muslims in the world today who do not openly espouse or approve of murderous violence, but who are careful not to condemn the violences of their compatriots.

Such noncommittal acquiescence to or implied sympathy for violence is especially disturbing when seen in residents of the free world. Newspaper columnist, Charles Krauthammer, wrote bitterly about this phenomenon in the United States a month-and-a-half after September 11:

> Imagine if 19 murderous Christian fundamentalists hijacked four airplanes over Saudi Arabia and, in the name of God, crashed them into the holy cities of Mecca and Medina, destroying the holy Kaaba and killing thousands of innocent Muslim pilgrims. Could anyone doubt that the entire Christian world—clergy and theologians, leaders and lay folk—would rise as one to denounce the act? ... And yet after Sept. 11, where were the Muslim theologians and clergy, the imams and mullahs, rising around the world to declare that Sept. 11 was a crime against Islam? Where were the fatwas against Osama bin Laden? The voices of high religious authority have been scandalously still ... Hence that great post-Sept. 11 oddity: Deafening silence from the spiritual authorities of Islam, obsessive chatter from Americans, largely Christian, filling that silence with near apologetic professions of good faith and tolerance.[42]

From within the ranks of Muslims, Salman Rushdie raised a similar voice. He calls the issue about Islam in a straightforward way:

> If this isn't about Islam, why the worldwide Muslim demonstrations in support of Osama bin Laden and Al Qaeda? Why did those 10,000 men armed with swords and axes mass on the Pakistan-Afghanistan frontier, answering some mullah's call to jihad? ... Of course this is "about Islam" ... highly motivated organizations of Muslim men ... have been engaged over the last 30 years or so in growing radical political movements out of this mulch of "belief." This paranoid Islam, which blames outsiders, "infidels," for all the ills of Muslim societies, and whose proposed remedy is the closing of those societies to the rival project of modernity, is presently the fastest growing version of Islam in the world.[43]

We were discussing Daniel Pipes in a previous chapter. He is known as a severe critic of Islam for its terrorism, and his opinions as a strategic analyst must command respect, even as it is always fair and important to question and discount to an extent opinions from any source that becomes identified very strongly and repeatedly with a polarized position. Pipes has not only been a severe critic, but has become known as strident and at times downright prejudicial against Islam. Since he is opposing Islam for its terrorism, and his positions are basically grounded in facts and responsible evidences, he needs to be listened to. And yet there is a tone of Islam-bashing in his writing that conjures up memories of bigots toward whichever peoples. Thus, we saw earlier how Pipes makes a point far too strongly when he moves from a legitimate warning about the totalitarian violent threats of the Islamic movement to a gross and inflammatory generalization that "all" Islamists "must be considered potential killers."[44] The very language construction deeply offends and contradicts peacemaking efforts. The point that the militant Islamic movement is today seeking to dominate the world is obviously true. But at the same time, I do sympathize with the position of the Arab American Institute (AAI) that Pipes is a bigot. The Arab American Institute, which is "committed to the civic and political empowerment of Americans of Arab descent" criticizes Pipes sharply: "Time and time again, he has used his voice to denigrate, ridicule and malign Arab Americans, American Muslims, Arabs and Islam itself." In fact, they suggest that he displays "a bizarre obsession with all things Arab and Muslim . . . hatred and bigotry."[45] The Council on American-Islamic Relations calls Pipes "the nation's leading Islamaphobe." A profile of Pipes on the Web site "MotherJones.com" says that he frequently declares that "militant American Muslims intend to mount a second American revolution and impose Islamic law," and in this connection he has criticized President Bush for referring to Islam overall as a "peaceful religion," for example in his post-September 11 address to the nation.[46]

I am personally so frightened and object so strongly to Pipes' statement that *all* Muslims must be considered potential killers that I have to agree with the criticisms. Yet, as I said, I will also continue to read and draw from his analyses. Pipes is a significant person. It was mentioned earlier that, by nomination of President George W. Bush, he was on the Board of the U.S. Institute of Peace, an institution which I dearly love and respect, and for whose establishment I campaigned hard years ago as a young peace researcher. I too would have opposed Pipes' appointment, but I will also pay attention to his learned views.

In another article the same year, Pipes made his important point less offensively. In response to statements that are heard periodically, including by the U.S. government, that "the vast majority of Muslims do not condone terrorism," he wrote:

> *Well, sort of . . .*
>
> But those spokesmen are not telling the whole story, for Islamists consider suicide as not just legitimate, but highly commendable when undertaken for reasons of *jihad* (holy war). Going into war knowing with the certainty that one will die, they argue, is not suicide (intihar), but martyrdom (istishhad), a much-praised form of self-sacrifice in the path of God, a way to win the eternal affection of the houris in paradise.
>
> A leading Islamist authority, Sheikh Yusuf Qaradawi, recently explained the distinction this way: attacks on enemies are not suicide operations, but "heroic martyrdom operations" in which the kamikazes act not "out of hopelessness and despair, but are driven by an overwhelming desire to cast terror and fear into the hearts of the oppressors."
>
> In other words, Islamists find suicide for personal reasons abominable, suicide for jihad admirable.[47]

Jewish writers (like myself) have every right to be heard respectfully, while at the same time it is only fair that we should be recognized as possibly inclined to some prejudiced negative view of Islam as such, along with the legitimacy of our opposition to the strong linkages that do exist between Islam and terrorism, for we have been frequent victims of Islamic killings. Jews naturally also are not likely to be among those who will appreciate any heroism and legitimacy in terrorism from any source, since the preponderance (but not the totality) of Jewish tradition has always been on the side of reverence for life and prohibition of murder.

From within Jewish ranks, a well-thought-of professor of Jewish thought at the Hebrew University of Jerusalem, himself an orthodox Jew, Aviezer Ravitzky, has cautioned adamantly against Jewish or Israeli participation in any demonization of Islam. He warns that Israel must not strengthen the religious dimension of its political battles with neighboring Islamic countries, nor dare it contribute to the impression of an "ultimate conflict" between civilizations. Otherwise, Ravitzky warns, the Palestinian-Israeli political conflict can be transformed into a deadly religious conflict. Ravitzky seems motivated most of all by a wish to protect Israel from a Muslim crusade, but as a peace-caring person, he also seems to be seeking to contribute to the possibility of avoiding a global clash between violent Islamic countries and the rest of the world.

Nonetheless, because he is a rational man, he cannot help but acknowledge how very real Muslim violence already has become:

> True, the murderous form that radial Arab Islam is currently assuming before our eyes is suffocating hope from one minute to the next. True, Muslim nations and Muslim groups are deeply involved in the violent conflicts that are raging around the world and not only in our region. And this, after all, is the declared aim of the leaders of extreme Islam: to divide the world into two polar camps that will be locked in a battle to the death—the great Muslim "nation" and the "Jewish-Crusader alliance" (in bin Laden's words).[48]

Personally, I do not believe Jews can remove themselves from this battle, if only because Israel and the Jews have been chosen by the Muslims among their favored enemies. But I also do not believe that Jews *should* remove themselves from the larger battle between protectors of the lives of all peoples and the transnational genocidal terrorists. In my opinion, this is a battle that cannot and should not be sidestepped by anyone.

Robert Wistrich, born in Kazakhstan and educated in London, is a Jew who is now resident in Israel and is also a professor at Hebrew University where he directs the Center for the Study of Antisemitism, to whom I also referred earlier. He is a distinguished scholar of politics and philosophy who has written extensively on subjects such as the philosophy of Nietzsche and fascist thinking. Writing after September 11, Wistrich projects the central belief system of the Islamic terrorists as far more than a battle for self-defense against a nasty global enemy, but as an ideology that is similar to the ideology of previous fascists, like the Nazis, of hatred, anti-Semitism, and projective conspiracy against all the "other" "godless" antagonists of Islam. Note also Wistrich's frightening observation that much of the Muslim world, that is, also Muslims who are not themselves active terrorists, view the suicide bombing murders of September 11 with acclaim:

> The Islamic terrorist perpetrators of this act, like the Nazis and fascists 60 years ago, speak a language of unquenchable hatred for the Jewish people, for America and the West, indeed for civilization itself. They, too, enjoy—at least in the Muslim

world—the acclamation of significant sectors of the population . . . The conspiracy theory at its heart, which links plutocratic capitalism, international freemasonry, Zionism, and Marxist Communism, is almost identical with the mythical structure of Nazi anti-Semitism. For contemporary jihadists, a "Judaized" America and Israel, together with heretical, secular Muslim regimes are the godless spearhead of these dark occult forces that seek to destroy Islam and undermine the cultural identity of Muslim believers.[49]

A report in the *London Daily Telegraph* following September 11 also offered the conclusion that on the whole, at least in the world of what might be called Saudi-affiliated Islam, the radicals who want a violent struggle against their antagonists (Americans and Israelis at the top of their list) have won out in Islamic culture, and as such also have adopted suicide bombers as heroic and martyrs.

Suicide operations caught the Arab imagination in 1983, when Lebanese Shi'ite Muslim guerrillas trained by Iran blew up 241 American servicemen and 58 French paratroops in a simultaneous operation in Beirut. The technique—and the cult of martyrdom characteristic of the Shi'ite branch of Islam—was transferred to the Palestinians, leading to a series of bombs in Israeli buses and market places. Islam condemns suicide as a way to hell and damnation . . . Islamic scholars have debated whether blowing yourself up constitutes suicide or martyrdom. Some Saudi scholars continue to denounce suicide as a sin, but the argument has been won by the radicals who see it as a legitimate means of jihad, or holy struggle. The term "suicide bomber" has been replaced with "martyrdom operation." Such is the prestige of the suicide bomber that no one in the Palestinian territories would dare to raise a voice against the practice.[50]

THE DEADLY VIOLENCES OF ISLAM AGAINST ISLAM

One would wish at least that the differentiation between Shi'ite and Sunni would give us a division of the Islamic world along an axis that would differentiate between a group who espouses martyrdom-terrorism and a group who does not, but alas it is not so. The division between these two giant branches of Islamic faith in itself is a repeated focus of enormous hatred, battles, persecution, and full-blown murderous terrorism of one against the other. Islamic suicide bombers explode not only against westerners, Americans, and Jews-Israelis. Much of the suicide bombing also concerns open warfare and terrorism between Sunni Muslims and Shi'ite Muslims. Although only 10–15 percent of the world's 1.3 billion Muslims are Shi'ites, that means a not-at-all-insignificant 130 to 200 million people. The Shi'ites are a majority in several countries including Iran and Iraq, they are the largest religious community in Lebanon, and a sizable minority in a number of countries including Saudi Arabia.

Wahhabi Sunnis, who dominate Saudi religious affairs, have declared Shi'ites "infidels," the magic word we have seen which justifies murder. Anti-Shi'ite beliefs have spread to South Asia, Afghanistan, and Pakistan. In the latter two countries, there have been widespread killings of Shi'ites including bombing of their mosques. According to one analyst, many of the Sunni militants are linked with Taliban and Al-Qaeda. "It is a network of Arabs and non-Arabs, South Asians and Middle Easterners, Wahhabis and non-Wahhabis. And if these men succeed in starting a sectarian civil war, it will quickly spread beyond Iraq's borders."[51]

In Saddam Hussein's Iraq, despite the Shi'ite majority, it was the Sunni who held the ruling hand for all the years of Saddam's rule, and many Shi'ites found their way into the numerous genocidal mass graves of Saddam that were discovered after his downfall. In postwar Iraq, with the fall of the Sunni power as governors, it was at first both Sunni resistance to the American occupation and to the emergence of the Shi'ites in positions of significance that were being attacked repeatedly, including by devoted suicide bombers. See, for example, the devastating coordinated attacks in both Baghdad and Karbala during religious ceremonies on March 3, 2004.

One year after the United States-led force invaded Iraq and overthrew Saddam Hussein, Iraq moved on to the center stage of suicide bombing in the world. Up until March 20, 2004, there were 660 killed in suicide bombings, which, for example, is far more than in the three and a half years of Palestinian suicide attacks against Israel where, just about to the same date, the death toll had been 474 (including the bombers) in 112 cases of Palestinian suicide bombings. Press reports note that not all suicide-bombing attacks in Iraq are to be credited specifically to Al-Qaeda. Also involved were not only Saddam regime loyalists, but also terrorists belonging to Ansar al-Islam—a group believed linked to Al-Qaeda, foreigners who had come into Iraq with their agendas for fighting against the presence of the infidel United States and Britain and the possible stabilization of a democratic regime in the Arab world, and Sunni fighting Shi'ites.[52] Adding to the bizarre and deadly situation, there then also emerged another deadly intifada led by an anti-American Shi'ite cleric, Moktada al-Sadr, who organized huge militias and launched powerful attacks on U.S. coalition forces. According to one analyst, al-Sadr was trying to oppose the power of another Shi'ite political group that was led by a rival cleric, which has been chosen to head the Iraqi government the United States proposed to install a few months later.[53]

What a mess! Together, there emerges a frightening array of ever-splintering groups of Islamic "extremists" and "fundamentalists" of all sorts who share not only their wish to destabilize a possible American-sponsored regime along some-what democratic lines, but also are celebrating a blessed opportunity to fight and kill. For too many, like the practitioners and perpetrators of Nazism, Stalinism, and Khmer Rouge all of which became cultures of killing, today's terrorism in contemporary Islam, including suicide bombings, is also a culture-wide way of life so to speak for large parts of the population.

So we return to the original question framing this discussion: Is all of Islam to be condemned for the growing worldwide terrorism issuing from Muslims?

God forbid.

But this does not mean that we do not face the presence of a radical Islamic philosophy and culture of violence and jihad in many large parts of Islamic culture. The fact is that there is widespread transnational genocidal terrorism by many Islamic groups in many societies around the world.

It is long past time for Muslim individuals, mosques, religious leaders, and communities to take believable and firm stands against suicide bombing and terrorism, certainly beginning with Muslim citizens in democratic countries. The facts of death in our world today make it legitimate, and not a disgraceful act of prejudice, to attribute to worldwide Islam as a whole great dangers of murderous violences, and to intensify security procedures based on these objective facts without their representing bias or discrimination.

Again here I come under the attack of one of my liberal critics, in whose opinion, after I had been "much better" in acknowledging that there are pro-life forces in Islam, I lost it all again here in a "take away message that is unbelievable." I don't think so at all. It is the same issue that is dogging us over and over again. Does respect for another religion mean denying the history and current patterns of violences in its name by many of its adherents? Are the very tangible dangers of suicide bombers not to be real for democrats and liberals too? I certainly think so as I meet friends who have lost dear ones in suicide bombings in my city, or as I step into a restaurant to dine in Jerusalem, or board airplanes outside of Israel in different parts of the world.[54]

Irshad Manji, a Muslim, author of *The Trouble with Islam*, says that we need to be very careful not to let our democratic principles and convictions trap us into being irreparably damaged by totalitarians who exploit democratic openness as an entry point for more attacks.

> As Westerners bow down before multiculturalism we anesthetize ourselves into believing that anything goes. We see our readiness to accommodate as a strength—even a form of cultural superiority (though few will admit that). Radical Muslims, on the other hand, see our inclusive instincts as a form of corruption that makes us soft and rudderless. They believe the weak deserve to be vanquished ... We know the dangers of taking Islam literally. By now we should understand the peril of taking tolerance literally.[55]

Obviously, in democratic societies, it is also crucial to conduct such security operations within the law. The fight against terrorism needs to be conducted respectfully and in a spirit of mutual cooperation with the people being investigated, however much this requires even in democracies going against the natural trend of power to expand and head into the range of sadistic acts. For security today in our world is the protection of all of us, very much including Muslims, against those of us human beings who are rotten enough to take lives. The war that is developing is indeed between a culture of death and a culture of life, and our strongest weapon is a genuine democracy that knows how to defend itself.

Promoting a New Worldwide Constituency for Human Life and Making Suicide Bombing Unattractive and Unacceptable

The double-decker buses of London and the subways of Paris, as well as the co-vered markets of Riyadh, Bali and Cairo, will never be secure as long as the Muslim village and elders do not take on, delegitimize, condemn and isolate the extremists in their midst.   —Thomas Friedman, *International Herald Tribune*[1]

Al Qaeda has become Al Qaedaism . . . What had been a relatively small, conspira-torial organization has mutated into a worldwide political movement . . . Al Qaeda [is] . . . a kind of spectacular terrorism carried to a level of apocalyptic brutality that the world had not before seen.   —Mark Danner, author of *Torture and Truth: America, Abu Ghraib and the War on Terror.*[2]

There should be no illusions about what we are facing in our world. Terrorism in general and suicide bombing in particular are on the rise as the newest forms of destruction, and the dangers of uses of WMD by terrorists and suicide bombers are not insignificant. The commission established by the United States to investigate the attacks of September 11 gave its report in 2004, with a conclusion that an attack "of even greater magnitude . . . is possible, even probable."[3]

Some ideas that have been reported to have been raised in Al-Qaeda circles are reported to include taking over a nuclear launcher in Russia and forcing personnel to fire a nuclear missile at the United States, attacking Jews who live in Iran with gas, and crashing a hijacked airliner into an airport terminal or a city.[4] Al-Qaeda leaders are thought to have considered hijacking twelve airliners in Southeast Asia and blowing them up in midair over the Pacific at the same time that the September 11 attacks took place in New York and Washington. They also are said to have considered crashing planes into American targets in Japan, Singapore, or South Korea.[5]

The world clearly has a long complex battle on its hands.

Suicide bombers, like all terrorists, need to be fought with powerful and clever intelligence and detective work, and by military, police, and other security personnel. A tremendous amount of intelligence work is called for: checking the comings and goings of people at international ports, tracking the organizational structures of groups and institutions that are potentially providing the infrastructure to terrorist groups, monitoring movements of funds between countries, watching for changes in "chatter" on communication nets between suspect groups, and much more. A wide variety of people and devices are needed: security guards (what a growth industry for our times!), labyrinth-corridor entrances to public buildings, metal detectors, body checks, I.D. checks, special antiterrorist police, antibomb squads, explosive-sniffing dogs, roadblocks, and more and more innovative means for identifying and heading off incipient terrorist activities are now essential means of self-defense for civilized people in our times.[6]

Still, in the long run, what is no less needed and could even prove to be more effective in limiting suicide bombers are ways of mobilizing greater criticism and rejection of suicide bombers in the minds of people around the globe, as opposed to their being welcomed, honored, supported, or even "understood" by too many peoples, nations, and religions. Marc Sageman was a CIA case officer for several years in Afghanistan who then became a political scientist and psychiatrist. He collected data on 400 terrorists and concluded that 75 percent came from the upper or middle class, 90 percent from intact families, 63 percent had gone to college, 75 percent were professionals or semi-professionals—most of them in engineering and science professions, 73 percent were married. "These are the best and brightest of their societies in many ways." He also noted that at the time they first joined the terrorist culture, they were not very religious. Sageman concluded that there is no "profile" to the bombers, "just" similar pathways to joining the jihad.[7] My own reading is that Sageman has, in fact, put his finger on a profile after all. Many of the terrorists are young capable people, who are educated, ready for a conventional work life, but who are hungry for meaning and/or group connection and solidarity, and who are exposed to a cultural message that honors violence not only as legitimate but as a fulfillment of a life's purpose. The powerful conclusion that is suggested by such data is that the antidote to terrorism must not only be a resolute intelligence or police or military battle to head off and defeat as many terrorists as possible, but a cultural battle to win over hearts and minds to commitments to life. We need to advance the values of antiviolence and nonviolence, and the treasuring of lives of human beings of all ages and races. These are positive cultural values that need to compete with the automaticity of cultural idealization of power, conquest, warmaking, and empires of destruction.

It is Sageman's overall conclusion that interests me the most at this point in our work. As several others have concluded, Sageman observes that on a political level Al-Qaeda today is more of a network than an organization, and that the network "is held together by a vision," of a fundamentalist Islamic state which Sageman calls "the Salafi state." He therefore concludes:

> A fuzzy, idea-based network really requires an idea-based solution. The war of ideas is very important and this is one we haven't really started to engage yet.[8]

It is to a war of constructive ideas that I seek to go in the conclusion of this book.

THE LIMITS OF FREE SPEECH FAVORING SUICIDE BOMBING IN A DEMOCRATIC AND SANE SOCIETY

A fascinating and important problem that in some sense continues our discussion of whether or not suicide bombers are to be considered disturbed is whether or not a democratic society can allow free speech in favor of suicide bombing.

Say it is many years ago in the 1930s in a democratic country like the United States, and the police overhear a person giving a talk to a crowd in a park in which he preaches ramming airplanes into tall buildings, or poisoning the water supply of a city and bringing about thousands or millions of deaths. It is quite likely that the speaker would have been picked up and taken to the emergency room of a psychiatric hospital. Once seen in the psychiatric context, there is no doubt at all in my mind that he would have been diagnosed as a paranoid schizophrenic with persecutory-homicidal delusions, and would have been put away.

Nonetheless, even many years ago, in democratic countries, *IF* said speechmaker was the designated Official Speaker of a legitimate political party or even an up-and-coming protest group, and certainly if his talk was in the context of a proper rally of his party or group, more than likely he would *not* have been taken in for psychiatric observation. The Hitlers of yesteryear, the neo-Nazis of today, the sympathizers and supporters of Stalinist Communism in its time, or the fiery Islamic imams of today who preach the overthrow of the infidel Western world for the most part are granted for the longest time (too long a time, in my judgment) the protection of free speech in democracies.

In their devotion to the magnificent principle of free speech, democracies often make the mistake of going too far to an extreme that fails to discriminate when free speech is being used to legitimate deadly violences, as well as to overthrow the very democracy itself and replace it with a totalitarian way of life. Messages approving or even that actually call for terrorist actions may be allowed to be delivered to large publics without being interrupted on the grounds of being an illegal incitement to violence that is unacceptable to the community, a disturbance of the peace, and/or an evident psychiatric disturbance. It can take democracies a very long time before they awaken to the real threats of fundamentalists who clearly intend violence, terrorism, and revolution to destroy as many people as possible and, of course, also to destroy the democracy. Terrorists unhesitatingly use the principles of democracy to destroy the very structure that was created to protect the rights of everyone including them.

Robert A. Pape, author of *Dying to Win: The Strategic Logic of Suicide Terrorism,* compiled a database of 315 suicide bombers during the period 1980–2003. He says "Democracies are uniquely vulnerable to suicide terrorists."[9]

Michael Rubin, the editor of the *Middle East Quarterly*, has concluded that dictators and terrorists have taken notice and adopted some of the rhetoric of democracy while continuing in their ways of making death. He warns that, "The sincerity of terrorists should no more be trusted than that of dictators. They may adopt democratic rhetoric, but words are cheap." Rubin gives an example how in Egypt American diplomats were holding talks with the Muslim Brotherhood (the terrorist group that assassinated Sadaat and has killed thousands of others), but not long after the diplomats' visit the terrorists detonated a bomb in a popular market and sprayed a tourist bus with bullets. According to Rubin, terrorist mastermind, Abu Musab al-Zarqawi, cited American outreach as evidence of weakness: "The severe blows you deal this enemy, by the grace of Allah, forced America to beg for negotiations," al-Zarqawi said.[10]

In a democracy all groups have a wide range of rights to speak their ideas, but this should only be up to a point that falls short of espousing and inciting violence. Many liberal supporters of terrorists who respect the sometimes-legitimate grievances of the terrorists completely miss the point that if the terrorists have their day, there will be no more machinery for democratic discussion and protest thereafter, and that the very same liberal supporters themselves will be happily eliminated!

Of course, there are very serious dangers of acting against threats to public safety prematurely or overly severely, certainly without proper legal safeguards. The horrifying McCarthy period in the United States is an example of a runaway fascist political process that literally destroyed many lives and damaged the fabric of American society for many years. For many of us, it was also a vital lesson about the very real dangers of a possible sudden eruption of fascism even in a great democracy, and the need to be constantly vigilant against totalitarian processes and leaders. Senator Joseph McCarthy was the mad-hatter Hitlerian-figure who was a devastating threat to democratic institutions. But it was to take no less than several *years* before public awareness in America could take in that McCarthy's totalitarian tactics were aided and abetted by a long list of fascist liars and demagogues, including the-then superdangerous director of the F.B.I., J. Edgar Hoover, along with Special U.S. Attorney, Roy Cohn, and many others on all levels of the government who are always there, in every bureaucracy, waiting to serve and even to outdo their totalitarian masters in their policies when these gain power in society.

Every democratic society that faces actual threats of terrorist violences necessarily must also face very difficult, and to some extent unsolvable, tensions between its democratic values and the need to protect oneself against the dangerous evils that issue from murderous revolutionaries and terrorists who are really out to kill citizens as well as to destroy the structure of democracy.

Today, in the wake of September 11, there are many Americans who are concerned that new security procedures will violate too many basic human rights, especially of Muslim-Americans, but not only them. Liberal thinkers and caring people are often in great pain about these situations. A good person can wish so much for a decent world that he or she wants to believe that people cannot be so bad that they will destroy other human beings. The argument becomes that if only the terrorists will be treated fairly and respectfully, they will do us no harm. Unfortunately, this is not true. Fascists and terrorists go on with their schemes to destroy life and to take over society no matter how well they are treated. The police and army forces then begin to act against the terrorists, but inevitably they make mistakes in misidentifying innocent people, and inevitably they too use excessive and even stupidly brutal force and violate many civil rights. The next thing that happens is that good people become upset at the police excesses as they should, and now they also try to explain away the terrorists' dangerous actions as their understandable responses to the society's oppression and excessive brutality against them. But they are wrong. Protests against the authorities' degradations, brutality, and violations of human rights are very important and require a full hearing, but the harshness and brutalities of the society defending itself are *not* the causes of fascist and terrorist threats. The terrorists are an evil force in their own right.

Following the four suicide bomber attacks on London on July 7, 2005, which were followed by four unsuccessful attempts at replicating the attacks on July 21 in all of which the explosive material failed to blow up (and which gave Scotland Yard an unusual opportunity to arrest and interrogate living suicide bombers), the United Kingdom's leader, Prime Minister Tony Blair, announced a series of major new proposals to curtail terrorism at its source. After many years of reports of imams in the United Kingdom preaching terror and violence, and mosques serving as gathering points if not as training centers for future terrorists like Richard Reid, the "airplane shoe bomber" who had been arrested trying to blow himself up on a plane, the prime minister proposed new measures to close mosques and to deport imams who fostered hatred and violence. Blair said he would outlaw Islamic organizations and that people "whose activities or views pose a threat to Britain's security" would be kept out of Britain. The Prime Minister said that Britain needed to amend its human rights legislation to enable deportations of non-Britains with known terrorist sympathies, a policy that at present is forbidden under the European Human Rights Convention. Blair said the grounds for deportation would include "fostering hatred, advocating violence to further a person's beliefs or justifying or validating such violence."[11]

> Coming to Britain is not a right. And even when people have come here, staying here carries with it a duty. That duty is to share and support the values that sustain the British way of life. Those that break that duty and try to incite hatred or engage in violence against our country and its people have no place here.[12]

The prime minister also called for new measures aimed at Islamic Web sites, bookstores, and centers that preach violence. "Let no one be in any doubt," he said. "The rules of the game are changing."[13]

Irshad Manji, whom we have previously met as a Muslim woman who publicly calls for major reforms in Islamic culture, commented very positively on the announcement of new measures: "For a European leader, Prime Minister Tony Blair of Britain has done something daring. He has given notice not just to the theocrats of Islam, but also to the theocracy of tolerance."[14]

THE PROBLEM OF ISLAMIC PREACHING AND EDUCATION FOR TERROR AND SUICIDE BOMBING

A satiric article was published in the London daily *Al-Hayat* by the Egyptian playwright Ali Salem, in which he sarcastically suggests opening a kindergarten to teach terrorist values:

> I will say to them: "Kids, don't believe that others worship the same god as we; they are infidels who worship other deities. You must always think of ways to force them to worship whom we worship—the others are foreigners, and foreigners are infideis. The task for which I am preparing you is to purge the world of 'them.' This is your holy message: Don't believe the story that they stick to about freedom, democracy, human rights, progress, and civilization; they are liars and deceivers. They hate us because we are better, greater and stronger than they.
>
> "Dear children: Hate the beaches. Hate the flowers and the roses. Hate the wheat fields. Hate the trees. Hate music. Hate all manner of artistic, literary, or scientific endeavor. Hate tenderness. Hate reason and intellect. Hate your families and your countrymen. Hate others—all others. Hate yourselves. Hate your teachers. Hate me. Hate this school. Hate life and everything in it."
>
> "Go on, get to class."[15]

Anyone who reads the news and certainly anyone who has made a serious inquiry into the ways of Islamic culture will know that there are longstanding powerful themes at work in the culture of violence as a way of life. Moreover, the violence is accompanied by a great deal of degradation of the enemy as no less an object of the violence than killing the other or winning a battle. Americans in Iraq, civilians as well as soldiers, have been the objects of vicious terror attacks as well as joyful displays of severing of heads and dismembering of bodies. Saddam was previously legendary for sending home to the family of one of his victims their body parts in a plastic bag—with a government bill for services rendered to boot. (In general, Saddam had a flair for combining state ceremony and services with his flagrant cruelties, for example, shooting members of his cabinet or the parliament during meetings and having their bodies hauled off conspicuously as unforgettable lessons in civics.) Israel has also been the site of brutal Palestinian mob lynching and mob dismemberment of living and dead soldiers. It is an old tradition in Muslim culture. One remembers, for example, the practices of Arab killers in the previous century who would leave the dead victim with his cut-off sexual organ in his mouth (this is not to say that genital mutilation is exclusive to this society, of course). That will teach him something or other, and certainly, it will teach, degrade, debase, and terrify his living countrymen.

The larger meaning of these aspects of Muslim culture is that in many places in Islam, violence is honored, valued, celebrated, and lionized.

Of course, we in the West too have more than our share of problems with violence in our culture where our rates of domestic violence, criminal violence, and murders, certainly in American cities, are frightening and a disgrace. In a way such violence is our way of life. According to many critics including myself, we are also world experts in mass media displays and literally education for a wide variety of cruelties and violences.[16]

On the other hand, normatively and legally, for the most part in the West, one is not allowed to incite violences and even the cruelty of warfare is not to be practiced with open celebrations of or displays of sadism. There is, of course, an age-old sense of triumph and victory in defeating one's military enemies, but open display of joy at their deaths and certainly torture and murder of the enemy's civilians and innocent bystanders are not generally allowed. When sadism and celebration of violence are exposed, as they were by the U.S. troops in Iraq, they are often punished.

My forever-imaginative mind suddenly races off to a fantasy of a messianic world in which both Islam and the West would regulate their respective media promotions of violence. In the West, this would mean not having TV and movies pandering to violence in daily life and portrayals of criminality as an almost superhonorable profession. In Islam it would mean changing the basic educational messages and images for children on TV—including open-and-shut praise of violence against infidels, stopping widespread practices of recruiting children as shahids, and canceling the heroic status of shahids of all ages. Would that the West and Islam could make a deal!

I continue my free associations with an image of a confrontation at high noon between a Mafia killer from our West and an Islamic suicide bomber drawing guns on each other. My mind asks playfully whether this could be the predicted war between our civilizations? I honestly think I'd like them to shoot one another!

Much of Islamic culture supports violence qua martyrdom. The following is a newspaperman's description in 2001:

> In Hamas-run kindergartens, signs on the walls read: "The children of the kindergarten are the shaheeds (holy martyrs) of tomorrow." The classroom signs at Al-Najah University in the West Bank and at Gaza's Islamic University say, "Israel has nuclear bombs, we have human bombs."
>
>   At an Islamic school in Gaza City run by Hamas, 11-year-old Palestinian student Ahmed ... [says], "I will make my body a bomb that will blast the flesh of Zionists,

the sons of pigs and monkeys . . . I will tear their bodies into little pieces and cause them more pain than they will ever know."

"Allahu Akbar," his classmates shout in response: "God is great."

"May the virgins give you pleasure," his teacher tells, referring to one of the rewards awaiting martyrs in paradise. Even the principal smiles and nods his approval."[17]

The sporting lives of many children in Palestine have been devoted to "little leagues" of preparing to be terrorists and suicide bombers when they grow up—obviously not necessarily to a very advanced age.

- In the Palestinian Authority, each of twenty-four soccer teams was given the name of an honored terrorist or of a terrorist group, such as the suicide bomber's wing of Hamas.
- A tournament for 12-year-old boys was named after the suicide bomber who murdered Israelis gathered to celebrate the Passover Seder at a hotel.
- Palestinian summer camps also carry the names of suicide bombers, let alone are hotbeds of celebration and role-play rehearsals of the roles of shahid suicide bombers.
- Palestinian kids play or trade cards celebrating various terrorists, including the indomitable Osama bin Laden.[18]

What is also clear is that the games of violence are deadly real and not some split off arena of fantasy for dear little children to discharge their aggressions and express their religious and national loyalties. One of the major defenses of our own Western world with our horrible diet of violences is as if to assign the media a role of a fantasy outlet. Up to a point this does work. Our media viewers are expected to be sufficiently mentally healthy to know the difference between fantasy and reality—*woops, so sorry, those kids in Columbine forgot!* One has to be very foolish not to realize that American media do pollute us with violence, but at least they are officially intended as entertainment and fantasy. In Palestine and some other places in the Arab world, the kids know they are expected to be terrorists for real.

Dr Eyad Sarraj, the director of the Gaza Community Mental Health Program (GCMHP), warns that children in the territories now dream of martyrdom, or *shahada,* 'the way normal kids in the U.S. dream of going to Disneyland' . . . Suicide bombing is also a short-cut to glory for kids, who have a fuzzy notion of mortality . . . According to an opinion poll conducted in April by the Bethlehem-based Palestinian Center for Research and Cultural Dialogue, 76.5 percent of Palestinians support suicide bombings within the Green Line . . . Itamar Marcus argues the Palestinian Authority has been consciously feeding this cult of martyrdom. The director of the Jerusalem-based Palestinian Media Watch, has over 7,000 video cassettes of broadcasts—news programs, politically charged music videos and pastiches of random violence—recorded from Palestinian Authority TV since 1997. . . .

Some call for outright martyrdom. One music video broadcast some 500 times in 2001 shows a child surrounded by his playmates presenting his father with a note telling him that he will become a *shahed*.

In 2002, Palestinian TV ran a video clip starring Muhammad al-Dura, the famous 12-year-old killed accidentally in a September 2000 gun-battle between Israeli soldiers and Palestinian gunmen in Gaza. In the video, a child actor playing al-Dura runs in what is meant to be Paradise and beckons little children to join him. There is a lit-up ferris wheel in the distance—shades of Disneyland.[19]

When Israelis are murdered, Palestinian children have been given candies to celebrate, and candy vendors sell toy hand grenades in Palestinian streets.[20] Exhortations, instructions, and celebration of violence are the language of the leadership for people of all ages. Fiery, ominous Abdel Aziz Rantisi, who replaced the assassinated Sheikh Yassin as the head of Hamas before himself being assassinated by Israel, had promised, "Bodies will continue to blow up in the depth of the Zionist entity."[21]

The funerals of martyrs are the biggest and best shows in town, truly wonderful occasions for crowd joy and recommitment to more and more cruel vengeance. Hundreds of thousands of the overall relatively small population of Palestinians can pour into the streets for a kind of frenzied celebration of the death of the martyr and a fervor of fellowship in intentions of revenge. It is certainly as "good" a crowd as at any World Series game. Even Yasser Arafat's funeral, which was planned as a communal ceremony, got so out of hand that Palestinian authorities had to steal the body away for quick burial and canceled all the planned ceremonies and talks.

The recruitment of more and more terrorists is, of course, an important task for Muslim cultures and nations that are engaged in active terrorism. The *London Daily Telegraph* carried the following description of what they called "bin Laden's recruitment video":

Osama bin Laden's recruitment video ... is a great propaganda film—the kind that you can't get out of your head ... He uses the most sophisticated western film-making techniques: It's as if Guy Ritchie, Sylvester Stallone and Spielberg have banded together to make jihad, the movie ... In slow motion, and in time to the music, Israeli soldiers beat two women with sticks, until one falls to the ground. The soldiers carry off screaming men, as if they are so much rubbish. Then, they strike a little boy with such force that he crumples to the ground. These images, and similar ones, are repeated over and over, until the violence seems unending ... Throughout, he is screaming tearfully over the music: "Your sister goes to bed honourable and wakes up violated, raped by the Jews."[22]

Possibly the most powerful source of inspiration and education for violence in the Muslim world are the imams regarding whom we opened this discussion of what the boundaries of free speech should be in democracies under attack by terrorism. The imams preach blood-curdling, God-mandated-and-blessed calls to destroy the infidel Americans and Zionists. Allah becomes the fuehrer in these pronouncements who commands, leads, and blesses his devoted emissaries to dispense God's terror and death.

For millions of us in this world there is an archaic power to religious imagery. Religious motifs inspire us with experiences of fellowship and reaffirmations of our sense of identity with our religious and often also our ethnic community. From our earliest childhoods, through our participation in our mosques, churches, and synagogues, many of us are imbued with an almost overpowering sense of awe about what our gods promise us and demand of us. Reactivation of the power of these early imagoes in later years can touch the heart of many a confirmed secularist, let alone the hearts of believers and practicing members of the faith. Moreover, in a largely traditional society, excluding oneself from identifying with and practicing the consensual faith has serious political or practical consequences as well.

The following are excerpts from an official Friday sermon on Palestinian Authority (PA) TV, on May 13, 2005. The preacher is Sheik Ibrahim Mudeiris, a paid employee of the Authority:

> Jews are responsible for all wars and conflicts . . . Do not ask what Germany did to the Jews but what the Jews did to Germany. True, the Germans killed and burned Jews but the Jews exaggerate the numbers to gain propaganda advantages and sympathy.[23]
>
> Israel is a cancer spreading through the body of the Islamic nation, and the Jews are a virus resembling AIDS, from which the entire world suffers . . . We have ruled the world before, and by Allah, the day will come when we will rule the entire world again. The day will come when we will rule America. The day will come when we will rule Britain and the entire world—except for the Jews. The Jews will not enjoy a life of tranquility under our rule, because they are treacherous by nature, as they have been throughout history. The day will come when everything will be relieved of the Jews—even the stones and trees which were harmed by them. Listen to the Prophet Muhammad, who tells you about the evil end that awaits Jews. The stones and trees will want the Muslims to finish off every Jew.[24]

Such venom spews forth from many an imam in today's mosques around the world, and any number of the case histories of terrorists—including some of the September 11 suicide bombers—record the apparently definitive roles of zealous jingoistic imams in forging the readiness, will, and courage of the terrorists to embark on their deadly missions. Such imams appear not only in Islamic countries but also in many countries of the West, including the United Kingdom, Germany, and France, in effect in all countries where there is a Muslim population.

Marc Sageman, whom we saw earlier had studied 400 terrorists, concluded that they had "clustered around ten mosques worldwide that generated about 50 percent of my sample. If you add . . . two institutions in Indonesia, twelve institutions generated 60 percent of my sample."[25]

Steven Stalinsky, the Executive Director of the Middle East Media Research Institute (MEMRI), filed a report on the contents of thirty major Palestinian sermons from 2000–2003. Each khatib (preacher) is a paid employee of the Palestinian Authority. According to Stalinsky's report, the sermons, which are broadcast live every Friday at noon from mosques under control of the PA, and are shown on PA television, all had the following common themes: calls for the destruction of the United States—which is described as the leader of a Crusader [Christian] war against Islam, honoring shahids and extolling the reward of the martyrs, educating children to martyrdom, hatred of Jews and Israel, and calls for the killing of Jews.[26]

As we have seen, it is only relatively recently that the subject of the preachings of imams has begun to receive the attention of Western governments, some of which have begun to monitor the preachings of imams and to institute legal proceedings for the deportation of extremists who preach jihad violences. At stake here is a fundamental issue in the theory of democracy and free speech. Should there be any limits on the rights of anyone to free speech in democracies? The purists believe that truth will come out, that a free play of all ideas in a democracy will lead to the disgrace and rejection of antidemocratic prejudices, and that in the long run *not* regulating and restricting the free speech of anyone strengthens a democracy. I wish they were right, but I believe they are not. As I wrote earlier, I believe that the ideologues who are committed to the overthrow and eradicating of democracy should not be entitled to use the wonderful democratic safeguards of free speech to destroy democracy.

How the laws for monitoring and enforcing controls over incitements to violence should be worked out with least damage to the key institutions of a democracy is a fascinating subject. I am quite convinced that it is doable, but clearly it needs to be done wisely, with many legal safeguards, and with great care to monitor the dangers of excessive runaway state powers. The process of monitoring has to be done keeping an eye on the real goal, which is to protect freedom and democracy, including freedom of thought, dissent, anger, and protest, and including healthy and troubling attacks on the democratic government because that is the essence of the privilege of free speech. But free speech should not include allowing plots to kill people or to destroy and overthrow the very democratic government and society from which one is benefiting. The fact that regulating bigoted incitements to violence is a tough line to walk does not mean that it can't be done. Committed ideologues of Nazism, Communism, or bin Ladenism must be treated as advocates of criminal terrorism.

Combining free speech with the additional very special freedom to worship one's gods in any way one chooses puts a further heavy weight on the issue of regulating the teachings and sermons of religious leaders. To some extent, in order to honor the value of freedom of religious worship, the borders of free speech deserve to be expanded somewhat in bona fide religious settings, but the principle still applies that holy leaders too cannot be allowed to preach murder, sedition, terrorism, and violent revolution. I am convinced that wise safeguards can be worked out to enforce such a policy within a democratic society without insulting or weakening basic freedoms.

Slowly but surely there is developing a readiness of sane countries to monitor the sermons of imams. Even a nondemocratic Arab country like Saudi Arabia has done so because so much of Islamic terrorism has set as its goal the overthrowing of the Saudi government in order to remake Saudi Arabia more in their fundamentalist image. On March 18, 2004, no less than 900 Saudi imams were suspended for preaching violent jihad. Authorities had previously suspended 1,357 religious officials in the previous year, including 517 imams.[27] Saudi religious authorities also set up training programs for imams to improve the standard of their sermons.

France has "kicked out dozens" of imams since 2001, according to the *New York Times*, which identifies France as having the largest Muslim population on the continent. According to Interior Minister, Dominique de Villepin, France has also resolved to support a government-sponsored Muslim Council to train imams in moderation so as "to encourage the emergence of a tolerant 'French Islam.'" The *Times* story comments that although many other European countries have been more tolerant, the subject of Islamic preachers encouraging terror constitutes "a thorny issue that most countries across Europe are facing as they struggle to fulfill the needs of their growing Muslim populations and protect traditional civil liberties while trying to curb the spread of extremist Islam thought."[28]

In China too, where the government is concerned about a separatist Islamic movement in Xinjiang Ulghur Autonomous Region inhabited by the Ulghurs, who are described as a Turkic people with their own language and distinct Islamic culture, the government has set up a China Islamic Association. The purpose of the association is also a positive one of spreading Islam but in a context of countering "religious extremism," and it is to monitor and supervise sermons by imams. (However, one BBC reporter predicted that the government would fail: "Central Asia's Muslims never did build their mosques and minarets in Chinese style," said the reporter.)[29]

As noted, in democratic countries, but probably especially in the United States where the principle of free speech tends to be held almost inviolate by many people, monitoring raises strong concerns about violating time-honored traditions of freedom of speech and religion. It seems to me that one constructive solution could be to encourage and even legally to require Islamic associations themselves to monitor the preaching of their imams to locate where the contents of their teaching fall on a continuum of understanding and sympathizing with violence as a political and social protest. Personally, I suspect that in the long run some modification of laws of free speech will be needed in respect of incitements of violence. I do not believe that a democracy can actually allow approval of violence and certainly not incitement of violence. My own judgment is that the ability to protect basic freedoms while at the same time monitoring calls for violence and for the destruction of democracy actually will mark a new stage of maturity in the construction of democracies, and in our basic theory of democracy, rather than a setback for freedom.

Finally, there is also a major cultural issue in Muslim countries which spawn prejudice and hatred without necessarily calling immediately for terrorism and violence. In the long run, such prejudice and hatred clearly make for violence some day and some place in the not distant future. Strangely, major cultural contributions to prejudice and violence will be found in some places in the Islamic world where at the same time active terrorism is strongly repressed. Thus, Egypt has disappointingly allowed legitimation of blatant anti-Semitism in several of its universities over the years. Egyptian TV has produced an anti-Semitic series based on the classic anti-Semitic document, *The Protocols of the Elders of Zion*, including a scene "depicting top Jewish leaders ritually slitting the throat and murdering a Christian boy to drain his blood for Passover Matzah" that was aired nightly on prime time throughout the Arab world. The series was described by the Simon Wiesenthal Center as "a multimillion dollar hate extravaganza."[30] At the same time, Egypt, which has seen any number of deadly terrorist attacks including the assassination of its peace-seeking President Sadat, cracks down fiercely on the Muslim Brotherhood.

In the Arab world, primitive anti-Semitic blood libels have been continued at the highest levels of several governments. Long ago 1840 saw a famous blood libel erupt in Damascus. The Jews were accused of murdering a monk and his Muslim servant in order to use the blood to bake matzah for Passover.[31] 150 years later the blood libel continues to be circulated. Thus, in 1986 Syrian Defense Minister Mustafa Tlass published a book about the murder of the monk that repeats the accusation that the Jews murdered the monk to use his blood. In November 2000, a long article appears in the semiofficial Egyptian newspaper, *Al-Ahram*. The author says that he heard stories in his childhood about the Jews using the blood of victims but he never believed them until he read the book by Mustafa Tlass. He then concludes the article with a contemporary update as to Jews' thirst for blood for their Passover food as follows:

> The bestial drive to knead Passover matzahs with the blood of non-Jews is [confirmed] in the records of the Palestinian police where there are many recorded cases of the bodies of Arab children who had disappeared being found, torn to pieces without a single drop of blood. The most reasonable explanation is that the blood was taken to be kneaded into the dough of extremist Jews to be used in matzahs to be devoured during Passover.[32]

The *London Daily Telegraph* reported in November 2003 that a textbook, *Islamic Culture*, originally published by the Palestinian Authority under Arafat in 1994, was being republished in 2003 despite earlier pledges by the Palestinians that it would be replaced. The book is written at the high school level. It explains "jihad" as noble war "for the sake of Allah and for His glory." It explains "shahada" as martyrdom. A suicide bomber sent to kill civilians in Israel is celebrated: "If a Muslim is blessed with shahada and honour, his soul returns to its Creator to live a different life, content with the rewards and honour bestowed upon it, a life of grace thanks to Allah." The frontispiece of the book gives the official imprint of "The Ministry of Education in the Palestinian Authority."[33]

A welcome positive example of constructive government intervention against bigotry in an Arab country was also reported by the Wiesenthal Center. The President of the United Arab Emirates closed down a think tank which carried his name for violating the "principles of interfaith tolerance" by hosting a Saudi professor who alleged that "Jews used human blood to prepare holiday pastries." The same center had also hosted notorious Holocaust deniers, Britain's David Irving, and France's Roger Garaudy.[34] Unfortunately, such stories of constructive government intervention are not yet very common.

THE PRACTICAL IMPLICATIONS OF A MENTAL HEALTH POINT OF VIEW ABOUT SUICIDE BOMBERS

Does mental health have anything to contribute to these issues? Similar to what I said in the earlier discussion about mental health concepts giving us a basis for defining suicide bombing as pathology because it is antilife, I think the answer is very much so.

Using a criterion of respect for life as the essence of mental health, and a significant readiness to destroy life as the essence of mental disturbance, mental health offers a perspective that can guide our responses to dangerous fundamentalist sponsors of terrorism already from their ominous *early* stages. A mental health system that is not afraid to stand for the integrity of human life and against the destruction of human life offers a conceptual framework that defines clearly the sickness and wrongness of ideas and actions that espouse or celebrate murder. I think that it is a healthier basis for society than an overly permissive allowance of "free speech" that legitimates killing, honors it, or even sympathizes with its "cause" in a way that subtly condones killing. A clear-cut mental health definition of incitements to violence as unhealthy and abnormal can provide another source of support in a culture for defining such behaviors as requiring public intervention for the health and safety of the community.

One needs to ask at what point should people get picked up by the police and brought before the courts instead of mental health systems and at what point should people be sent over for diagnosis to the psychiatric emergency rooms? These are important problems which I think can be worked out reasonably, with proper legal safeguards against much of the abusiveness that is seen regularly in *both* the criminal justice and mental health systems, for, sadly, any system that exercises a serious measure of power over people is going to be drawn toward its own potential for excessive and abusive use of power, and requires careful supervision and legal monitoring. Personally, I think the criminal justice system should get the first priority whenever actual overt threats against life and limb are in the offing. In everyday life, practicing psychotherapists who are working with a patient also must call in police when real violence has taken place or is threatening. The management of actual crimes of violence and threats of crimes in a society is first of all the job of the criminal justice professionals. As a practicing psychotherapist myself, I have had occasions when I have called the police to ask them to take away a handgun from an explosively angry man.

I think that we need to develop procedures for the police to be called in whenever a person promotes murder in public talks, whether in public parks, and even in official political rallies, and even in houses of worship. Rather than allow fascists and terrorists to take advantage of a democratic society to spread a virulent message of hate and calls to violence, incitements to violence should be known to be illegal anywhere and everywhere and should be persecuted promptly. The Hitlers, Stalins, bin Ladens, and their supporters should be brought in *early* before the bars of decent societies. Of course, if the killers-to-be know we mean business, they will go underground more readily, which I think is fine in itself since society will benefit by being less polluted by their incitements. The larger benefit is that once it is known that incitements to violence are not allowed by a democratic society, many more ordinary people will be more reluctant to join the terrorists. Without the tacit honor and excitement and a pseudocover of being a legitimate protest group or a kosher religious setting, organizations of violence and terrorist forces of evil will have to go underground where it will be up to police and counterterrorism forces to uncover them and bring them to justice. For the sake of people's lives and the survival of democracy, the earlier they are outlawed the better.

Again let it be entirely clear that in my espousing a get-tough policy against terrorists and suicide bombers and against all active espousals and organizers of violence that exploit our democratic institutions of free speech in the media, in academic bodies, or the freedom to preach in temples, churches, and mosques, I am *not* unaware of the dangers to genuine free speech and democratic debate. Personally, I will redouble my own activity and contributions to a wide range of civil liberties, watchdog groups, and agencies during any critically sensitive period like today when vital personal freedoms have to come under a greater scrutiny and control of authorities. Like all dispensers of power, regulatory authorities in democracies can be counted on to go too far in their abuses of democratic rights. But first and foremost, I want it to be clear that the terrorists and suicide bombers *really* intend to kill us, as they have done, and to kill our democracies, and we are going to be stupid and many of us dead if we don't fight back hard as early as possible.[35]

PROMOTING A CULTURE OF LIFE

The culminating question of our deliberations on suicide bombers is whether we believe there are any possibilities of fighting terrorists and their culture of death on the level of culture.

Fighting on the level of culture and for a change in cultural mindsets is probably more possible in today's world than ever before given the overwhelming penetration of mass media everywhere. Of course, this means getting the messages to reach the target populations with whom we desire to communicate the most—which is far more easily done for Muslim populations living in non-Arab countries, but if well planned is also conceivable in our day and age in the heartlands of Arab countries. It also means employing the wisest, most thoughtful, creative, and culturally-attuned communicators to design the messages and how they are to be delivered, for example, within religious motifs in the voices of respected religious leaders of the society and culture being addressed, through tasteful and appropriate media graphics and music, in the voices of respected and beloved folk heroes of the target culture, in wise appeals to archetypal universal concerns such as for the lives and health of one's children and families (however much such themes are ostensibly pushed aside as irrelevant in warrior societies and cultures that are obsessively committed to propagating their ideology at any expense).

Modern media are increasingly influential in Muslim countries as in the Western world.

A Bahraini author and journalist has pointed out that the specific message of recruitment of suicide bombers also has been globalized. Writing in the Saudi daily *Al-Yawm* in an article titled "The globalization of Islamic suicide," Sawsan Al-Sha'er wrote how the extremist Islamist groups are taking advantage of global communications to recruit suicide bombers. This article was published in May 2005 or shortly before the Al-Qaeda attacks on London, and in it Al-Sha'er predicted the spread of suicide bombers to Britain as well.

> All that is needed for recruiting [suicide bombers] is mass communications, to spread the Islamist slogan. Today, the centers for recruiting [suicide bombers] are no more than websites or satellite television channels, to which the youth connect from internet cafes, scattered throughout our Arab world, that have boosted the still-active traditional recruitment centers concealed in the mosques in far-flung villages ... The websites disseminate emails with murderous pictures and ideas that turn a man into a ticking bomb ... Expect the English 'Islamist' version of exploding suicide bombers soon. This is the globalization of the suicide culture.[36]

bin Laden himself is a global media star. The voice and especially video tapes of bin Laden and his chief assistants are in today's world of suicide bombing and terror dramatic news bulletins that call the world to attention. The appearances of bin Laden and company are virtually star dramatic performances that should not be missed by entertainment buffs, and as- if equivalents to heralded appearances by presidents and other heads of state. One must envy bin Laden for achieving powerful programming on the very low budgets of home-camera productions!

The democratic world that cares for human life needs to mount winning culture campaigns in an opposite direction. We will need to arrive at a real understanding that the battle for evolution of a more decent human being on our planet is deeply important alongside of all the intelligence, police, security, and military measures we must employ against suicide bombers. A cultural campaign will call for the commitment of a great deal of resources, the efforts of many interdisciplinary teams—news, entertainment, public opinion, media, advertising, and public relations professionals, and also culture-knowledgable sociologists and anthropologists.

Earlier we saw a remarkable mini-experiment in treatment where an Israeli doctoral student, Anat Barko, created a process of attempting to influence the thinking of five handlers of suicide bombers whom she was interviewing in their prison cells to experience more of the emotional-moral meanings of the suicide bombings, especially as they involved victims who were innocent members of families. In this small experiment, she reported that there was a perceptible shift in the moral sensitivity of her subjects as a result of the way in which she reinforced more decent human emotions. She concluded that we ought to cultivate broad cultural efforts to enhance humanization of victims by giving them more complete names and faces. She also proposed appeals to mothers in the suicide bombing communities, in this case Palestinian women, to try to get across to them a message of the significance of the lives of innocent family members who would be wiped out in suicide bombings. Barko observed: "It appears that the mother is an unusual key figure [for the handlers of suicide bombers]...When they speak of mother, they themselves are capable of crying, generally out of real sympathy and great appreciation for the mother's day-to-day struggle on behalf of family members."[37]

An apparently Muslim writer in *Newsweek*, Fareed Zakaria, has written that "suicide bombers can be stopped." In his judgment, a clear differentiation needs to be made between the suicide-bombing activists, whom we need to attack and overcome, and the surrounding population from which they come, and that however much the suicide bombers represent them, the larger population needs to be befriended, given social welfare supports, and treated respectfully in genuine negotiations about its political definitions of its grievances. Zakaria proposes that such a policy can lead to suicide bombing giving way to political negotiations and even coexistence.[38]

Two social scientists, Louis and Taylor also echo the above proposal that the West would do best "to divorce the sympathies of Arabs and/or Muslims from the terrorists by showing much greater respect for moderate Muslim norms and by ostentatiously aligning themselves with non-terrorist Muslims."[39] The renowned Egyptian playwright, from whose satire on opening a kindergarten to teach terrorist values we quoted earlier, proposed in a open letter in *Al-Hayat* that

> The Palestinian people now need political leaders—ordinary men and women who yearn for life more than they yearn for death. Political leaders who do not send a child to blow himself up for the sake of Allah, but send him—for the sake of life, the life of their people—to school, in hope that in another few years he will become a person who is useful to his family and his people. The time has come to live, not die, for the sake of our land and our family.[40]

In an extensive Rand Corporation review of the possibilities of greater partnership with a civil democratic Islam, Cheryl Benard analyzes how the concept of democracy is viewed as a possible direction toward which to evolve by less extreme groups in Islam which she defines as "conservative traditionalists," but is intrinsically not acceptable to more fundamentalist Islamic groups whom she defines as "scriptural and radical fundamentalists."

These are the ways democracy is defined by such groups according to Benard:

	Radical Fundamentalists	Scriptural Fundamentalists	Conservative Traditionalists
Democracy	A wrongful creed. Sovereignty and the right to legislate belong to God alone.	Islam is a form of democracy. The West has no right to define what democracy should be like, and the Islamic form is superior because it rests on the only correct and perfect religion.	There is some room for democratic instruments in the interpretation of Islamic practice, in community life and in certain sectors of public life.

Nonetheless, Benard adopts a quite forward-looking policy toward Islam in which she calls for a constructive "nation-building strategy" to modernize Islam. Among the steps she proposes are the following:

- Delegitimize the immorality and hypocrisy of fundamentalists
- Encourage investigative reporting into the corruption of their leaders
- Criticize the flaws of traditionalism, especially its promoting backwardness
- Support the modernists and secularists
- Back the traditionalists tactically against the fundamentalists
- Consistently oppose the fundamentalists
- Assertively promote the values of Western democratic modernity
- Encourage secular civic and cultural institutions
- Focus on the next generation
- Provide aid to states, groups, and individuals with the right attitudes

Once we become committed to a task of promoting new worldwide appreciation of human life and its sacredness, I have little doubt that our fertile and brilliant human imagination can create many intriguing and appealing techniques and programs for getting the message across.

In the following chapter, I am going to propose one such initiative that places at its center the respected leaders of many of our world's religions, including, of course, Islamic religious leaders.

The initiative I propose is intended as a major proposal in its own right, but it is also intended to be one illustration of many possible initiatives that human ingenuity, on behalf of decency, might undertake rather than our letting our civilization go downhill without a battle for life.

A Proposal for a "Worldwide Campaign for Life" by the Leaders of Many Religions and Other World Leaders and Heroes

That the goals of the global jihad movement are transnational has recently been affirmed in a letter by Al Qaeda's No. 2, Ayman al-Zawahiri, in which he calls for the establishment of a caliphate "in the manner of the prophet," to be spread over as many countries as possible. The countries affected by suicide attacks must step up the battle for the hearts and minds of alienated young Muslims.   —Assaf Moghadam, Suicide bombers go global, *Boston Globe* and *International Herald Tribune*[1]

Bangladesh: The Khtab of Baitul Mukarram National Mosque Moulana Obaidul Huq has requested the khatibs and imams of about 300,000 mosques of the country to highlight the prohibition of inhuman acts in Islam, quoting from the Holy Quran and Hadith . . . The khatibs and imams of all mosques in the country will deliver sermons during Friday prayers today pointing out the teachings of Islam, a religion of peace, against violence and suicide bombings . . . He also urged the imams to bring out processions in their respective areas to mobilize public opinion against suicidal bombing.   —*The Independent,* Bangladesh[2]

"So I say it is upon you oh Muslims, and you are neighbours to those who are not Muslims . . . it is upon you to announce that you are free from them in the papers, upon the radio, in the lectures in the masjid, in the Friday sermons, so that your neighbours may know—the non Muslims—that these events from bombings and kidnappings and assassinations are not from Islaam and have nothing to do with Islaam rather they are strange ways even if the people practicing them may be Muslim. So that your neighbours may know that the religion of Islaam is a religion of gentleness . . . "   —Shaykh 'Ubayd al-Jaabiree, a Salafie leader in London[3]

Suicide Bombing and our Commitment to Peace Making—An Emergency Resolution of the 2005 General Assembly of the Christian Church (Disciples of Christ): And if one member suffers, all the members suffer together (I Corinthians 12:26). We remember that Jesus drew innocent children around him to assure them protection and to focus the disciples on the sanctity of life that is known through opening ourselves to the realm of God (Luke 18:15–17).

WHEREAS, there has been a significant increase in suicide bombings . . . with an expansion to target civilians in non-combatant areas; and WHEREAS, suicide bombers reflect the alienation of their communities from other parts of the human family . . . The 2005 General Assembly of the Christian Church (Disciples of Christ) reaffirms our commitment to the World Council of Churches Decade to Overcome Violence opposing violence of all kinds—and a particular form of violence, suicide bombing as offensive against the sanctity of life.[4]

The Pope has called terror a deadly fusion of nihilism and fundamentalism: "The nihilist denies the very existence of truth, while the fundamentalist claims to be able to impose it by force. Despite their different origins and cultural backgrounds, both show a dangerous contempt for human beings and human life, and ultimately for God himself." —Pope Benedict XVI[5]

I want to propose a worldwide campaign for respecting human life that places at its forefront the leaders of a great many of our world's religions standing and working together to change the images people hold of life. This campaign would be worldwide and for all of us on our planet, but obviously I have in mind at this juncture of history especially its potential contribution to Islamic societies and a possible contribution to reducing suicide bombings as well as reducing the prospects or at least the extent of the developing war between cultures.

It seems to me that, come a good Messiah, were the religious leaders of what is today a suicide-bombing culture to issue encompassing and effective prohibitions of suicide bombing as being in violation of their gods, the impact on many suicide bombers could be a very significant one.

In the case of Islam, as we have seen, there are at least two levels of prohibition beckoning from within the culture, one of Islamic religion forbidding the person to act against himself or herself in suicide, and the other the Islamic prohibition against spilling the blood of others unnecessarily. But obviously the political will and possibility of a life-respecting and peace-seeking mode by Islamic religious leaders in the countries which "entertain" suicide bombers have been lacking, and who knows if realistically taking such a position might not put a religious leader's life at risk?

First, one has to know and believe that some degrees of meaningful ecumenical cooperation between non-Islamic faiths and Islam already *does* take place in various contexts in our world.

I am going to tell the stories of no less than four recent ecumenical gatherings in which leaders of many faiths, including Islam and alongside of them Jewish religious leaders—sometimes even in virtual embraces of the two—affirmed with reverence and joy the sacredness of all human life.

As will be seen, the caliber of many of the religious leaders participating was even hugely impressive, including leading imams at the top of their hierarchy and chief rabbis. And yet the overall impact of these congresses has not been great.

I wish there were an interactive computer linkage by which the reader in turn could signal whether he or she knew of each of these congresses with their distinguished clerical participants and how moving and meaningful these events were for them. My hunch is that fewer than half even will have known, let alone that the image product or memory impact that is left today is minimal, despite the fact that quantitatively, the worldwide press coverage of these events was very extensive.

I think one reason for the limited impact is that there were one-time events that achieved coverage at the times they occurred, and then both the press and the very religious groups that participated forgot about them. Another reason these events are little known, I think, is that they were exotic interesting stories about religious leaders that didn't include or touch the little people in their everyday lives. Later in the discussion of our proposal for a worldwide campaign, we will discuss this critical issue of impact on people and cultures.

In the process of describing the first of these ecumenical gatherings, we will also allow ourselves to be drawn aside to follow a fascinating-terrible story of one Islamic religious leader who came, saw, participated in the moving joint declaration of the sacredness of human life, went back home (to Egypt), first withdrew his decent affirmation, and then went on to bestow sacramental blessings on the suicide bombers—especially against the forever-accursed Jewish/Israelis, may their sacred lives be destroyed. This story as a feature-like story is certainly intriguing and a good read, but more than that it will keep us in a down-to-real-life perspective that an effort to bring together heads of religions in itself requires great concentration of efforts, dedication, and wisdom. Promoting world awareness of such developments in order to effect real culture change requires an even greater mobilization of wise leadership, a fascinating array of professional specialists in media communications, public opinion, advertising, psychology, sociology, anthropology, education, political science, world government, the religious leaders themselves, and also world business leaders as well as the economic resources for a sustained winning campaign over a period of several years if not decades— which is very different than a several-day congress even if it receives good media coverage.

I think this real-life story of the profound betrayal of the conference of religious leaders by this cleric also will help to keep us on our toes and help us not to fall asleep as it were during pontifical sermons about the godliness of life. There is a deeply rooted split in most religions between an idealistic and self-comforting "goodness" in prayer for human life in the church and a person's subsequent behavior in a real world where, after praying, many a churchgoer (read mosquegoer, or templegoer as well) decides to send people up in chimneys, blow up people in airplanes, or systematically slaughter one's neighbors with machetes. One of the British-born Muslims who was arrested for the plot to bring down

U.S.-bound planes in August 2006 was described as "a caring and strict devotee of Islam," and according to reporters his friends couldn't possibly countenance [that he] could have been mixed up in anything involving violence. An especially close childhood friend said, "I can't believe it because he was such a good person."[6] I urge the reader to regard the proposal we are developing with a wide-awake realism and not too simply as a comforting fairytale, however well intended, of wolves and lambs joining together in a humane kingdom.

The Alexandria Conference and Declaration (2002)

In January 2002, an inspiring ecumenical event took place in Alexandria, Egypt, when a dozen prominent Christian, Jewish, and Muslim religious leaders issued a joint declaration declaring the killing of innocents a desecration of God's name and defamation of religion.

The three-day gathering deep in the Middle East was organized by a very unlikely religious leader, the United Kingdom's Archbishop of Canterbury, George Carey. The declaration was called the "First Alexandria Declaration of the Religious Leaders of the Holy Land." It included a seven-point pledge by the leaders to use their "religious and moral authority to work for an end to the violence and the resumption of the peace process."[7]

The conference resolved:

> According to our faiths, the murder of innocents—in the name of God, as it were—is a desecration of his Holy name and a desecration of religion in this world. Violence in the Holy Land is an evil that demands the absolute opposition of all people of faith. We strive to live together as neighbors in mutual respect for the historical tradition and religious legacy of each people.[8]

The conference was given the full public backing of Egyptian President, Hosni Mubarak. Moving photographs of the event showed the religious leaders in their respective colorful traditional clerical clothing standing alongside each other announcing their accord.

The Unhappy Story of an Islamic Religious Leader: Unhappily, only a few weeks later the senior Egyptian cleric who had participated in the Alexandria conference announced his retraction and withdrawal from the ecumenical group. In fact, the same religious leader has since been responsible for more than one religious ruling legitimating suicide bombings. We saw one such ruling earlier that specified, with what I would say ironically might still be considered a degree of humanism, that suicide bombings were legitimate only if directed at soldiers but not at women and children (in the source material in my hands, I couldn't quite figure out where this left us other men who weren't soldiers, but I fear the worst).[9] So the touching example of the Alexandria conference that I gave is not exactly an optimistic one, and even underscores how far away we are from genuine ecumenical cooperation. Still, even the abortive effort is instructive of what can be attempted and what might yet be possible.

The "case history" of the religious leader in question, the "Grand Sheikh of the Al-Azhar mosque," Sheikh Muhammad Sayed Tantawi, particularly saddens me and angers me. I suspect in part my strong reaction in this case is because I was thrilled and encouraged by Tantawi's participation in the Alexandria conference and its joint Declaration by Christians, Muslims, and Jews, and subsequently I was deeply disappointed by his pulling back from the declaration and the original intention of the religious leaders to develop an ongoing "Alexandria process" over the coming years. And then, adding fearful insult to injury, came progressive exhortations by the same Tantawi even blessing and legitimating theologically various degrees of murderous suicide killing. Too much![10]

As I said, I am purposely interrupting the narrative building toward my optimistic proposal to initiate a new worldwide ecumenical process for peace with a "dirty story" of a religious leader who first stood with us and then returned to espouse and bless the suicide bombers. This is a true story that must be faced in its own right, and it is also an illustration of the many forces in religious cultures that promote making death. The story will help us to avoid naiveté, illusion, overinnocence, and kitsch. The proposal for a worldwide campaign to effect culture change will be very hard work, and not a starry-eyed piece of romantic idealism to help us go to sleep happily toward the end of a scary book on suicide bombers and the WMD that are in the offing for humanity today.

Tantawi on Suicide Bombings: Here is a recap I have put together of Tantawi on suicide bombings. The sources I have accessed do not necessarily give the definitive dates for the changes in Tantawi's positions as they first took place, but they seem to portray the timeline of how one source described sarcastically, "Sheikh Tantawi grows in office":[11]

Two months after September 11, 2001:

George W. Bush knows that Islam is a religion of peace because Sheikh Muhammad Sayyid Tantawi said so. Two months after the September 11 terrorist attacks, the President told the United Nations that Tantawi, "the Sheikh of Al-Azhar University, the world's oldest Islamic institution of higher learning, declared that terrorism is a disease, and that Islam prohibits killing innocent civilians."[12]

December 4, 2001:

Speaking at a press conference in Cairo, the sheikh, who is acknowledged as the highest spiritual authority for nearly a billion Sunni Muslims, said Islam condemned terrorism in all its forms... He says that in the name of Islamic law he rejected and condemned the aggression against innocent civilian people, regardless of whatever side, sect or country the aggression came from... He said that... Muhammad told his soldiers not to kill women or young boys or those who were worshipping.[13]

January 2002 is when the Alexandria conference takes place. In February, Tantawi is still being praised for his participation and contribution to the Alexandria Declaration, but by April he is being criticized for changing his mind.

February 1, 2002:

According to the London-based Arab press, there were many conflicts during the discussions [in Alexandria] . . . Perhaps the most important element in the declaration was the statement that all the monotheistic faiths prohibit the killing of innocents and regard it a crime, and all faiths and believing people should condemn violence . . . Last but not least, the meeting showed much about Sheikh Tantawi. Well before the September 11 attacks—in fact, since his appointment to his senior position as Sheikh al-Azhar in 1997—he succeeded in gradually returning al-Azhar to the leading role in orthodox and moderate Islam, despite all the criticism from popular radical Islamic scholars in Egypt and elsewhere in the Arab world. Al-Azhar has done this with much support from the Egyptian regime, but with substantial personal courage as well.[14]

April 4, 2002:

Unfortunately for Bush and others who trumpeted Tantawi's words around the globe . . . this sheikh whom the BBC called "the highest spiritual authority for nearly a billion Sunni Muslims" has now changed his tune . . . Tantawi has grown in office . . .

On April 4, 2002, an Arabic-language Web site connected to Al-Azhar stated that Tantawi has "demanded that the Palestinian people, of all factions, intensify the martyrdom operations [that is, suicide bombings] against the Zionist enemy, and described the martyrdom operations as the highest form of Jihad operations. He says that the young people executing them have sold Allah the most precious thing of all." . . . Tantawi, Bush's imam of peace, thus joins "Yasir Arafat" in the Hall of Fame of Islamic dissemblers. Both are extremely adept at telling the Western media what it wants to hear—and then doing likewise for the Arabic press, contradictions be damned.[15]

April 17, 2002:

The Anti-Defamation League reported further on the same talk by Tantawi: [Sheikh Tantawi] emphasized that every martyrdom operation against any Israeli, including children, women, and teenagers, is a legitimate act according to [Islamic] religious law.[16]

April 22, 2002: One new report seemingly resolved the contradictions in Tantawi's stands by underscoring that he deplores the killing of civilians unless they are Israelis:

Mohammed Sayed Tantawi is not an unknown figure to the Western press as he was quoted extensively as President Bush's imam of peace after the attacks on September 11th when he declared: "It's not courage in any way to kill an innocent person, or to kill thousands of people, including men and women and children." And the reporter adds sarcastically, "Unless they happen to be Israelis."[17]

December 27, 2002:

Dr. Mohammed Sayyed Tantawi, the Egyptian al-Azhar Sheikh, is the most senior religious authority of Sunni Islam. He is also closely connected to the Egyptian political establishment. In a recent interview . . . granted to the *Quds Press Agency* on 27 December 2002, as reported by the London-based daily al-Quds al-Arabi: . . . [he] authorized such acts when performed in the framework of the Palestinian struggle. The Sheikh . . . until then had reservations about women carrying out suicide bombings.

- The Sheikh stressed that the suicide attacks carried out by members of the Palestinian resistance are acts of sacrifice intended for the sanctification of Allah, whether performed by men or by women.
- The Sheikh even allowed women who engage in "suicide activities" to make concessions on their traditional attire [e.g., the compulsory veil], if such are needed to warrant the success of the suicide bombing.
- The Sheikh stated: "There is no difference between male and female when [it concerns] defending religion, homeland, self-respect, dignity and property; no difference whatsoever."[18]

The same reporter who had noted sarcastically that suicide bombings were anathema religiously continued with an overall observation about Islamic moderation: "It grows ever increasingly apparent that to ally with 'moderate Islam' is about as effective as coalition building with the lands of Narnia, Middle Earth and Utopia. In contradistinction to erroneous stories of Mark Twain's death—reports of moderate Islam's existence have been greatly exaggerated."[19]

Intriguingly, Tantawi continued a similar pattern of zigzagging contradictions of himself with regard to his views on the U.S. invasion and presence in Iraq. At least in the early stages of the U.S. presence in Iraq, the sources available to me show Tantawi tilting toward not condemning the United States as strongly as many of his compatriots, and he therefore came under the attack of his compatriots.[20]

Not surprisingly, some press reports about Tantawi end up being full of contradictions as well, and sometimes it is hard to know what one is reading, whether Tantawi really has changed the views between which he is flip-flopping, or the press reporter has cited the wrong date or made another reporting error. As late as July 2003, which is a date after Tantawi had called for suicide killings of Israelis, BBC reported as follows:

In July 2003, one of the world's most influential Islamic leaders condemned all attacks by suicide bombers at an international conference for Islamic scholars. He said those who carried out suicide bombings were the enemies of Islam, that suicide attacks, including those against Israelis, were wrong and could not be justified. He called on

Muslim nations to open themselves to dialogue with the West saying Islamic nations should "wholeheartedly open our arms to the people who want peace with us."

"I do not subscribe to the idea of a clash among civilizations. People of different beliefs should cooperate and not get into senseless conflicts and animosity," Sheikh Tantawi said. "Extremism is the enemy of Islam. Whereas, jihad is allowed in Islam to defend one's land, to help the oppressed. The difference between jihad in Islam and extremism is like the earth and the sky."[21]

How well said and beautiful! *But will the real Tantawi please stand up?*
I conclude that my disappointment and anger at Tantawi are as great as were my appreciation and admiration at his original participation in Alexandria and his original statements against suicide bombing. I have no idea what are the various motives of Sheikh Tantawi. But I do want to be aware that coming out for peace in the Middle East has been known to be a very risky business, and to consider that this risk *may* be involved in Tantawi's changes of positions. The late Egyptian President Sadat and Israeli Prime Minister Yitzhak Rabin both paid with their lives for their respective greatness in leadership for peace.[22]

The Kazakhstan Congress and "United Nations of Religions" (2003)

Happily, in addition to the Alexandria Conference there have also been other ecumenical gatherings. The next event I will describe in far-off Kazakhstan does not get as much recognition in the West as it genuinely deserves, but it definitely was not ignored. Both Alexandria, which I just reported, then Brussels, and then Seville which will be the next reports after this one in Kazakhstan, did receive stronger coverage in the Western press than Kazakhstan, but I think in large part they also were treated as flash-in-the-pan one-day curios rather than as genuine inspirational events, and then they too were promptly forgotten. All four congresses did not really get recognized as important statements of the real possibilities of bringing religious leaders in our world together. My view is that each one of these events can be a true inspiration that challenges us to creative thinking and efforts to bring to our world more lastingly a message of shared peace-seeking by different faiths.

In September 2003, a major religious conference was held in the former Soviet state of Kazakhstan under the active sponsorship of Kazakh President Nursultan Nazarbayev who believes "that Kazakhstan, which is home to more than 3,000 religious organizations covering 40 denominations, is the best place for interreligious dialogue."[23] Key leaders of eighteen faiths agreed to meet regularly under a banner of a "Congress of World and Traditional Religions." One delegate hoped the group would translate into a "United Nations of Religions." Speeches touched on how to address differences between religions, the need for more dialogue, and the issue of terrorism.

The secretary-general of the Muslim World League, Sheikh Abdullah Al-Turki from Saudi Arabia said the Koran prohibits any acts of violence. He told the delegates, "Islam is against all killing that is without a just cause. We cannot accept those who say that Islam is a religion that kills or harms others." Sheikh Al-Turki said Muslims also oppose those who use religion for political purposes.

The senior Jewish representative at the conference was Jonah Metzger, the chief rabbi of Israel. He spoke of the need for greater understanding between faiths . . . Seated nearby were the delegations from Saudi Arabia, Iran, Pakistan, and Egypt . . . Metzger invited all of those present to come to Jerusalem, which he respectfully called by its Islamic name of "Al-Quds."[24]

Also attending were Hindus from India and their historic adversaries, Muslims from Pakistan, delegates from Russian Catholic and Orthodox churches, Taoists and Buddhists from China, and a Shinto delegation from Japan.

Nice!

Admittedly, this congress too was marred by expressions of injustice and unresolved conflicts. Even at our best, we humans rarely seem to miss out on messing up and insulting or excluding someone or other. Thus, the religious leadership of nearby Ukraine was not invited; and no less than a Muslim news source pointed out that Baptists were not invited.[25] (To me the omissions are reminiscent of the failure a few years ago to invite representatives of Armenia to an international conference on the Holocaust in Stockholm that was initiated and sponsored actively by the Swedish Prime Minister primarily for leaders of many governments, but at least this serious exclusion was corrected in a follow-up conference in 2004.) In addition, the sponsor of the Kazakhstan conference, President Nazarbayev, is by all Western standards, like the leaders of many other not-really democratic countries, a covert dictator who has manipulated pseudoelection processes to stay in power. At the same time it is hard not to be moved by the fact that Nazarbayev himself is a Muslim. Rev. Minoru Sonoda, director of the Association of Shinto Shrines in Japan commented: "Nazarbayev has pledged to build a palace for the new organization so that 'all religions can enter and leave through one door.'"[26]

At this writing, I do not know of such a palace, or whether an organization of a new world body of religions are being developed further in Kazakhstan.

The Brussels "World Congress of Imams and Rabbis for Peace" (2005)

A third noteworthy ecumenical conference in recent years took place in Brussels in January, 2005. The conference featured rabbis and imams along with Christian clergy against religious extremism seeking means for religious leaders to contribute to lessening the bloody conflict between Palestinians and Israelis. It was sponsored by the organization Hommes de Parole and hosted more than 200 rabbis and imams as well as Christian clergy from all over the world. Its message was that "religion does not send people out to kill and that anyone who takes a life in the name of religion transgresses a commandment of God."[27]

The conference concluded with a pledge that the Jewish and Muslim clerics would work to put an end to bloodshed between Israelis and Palestinians and would struggle with all their might against hatred, ignorance, and extremism on both sides. When the declaration was read, the participants got to their feet and applauded.

A moving newspaper account describes many of the rabbis as never having met with imams, and how at first they ate at separate tables "Jews here, Muslims there, eyeing each other suspiciously"; but then a day later they had moved closer, and then a second day later "they were sitting together and even taking pictures arm in arm"; and by the end of the conference "they were praising each other's faith."

The imams represented most of the countries of Africa and Asia and were dressed in traditional robes and head coverings in a rainbow of colors. The former president of Indonesia, Abdul Rahman Wahid, about whom we learned earlier, had to cancel coming to the conference because of vast tsunami damage to Indonesia. The same tsunami gave the religious leaders an opportunity to stand and bow their heads in silence in memorial for the tsunami victims.

The reporter's account photographs the amazing moments that followed.

Suddenly, Rabbi Shlomo Chelouche, the chief rabbi of Haifa, recited a short prayer for the victims. When he finished, all those present said "amen."

Then Zimer Omar Farouk Turna, the former mufti of Istanbul, recited verses from the Koran.

No sooner did he finish than Rabbi Yosef Azran, chief rabbi of Rishon Lezion, chanted a psalm, his voice choked with tears. When the moments of silence were over, the hundreds of clergy in the room remained standing. Some wiped away a tear.

"This proves that rabbis and imams can work together for a common goal," said Rabbi René Sirat, the former chief rabbi of France. "In all my years as a rabbi, I never experienced a moment like this," Sirat added, invoking the traditional Jewish blessing for reaching a special milestone.

Hojat al-Islam Muhammad Mehatali, a senior Iranian cleric, looked at his colleagues in amazement. "These moments were the cream of the whole conference," he said. "Where have you ever seen Muslims and Jews praying as if they were one family?"

At the end of the conference the clerics held hands together and sang a Hebrew song about bringing peace, *Hevenu Shalom Aleichem.*

When I spoke to the reporter whose beautiful description of the conference I wanted to quote to get his formal permission, he told me that this was a story where "my feelings just welled up and poured into my writing." To this day, he remains deeply moved by the scenes he saw.

The Seville Second World Congress of Imams and Rabbis for Peace (2006)

A fourth ecumenical conference on which I will report took place in Seville, Spain, in 2006, also sponsored by Hommes de Parole, a peace foundation in Paris.[28] Seventy-two Muslim clerics and seventy-two rabbis took part in a three-day meeting. Of the imams, twenty were from Gaza and the West Bank, headed no less than by one of the Hamas founders, Sheikh Falouji—although Falouji had withdrawn from Hamas in 1996 and moved over to the Palestinian Authority. But the same Falouji was quoted as saying that Hamas did want "to hold a dialogue with the participation of Jewish and Muslim religious leaders."[29] Newspaper reports delighted in portraying some of the imams and rabbis pouring coffee for one another, trying out their English language skills with one another, or otherwise moving easily in one another's spaces. "In the open spaces of the hotel on the outskirts of Seville, rabbis in black coats and hats mingled freely with Muslim clerics in cloaks and turbans."[30]

Not surprisingly, there were tensions at this conference, but the clerics exercised good will and were careful not to bring to a divisive incident. Thus, a few Muslim religious leaders walked out when Israel's Chief Rabbi, Yona Metzger, spoke at the opening ceremony. They objected to what they called his admonishing them for bin Laden, and characterized Metzger's remarks as offensively superior. But the imams were careful that their protest was muted so as not to disrupt the ceremony. A second tense sequence took place when several Muslim speakers protested the Israeli occupation of Arab lands and spoke of the suffering of the Palestinians. The heading of the Hebrew-language report of the conference in *Haaretz* reads, "The smiles on the faces of the rabbis and imams disappeared when they began to speak of the occupation." Overall, the conference was reported to be a successful experience.

DEVELOPING A "WORLDWIDE CAMPAIGN FOR LIFE" BY THE LEADERS OF MANY RELIGIONS AND OTHER WORLD LEADERS AND HEROES

I now want to propose going one huge step further to mobilize an *ongoing worldwide ecumenical campaign* against killing.

Would that we were able to mount a truly impressive, creative, and touching worldwide campaign of the leaders of many of the world's religions, of course including Islam, who would join together not only in a single pontifical manifesto but in a carefully designed and well-promoted long-range "Worldwide Campaign for Life." Such a campaign would take shameless advantage of the archetypal power of the images of the vested official leaders of the established churches of many different religions.

In such a campaign, the imams, ministers, priests, rabbis, and leaders of all faiths would repeatedly link arm within arm and celebrate the sacredness of human life for all peoples of all religions.[31]

In any given culture, we know that the indigenous power of any people's religious leaders is considerable. Millions of people everywhere in our world carry deep within them inner rules and memories from childhood that one must obey God's commands as delivered to us by His designated holy leaders.[32] The basic image-messages the religious leaders would be delivering to the people of the world will continue a powerful early message that God and his prophets command us to treat life as a sacred creation, and that it is in His name that we are ordered, "Thou shalt not kill!"

Such a worldwide campaign would include many leaders of different religions joining together on behalf of life taking a full-voiced stand for life and against suicide bombing. Picture the world watching these venerable messengers of God standing together, speaking together, singing together, worshipping together, dancing together, and visiting the wounded and crippled survivors of suicide bombings together. A powerful chorus of living "angels of life" will be impacting on our world through the overwhelming communication power of contemporary media.

A heartwarming local peace festival for Jews, Christians, and Muslims, called "Sulha Way" ("Sulha" is forgiveness in Hebrew and Arabic) takes place in Binyamina, Israel, annually. *Haaretz* described the fourth such gathering in August 2004 as drawing 2000 people. "Jewish and Arab children played together, [there were] uplifting speeches by Sufi sheikhs and Orthodox rabbis and concerts by Arab and Jewish bands. The event is named after a traditional Arab ritual for reaching reconciliation between warring families. Among the attendees were a Tibetan monk and several guests from South Africa, northern Ireland, and England. Sulha coorganizer, Radash Eliyahu McLean, an American immigrant to Israel . . . was inspired to enter peace work partly by the death of a Jewish friend in a suicide bombing."[33]

In the campaign I envision, the respected religious leaders would not speak only once nor even only a few isolated times at long-separated intervals. I propose that the "Worldwide Campaign for Life" be conducted as a vigorous worldwide educational advertising campaign continuously over a period of several years with a well-planned sequence of media promotions delivered repeatedly to reading, listening, and viewing audiences in every country one can reach.

This is a good moment to be reminded once again that there are major Islamic leaders who do condemn terrorism. Thus, after the horrific decapitation of an American in Iraq, in a public display similar to the earlier beheading in Pakistan of *Wall Street Journal* reporter, Daniel Pearl, a group of American Muslim leaders issued a strong statement that "the images of the brutal murder of Nicholas Berg are a shocking and horrific symbol of the men of violence that do not represent Islam. This is not only a heinous crime but utterly repugnant to the Islamic rule of law . . . The horrific killing of Nicholas Berg . . . highlights a struggle with Muslim society . . . With our common humanity we seek to create a better understanding between members of many faiths and cultures through positive and constructive dialogue."[34] The signatories are a distinguished and impressive group of Muslim intellectuals and professionals in the United States. Are they—as happens in some societies—an intellectual elite that is removed from the day-to-day community of Muslims and real-life politics in that community? And as Americans, are they largely irrelevant to Muslims in Europe, the Middle East, and elsewhere? Or is their message not only fine in its own right but a spokesman of a real possible cultural trend in Islam in other parts of the world as well?

There are voices of criticism of terrorists in other Arab countries, including in Morocco, the Gulf States, Jordan, Lebanon, Egypt, and Saudi Arabia.

Rachid Benzine is a French-Moroccan intellectual who denounces Islamists as imposters who are interpreting the Koran in extremist ways. He insists that by acknowledging the historical roots and contexts of the Koran, Muslims can reconcile its texts with modern values such as democracy and human rights.[35]

According to an excellent survey report by John Kifner in the *New York Times*, following the terrifying murders of hundreds of children in Beslan, Russia, there was "an unusual round of self-criticism and introspection in the Muslim and Arab world."[36] The following are some of the examples cited:

- An especially powerful and inclusive criticism came impressively, from the general manager of the second most influential Arabic satellite TV network, Al Arabiya. "It is a certain fact that not all Muslims are terrorists, but it is equally certain, and exceptionally painful, that almost all terrorists are Muslims," said Abdel Rahman al-Rashed, writing in a pan-Arab newspaper, *Al-Sharq Al-Awsat.*

  Rashed then cited a whole string of suicide bombings all over the world, including in Muslim countries, and added: "The majority of those who manned the suicide bombings against buses, vehicles, schools, houses and buildings, all over the world, were Muslim," he wrote. "What a pathetic record. What an abominable 'achievement.' Does this tell us anything about ourselves, our societies and our culture?"

  Rashed also attacked explicitly and vociferously Sheikh Yousef al-Qaradhawi, a senior Egyptian cleric we noted earlier who legalized the suicide bombings of Jews, including civilians. Rashed does not mention the Israelis, but criticizes another fatwa by al-Qaradhawi that calls for killing American military and civilians in Iraq. "Let us contemplate the incident of this religious sheik allowing, nay even calling for, the murder of civilians," he wrote. "How can we believe him when he tells us that Islam is the religion of mercy and peace while he is turning it into a religion of blood and slaughter?"

- A Kuwaiti newspaper columnist also criticized the cleric "and others of his kind who, instead of defending true Islam, encourage these cruel actions and permit decapitation, hostage-taking and murder."

- The editor of a Lebanese newspaper wrote that without denying their identification with Palestinians fighting Israel, "all of us today are dehumanized and brutalized by the images of Arabs kidnapping and beheading foreign hostages."

- A Jordanian newspaper columnist wrote that the murderers of civilians in Iraq, commuters on trains in Spain, passengers on airliners, and the children in Beslan "are Arabs and Muslims who pray, fast, grow beards, demand the wearing of veils, and call for the defense of Islamic causes. Therefore we must all raise our voices, disown them and oppose all these crimes."
- In Egypt, a government newspaper said that the "propagandists of jihad succeeded in the span of a few years in distorting the image of Islam. They turned today's Islam into something having to do with decapitations, the slashing of throats, abducting innocent civilians and exploding people."

It took the enormous human tragedy of hundreds of dead children in Beslan to release such voices, but they are an impressive array—far from an intellectual elite in America or elsewhere in the Western world; these are leaders of society in Islamic countries.

The initial work of gaining the participation of clerics of all faiths, and the initial work of enlisting the cooperative participation of national media outlets are major parts of the project which have to be planned and launched very thoughtfully. Who would lead such a campaign? An ecumenical religious group such as the World Council of Churches could provide an opening platform of cooperation between many different faiths. But I would also look beyond religious bodies as such to other perhaps "higher" levels of international cooperation which convey all the more that many—perhaps almost all—peoples of the world are joining together in this campaign to end the disgusting killings by suicide bombers.

In other words, I suggest that the venerable and powerful religious leaders themselves would be sponsored by more inclusive world organizations, thus building even more powerfully the anthem that "everybody loves life." Backing up the religious leaders now would be leaders of the international community, such as the U.N. Secretary General, ambassadors to the United Nations, and heads of international and national health organizations. For what I imagine would be the price of one missile or one atom bomb or one space ship, a marvelous worldwide media campaign could be developed over an extended period of several years, for example under the auspices of the United Nations, and with the cooperation of other universally respected agencies such as the International Red Cross (cooperating with its variants such as Red Crescent and Red Magen David) and other national health agencies to announce, teach, and celebrate the honoring of life.

I would further mobilize additional respected leaders and former leaders of countries all around the world in support of the "Worldwide Campaign for Life." Moreover, I would not stop at the great religious and political leaders of each culture. In each culture, I would further mobilize from the indigenous community celebrated current folk heroes such as folk singers, sports heroes, respected military heroes, admired business leaders, heroes in medicine, and so on in all the pursuits of life, and work with them creatively to build a series of advertising projects for the "Worldwide Campaign for Life," in their country and everywhere. This campaign would be conducted around the world in many of the different languages of our world with music and movement and color.

Famed American jurist, Alan Dershowitz, has asked why certain regimes and cultures become devoted to suicide bombings and others do not, and his answer is that the leaders of cultures and societies make the most difference.

> The answer lies in differences among the elite leadership of various groups and causes. The leaders of Islamic radical causes especially the Wahhabis advocate and incite suicide terrorism, while the leaders of other causes advocate different means. Recall Mahatma Gandhi and Martin Luther King, Jr., whose people were truly oppressed but who advocated non-violent means of resistance . . . The real root cause of suicide bombing [is] elitist incitement by certain religious and political leaders who are creating a culture of death and exploiting the ambiguous teaching of an important religion.[37]

I believe that were the truly visible top leaders of *many* churches in the world to get together in a powerful, active, and cleverly appealing promotion of the sacredness of human life, and *restatements* of the ancient theological principle that killing is forbidden by our gods; and if an international political leadership would link up with them, and if renowned and beloved public heroes in each indigenous culture, including singers, sports heroes, admired leaders of medicine, and other heroes in the national collective memory would join them in pro-life messages; and if the media and advertising professions would be enlisted in helping to create newly attractive ways for disseminating a message of the sacredness of life in folk songs, slogans, on computer screens, and in public pageantry of all sorts; many plain people all over the world would respond. Hitler won over the German people with an undeniably beautiful and stirring pageantry (damn him!). Years later, we would commit the most powerful pageantry and symbolism to a campaign against all that terror and suicide bombings stand for.

Following the July 7 four suicide bombing attacks in London (and prior to the July 21 four repeated bombing attempts which failed), an ecumenical religious ceremony was held in which the leaders of Islamic, Jewish, and Christian faiths participated together. A central purpose of the gathering was to draw a distinction between Islam as a religious faith and Islam as an identity for many terrorists. Participants included Sheikh Zaki Badawi, the head of Britain's Council of Mosques and Imams, Jonathan Sacks, the Chief Rabbi of the United Kingdom, Rowan Williams, the Anglican Archbishop of Canterbury, Cardinal Cormac Murphy-O'Connor, the Roman Catholic Archbishop of Westminister, and David Coffey, the Moderator of the Free Churches.

Sheikh Zaki Badawi said:

> Anyone claiming to commit a crime in the name of religion does not necessarily justify his position in the name of that religion. People do things in the name of Islam which are totally contrary to Islam.[38]

There are also many plain people in the world who do not want their lives destroyed and are waiting to voice their protests of suicide bombings. After the three bombings in Sharm El Sheik, Egypt, in July, 2005, *Haaretz* reporter, Yoav Stern, reported that "thousands of workers and residents took to the streets in Sharm in a protest rally against the suicide bombers . . . 'Stop Killing Innocent People—Sharm is a City of Peace,' they wrote on placards."[39]

A perfectly silly sports story in the *New York Times* tells us how the excitement of a victorious sports fan can be channeled to excitement and hope about making this a better world in respect of far more serious issues. Samantha Power is a Pulitzer-Prize winning author of an excellent book on the world's failures to confront genocide and a Harvard University lecturer. She spoke of becoming so excited when her beloved Boston Red Sox won the World Series in 2004 for the first time since 1918: "Suddenly all things seem possible." said Power. "For ordinary people . . . now anything can happen. I feel more ambitious and more encouraged about things other than the Red Sox because of this sense that things can be turned around. Maybe we can make America a moral force in the world, maybe we can stop genocide. For those of us who live with lost causes, it's a very inspiring perspective shift."[40]

How many combinations can we create of voices against destruction of life? Imagine clergymen together with sports heroes, health heroes who have solved major illnesses and diseases with political and civic leaders, folk singers with military heroes, or religious leaders again with international business leaders, including the baby-faced millionaire entrepreneurs of today's start-ups in their jeans. The possibilities appear endless, and they also beckon with a kind of lightness and pleasure of a feeling of celebrating life. The message in support of life would be transformed into a kind of global merchandising campaign that builds steadily a momentum for penetration into the far corners of our globe which seeks to create a new consensus in the evolution of man's consciousness about what it is to be *human*.

It is a grand conception that at its core is amazingly simple. One respected national religious leader in the United States told me he was surprised by the thought that such a huge project was possibly quite doable. "It's a long shot in a way, but it has a clarity and straightforwardness to it and a message of hope that so many people yearn for. It could possibly do much good."[41]

2003 was a bloody demoralizing year of suicide bombings and terror in Israel and Palestine. Nonetheless, many Israelis and Palestinians nonetheless made Herculean efforts to design and express their support for blueprints for peace. One initiative was a "People's Voice" petition, initiated by a former head of Israel's security service (Shin Beth), Ami Ayalon, along with the president of Al Quds University in Jerusalem, Sari Nusseibeh. A second project, the "Geneva Initiative" was led by a former Minister of Justice and Deputy Foreign Minister of Israel, Yossi Beilin, and a former Minister of Information in the Palestinian government, Yasser Abed Rabbo.

An impressive statement of support for both initiatives was organized by the International Crisis Group and was published in the *International Herald Tribune*. The signatories included a former secretary general of the United Nations, a former secretary general of NATO, a former president of the EC, a former U.N. High Commissioner for Refugees, a former president of the International Red Cross, former presidents of Finland, Costa Rica, Brazil, Switzerland, U.S.S.R., South Africa, Philippines, Ghana, Ireland, Cyprus, Mexico, former prime ministers of Sweden, Belgium, India, Australia, Netherlands, France, Finland, Poland, former foreign ministers of Indonesia, Canada, U.S.S.R., Algeria, United Kingdom, France, Czechoslovakia, Denmark, Australia, Germany, Poland, Armenia, Japan, Yugoslavia, Italy, Thailand, Colombia, Finland, Guatemala, the Netherlands, Norway, Malta.[42] It is an impressive and heartwarming group of leaders. This is an example of the broad international cooperation I envision, but as I said at the core of the campaign I am proposing are the representatives of the many religious constituencies in this world, very much including Islam, to help convey a message that at long last mankind's many religions have found in common cause to protect God's creation of life—the human being.

The "Worldwide Campaign for Life" that I propose will cost some considerable money, but in truth it would be amazingly inexpensive compared to expenditures for the simplest megaweapons, which the suicide bombers *will* be aiming to use to destroy millions of people as soon as they can. The proposal of a "Worldwide Campaign for Life" is a naive proposal, with an innocence and charm akin to "naive art," but it is far more attractive than waiting passively for the equally unimaginable pictures of apocalyptic deaths of millions which, all too realistically, seem to lie ahead of us as the natural outcomes of an unchecked process of transnational genocidal terrorism.

The stakes are big. September 11 in 2001, to which I refer repeatedly, was so overwhelmingly devastating, both as a massive and unbelievable event in its own right and as a portent of the bigger and worse that are coming, that many of our minds cannot retain an active memory of its realness. It's like a bad dream that can't be true; or like an important folk tale but not something that really happened. But of course it is very real. Thus, Fareed Zakaria sees the danger:

> Technology means that small numbers can still do great harm. Even al-Qaeda's demonstrated genius for organizing damaging coordinated multiple attacks on a large scale, and in my opinion likelihood of their use of WMD, I foresee the grave possibility of a worldwide conflict and its hell of human suffering in the coming years.[43]

Given the nature of the beast, which is the limited likelihood of a significant evolution of human nature in the immediate future; and the likelihood of only limited improvement in the system of world governance with respect to a common will and ability to confront terrorism with rapid and powerful police, military, and legal actions; and yes, the great likelihood of WMD becoming available to committed terrorists who desire strongly to create an apocalyptic hell; *we need to prepare ourselves for the overwhelming likelihood that hell is going to happen.*

The National Intelligence Council, a strategic arm of the U.S. government, studies likely and possible scenarios of the future. In its "2020 project," it notes than an earlier report's prediction about the increase in world terrorism has been borne out. That prediction had been: "Between now and 2015 terrorist tactics will become increasingly sophisticated and designed to achieve mass casualties. We expect the trend toward greater lethality in terrorist attacks to continue.[44]

Here, for example, is one of the scenarios studied in the 2020 project. It is far more overwhelming than the word-pictures I have been drawing so far. The number used by this high-level professional group of strategists defies our imagination. Yet in truth, it is a reminder that in our past "old-fashioned" ways of killing, we humans have already murdered *hundreds of millions* of us, so why not a possibility that many millions will die in one concentrated blow or sequence such as the biological warfare envisioned here?

> The murder of 25 million people in the mid-2010s by the self-proclaimed Agent of God who created the genetically modified Congo virus, finally woke up the world to the realization that an individual acting alone could create and use a weapon of mass destruction.[45]

Nonetheless, the grim prospects for the future don't mean that I want to give up. On the contrary, I want to try that much harder to pull off a miracle and stop the destruction, and/or to be ready to respond to the crisis of a disaster that will have taken place by moving ahead with important new developments in world government and world culture that will prevent still more disasters.

I would propose an ecumenical "Worldwide Campaign for Life" as a major international initiative of the twenty-first century. There is every reason to hope and believe that people can be touched by messages of faith and inspiration, especially from their own respected religious and culture leaders. Even in politically repressive cultures where there are few to no voices against suicide bombings, we have every reason to believe that there awaits a measure of ambivalence within what Habib Malik referred to so beautifully as the universal human experience of "moral universals and . . . natural laws."[46]

Amazingly, a Saudi Arabian columnist for the newspaper *Al Riyadh* published a statement in his paper, and then an English translation in the Western press, calling for an end to "deep-rooted Islamic extremism in most schools and mosques, which have become breeding grounds for terrorists." He told how previously he had called for "freedom of speech and criticizing Wahhabism, Saudi Arabia's official religious doctrine," and as a result had been sentenced to seventy-five lashes on the back, but that he had decided not to go to the police station to receive the punishment. He writes that, paradoxically, it had been during an earlier period in jail as a youngster who had set fires against heretics who opposed Wahhabism, that he had come with "wrenching disbelief" to the conclusion that "Islam was not only Wahhabism, and that other forms [of Islam] preached love and tolerance." *What a brave man!*[47]

Of course, there shouldn't be any doubt that the reactionary forces in many societies will understand that the "Worldwide Campaign for Life" is an assault on their "racket." They will fight back and hard, politically, propaganda wise, quite likely even with terrorist means in some societies. It has to be clear that there is a wing of religious leaders in many faiths who are adamantly in favor of violence. Thus, the recent joint Israeli-Palestinian peace proposal of the Geneva Peace Accord or Geneva Initiative to which we referred a little while ago was denounced by the hardliners on *both* sides. There are plenty of distinguished clerics (sometimes it seems to me that for some reason we tend to identify most clerics as "distinguished") who, when the truth is told, *want wars!*

A committee of 250 rabbis called Pikuah Nefesh, or Preservation of Life, said Israelis who had signed the Geneva document should be considered traitors who deserve to be "cast out from human society and brought to trial." And Dar al-Fatwa, a Palestinian institution that specializes in Islamic law, issued a fatwa, or religious edict saying it would be improper for Muslims to relinquish claims to land lost in wars with Israel.[48]

But that's the point of a "Worldwide Campaign for Life." It is to stand innovatively, attractively, and courageously against the tried and true paths of a culture of destruction and its faithful adherents.

Periodically there are reports not only of suicide bombers who are intercepted by excellent police-military intelligence before they execute their mission, but also of some would-be suicide bombers who seem to make it easy for security personnel to arrest them, including instances where the suicide bomber appears to be in a disoriented trance, or some cases where they seem to freeze into inaction, and occasionally even blessed occasions where the bomber experiences a moving spiritual redecision not to kill.

One such inspiring case occurred when a woman suicide bomber turned back from her mission in a spiritual moment of inspiration.[49] A 20-year-old Palestinian student of business administration, Arien Ahmed, had been educated in a Lutheran high school in Bethlehem. It was May 22, 2002. Ahmed was taken out from a lecture on marketing at Bethlehem University and given a backpack loaded with explosives and shown how to trigger the bomb inside. Together with another would-be killer, a 16-year-old boy who was a son of a lawyer educated in Wisconsin, they were sent in a broken-up car on to their missions.

> Ms. Ahmed was . . . starting to wonder, as she walked along the pedestrian mall [in Rishon le Zion, Israel] if she was doing the right thing, or if hell rather than heaven awaited her . . .
>
> "I look at the sky," Ms. Ahmed recalled . . . speaking English as she described a kind of awakening. "I look at the people." She said she remembered a childhood belief, "that nobody has the right to stop anybody's life." Ms. Ahmed, a rare exception among suicide bombers, turned back . . .

Her recruiters simply told her that she would rejoin her slain fiancé, Jaad Salem, in paradise, a notion she recalled thinking stupid even at the time . . .

Ms. Ahmed said she wanted to be interviewed to discourage other Palestinians from conducing suicide attacks, and to gain sympathy for herself . . . In high school she took part in joint discussions with Israeli students, and she made some friends among them. "Maybe if I check my e-mail, I will see e-mail from them," she said smiling.[50]

In a BBC TV documentary referred to earlier, another story was told of a man who changed his mind and did not complete his suicide-bombing mission. He describes how he had gone to look at the area in which he was to explode himself and then, "I saw a group of kids playing. To be honest, that's when I decided I wouldn't do it." He also said:

It crossed my mind that some people did not deserve to die, Jews who wanted peace. I was going to kill and didn't know if any of these people would be around. I could not think clearly . . . In my heart I felt that I didn't want to carry out this operation. I didn't want innocent people and young people to get killed . . . God inspired me to go home.

The narrator of the documentary comments, "In his heart he is not a suicide bomber, he is not obsessed with death and despair."[51]

There are also the voices of some convicted terrorists who teach us of the possibilities of profound philosophical changes. Earlier we referred to one, Samir Kuntar, who has been held in an Israeli jail for terrorist murders in 1979, and who in 1995 told an *Haaretz* reporter that while in jail he underwent a basic change in his thinking and resolved that the Palestinians must give up violence including against themselves within their own community. Kuntar recounted that the change in him came about when he learned of the Holocaust. He was shocked. "I felt a powerful reaction I can't describe," he said. He was moved to his decision that "the Palestinian nation, must make a moral correction."[52]

Let there be no question that active terrorism needs to be fought militarily first of all. The call for a "Worldwide Campaign for Life" in no way justifies a pie-in-the-sky naiveté and innocence. Thus, for all that we previously saw Habib Malik inspiring us to trust in a timeless human conscience, we also noted his cautions against believing naively that overtures to peace will be received in good faith by many Islamic leaders. "The Islamic establishment on the whole . . . remains conservative and unyielding" and is unmoved by overtures to ecumenicism and peace, Malik warns; and he cautions against "Western apologist academics, ecclesiastical wishful thinkers, reaching out to conduct religious dialogue, or embarrassed policy planners attempting to soften the image of some of their brutal allies in the name of a vague multiculturalism . . . who, out of ignorance or design, continue to push for dialogue with this mirage of moderation." He adds chillingly, "Whenever Islam meets non-Islam, there is blood spilled," and asks, "Is there something within [Islam's] system that makes it perhaps unable to coexist?"[53]

Yassin Musharbash writes in *Der Spiegel* about his interviews of a Jordanian journalist, Fouad Hussein, as someone who spent time in person with Al-Qaeda's leader in Iraq, al-Zarqawi, and who has been in extensive contact with the movement. In an article entitled, "What al-Qaeda really wants," Musharbash describes a long-range multi-sequence plan which is to reach its "Fifth Phase" in 2013 when an encompassing Islamic state is declared, and its "Seventh Phase" by 2020 when a "definitive victory" is achieved and "the rest of the world will be . . . beaten down" by Muslims and the Islamic state.[54]

An eloquent Buddhist wrote in the *Wall Street Journal*, "I'm a Buddhist, but not a Pacifist in War on Terror." He saw first of all great inspiration in the decency and humanity of many people's responses to September 11. But he then goes on to recognize that the actual terrorist suicide bombers have to be fought by military means.

> So what is a reasonable person to do? . . . Passive resistance isn't going to work with the Islamic terrorist network . . . Absolute pacifism barely exists in the real world. None of the antiwar folk that I know object to the idea of a police force in their communities (although some are critical of police procedures). If there were a hostage situation in their local school, and a maniac were brutally killing teachers and pupils one by one, very few so-called pacifists would say the police should not use force . . . Frankly speaking—and I speak for no one but myself—if you put a rifle in my hands and somehow got Osama bin Laden into the crosshairs, I, as a Buddhist, would endeavor to place the bullet right between his eyes.[55]

New and stronger legal tools against suicide bombers are needed at every level of national and international legal systems. Earlier we noted that a group of scholars has been circulating a petition to identify suicide bombing as a *war crime*[56]; and that the Simon Wiesenthal Center has proposed that the United Nations declare suicide bombings crimes against humanity. The leaders of the Wiesenthal Center have been actively personally lobbying international leaders, including the Pope, EU leaders, the Present of Russia and others. In a recent statement, Rabbis Marvin Hier and Abraham Cooper, deans of the center said:

> Suicide attacks have become the crime of the 21st century . . . Today, there is no greater danger facing our world than the scourge of suicide bombing and international terrorism. If there is any hope of preventing future mass murders of innocent children, the U.N. must pass a resolution that would treat Islamist terrorist networks carrying out these attacks as international pariahs and outlaws.[57]

Obviously, there will be resistance, cynicism, counterpropaganda, and in effect a battle of all that is anti-human and pro-destruction against all efforts to spur the human race on to evolve a new level of respect for life. The kind of "Worldwide Campaign for Life" I propose would itself become a setting for a major battle between the forces of fascism and the forces of democracy.

Such a global campaign for life itself would be a collective magnification of a process that each individual is called upon to do in his or her own mind on an everyday level, which is to choose whether to be a walking fascist-mind case of power-seeking and evil inside of one's own self and/or toward others, or to be a democratic-mind leader who works for the protection of life and a good quality of life for oneself and others.[58]

So long as hate is taught in the schools of a society and legitimated and celebrated, there can be little hope. We have seen that there are Muslim countries where very young children are taught in schools and summer camps catechisms of hate of the Jews and the West. Here is an example:

Who do we hate?
—We hate the Jews.
Why do we hate the Jews?
—Because they are pigs and dogs.

One friend of mine has commented: "They are socialized into a way of life where the value of life is different than it is for us in the West. The humanity into which we are all born is being eradicated day after day. When an idea of any sort becomes greater than the human being and the idea takes over the person rather than the person remaining in charge of their mind, it is madness."[59]

Nonetheless, it is also one of the firm contributions of the social sciences to the successful resolution of prejudice and intractable conflicts that we have learned that if people are exposed to new messages of peace and reconciliation by their leaders and in their cultures, changes in attitudes and behaviors *can* follow in amazingly short periods of time. After the Holocaust, who would have believed that the Jews would enter into renewed positive relationships with Germans? (Prime Minister David Ben-Gurion made a strategic decision early in Israel's history to lead in this direction.) In the United States, how many years ago did it seem inconceivable that black Americans would hold the highest diplomatic and security positions in the cabinet, or that a Jew would run as candidate for vice-president?

Even assertive behaviors by common people against prejudice have been shown to have a powerful influence on others observing them. Social science researches for many years have shown that the creation of nonprejudiced norms is most accelerated by people seeing and hearing others stand up against prejudice and for wholesome values.[60]

All incitements of violence have a good deal in common with one another, of course. They are fellow travelers that lower moral resistances to doing harm to fellow human beings. In the areas of racial, ethnic, religious, or other group prejudices, each encouragement and legitimation of violence in effect reminds one of other target groups as well and encourages a generic prejudice against many and various peoples. The Simon Wiesenthal Center has been producing an annual CD-ROM report which reports on "digital terrorism and hate" on the Internet as "a key propaganda weapon marketing tool and fundraising engine for supporters of terrorist groups such as al-Qaeda and Hamas as well as neo-Nazi, skinhead and other hate groups." The report includes some of the online recruitment videos used to attract new inductees into the cults of terrorism. It also presents hate games where "users can gun down illegal aliens at the U.S.–Mexico border in Border Patrol, shoot Blacks in Niggaz Doom, hunt down Jews in Duck Hunt, and gas Turks in KZ Manager."[61]

Intriguingly, long before a millennium of Peace on Earth and an end to suicide-bombing terrorism might come to be, a "Worldwide Campaign for Life" might at least contribute to some reductions in other everyday violences such as domestic violence, life-threatening driving, or violence in sports events. In any case, suicide bombings will diminish and cease wherever we are successful in turning the culture and its public opinion against them. A 2003 report to the U.S. Congress makes the point we have been emphasizing very strongly, that fighting suicide bombers means fighting all the cultural conditions which allow and legitimate suicide attacks.

> Suicide attacks . . . are usually carefully recruited, indoctrinated and then targeted by organizations. It is important, therefore, to concentrate on analyzing the culture and structure of the organization when fashioning a response . . . While the organization is predominant in the execution of the attack, over time it cannot recruit and sustain itself without the acquiescence of the large society . . . Suicide attacks cannot occur in a population that does not provide individuals who are willing to die for the cause . . . Preventing imminent attacks would include policies that alter the political, cultural and socio-economic contexts that perpetuate suicide attacks.[62]

Eminent Holocaust scholar, Yehuda Bauer, is very clear, and frightening, not only to Jews but also to all peoples, when he concludes:

> International Islamic terror is ideologically based, and endangers the entire world.

Yet, Bauer immediately emphasizes that the solution cannot come from military force but—

> The sole possibility of fighting an ideology of mass murder disseminated by radicals is to encourage the opposition to them within their own people and faith. There are many public figures in the Muslim world, which numbers some 1.2 billion people—about one-fifth of the human race—who are seeking ways to contend with radicalism without abandoning their culture and religion. The West, and the Jews as part of it, cannot approach this issue in a patronizing or condescending manner, but out of respect for the traditions of the Islamic world.[63]

Writing about contemporary terror, the director of Hebrew University's Center for the Study of Antisemitism observes: "Europe has barely had a glimpse of the kind of merciless terror against innocent civilians that Israel has had to face for years." At the same time, he credits *most* Muslim communities in the world as consisting of "decent, law-abiding citizens." He adds that, "The tragedy is that the Muslim majority does not speak up. It has been silenced or intimidated by the fundamentalists. We have to find a way to reach out to them."[64]

In the London Arabic language daily, *Al-Sharq Al-Awsat*, renowned Sudanese author and literary scholar Al-Tayyib Salih castigated Islamic extremists' use of violent means to achieve their ends. In the touching style of Islamic legends, he recounts:

> The prophecy that our great leader 'Uthman Ibn' Affan, may Allah be pleased with him [made] in the year 35 or 36 of the Hijra has come true. He made this prophecy when the wild mob that came from distant regions of the kingdom, from Egypt and Iraq, entered his home, having decided to kill him . . .
>
> "If you kill me, you put the sword to your own neck, and then Allah will not lift it from you until the Day of Resurrection . . . and Allah will never remove discord from amongst you . . . "
>
> They murdered him, and their murder of him was tantamount to the crushing of the symbol of consensus in the [Islamic] nation, and the violation of its sanctity, and the tearing to shreds of the garment of awe and reverence without which the ruled cannot be pleased with the ruler . . . With this deed, they transgressed all bounds and trampled all that is sacred. And indeed, we see after that deed how . . . throughout Islamic history to this day . . . those same evil spirits returning with different masks, garb, and forms, using a new language with diverse tongues, holding implements of destruction which are capable of more destruction and more widespread damage . . .
>
> Collective rage is a combination of little truth and much falsehood, and dubious leaders who bewitch the hearts of the gullible and fan the flames of grievance and alien hands weaving plots in the dark with no aim but to undermine the foundations of society . . .
>
> This is a hidden evil against which reasonable people must unite . . . This can be [accomplished] only by wisdom, prudence, knowledge, honesty, and frankness. It's either this or clear deterioration.[65]

Afterword: Inshallah

Is there a chance of averting a war between the civilizations of death and life? I doubt it. As I have said, I think the war has already begun and is warming up.

I also fear it's only a matter of time (and it could be a short time) before a Weapon of Mass Destruction takes a terrible toll of some people somewhere on our planet. In this respect, I can only hope that the extent of the massive destruction nonetheless will be localized and limited rather than there being more catastrophically widespread megadestruction; and I can pray that the tragedy and fright of the disaster that will have taken place will mobilize the world for major new steps toward controlling terrorism and war.

Still, *maybe, maybe* we will have the unexpected good luck that there won't be a WMD attack. And *maybe, maybe* there will be a godsend of a world-level leader of the stature of a Martin Luther King or a Gandhi who will lead the world toward a new idealism, and there will be a giant leap forward in the world's governing system that will lead to much more effective international cooperation against terrorism, including a growing number of Islamic countries who will join the battle against terrorism. *Inshallah.*

Or *maybe, maybe* alien people will have arrived on Earth, and the resulting dynamics will be a stronger human species which learns how to effectively limit violence.

Or *maybe, maybe* a worldwide culture change will be achieved by the kind of campaign I have proposed of a *"Worldwide Campaign for Life"* which will result in discernible rejection of terrorists and acts of terrorism by much of the world, and a notable reluctance of people to become terrorists.

Inshallah. I can pray and dream, even though I am bracing myself for more of the war between the civilizations of death and life.

Sometimes I even imagine that, of all major conflict zones in the world, it will be the Middle East which will surprise us and "break out in peace" in the coming years. I think of how there are so many capable Palestinians who have completed a fine Western education who want to be partners with Israelis in creating a real economic and physically safe Garden of Eden in the Middle East. In my hope scenarios, the flourishing Palestinians then become the object of great envy of the Arab world, along with other flourishing Islamic states already committed to peace, and the star of terrorism in the rest of the Arab world begins to wane.

Let there be no doubt. Some decent and hopeful things are happening continuously including in the Arab World. In addition to the many examples of Islamic voices and leadership for peace given throughout the book, here are three more previously unexpected developments:

- March 27, 2004: 155 Palestinians publish an announcement in the newspaper *Al-Ayyam* calling for a popular nonviolent intifada. Of course, the Al-Aqsa Martyrs Brigades stated their absolute opposition to this "path that weakens the Palestinian stand and serves the occupation."[1]
- October 21, 2004: A seminary in Cairo with the participation of Arab intellectuals from Egypt, Syria, the Philippines, Tunis, Yemen, and the United States calls for an "intellectual jihad against the extremists, radicals and zealots who have hijacked Islam and turned it into a means of intimidation and terror all over the world."[2] Of course, the call was met by immediate protests from establishment clerics, including Sheikh Tantawi who "harshly attacked the seminar and its participants" as "a mark of shame and a disaster," that the participants "have a destructive influence on Egyptian society and they must be stopped and brought to trial." (Thank you again, Sheikh of destruction.)
- October 24, 2004: Two liberal Arab websites publish a manifesto written by Arab liberals in which they petition the United Nations to establish an international tribunal that would prosecute terrorists, as well as people and institutions, primarily religious clerics, that incite terrorism.[3] The idea to petition the United Nations with this request was raised by Jordanian writer and researcher, Dr. Shaker Al-Nabulsi in early September 2004 in response to the fatwa issued by Sheikh Yousef Al-Qaradhawi, whom we have seen as a leader and one of the important religious authorities in Islam, who call for the abduction and killing of U.S. citizens in Iraq. The idea to petition the U.N. was developed and written up by Al-Nabulsi, a Tunisian intellectual, Al-'Afif Al-Akhdhar, and former Iraqi Minister of Planning Dr. Jawad Hashem.[4]

Regrettably, I believe that overall we will be seeing the world situation getting worse before we are able to make some major new steps toward a less violent world.

And yet can't a person dream of a less violent and murdering world, and do everything possible to bring about such a world?

I do. And I pray: *May He who brings peace to the celestial bodies above bring peace to all the peoples of our world* (a version of a Jewish prayer).

Inshallah (*May it be the will of Allah* in Arabic).

Representative Suicide Bombings around the World

The following is a list of representative suicide bombings, especially since September 11, 2001, including some of the major wake-up calls preceding September 11.[1,2] Suicide bombings in Iraq have become so numerous that they have become problematic for this compilation of representative events.

- There are too many events of suicide bombing to list.
- There are so many major events of suicide bombing that it becomes virtually impossible to select a small number as the representative events.
- Suicide bombings have become so entwined with other types of terror attacks, such as car bombs or remote-triggered explosions, that the listing of representative suicide bombings at times requires much more complex descriptions of integrated terror attacks that include multiple types of attackers and weapons.

As this book goes to press, it is reported that 3,438 Iraqi civilians died violently in July 2006 which is more civilians than were killed in any previous month. An average of more than 110 Iraqis were killed in various forms of violence each day in July. At least 17,776 civilians died violently in the first seven months of this year.

♦ MARKER EVENTS

These items are events of suicide bombing that have been recognized as relatively significant transitional events in the history of suicide bombing and contemporary society.

■ SUPER MARKER EVENTS

These events represent major incidents of suicide bombing that are especially memorable and possibly even watershed events.

1983

Beirut, Lebanon	October 23, 1983	241 U.S. military personnel killed; more than 100 wounded
		58 French military personnel killed, 15 wounded

An explosive-laden truck is used in a devastating suicide bomb attack on the U.S. Marines Building. The Marines had been in Beirut on a peacekeeping mission since the middle of the previous year. "The explosion lifted the entire building off its foundation" (–Congressional Research Service, August 2003). Within minutes, the headquarters of the French paratroopers, also part of international peacekeeping efforts, is hit in a similar manner. The attacks were by the Islamic Revolutionary Movement.

1993

Sri Lanka	May 1, 1993	President killed

President Ranasinghe Premadasa blown up by suicide bomber of the Liberation Tigers of Tamil Eelam (LTTE)

1998

Nairobi, Kenya	August 7, 1998	263 dead and over
and Dar es Salaam, Tanzaniya		400 injured

Bombings at two U.S. embassies in Africa in separate locations 700 kilometers from each other at nearly the same time, a pattern that is to emerge as a hallmark of Al-Qaeda operations. In the first, the car bomber escapes at the last minute from the bomb-laden car, throws a grenade, and car crashes into embassy. In the second, the bomber detonates himself.

1999

Sri Lanka	December 18, 1999	27 killed, President wounded

President Chandrika Kumaratunga is wounded in a suicide assassination bid by Tamil Tigers

2000

Aden, Yemen   October 12, 2000   17 killed, 39 wounded
Suicide attack blows a 40 by 40 foot hole in USSS Cole anchored in harbor of Aden; U.S. intelligence sees similarities between blast which was executed with great sophistication in explosion at two U.S. embassies in East Africa in 1998

2001

Tel Aviv, Israel   June 1, 2001   22 killed, many wounded
Suicide bomber explodes self among teenagers lining up to enter a nightclub

Jerusalem, Israel   August 9, 2001   15 killed, many wounded
Suicide bombing in pizzeria in downtown Jerusalem

Opposition Base in   September 2, 2001   4 dead
Northern Afghanistan
Suicide bombers believed to be Algerians pose as television journalists to conduct an interview with Shah Massoud, a former defense minister who was Afghanistan's anti-Taliban alliance leader; Massoud is killed

■ **September 11, 2001: USA—New York and Washington, DC, 3000 killed, scores wounded**

Two hijacked U.S. airliners crash into the Twin Towers of the World Trade Center in New York, which, amazingly, collapse shortly afterwards. A third hijacked plane crashes into the Pentagon, while a fourth plane which is suspected to have been intended to crash into the White House or the Congress comes down in rural Pennsylvania after passengers heroically fight back. The four superbly coordinated attacks were carried out by Al-Qaeda under Osama bin Laden, notwithstanding insane conspiracy theories that either the United States or Israel or both were the real perpetrators, or hired the killers, or something or other.

Srinagar, India   October 3, 2001   38 people killed, at least 60 wounded
Suicide bomber blows self up at the gate of the legislature in Srinagar, the summer capital of the Muslim-majority state of Jammu and Kashmir

Colombo, Sri Lanka   October 29, 2001   5 killed, 20 wounded
Suicide bombing attempt on the life of Prime Minister Rathnasiri Wickremanayake

Oil Tanker, off the   October 30, 2001   3 killed
coast of Sri Lanka
Tamil suicide bombers rammed a boat loaded with explosives into an oil tanker off the northern coast of Sri Lanka

Jerusalem, Israel   December 1, 2001   10 killed, 150+ hurt
Bombing on Ben Yehuda Street in the heart of West Jerusalem, Hamas claims responsibility

Haifa, Israel   December 2, 2001   15 killed, 40 hurt
21-year-old Palestinian plumber boards a bus and detonates explosives filled with nails, Hamas takes credit

2002

Tel Aviv, Israel   January 25, 2002   25 people hurt
Cafe, Islamic Jihad's Jerusalem Brigades took credit

Jerusalem, Israel   January 27, 2002   2 killed, 111 hurt
Jaffa Road, Wafa Idress, 28, from the Al-Amari refugee camp near Ramallah, was the first Palestinian woman bomber

Jerusalem, Israel   March 2, 2002   9 killed
Bar Mitzva celebration in ultra-Orthodox neighborhood of Jerusalem, 5 children among dead

Jerusalem, Israel   March 9, 2002   13 killed, 50+ hurt
Suicide bomber explodes in Cafe Moment, crowded with young people, *near the prime minister's residence*

Netanya, Israel   March 27, 2002   29 killed, 100+ hurt
Suicide bomber penetrates Park Hotel where family groups are gathered for Passover seder

Jerusalem, Israel   March 29, 2002   2 killed, 20 hurt
Kiryat Yovel supermarket, an 18-year-old female who was engaged to be married, Al-Aqsa Martyrs Brigades took responsibility

Haifa, Israel   March 31, 2002   15 killed, 44 hurt
Bombing in Maza Restaurant run by Israeli Arabs

Jerusalem, Israel   April 12, 2002   6 killed, 90 wounded
20-year-old female bomber from Bethlehem detonates herself at a bus stop near the Mahane Yehuda central open-air market, she is a Tanzim operative

Rishon Lezion, Israel   May 7, 2002   16 killed, 60 hurt
Snooker club

Karachi, Pakistan   May 9, 2002   11 people killed, at least 4 wounded
Suicide car bomber strikes against French engineers and technicians supervising the construction of a submarine for Pakistan; Karachi is the scene of the earlier murder-beheading of Jewish-American Wall Street Journal *reporter, Daniel Pearl.*

Chechnya, Russia   May 12, 2002   50 killed, many hurt
Two suicide bombers drive a truck full of explosives into a government compound

Jerusalem, Israel   June 19, 2002   19 killed, 50+ wounded
Bus packed with schoolchildren and commuters

Tel Aviv, Israel   September 19, 2002   6 killed, 50 wounded
Bus bombing near central synagogue

♦ Bali, Indonesia   October 12, 2002   193 killed
*Just before midnight a suicide bomber blows himself up inside Paddy's bar on
Kuta beach killing 9 people. A few minutes later a parked van packed with bombs
explodes outside the nearby Sari Club, killing 193 people. A third bomb explodes
about a minute later near the U.S. Consulate a few miles away, no one is hurt.
Al-Qaeda claims responsibility for Bali. The* Asian Wall Street Journal *reports that
"al-Qaeda operatives had met regional Islamic extremists in southern Thailand
in January and proposed a series of attacks on bars, nightclubs and resorts across
South East Asia."*

Hadera-Afula road,   October 21, 2002   4 killed, 50 wounded
Israel
Suicide bomber explodes on a bus, Islamic Jihad takes responsibility

Jerusalem, Israel   November 21, 2002   11 killed, 49 wounded
Kiryat Menachem suburb

Grozny, Russia   December 27, 2002   80 killed
*Chechen suicide bombers destroy four-story local government headquarters as
three unidentified terrorists drive their bomb-laden vehicles into the Grozny
headquarters complex of the Moscow-appointed Chechnya administration. The
bombers managed to get past all obstacles easily because they were dressed in
Russian military uniforms with officers' insignia, their two vehicles had military
license plates, they presented proper identification papers and official passes, and
they did not look like Chechens.*

2003

Riyadh, Saudi Arabia   May 12, 2003   35 killed
*Suicide bombers in vehicles shoot their way into expatriates' housing area in
capital of Saudi Arabia as residents sleep*

Znamenskoye,   May 12, 2003   59 killed, scores wounded
Chechnya
*Two suicide bombers drive a truck packed with explosives into a government
building*

Iliskhan-Yurt, Chechnya   May 14, 2003   18 killed, 145 wounded
Female suicide bomber blows herself up during religious festival

Casablanca, Morocco   May 16, 2003   45 dead, about 60 wounded
Bombers set off at lease five coordinated blasts, among the 45 dead are 12 suicide bombers

Chechnya, Russia   June 5, 2003   at least 18 dead
Female suicide bomber kills herself on a bus packed with Russian air force personnel just outside Chechnya

Jerusalem, Israel   June 11, 2003   17 killed, at least 100 wounded
Suicide bomber disguised as an Orthodox Jew blows up bus near open-air market, Hamas takes responsibility

Quetta, Pakistan   July 4, 2003   at least 48 dead, about 100 wounded
Sunni suicide attack at a Shi' ite Muslim mosque in the southwestern Pakistani city where 2,000 worshippers had gathered for Friday afternoon prayers; Shi' ites are about 20 percent of Pakistan's Sunni-dominated 145 million population.

Moscow, Russia   July 5, 2003   17 dead, 60 wounded
Two Chechen women suicide bombers blow themselves up at a Moscow rock concert

Mozdok, North Ossetia,   August 1, 2003   50 killed
Russia
Suicide bomber detonates a truck packed with explosives at a military hospital in southern Russia, Chechens responsible

Jakarta, Indonesia   August 5, 2003   12 killed, 150 wounded
Suicide bomber in car tears through the luxury JW Marriott Hotel and surrounding buildings in Jakarta's main business district, Jemaah Islamiah, a radical Islamic group linked to Al-Qaeda, is implicated

Baghdad, Iraq   August 19, 2003   23 people killed
Attack occurs at the Canal Hotel, dead included the top U.N. envoy to Iraq

Najaf, Iraq   August 29, 2003   83 killed, 175 wounded
Attack occurs at the Iman Ali Mosque in the Shi' ite holy city of Al Najaf, among the dead was the Shi' ite Muslim Leader, Ayatollah Muhammad Bakr al-Hakim

Jerusalem, Israel   September 9, 2003   7 killed, many wounded
Cafe Hillel on Emek Refaim Street, the dead included the Medical Director of Emergency Medicine at Shaarei Zedek Hospital and his daughter on the eve of her wedding

Haifa, Israel   October 4, 2003   25 dead
Palestinian woman suicide bomber blows herself up in a crowded Israeli beach restaurant, Maxim, owned and frequented by Arabs and Jews

Baghdad, Iraq   October 9, 2003   8 killed
Two suicide bombers attack police station in Shi'ite Muslim district of Sadr City, northeast of Baghdad

Baghdad, Iraq   October 12, 2003   7 killed, more than 35 wounded
A suicide car bomb exploded at a parking lot outside a hotel used by members of Iraq's Governing Council, as well as by many Americans

Baghdad, Iraq   October 14, 2003   1 killed, 10 wounded
Suicide bomber explodes outside the Turkish embassy in Baghdad

Baghdad, Iraq   October 28, 2003   at least 34 killed, 230 wounded
Suicide bombers strike four times in rush hour in attacks aimed at Red Cross offices and three police stations

Riyadh, Saudi Arabia   November 9, 2003 18 people killed, 120 wounded
Al-Qaeda suicide bombers devastate the guarded 200-villa Muhaya complex in the Saudi Arabian capital

Nassiriya, southern Iraq   November 12, 2003   19 Italians and 9 Iraqis killed,
                                                 at least 100 wounded
Suicide car bombers devastate Italian military police base

Istanbul, Turkey   November 15, 2003   25 killed, 300 wounded
Two coordinated suicide car bombs explode outside two synagogues during prayer services

Istanbul, Turkey   November 20, 2003   at least 27 dead, more than 400 wounded
Two explosions at the HSBC Bank headquarters and the British consulate, Britain consul general is among the dead, Turkish Islamic group linked to Al-Qaeda originally intended to hit an Israeli ship

Islamabad, Pakistan   December 25, 2003   13 killed, 46 wounded
Attempt on life of President Pervez Musharraf, second bomber was an Afghani with membership in Afghan Jihad

Karbala, Iraq   December 27, 2003   13 killed, 45 injured
Bombing is executed in a Shi'ite Holy city

2004

Erez checkpost, Gaza,   January 14, 2004   4 killed
Israel
A young Palestinian mother of two toddlers, a 3-year-old son and a 1-year-old daughter, feigns a limp and claims she is requesting medical help (she also tells soldiers she had a metal pin implanted in an operation that would set off the

metal detector) blows herself up at a security inspection point for Palestinian workers

| Baghdad, Iraq | January 18, 2004 | at least 32 killed, more than 60 injured |

Suicide car bomber blows up his vehicle at a main gate to the U.S. headquarters compound as hundreds of people lined up to enter the building to begin their work day

Kabul, Afghanistan

	Summer 2003	4 German soldiers killed
	January 27, 2004	3 Canadian soldiers killed, 11 wounded
	January 30, 2004	1 Canadian and 1 British soldier killed

Suicide bombers attack international peacekeeping forces; there were no suicide bombers in years of Afghan jihad against Soviets, or in the Northern Alliance's battle against the Taliban

| Irbil, in Kurdish area, Iraq | February 1, 2004 | more than 100 dead, hundreds wounded |

Two coordinated suicide bombers strike the offices of two Kurdish political parties as party leaders receive hundreds of people gathered to celebrate a Muslim holiday, the Feast of the Sacrifice; the two attacks deliver devastating blows to the political leadership of the Kurdish people

| Iskandriya, Iraq | February 10, 2004 | at least 54 killed, about 75 injured |

Suicide car bomber explodes outside a police station, the dead and wounded are civilians waiting to apply for police jobs. A senior officer with tears says, "These people who were killed came here to put food on their table and they died" (New York Times).

| Baghdad, Iraq | February 11, 2004 | at least 47 killed, dozens wounded |

Suicide car bomber explodes outside recruiting station of Iraqi Army headquarters next door to the volunteer center of a Shi'ite political party and near the main railway station. A U.S. Army colonel tells Reuters, "It was aimed strictly at Iraqis."

| Kirkuk, Iraq | February 23, 2004 | at least 10 killed, at least 50 injured |

Suicide car bombing at police station, Kirkuk has a heterogeneous population of Arabs, Kurds, Christians, and Turks surrounded by some of the richest oil fields

| Baghdad and Karbala, Iraq | March 3, 2004 | more than 140 people dead, unnumbered hundreds more injured |

An amazing coordinated series of suicide bombs and mortar attacks rips through Shi'ite Muslim religious ceremonies both in Baghdad and in the city of Karbala, about 80 km south of Baghdad, where there are at least five powerful blasts among the pilgrims who had flocked to pray on their holy days. In Baghdad, one suicide bomb blasted at the gates of a shrine, another bomber then blew himself up inside the shrine, and as the crowds ran screaming, a third bomber struck – the bomber had planted himself at the mouth of the doors, and the explosion ripped into the trapped crowd.

■Madrid, Spain

March 11, 2004   191 dead, hundreds wounded
April 4, 2004   5 dead, 15 wounded

Spain's "3/11" saw ten bombs ripping apart four commuter trains in three stations near simultaneously in the Al-Qaeda tradition. For Spain and Europe, 3/11 was seen as a definitive announcement of the threat of Al-Qaeda everywhere on the European continent as on other continents. There was no need to carry out the above bombings as suicide bombings, but on April 4 when Spanish Special Forces and police caught up with what they believe was the main leadership group of the bombings, the terrorists opened fire and resorted to suicide bombing, killing four of them and one Special Forces agent.

Tashkent, Uzbekistan   March 28, 2004   20 killed in shootout,
                                                                                     5 killed earlier in suicide bombings

20 terrorists die in a shootout at an alleged terrorist bomb-making hideaway after 2 suicide bombings that killed 3 policemen; Wahhabis of a branch of Al-Qaeda are responsible, according to Interior Ministry. Movement intends to establish an Islamic state in area (Ferghana Valley) which straddles Uzbekistan, Kyrgyzstan, and Tajikistan.

April 12, 2004, *Newsweek:*
"Since the Iraq war began, at least 48 suicide bombers have killed more than 700 people."

Riyadh, Saudi Arabia   April 21, 2004   at least 9 killed, 60–125 wounded
Two car bombers parked about 50 feet from the headquarters of Saudi Arabia's police force

Karachi, Pakistan   May 6, 2004   at least 14 people killed,
                                                                                     100 wounded

Suicide bomb attack in a packed Shi'ite mosque during Friday prayers. "The wounded lay screaming for help on bloodstained carpets in the mosque while dazed worshippers stumbled out" (Associated Press).

Baghdad, Iraq   June 15, 2004   at least 13 people killed
Suicide bomber rams a truck full of explosives into a convoy of foreign contractors

Baghdad, Iraq   June 17, 2004   at least 35 dead, 138 wounded
Powerful suicide car bomb rips into a throng of men waiting to sign up for new Iraqi Army outside its main recruiting station

Baghdad, Iraq   July 28, 2004   70 people killed, about 55 wounded
Suicide bomber detonated an explosive-packed sedan in street; he was aiming at new police recruits, but killed scores of ordinary Iraqis busy with their morning

Moscow, Russia   August 25, 2004   90 dead
Two Russian passenger jets crashed almost simultaneously: Flight 1047, a Tupolev 154 crashed near the southern city Rostov-on-Don with 46 people on board; Volga AviaExpess Flight 1303, crashed about 100 miles, or 160 kilometers, south of Moscow, killing 43. Two Chechen women are presumed to be possible suicide bombers. In the past two years, women known as "black widows" said to be avenging the deaths of husbands, brothers, or sons in Chechnya, have been involved in some of Russia's most spectacular suicide attacks, including the bombing of a subway train in Moscow in February that killed at least 41. A Web site of a group calling itself the Islambouli Brigades of Al-Qaeda claimed responsibility for both crashes.

Kabul, Afghanistan   August 30, 2004   8 killed
Explosion tears through the office of an American security contractor that provides security for Afghanistan's president, Hamid Karzai and works for the U.S. government in Iraq. Two Americans and a suicide bomber were among the dead.

Moscow, Russia   August 30, 2004   at least 8 people dead, 10 wounded
A female suicide bomber exploded a car outside a central Moscow subway station in an area between the entrance to the station and a supermarket-department store complex. The blast came a week after two Russian passenger planes exploded simultaneously killing all ninety people aboard.

Beersheva, Israel   August 31, 2004   16 dead, 100 wounded
Two buses are exploded by two suicide bombers in the center of the city within twenty seconds of each other. This was the first 'successful' suicide bombing in Israel in six months. The Hamas claims responsibility and defines the bombings as revenge for the assassination of their leader, Sheikh Yassin and then his successor, Dr. Abdel Aziz Rantissi. Palestinians in Gaza dance in the streets in joy.

■**Beslan, Russia   Sept. 1–4, 2004   326 dead (including about 20 of 30 attacking suicide bombers), at least 172 of them children, 727 wounded, about half of them children**
More than 2 dozen Chechens seize 1,200 hostages, mainly children, at a school in southern Russia. The terrorists hid their weapons in the school weeks earlier. Not all the attackers realized their mission was to seize a school, and when at least one objected, he was shot dead by the leader of the attackers. A 52-hour standoff between Russian troops and the attackers ended when one of many bombs laid out by the Chechens in the school gymnasium exploded apparently in error.

Taking advantage of the panic, children began to escape through windows, the attackers shot at them, and the Russians fired back.

Sinai, Egypt   October 7, 2004   33 dead
Terrorists attacked three Sinai resorts including tearing the frontage off the Taba Hilton just outside of Eilat, Israel. Two of the attacks were by suicide bombers, and one attack somewhat further south in Nuweiba on the Red Sea was by booby-trapped cars detonated by remote control.

Baghdad and Mosul, Iraq   December 4, 2004   14 killed, at least 59 wounded
Suicide attackers carried out a string of car bombings against Iraqi policemen in Baghdad and Kurdish militiamen in the north. In Baghdad, insurgents unleashed two suicide car bombs nearly simultaneously at a police station just across the street from a checkpoint leading into the heavily fortified Green Zone, the seat of American and Iraqi power in Baghdad. A policeman who survived the attack, said that a "suicide car bomber sped into our police station" (Haaretz, from the Associated Press). In the northern city of Mosul, a suicide bomber pulled his explosive-laden vehicle alongside a bus bringing Kurdish fighters into the city. The latest attacks were particularly audacious and sent a clear message that the insurgents can strike wherever they choose.

Karbala, Iraq   December 19, 2004   14 killed, 52 wounded
A suicide bomber detonated his vehicle amid minibuses at the entrance to the city's bus terminal. This attack came on a day when at least 50 more people were dead from a variety of attacks in three large Iraqi cities, including Baghdad and Najaf.

Mosul, Iraq   December 22, 2004   22 dead, 69 wounded
A suicide bomber blew himself up in a U.S. military dining tent near Mosul. He was probably wearing an Iraqi military uniform, the U.S. military said. A U.S. general in northern Iraq acknowledged that the bomber may have gotten through the process conducted by United States and Iraqi authorities to check the backgrounds of Iraqis joining the security services. Ansar al-Sunnah Army, a military group, claimed responsibility for the attack in a statement reiterating that it was a suicide bombing: "God enabled one of your martyr brothers to plunge into God's enemies inside their forts, killing and injuring hundreds," the group said on its Web site. The blast was the deadliest single attack on a U.S. base to date, hitting the dining tent at lunchtime.

Baghdad; Tikrit, and   December 27, 2004 9 killed, 67 wounded in Baghdad
Samarra, Iraq
A suicide car bomber sets off a huge explosion outside the Baghdad headquarters of the nation's largest Shi'ite political party. The leader of the party, Abdul Azis al-Hakin, who has emerged as one of the country's most powerful political figures in the run-up to national elections next month, was inside the building but unhurt in the blast, which was felt across central Baghdad.

Baghdad, Iraq   December 28, 2004   at least 25 people killed
At least 25 Iraqis were killed in a string of other types of attacks, including one in which 12 policemen's throats were slit in their police station near Tikrit. In the central city of Sumarra, a suicide bomber detonated his car in the city center wounding ten people including three children.

2005

Iraq: A ceaseless wave of suicide bombings and car bombs swept Iraq in the months preceding the scheduled first democratic elections, and then continued with the expressed intent of toppling the emerging Iraqi government as an accomplice of the United States even after the very successful elections in which a high percentage of Iraqis did vote

Baghdad, Iraq   January 4, 2005   governor assassinated, 11 killed
Unidentified gunmen open fire on governor's convoy in Baghdad's northern neighborhood of Hurriyah; suicide bomber attacks a police checkpoint. "The shooting of Governor Ali al-Haidri in a roadside ambush showed insurgents' power to strike at the heart of the governing class" (International Herald Tribune).

Baghdad, Iraq   January 21, 2005   at least 4 killed, 16 wounded;
                                                 at least 14 killed, 40 wounded
A suicide bomber detonated an ambulance at a Shi'ite wedding party in a village near Youssifiyah, 20 km south of Baghdad. Simultaneously, a car bomb exploded outside a Shi'ite mosque just after morning prayers on the second day of a Muslim holiday. Akeel Kamil, who owns a nearby telephone shop, said: "When the worshippers finished prayers, they detonated" (International Herald Tribune).

Basrai, Iraq
"It's not the man who exploded himself who is a martyr," said Jasmin, a friend of a wounded man from a suicide attack, as the body washer wiped dried blood from his friend's wounds. "He wasn't a true Muslim. This is the martyr. What religion asks people to blow themselves up? It's not written in the Koran."—Following a suicide bombing at a polling place on the first election day on January 30, 2005 (*New York Times*).

Baghdad, Iraq   February 18, 2005   at least 29 killed, 58 wounded
Suicide bombers attacked two mosques in and near Baghdad as Shi'ite Muslims prepared for Ashura, the holiest day of the year for Shi'ites. The attacks took place as worshippers were in their prayers. In the first of the blasts, a suicide bomber wearing either a belt or vest of explosives was stopped by a security guard at the front gate to the mosque ... As the guard grappled with the man, he set off the explosive. One of the wounded in the second blast said he had been late for prayers and was walking quickly into the mosque when the blast occurred. "I found myself on the ground completely paralyzed." He added: "They will fail. They will go and we will stay" (New York Times).

Hilla,   February 28, 2005   at least 106 dead, 133 wounded
south of Baghdad, Iraq
A suicide bomber blew himself up in a crowd of police and Iraqi national guard recruits south of Baghdad. "People were queuing up to be checked medically in order to become policemen. A car came . . . and exploded . . ." (Associated Press).

Mosul, Iraq   March 10, 2005   at least 36 people killed
A suicide bomber blew himself up inside a Shi'ite mosque in the northern Iraqi city of Mosul. Mosul has been a hotbed of insurgent activity and the scene of many bombings, drive-by shootings and assassinations against the country's security services, the Shi'ite majority and people thought to be working with U.S.-led forces.

Doha, Qatar   March 20, 2005   1 killed, 16 wounded
In first suicide bombing in an Arab Emirate, an Egyptian suicide bomber believed to be associated with Al-Qaeda drove a car loaded with explosives into a theatre in the capital city, Doha. Qatar provided a command headquarters for U.S. troops in the invasion of Saddam's Iraq.

♦ Baghdad, Iraq   April 29, 2005   at least 20 killed and at least
                                                                          65 wounded
Four suicide car bombings in quick succession in Baghdad. The first suicide bombing hit an Iraqi army patrol, the second a police patrol, and the third and fourth hit different barricades near the headquarters of the police special forces unit. The suicide bombings were joined by other attacks across Iraq killing at least forty-one people and wounding more than one hundred in a single day.

Cairo, Egypt   April 30, 2005   7 wounded
Suicide bomber explodes himself in a shouk (bazaar) near the Egyptian National Museum aiming at tourists milling in the area. An hour later, his sister and his fiancée open fire on a bus full of tourists and injure another three people before they are killed—according to one report the sister herself shoots the fiancé and then sets out to kill herself before being shot by security forces.

Erbil, Iraq   May 4, 2005   at least 60 killed, about 150 wounded
A suicide bomber pretending to be a job seeker blew himself up outside a police recruiting center in the Kurdish provincial capital, Erbil. The attack was the second postwar strike of its magnitude in the normally calm Kurdish territories, where the disciplined Kurdish militia, the Pesh Merga, enforce a strict system of checkpoints and racial profiling intended to keep out terrorists.

Iraq.   May 9, 2005:
Suicide attacks have killed about 300 people in the past 10 days according to senior American officials. 135 car bombs exploded in April, up from 69 in March, and more than in any other month in the two-year American occupation. For the first time last month, more than 50 percent of the car-bombings were suicide attacks, some remotely detonated, suggesting that

Iraqis, who typically do not use that tactic, are being forced or duped into driving those missions, an American general said.

Baghdad, Iraq   May 12, 2005   86 killed, many wounded
In a series of attacks, 86 people were killed in one day. A suicide bomber exploded a car bomb in the busy, ethnically mixed eastern Jadida district of the capital, at least eight cars and a bus were caught in the blast which blew out windows and storefronts and sent street vendors' stalls flying. The last attack was a suicide bombing in a car loaded with explosives near a residential building. In April alone there were 67 suicide killings in Iraq.

Islamabad, Pakistan   May 27, 2005   at least 18 killed, 67 wounded
A powerful explosion, apparently set off by a suicide bomber, ripped through a crowded gathering at a Muslim shrine in the outskirts of Islamabad, the Pakistani capital, at the shrine of Shah Abdul Latif Kazmi. Kazmi was popularly known as Bari Imam, a seventeenth-century Sufi saint famous for his teachings of religious harmony and tolerance. The shrine is in a village near the diplomatic enclave in Islamabad which Shi'ites and Sunnis attend equally. According to the International Herald Tribune, "Muslims belonging to the Shi'ite and Sunni sects generally live in harmony, but violence between extremist groups from both sides has left hundreds dead. Shi'ites make up 20 percent of Pakistan's population while Sunnis make up 77 percent."

Fallujah, Iraq   June 23, 2005   4 dead (1 woman), 13 wounded
                                                                  (11 women)
Suicide bombing of a vehicle filled mostly with female U.S. Marines who perform security checks on women passing in and out of Fallujah

Baghdad, Iraq   June 28, 2005   4 dead, 4 wounded
Kirkuk, Iraq   2 dead, 4 wounded
A suicide car bomber killed an influential Shi'ite member, the interim speaker of Parliament and his son, as they drove to the capital. The attack that killed Dhari Ali al-Fayadh, his son, and two bodyguards was one of several around the country carried out by suicide bombers.

In Kirkuk, 290 kilometers north of Baghdad a suicide car bomber slammed into a convoy carrying the police chief, Brigadier General Salar Ahmed, killing one of his bodyguards and a civilian. Four others, including Ahmed and three of his bodyguards were wounded.

■**London, England   July 7, 2005   66 dead, over 700 wounded**
                                       also July 21, 2005
A series of four suicide bombings came almost simultaneously in the rush hour in three Underground stations and one bus. The attacks began at Liverpool Street Station when an explosion tore through a subway train 100 meters into the tunnel; continued at Liverpool Street, a hub which links the subway to overland trains; continued with a blast ripping through Edgware Road Station,

again 100 meters inside the tunnel; and concluded with an explosion on the upper deck of a bus at Tavistock Square.

Three of the bombers, Mohammad Sidique Khan, 30, Shehzad Tanweer, 22, and Hasib Mir Hussain, 18, were found to be born and educated in Britain, while the fourth, Germaine Lindsay, 19, was a Jamaican-born U.K. citizen. This coordinated attack became the British 9/11, "proving once and for all Britain's vulnerability to Moslem terror. The further shock for Britain was to learn the suicide bombers were not 'imported' from Al-Qaeda units overseas but were homegrown from the local British community" (International Herald Tribune).

A group identifying itself with Al-Qaeda claimed responsibility.

"Rejoice Islamic nation, Rejoice, Arabic world," said the group's statement on a Web site. "The time has come for revenge against the Zionist crusader government of Britain." (Statement on a Web site used often by Islamic militants, according to Elaph, a secular Arabic-language news Web site).

Two weeks later on July 21, Islamic terrorists struck again in what appeared an effort to repeat the same pattern of three attacks in the Underground and one on a bus, but this time all four explosive rigs failed to blow—the detonator caps exploded but not the explosives. The would-be suicide bombers fled the scenes. Their subsequent arrests, and arrests of others who were associated with them are expected to produce a great deal of counterterrorist information.

Baghdad and	July 10, 2005	at least 33 dead,
Kirkuk, Iraq		more than 74 wounded

A man with explosives strapped to his body blew himself up at an Iraqi military recruiting center in Baghdad as suicide bombers attacked three times in Iraq on this day. The explosion occurred as some 400 potential recruits were crowded outside the gate of the center. Another attack in Kirkuk occurred on a highway near a hospital; most of the casualties were people headed to Kirkuk General Hospital. A third suicide bombing took place along the Iraq-Syrian border forcing closure of a checkpoint.

Baghdad, Iraq   July 13, 2005 up to 27 dead, at least 21 wounded
A suicide car bomber sped up to American soldiers distributing candy to children and detonated his explosives. In September, 35 Iraqi children were killed in a string of bombs that exploded as American troops were handing out candy at a government-sponsored celebration to inaugurate a sewage plant in west Baghdad.

Baghdad, Iraq   July 16, 2005   71 dead, 156 wounded
A suicide bomber wrapped in explosives detonated himself next to a gasoline tanker south of Baghdad creating a devastating fireball. The bombing, one of the most deadly suicide attacks since the American invasion of Iraq, attacked a Shi'ite mosque and a crowded open-air market.

In Iraq, American military commanders have begun to refer to the suicide bomb as the "precision-guided weapon" of the enemy (New York Times).

Sharm El Sheikh, Egypt   July 23, 2005   88 dead, 55 wounded
Three nearly simultaneous bombings took place on a Saturday night after 1 a.m. Egyptian authorities attribute the first, at the Ghazala Garden Hotel, to a car bomb where the bomber drove his truck into the lobby. Another bomb exploded in a crowded coffee house in the market place, and a third at Movenpick Hotel. One Egyptian wounded said, "It is all the West's fault. They have destroyed us."

Baghdad, Iraq   July 24, 2005   at least 40 dead, 33 wounded
A suicide truck bomb exploded at a police station in the middle of a sandstorm cloaking buildings and streets with a thick layer of grit. The driver of the truck, loaded with 225 kilograms of explosives, rammed into concrete barricades outside the station before the vehicle burst into a ball of fire, incinerating people nearby and peppering them with shrapnel.

Baghdad, Iraq   September 14, 2005   at least 75 killed, 162 wounded
                                             full day death toll of 167
Suicide bomber explodes among day workers waiting for work at 6:50 a.m. in Aruba Square, one of Baghdad's largest Shi'ite districts. The bomber used a trick of luring the laborers to a van with promises of work and then blew it up. More bombings followed throughout the day – there were at least 14 bombings on this day, with a death toll of 167, the worst in a single day since U.S. occupied Baghdad.

"There are only two camps—the camp of truth and its followers, and the camp of falsehood and its Shi'ites. You must choose in which of the two trenches you lie ... Whoever is proven to belong to the Pagan [National] Guard, to the police, or to the army, or whoever is proven to be a Crusader collaborator or spy—he shall be killed ... This is his reward for betraying his religion and his nation, so that he shall serve as a clear lesson and a preventive warning to others."—the leader of Al-Qaeda in Iraq

Balad, Iraq   September 29, 2005   at least 60 dead, 70 wounded
Three suicide attackers detonated car bombs nearly simultaneously in a mainly Shi'ite town north of Baghdad before sunset hitting a bank, a vegetable market and another location in the center of Balad, about 80 kilometers north of the capital.

Bali, Indonesia   October 1, 2005   at least 25 dead, more than
                                                 100 wounded
Three near-simultaneous blasts at two packed seafood cafes on Jimbaran beach and a three-story noodle and steak house in downtown Kuta about 30 kilometers away ripped through three crowded restaurants on the Indonesian resort island of Bali. The bombings were suicide bombers, by the Al-Qaeda linked militant group, Jemaah Islamiya.

Amman, Jordan   November 9, 2005   at least 69 killed, about 115 wounded
*Bombs rocked three hotels in Amman: from U.S. hotel chains, the Grand Hyatt
and Days Inn, and the Swedish Radisson SAS. The three suicide attacks were simultaneous and hit minutes before 9 p.m. sending smoke bellowing into the streets
of Amman. The first bomber, at 8:50 p.m. struck the Grand Hyatt, completely
shattering the stone entrance. CNN reported an eyewitness saying the Jordanian
prime minister's car was at the Grand Hyatt at the time of the blast. A second
explosion hit the nearby Radisson SAS hotel where about 250 people including
Jordanian notables were attending a wedding reception. Jordanian officials arrested an Iraqi woman, Sajida Mubarak Atrous al-Rishawi, who appeared on
Jordanian TV confessing that it was she and her husband who entered the Radisson wearing explosive-packed belts during the wedding reception. Her husband
went to one direction and carried out his attack. while her trigger cord failed to
work. A spokesman for Al-Qaeda in Iraq, claimed responsibility for the attacks
and charged that the "tyrant of Jordan has made the backyard garden for the
enemy of religion: Jews and crusaders." Among the dead were Jordanians, Iraqis,
Indonesians, Chinese, Syrians and Saudi Arabians. In July, there had been a failed
multiple-rocket attack in Jordan against two American warships in the southern
port city of Aqaba.*

**"As a Jordanian I have been haunted by a gruesome, saddening portrait
of humanity, with its pitfalls garishly highlighted." —Munjed Farid al-Qutob,
*International Herald Tribune***

Baghdad, Iraq   November 10, 2005   at least 29 killed, 30 wounded
*A man wearing a suicide bomb belt walked into a bustling breakfast restaurant
in the heart of Baghdad and blew himself up. The bomber struck shortly after
9:30 a.m. in the Qadouri Restaurant, known for its traditional dishes of eggs and
meat and which is popular among police officers, and on the day of the attack was
packed with the usual breakfast crowd. Al-Qaeda in Iraq claimed responsibility for
the attack. The suicide bombing was the most lethal in the capital in two months
and was the worst strike in a day of violence in Iraq that left at least 35 dead and
more than 50 wounded. The attack occurred a day after three suicide bombings in
Amman killed sixty-nine people in a coordinated attack also claimed by Al-Qaeda.*

Khanaqin, Iraq   November 18, 2005   at least 65 killed, scores more
                                              wounded
*A pair of suicide bombers detonated explosive belts inside two Shi'ite mosques
in the northern Kurdish town of Khanaqin. The attack came as worshippers were
gathering for Friday prayers. It was the deadliest coordinated bombing in Iraq
in nearly three months, and came hours after two suicide truck bombs exploded
outside the Hamra Hotel, one of the most important and perhaps the most heavily
populated expatriate center outside the fortified Green Zone and houses many
foreign journalists. The blasts which killed at least six Iraqis and wounded at
least 60, completely reduced a neighboring apartment building to rubble. The
collapse of the apartment building sent a mushroom cloud above the Baghdad*

skyline. Closely resembling an attack last month on two other prominent hotels, it shattered any notion that journalists might have had about retaining a protected or neutral status in this war.

Abu Saida, Iraq   November 19, 2005 at least 48 dead, about 50 wounded
A suicide bomber exploded himself at a mourners' tent that was filled with visitors who came to mourn the death of a Shi'ite leader in a town near Baqouba in northern Iraq.

"Even by the bloody standards of this conflict, the bombing was particularly vicious, aimed at hospital workers and those going to visit the sick and infirmed."—as cited in following story from *New York Times*

Mahmudiya, Iraq   November 24, 2005   at least 30 killed, at least 23 wounded
A car bomb exploded outside the main hospital in the town of Mahmudiya. The bomb detonated as people were gathering in the morning at the front gate of the hospital. "Even by the bloody standards of this conflict, the bombing was particularly vicious, aimed at hospital workers and those going to visit the sick and infirmed."

Chittagong and Gazipur   November 29, 2005 11 killed, more than 100 wounded
Gazipur, Bangladesh   December 1, 2005
three suicide bombings in three days
The first two synchronized suicide bombings on November twenty-nine targeted a courthouse in Chittagong, a major southern port city, and a legal office in Gazipur, north of the capital, and the third suicide bombing went off near a meeting of lawyers at a government office in Gazipur. The second suicide bomber had disguised himself in a black lawyer's robe, and blew himself up inside the crowded Gazipur Bar Association office, where some 50 lawyers and their clients had assembled. The third bomber detonated explosives hidden in a tea flask. "Litigants are not feeling safe to come to the courts," said Rokanuddin Mahmud, a member of the Bangladesh Bar Council. "The environment of our administration of justice has been destroyed."

"I want to ask the mujahedeen: 'Do you slaughter your brother in the name of jihad?'" (as cited in following story from Baghdad in the *International Herald Tribune*)

Baghdad, Iraq   December 6, 2005   at least 36 police officers killed,
                                                      72 others wounded
Powerful explosions from a pair of suicide bombers ripped through the capital's main police academy.
    A trainer at the academy who was sobbing while lying on a marble bench in a hallway of Al Kindi Hospital: "I just want to ask, 'Is this jihad? Is this jihad against Iraqis?' I want to ask the mujahedeen, 'Do you slaughter your brother in the name of jihad?'" The attack was the deadliest in the capital in months.

The bombers, each armed with explosive vests, made their way into the academy despite what some officers described as meticulous searches at the entrances. They demonstrated an unerring knowledge of the layout of the compound and the procedures inside. After the first bomber detonated at about 12:45 p.m. in the courtyard, the second bomber exploded inside a shelter to which many of the officers had fled.

Baghdad, Iraq   December 8, 2005   at least 30 killed, at least
                                                      25 wounded

Two near-simultaneous explosions, at least one detonated by a suicide bomber, tore through a crowded bus in the capital's main bus terminal. The bus bombing occurred in the Nahda terminal in central Baghdad, which handles buses destined for the Kurdish North and the Shi'ite-dominated South. The bus was about to leave the terminal when the bomber, ignoring the fare collector's admonitions, forced himself on board. Bystanders heard a small explosion that appeared to come from the luggage hold, then saw the bomber detonate himself causing a fireball that engulfed the bus that killed most of its occupants and several people at a nearby food stall.

Baghdad, Iraq   January 4, 2006   more than 50 killed, at least
                                                      36 wounded

Insurgents killed more than fifty people as they unleashed car bombs and suicide attacks throughout central Iraq in the deadliest day since the national parliamentary elections three weeks ago.

In the most lethal attack they hit a favored and particularly easy objective – a burial service packed with Shi'ite mourners—killing at least 30 people and wounding 36 during a two-stage bombing of a funeral procession in Muzdadiya, 100 kilometers northeast of the capital. The first attacker, according to one witness, wore a slim bomb strapped to his torso and waded into a pack of grieving relatives surrounding the coffin. Shortly after the first attacker struck, a car bomber drove into the frantic crowd and exploded, killing more mourners. The victims at the funeral had come to pay last respects to a physician who was killed after he ignored warnings to stop treating members of the Iraqi security forces.

Karbala and Ramadi, Iraq   January 5, 2006   at least 100 killed, at least
                                                      124 wounded

Two new suicide bombings rocked Iraq in attacks at a shrine in the Shi'ite city of Karbala and a police recruiting station in the Sunni city of Ramadi. The killings come on top of attacks that left more than 50 people dead yesterday. In Karbala, the attack took place about 20 meters outside a shrine in the middle of a large crowd. The area is packed with vendors' stalls and the shrine had a higher number of visitors than usual. The bomber was wearing an explosive belt under clothing packed with metal balls, and was also carrying hand grenades, one of which failed to detonate. More than 60 Shi'ite pilgrims died just steps away from the Imam Hussein shrine in Karbala, one of Shi'ite Islam's holiest sites, when a terrorist detonated an explosive vest just after 10 a.m. Pools of blood and body parts were strewn about, and survivors shrieked and cried while people ripped benches from buildings to use as stretchers. The police chief in Karbala said the suicide vest had contained at least 15 pounds of high explosives and was studded with ball bearings that shot through the crowd to maximize the slaughter. Health officials said the dead included Iranian visitors and a 3-month-old baby, and that at least 63 people had been wounded. In Ramadi, the target of the attack was a line of about 1,000 potential recruits waiting to apply for a position in the Iraqi police force.

Tirin Kot, Afghanistan   January 5, 2006   at least 10 killed, at least
                                                        50 wounded

A suicide bomber blew himself up in a crowd of people in Tirin Kot, the capital of southern Oruzgan Province as the American ambassador was meeting with local officials. The explosion killed civilians in a market, which was busy with shoppers. Incidents of suicide bombings have increased in the last six months in Afghanistan. Afghans had not usually used this tactic, but there have been about twenty suicide attacks in Afghanistan, most of them in the last few months.

Baghdad, Iraq   April 7, 2006   71 killed, at least 140 wounded

Three suicide bombers, at least one of them a woman, exploded in a sea of worshippers at the main mosque of the most powerful Shi'ite political party in Iraq. The explosions at the Baratha Mosque in northern Baghdad took place just minutes after a prominent imam, Sheik Jalaladin al-Sagheir, delivered a speech. One bomb exploded at the front gate. Panic erupted and worshippers who had been trying to leave streamed back toward the main courtyard. Two other bombers slipped in during the chaos and exploded by the separate prayer areas for men and women. The well-guarded Baratha Mosque is the main religious center for the Supreme Council for the Islamic Revolution in Iraq, an Iranian-backed party that heads the Shi'ite bloc. It was clear that the explosions went to the very heart of the Shi'ites' sense of victimhood.

Dahab, Egypt   April 24, 2006   at least 30 killed, more than
                       April 26, 2006   115 wounded 2 suicide bombers
                                              dead, no victims

On April 24, suicide bombers exploded three bombs at a Sinai beach resort, killing twenty-one people, most of them Egyptians. The attack was the third in two years at a Sinai resort. It was also the third near a national holiday, in the present case, the anniversary of Sinai being returned to Egypt by Israel. On April 26, two suicide bombers struck near the main base of the multinational peacekeeping force near the Gaza border in Sinai killing themselves but causing no other casualties. The 1,800 peacekeepers monitor the 1979 Egypt-Israeli peace deal. A total of ten countries make up the force—the United States, Canada, Australia, Colombia, Fiji, France, Hungary, Italy, New Zealand, and Uruguay. Norway also provides the force with three officers, although it is not technically a member.

CONCLUSION: SUICIDE BOMBING IS A REDEFINITION OF THE LEGITIMACY OF VIRTUALLY ALL KILLING

Over the last few years, suicide bombings and other terror attacks have been constructed in an endless number of scenarios that invade every aspect of normal civilian life, from markets to eating places to cafes and dancing places, to schools, religious centers including during times of worship, medical centers, transport vehicles and transportation centers, political and other public gatherings, government offices, including where couples register to marry, and at weddings, funerals and mourners' tents, places to which people flee for safety after a first suicide bombing which is then followed by another suicide bombing in the would-be shelter—and more, wherever human beings congregate.

Moreover, every conceivable ruse is used by the suicide bombers who disguise themselves in any and every way that will gain them admission and close access to their intended victims: the suicide bombers appear as sick people seeking medical treatment, pregnant women on their way to appropriate obstetric care, ambulance drivers, religious people or clergymen, police officers, soldiers, newspaper or television journalists, tourists—whatever.

Warfare has been conceived to some extent as a joust of armies operating according to some rules that protect against promiscuous killings of unarmed civilians. However, contemporary terrorism allows for murders of nonmilitary targets and an induction of terror in the whole civilian population of the enemy as they go about their daily activities. Suicide bombing today is a newly powerful form of terrorism that has been extended to all walks and venues of life, including, as noted, those that were once held off limits to purposeful killing.

Suicide bombing in the early twenty-first century has become a message that all restraints, reservations and limitations, and all legal restriction such as the Geneva Conventions as well as any moral conventions that may have outlawed or delegitimized a given form of killing are now suspended and irrelevant. One major result is that humanity now lives in foreboding expectation that suicide bombers will be the ones who attack with the ultimate weapons of mass destruction.

---

[1] Experience shows that the number of killed and wounded are reported somewhat inconsistently by different news sources, and they are also approximate because some of the wounded die at a later date. The statistics also do not convey the pain, misery and grave handicaps and disabilities that plague many of the wounded for years to come if not for the remainder of their lives, as well as the enormous price paid by the families of the dead and wounded for many years after the event.

[2] All of the events in the list are from recognized international news sources, and can be accessed easily from many news archives. Up until the report of October 7, 2004, reports were drawn from a combination of individual news reports and from chronologies such as ReutersAlertNet/Chronology/Worst bomb attacks in 2003. Guardian Unlimited/Sri Lanka chronology, and others. From October 7, 2004 each report has been drawn from news reports of the specific event. The complete list of sources has been reviewed by the publisher and remains on file with the author. The publication sources of quotations used in special feature comments are give in the text.

Notes

Epigraph

1. Primo Levi Afterword in *Night of the Girondists. (De Nacht der Girondijnen) by Jacques Presser.* Translated from Dutch into Hebrew by Irit Varsano-Landman, Hakibbutz Hameuchad. Translated into English by Barrows Mussey. Harper-Collins. Levi's statement is as summarized by Nili Keren (January 7, 2005), Evil in the mirror, *Haaretz (English Edition)*, B10.

Selected Worldwide Case Incidents

1. Rory McCarthy (January 19, 2004), Suicide bomb at U.S. headquarters kills 20 and injures more than 100, *Guardian Unlimited*, Retrieved from the Web.
2. Frank Griffiths (July 11, 2005), Iraq suicide bombings kill dozens, *Moscow Times,* with attribution to the *Associated Press*, Retrieved from the Web.
3. Bassem Mroue (July 14, 2005), Twelve children killed in Iraq suicide bombing, *Jerusalem Post.*
4. Kirk Semple and, John F. Burns (July 16, 2005), All-day suicide bomb blitz claims 22 lives in Baghdad, *New York Times*, Retrieved from the Web.
5. *CNN.com* (July 17, 2005), Iraq suicide bombings kill 99, Retrieved from the Web.
6. Dan Eggen and Scott Wilson (July 17, 2005), Suicide bombs potent tools of terrorists: Deadly attacks have been increasing and spreading since September 11, 2001, *Washingtonpost.com*, Retrieved from the Web.
7. Robert F. Worth (September 14, 2005), 75 killed in Baghdad Blast; Amended Charter approved, *New York Times*; Richard A. Oppel, Jr. and Robert F. Worth (September 15, 2005), A wave of attacks kills 150 in Iraq. *International Herald Tribune,* pp. 1,4, with attribution to the *New York Times*; Robert F. Worth and Richard A. Oppel, Jr. (September 15, 2005), At least 20 killed by suicide car bombers in Baghdad, *New York Times*; Associated

Press (September 17, 2005), Nytimes.com. Car bombing at Iraq market leaves 30 dead. Each of the above stories was retrieved from the Web.

8. *Wikipedia Encyclopedia* (2004), Beslan school hostage crisis. Based on multiple reports from BBC, Russian press and government sources, and other reports as listed in the Encyclopedia, Last updated August 8, 2005, Retrieved from the Web, August 25, 2005. See also Associated Press (2004), Russia offers reward for information on rebels: Official promises use of 'preventive strikes' against terrorist bases, updated September 8, Retrieved from MSNBC.com, August 25, 2005.

9. YusufIslam.org.uk (2004), The Beslan Tragedy, September 2004: Yusuf Islam speaks out against the horrific Beslan school siege and its brutal ending.

10. Roni Shaked and Itzik Saban (June 21, 2005), After being stopped on her way to blowing up a suicide bomb in Soroka Hospital, this is what the terrorist tells *Yediot Achronot*: "I don't care if children will also die." Israeli secret service says that Wafa Samir Bas intended to blow herself up while standing up among the doctors who treated her in the past in Soroka Hospital. The terrorist: "I wanted to kill as many Jews as possible." *Yediot Achronot* (daily newspaper), pp. 2–3 (Hebrew).

11. Margot Dudkevitch (June 21, 2005), Female bomber planned to blow up at Soroka Hospital, *Jerusalem Post*, 1, 19.

12. *Yediot Achronot* story, op cit.

Preface

1. Full text of speech published in Iranian Students News Agency (Iran), October 26, 2005, Cited in Middle East Media Research Institute (MEMRI) (2005), Iranian President at Tehran Conference: "Very soon, this stain of disgrace [i.e. Israel] will vanish from the center of the Islamic world—and this is attainable." Special Dispatch—Iran, No. 1013, October 28.

2. Douglas Jehl and Thom Shanker (2005), Al Qaeda tells ally in Iraq to strive for global goals, Retrieved from the *New York Times*: nytimes.com, October 7; Bernard Haykel (October 11, 2005), Terminal debate, *New York Times*, Op-Ed, Retrieved from the *New York Times:* nytimes.com.

3. Alan Cowell and Dexter Filkins (August 11, 2006). U.K. foils plot to bomb U.S.-bound planes: Hundreds of flights held; 24 seized in broad sweep. *International Herald Tribune*, page 1. With attribution to the *New York Times*.

4. William K. Rashbaum and Eric Pfanner (August 11, 2006). Plan inivolved use of liquid explosives in hand luggage. *International Herald Tribune*, page 1. With attribution to the *New York Times*.

5. Raza Mumtaz, 'Pakistan Times' Executive Editor/UK Bureau Chief (August 11, 2006). 21 People Caged: Plot to blow up UK to US Airliners Foiled. *Pakistan Times*. "Top Story."

6. See on the Web: 10 Downing Street, *PM News*, August 14, 2006. Retrieved from www.number-10.gov.uk/output/page9949.asp.

7. Alan Cowell and Dexter Filkins, ibid.

8. Oriana Fallaci is a well-respected prize-winning but also controversial (for her strong negative views of Islam) Italian author and journalist who has been translated into many languages. In the United States, she has lectured at many universities including Chicago, Yale, Harvard, and Columbia. The quotation is taken from Oriana Fallaci (2005), "The enemy we treat like a friend" (Part 11), July 24. Retrieved from the Web:

www.mysteryachievement.blogspot.com/2005/07/enemy-we-treat-like-friend-part-ii.html. An
article by Oriana Fallaci published in *Corriere della Sera*.

9. Four suicide car bombings in quick succession in Baghdad. The first suicide bombing hit an Iraqi army patrol, the second a police patrol, and the third and fourth different barricades near the headquarters of the police special forces unit. The suicide bombings were joined by other attacks across Iraq killing at least 41 people and wounding more than 100 in a single day. *International Herald Tribune* (From News Reports: *AP, AFP*) (April 30, 2005), Spate of coordinated attacks in Iraq kills at least 41, p. 3.

10. Kirk Semple and John F. Burns (July 16, 2005), All-day suicide bomb blitz claims 22 lives in Baghdad, *New York Times*, Retrieved from the Web.

11. *Haaretz* (May 13, 2005) (with attribution to the *London Guardian*), 86 dead in a series of suicide bombings across Iraq.

12. Dan Eggen and Scott Wilson (July 17, 2005), Suicide bombs potent tools of terrorists: Deadly attacks have been increasing and spreading since September 11, 2001, *Washingtonpost.com*, Retrieved from the Web.

13. A very close acquaintance of mine, who is based in London, with whom I was discussing the tension of the pro and critical views of Islam that alternate in this book proposed to me that I get a Muslim coauthor for the book in order to "prove" further that this book is not at all against Islam as such. We then got into a playful fantasy that I would go to pick up a day laborer who waits at the borderline between East Jerusalem and West Jerusalem for Jewish employers, and after establishing that he has a good usable name like "Mohammed," I would bring him home for a day's work that would consist of my signing him up to the effect that he agrees to co-author the book. Even as we were laughing away at the progress of our fantasy, we realized that the poor guy would then be doomed to a high probability of being rubbed out for his collaboration with the West in my book's condemnation of suicide bombers. My friend then volunteered that we have to choose someone who is already dreaming of being a *shahid* (martyr), and at least we would be doing him a favor moving him toward his goal in life. At this point we didn't know whether to continue laughing or to be ashamed of our callousness, and so we stopped with a proper sense that we had now entered a zone of black humor that was no longer acceptable to either of us.

14. This information appeared in a critical article by the editor of *Akhbar Al-Yawn* (Egypt), Ibrahim Sa'dah, on January 1, 2005 who criticized the Arab Doctors' Association for aiding jihad warriors in Chechnya, Afghanistan, Iraq, and Bosnia, but refusing to help victims of the tsunami because it is "punishment from Allah," Cited in Middle East Media Research Institute (MEMRI) (2005), Editor of Egyptian Government Weekly: Arab Doctors' Association is aiding Jihad Warriors-but not Tsunami victims, Special Dispatch—Egypt/Reform Project, No. 846, January 13.

15. *International Herald Tribune* (July 11, 2005). The rationale of terror, p. 10.

16. Ibid.

17. Film (2005): *Human Weapon*.

18. Fallaci, "The enemy we treat like a friend."

Chapter 1

1. Excerpts from a show about the culture of martyrdom which aired on Al-Arabiya TV on July 22, 2005. Cited in Middle East Media Research Institute (MEMRI)

(2005). TV Program on the Culture of Martyrdom and Suicide Bombers on Al-Arabiya. Special Dispatch—Jihad & Terrorism, No. 961, August 19. To view this clip, visit: www.memritv.org/search.asp?ACT=S9&P1=807.

2. Jamestown Foundation (September 26, 2003), *Chechnya Weekly*, *4*, 34.

3. Manfred Gerstenfeld (May 2, 2004), The end of American Jewry's golden era, An interview with Daniel Pipes. *Post-Holocaust and Anti-Semitism, 20*. Jerusalem, Israel: Jerusalem Center for Public Affairs.

4. Samuel P. Huntington (1996), *The Clash of Civilizations and the Remaking of World Order*; and Bernard A. Lewis (2003), *The Crisis of Islam*.

5. *World Tribune.com* (September 10, 2004), Muslim group takes responsibility for 9-11: "We are so sorry," Web site: www.freemuslims.org.

6. Talya Halkin (February 18, 2005), Muslim scholar presents literary critique of suicide bombers, *Jerusalem Post, p. 6*. An extracted summary of the article in the *Jerusalem Post* appears on a Web site devoted to Sufism, a form of Islam devoted to a love of life and defines terrorism as abhorrent: Maryam: Tasawwuf Blog. Retrieved August 13, 2005.

Chapter 2

1. Roger Cohen (October 26, 2005), 10 reasons terror meets silence from Muslims, *International Herald Tribune*, Retrieved from the *New York Times*: nytimes.com.

2. Many of the examples given in this book of suicide bombers are from the unique suicide bombings of September 11 on the United States in 2001, the suicide bombings in London four years later on July 7, 2005, and many suicide bombings by Palestinians against Israel. These zones are my own natural life space, and they also are areas from which repeated in-depth news coverage and analyses have been available. However, the book also brings many other examples from other political-cultural settings other than the United States, the United Kingdom, and Israel.

3. John F. Burns (October 7, 2003), For bomber's parents, a smile for a goodbye, *International Herald Tribune*; Vered Levy-Barzilai (October 17, 2003), Ticking bomb: What made a young lawyer from Jenin enter a packed restaurant and blow herself up, killing 20* people and wounding dozens of others? The story of Hanadi Jaradat, the bomber from Maxim restaurant in Haifa, combines a tough family situation, religious zealotry—and revenge, *Haaretz Magazine* (English edition), pp. 10–13. (**The death toll has since risen to 21.*)

4. Yoav Stern (November 9, 2003), Nasrallah: Without freeing Kuntar [the name of the terrorist quoted] there will be no hostage swap [between Hizbollah and Israel]. Insert story: Kuntar in an interview in 1995: "I have changed." *Haaretz* (Hebrew). Kuntar, a Palestinian, is referring to the fact that the intifada provided a reason and in effect a cover for considerable killings within the Palestinian community itself, such as of alleged collaborators with Israel, where often enough the charges were contrived to justify a settling of other accounts.

5. Eric Hoffer (1951), *The True Believer: Thoughts on the Nature of Mass Movements,* New York: Harper.

6. Stanley Milgram (1965), Some conditions of obedience and disobedience to authority; Stanley Milgram (1965), Obedience (A Film); Stanley Milgram (1974), *Obedience to Authority: An Experimental View*; Philip G. Zimbardo (1973), On the ethics of intervention in human psychological research: With special reference to the Stanford Prison Experiment; Philip G. Zimbardo (1989), *Quiet Rage. The Stanford Prison Experiment Video;*

Philip G. Zimbardo and Allen Funt (1992), *Candid Camera Classics in Social Psychology: Viewer's Guide and Instructor's Manual;* Philip G Zimbardo, Christina Maslach, and Craig Haney (2000), Reflections on the Stanford Prison Experiment: Genesis, transformations, consequences, In Thomas Blass (Ed.) (2000), *Obedience to Authority: Current Perspectives on the Milgram Paradigm. S*ee in the latter book also a fascinating follow-up on both the Milgram and Zimbardo experiments.

7. Pape, Robert A. Pape (September 22, 2003), "Dying to kill us." *New York Times,* Sept. 22. The subsequent book is Robert A. Pape (2005). *Dying to Win: The Strategic Logic of Suicide Terrorism.* Pape's major point in the book, I think, is that every suicide terrorist campaign has had a clear goal that is secular and political.

8. Steven Emerson is the author of the documentary film, *Jihad in America,* aired by PBS on November 21, 1994, which won the prestigious George Polk Award. It was also named the "best investigative reporting in print, broadcast or book" by the Investigative Reporters and Editors Organization, and won other awards as well. Emerson was one of the small number of people who tried to warn the United States early on about a growing threat of a Muslim jihad in America which was to reach its dramatic height in the coordinated suicide bombing attacks of September 11, 2001. He described going to a mosque in Bridgeview, Illinois, a suburb southwest of Chicago. "I could tell immediately that we were deep in the heart of Hamas territory. The walls of the vestibule were covered with Hamas posters and recruiting literature showing masked gunmen brandishing automatic weapons. It was all in Arabic, but you could see daggers plunged into Jewish hearts wrapped up in American flags. They even had a library filled with militant terrorist videos and books." See Steven Emerson (2002), *American Jihad: The Terrorists Living Among Us.*

9. The best-known statement of a forthcoming clash between Islamic and non-Islamic civilizations is that of Samuel P. Huntington (1996), *The Clash of Civilizations and the Remaking of World Order.* We will be discussing this thesis later.

10. The following is the text of a petition that has been circulating on Internet in response to the rise of suicide bombers around the world, which calls on the international system to identify suicide bombing as a *war crime.*

> We insist that the United Nations, its Security Council and World Government Leaders declare that raising infants and children to become suicidal/homicidal bombers is a violation of fundamental human rights, a breach of the Geneva Convention and a war crime. We ask that those political, governmental, military, and religious organizations and their leaders and supporters be prosecuted by the International War Crimes Tribunal to the fullest extent of International Law.
>
> We have signed this position and sent it to people of all faiths, ethnic backgrounds and political beliefs with the hopes that the United Nations and World Leaders will not only vote to divest countries of their weapons of mass destruction, but act upon the immorality and criminally of raising of innocents to kill other innocents.

Petition to United Nations and World Government Leaders was created by Scholars for Peace in the Middle East and written by Dr. Edward S. Beck. Retrieved from www.PetitionOnline.com, October 2, 2003.

Independent of the above petition, the Simon Wiesenthal Center in Los Angeles also has undertaken a worldwide campaign to have the international community recognize suicide bombing as a *crime against humanity.*

> The Wiesenthal Center believes that designating suicide bombing as a "crime against humanity" gives the world an important *legal* tool to go after the infrastructure and

those who inspire this culture of death ... The hope is that with this new legal tool, it will be possible to hold accountable not only those groups that dispatch the terrorists, but also those who inspire the mass murder of innocents.

See *Response* (Winter 2003/2004), Simon Wiesenthal Center, Los Angeles.

11. Osama bin Laden, World Islamic Front (February 23, 1998), cited by Federation of American Scientists (2001), *Jihad against Jews and Crusaders: World Islamic Front statement*. Available from www.fas.org/irp/world/para/docs/980223-fatwa.htm [Original Arabic text version available: www.library.cornell.edu/colldev/mideast/fatwa2.htm].

12. See I.W. Charny (2006), *Fascism and Democracy in the Human Mind: A New Bridge between Mind and Society.*

13. In February 2003, Sheik Aba Hamza al-Masri was fired from his post at the infamous Finsbury Park mosque, one of London's largest mosques, by the British Charity Commission, which has the authority to oversee places of worship in the United Kingdom that receive charitable funds. The mosque, which was seen as linked with al-Qaeda, had been raided by British antiterrorist police who found false passports and credit cards. Among other sermons, the imam had called America's spaceship, Columbia, "a trinity of evil against Islam" because the astronauts included Americans, an Israeli and a Hindu, and called the loss of the Columbia spaceship "a punishment from God." BBC News [on the Web] (January 23, 2002). Mosque in the spotlight; BBC News [on the Web] (February 4, 2003), Imam fired from London mosque post. At this writing Hamza al-Masri has been reported jailed, after he continued to preach on the streets near the mosque following his being fired, and the United States has requested his extradition from the United Kingdom.

See further in the book more examples of imams preaching violence, and especially the discussion in Chapter 7 of the need for democratic countries to monitor and regulate such preaching which both sponsors violence and in the long run also threatens to undermine democracy.

14. Habib Malik (2003), Can Christians and Muslims relate in peace? Address to the Presidents Conference of the Council for Christian Colleges and Universities, February 2–4. Text retrieved from the Internet September 16, 2003 at the site of the Council for Christian Colleges and Universities. www.cccu.org/conferences/eventID.189/past_conferences_detail.asp.

15. See www.acampbell.org.uk (no date), The assassins of Alamut, Chapter 1, Prologue, p. 3 of 8 on printout, Retrieved from the Web May 17, 2004.

16. Edward Luttwak (2003), Asymmetric war: How the weak fight: The mice that roared: From the earliest times, small forces have found ways of wounding super powers, *Newsweek, Special Issues 2003 Edition*. December 2002–February 2003, pp. 24–25, quotation on p. 24.

17. Danny Rubinstein (December 15, 2003), The infrastructure of terror, *Haaretz* (English Edition).

18. Scott Atran (2003), Understanding suicide terrorism: Genesis and future of suicide terrorism, *Interdisciplines*, Retrieved September 23, 2003: www.interdisciplines.org/terrorism/papers/1/21#_21.

19. Ibid.

20. Ibid.

21. In the war between Iran and Iraq, Iran's Khoumeini sanctioned suicide (although we will see that it is traditionally forbidden by Islamic law) as legitimate and heroic by

sending tens of thousands of children as human mine detectors to clear mine fields and to march into combat directly against the Iraqis.

22. Yoram Schweitzer (2001), Suicide bombings: The ultimate weapon? Interdisciplinary Center, Herzliya, Israel, paper on Internet, August 7. See also Yoram Schweitzer and Shaul Shay (2003), *The Globalization of Terror*.

23. An Indian publication reported in August 2003: "Terrorist organizations in the Kashmir village have an all-new recruitment drive. They are now approaching senior citizens in the village to act as fedayeen (suicide bombers)." It is easier to persuade senior citizens, the report says. They are paid handsomely and promised their families will be looked after once the bombers themselves attain martyrdom for the cause of "freedom and Kashmir." Of course, the assumption also is that seniors will be able to move to their targets more easily. See M.K. Tayal (August 16, 2003), Senior citizens as suicide bombers, *Mid-Day*, Retrieved from the Web: imcindia [independant media center] (spelling of independant in source).

24. The suicide bombings in Iraq have included coordinated simultaneous suicide attacks on different targets. Thus, on October 27, 2003 "a series of suicide bombings shock Baghdad" with 34 killed and 224 wounded. "The attacks ... were part of a highly coordinated operation." Dexter Filkins and Alex Berenson (October 28, 2003), Baghdad suicide bombers kill 34: Series of attacks continue chaos in Iraq's capital, *International Herald Tribune*.The suicide bombings in Iraq were resumed with a vengeance only days after the capture of the arch tyrant, Saddam Hussein in December, 2003. No matter that he had murdered tens of thousands of Iraqis who were to be found after the invasion of Iraq in numerous mass graves! The Westerners had humiliated Saddam, Iraq, and all of Islam, and they would be made to pay the price.

25. Amy Waldman (January 15, 2003), Sri Lanka offers textbook cases for terror: Tigers are 'a most ruthless and disciplined group,' *International Herald Tribune*, p. 2, with attribution to the *New York Times*.

26. Ibid.

Of course, most Palestinians would reject out of hand that their suicide bombers are more dejected and any less nobly devoted to their cause. Thus, in Gaza's Jabaliya refugee camp, Salah Othman has been known as the "live martyr." He had joined in Hamas' suicidal attack on a Jerusalem bus during the first intifada and was shot in the head and back but he recovered. "This life—whatever we see now—for God, it's not worth the wing of a mosquito," he explained. "You cannot compare this life with the afterlife. It's like a drop in the ocean. Why should I waste the ocean for this drop?" He said he hoped his children would martyr themselves. "The new generation, they will be more fond of martyr attacks than the previous one," he said with satisfaction. See James Bennet (June 21, 2002), Rash of new suicide bombers showing no pattern or ties, *New York Times*, pp. A1, 10. On page 10, the article continues with spanner: Middleast turmoil: The human bomb, and the human loss; this is followed by headline: New suicide attackers are rising untrained from anger of the street.

27. Israel Radio News Magazine, Channel 2, December 17, 2003.

28. See Section: Cambodia, Genocide in. *Encyclopedia of Genocide,* pp. 129–136. This section includes the following entries and feature: Ben Kiernan (1999), The Cambodian Genocide and its leaders; R.J. Rummel (1999), Khmer Rouge and Cambodia; Alexander Laban Hinton (1999), Comrade Ox did not object when his family was killed.

29. R.J. Rummel (1999), China, Genocide in: *The Chinese Communist anthill.*

30. Eric H. Boehm (1999), The fates of non-Jewish Germans under the Nazis.

31. Gilad Margalit (November 18, 2004), A good uncle to bad nephews Hitler, A review of the film, "Downfall" by Bernd Eichinger.

32. Film (2004) *Der Untergang* [Downfall].

33. Jessica Stern (May 12, 2004), A Buzzflash interview with Jessica Stern, author of *Terror in the Name of God: Why Religious Militants Kill,* Retrieved from www.buzzflash. com/interviews/04/05/int04024.html.

Chapter 3

1. From a communiqué by Al-Qaradhawi intended for Arabic speakers as a "correction" to a *Der Spiegel* version that was intended for European readers the previous day that was posted on his Web site and published in the Qatari press (Qatari dailies, *Al-Raya, Al-Sharq*, and *Al-Watan*, September 28, 2005).

2. Khaled Abou el Fadl, a high-ranking sheikh, trained in Islamic law in Egypt and Kuwait is a professor at the School of Law at the University of California. He is further identified as on the board of directors of Human Right Watch, and it is reported that "since openly attacking Wahhabism, he has received regular death threats." Interview with Khaled Abou El Fadl, "Jihad Gone Wrong." Qantara.de, October 27, 2005, Retrieved from the Web: www.scholarofthehouse.org/jgowrinwikha.html, December 20, 2005.

3. Muzamil Jaleel (no date ?2002), Suicide militancy-II: Martyrdom, the prize for taking one's life, Retrieved from the Web: expressIndia: KashmirLIVE, on January 25, 2004.

4. Robert S. Robins and Jerrold M. Post (1997), *Political Paranoia: The Psychopolitics of Hatred,* quotation on p. 155. The authors credit the work of Martin Kramer (1990), The moral logic of Hizballah.

5. *Al-Aharam Weekly Online*, 647, July 17–23, 2003.

6. See Edward Said (September 27, 2003), Dignity, solidarity and the penal colony, *Asbarez Daily,* pp. 3, 10, quotation on p. 3.

7. State of Israel, Knesset Library, Topics on the Public Agenda (2003), The ideological basis of the phenomenon of suicide bombers, Retrieved from the Web, December 27 (Excerpted and translated from the Hebrew).

8. *About Islam* (2003), Suicide bombers: Why do they do it, and what does Islam say about their actions? www.islam.about.com, Retrieved September 20.

9. Thomas Fuller (September 7, 2004), Return of a Malaysian: Muslim-West divide is on Anwar's mind, *International Herald Tribune.*

10. Nassrine Azimi (September 8, 2004), The anguish of a faithful Muslim, *International Herald Tribune*, Views, p. 6.

11. Brian Knowlton (July 15, 2005), Muslims shift from violence, *International Herald Tribune Online*. Full results of the PEW Global Attitudes Survey are available online at www.pewglobal.org.

12. Ibid.

13. Middle East Media Research Institute (MEMRI) (2004), Sheikh Yousef Al-Qaradhawi in London to Establish 'The International Council of Clerics.' Special Report— Jihad & Terrorism Studies Project, No. 30, July 8.

14. Ibid.

15. Judea Pearl (July 20, 2005), Wellsprings of terror II: Islam struggles to stake out its position, *International Herald Tribune,* p. 8. King Abdullah II's address to the Amman conference can be accessed from www.MaximsNews.com. Judea Pearl is president of the

Daniel Pearl Foundation, an organization promoting intercultural dialogue that was named after his son, the *Wall Street Journal* reporter who was murdered in Pakistan in 2002. This article first appeared in the *Boston Globe*.

16. Bat Ye'or (1996), *The Decline of Eastern Christianity under Islam: From Jihad to Dhimmitude—Seventh–Twentieth Century*. See *The pre-Islamic Orient*, pp. 33–39; and quotations on p. 472 in Glossary. Bat Ye'or defines *dhimmi* as "indigenous Jews, Christians, and Zoroastrians who—subjected to Islam law after the Arab or Turkish conquest—benefited from the *dhimma*." The *dhimma* is defined in turn as "a protection pact or treaty granted by the prophet Muhammad to the Jewish and Christian populations whom he had subjected."

17. Ibid., quotation on p. 40.

18. Ibid. The concept of making a truce as a strategic device to recover from losses and gain political advantages while rearming and planning to renew combat has proven at times a real impediment to some peace efforts in the Israeli-Palestinian conflict. Some Israelis believe that there can be no trust in a truce agreement with Palestinians who could very well be working the truce to regroup their efforts to destroy the Jewish state.

19. Jacques Ellul (1996), Foreword to Bat Ye'or (1996), *The Decline of Eastern Christianity Under Islam,* ibid., quotation on pp. 18–19.

20. A Web site that continues Bat Ye'or's concepts is entitled, "Dhimmi Watch." It defines itself as a watching post looking at the "denial of equality of rights and dignity" which are part of regimes that follow traditional Muslim law (a *Sharia* regime) where "non-Muslims, primarily Jews and Christians ... are made subject to a number of humiliating regulations designed to enforce the Qur'an's demand that they 'feel themselves subdued' (Sura 9: 29)." The website correctly points out that in much of Western discourse it has been politically incorrect to point out the Islamic degradations of others: "To do so would offend the multiculturalist ethics that prevails everywhere today." I think this is a fair warning of a prejudice of the wanting-to-be-liberal West, but again I am impressed that the philosophy and material produced on this website overwhelmingly fails to present the peace-seeking sides of Islamic thought and of many leaders and practitioners of Islam. See www.DhimmiWatch, Retrieved from the Web May 15, 2004.

21. Steven Emerson (1998), Foreign terrorists in America: Five years after the World Trade Center bombing, February 24. Prepared statement of Steven Emerson before the Senate Judiciary Committee Subcommittee on Terrorism, Technology and Government Information, quotation on p. 2 of 31 pages of a printout from Internet.

22. Middle East Media Research Institute (MEMRI) (2004), Liberal Muslim scholar: The term 'jihad' is misunderstood by Islamist clerics, Special dispatch—Reform project, No. 699, April 23.

23. Ibid.

24. Ibid.

25. Danny Rubinstein (June 28, 2004), The price of the winning equation. *Haaretz* (English Edition).

26. Middle East Media Research Institute (MEMRI) (2004), Commander of the Khobar terrorist Squad tells the story of the operation, Special Dispatch—Saudi Arabia/Jihad & Terrorism Studies Project, No. 731, June 15.

27. Hamza Qablan Al-Mozainy (March 27, 2004), The culture of death is our schools. *Al-Watan*. Al-Mozainy is a lecturer at the Department of Arabic Language and Literature at King Saud University in Saudi Arabia. Naturally, this article is reported to have aroused strong reactions from clerical sources, including a religion teacher cursing the son of the

author of the article. Reported by Middle East Media Research Institute (MEMRI), June 10, 2004.

28. David Brooks (September 8, 2004), This cult of death is beyond any reason, *International Herald Tribune*, Views, p. 6.

29. Khairallah Khairallah (September 28–29, 2002), It's time for Arabs to face reality, *International Herald Tribune*. Adapted from an article in *The Daily Star* (Beirut).The writer is identified as a senior Lebanese journalist.

30. *New York Times* (June 21, 2002), Palestinian intellectuals call for halt to attacks.

31. *International Herald Tribune* (November 26, 2003), 9 charged as suspects in attacks in Turkey. Attributed to news reports from Reuters and AP. We have already referred to the significance of sermons in the mosques, and we will want to remember this constructive regulatory action by the Turkish government later in the book when we discuss government policies with respect to imams' sermons.

32. *The Age* (newspaper, Melbourne, Australia) (November 17, 2003). Newspapers given al-Qaeda statements, Retrieved from www.Theage.com.au

33. Muqtedar Khan (February 12, 2003), Memo to Osama bin Laden, Retrieved from the Web: *Islam for Today*.

34. Yosi Melman (June 27, 2003), The voice of cultural Islam: The fundamentalists are misconstruing Islam says Abdurrahaman Wahib, former president of Indonesia. *Haaretz* (English Edition), p. B2.

35. John F. Burns (October 7, 2003), For bomber's parents, a smile for a goodbye, *International Herald Tribune*, p. 10.

36. Baruch Goldstein, In *Wikipedia*, "the free encyclopedia," Retrieved from the Web, July 29, 2005.

37. March 5, 1994, Cited by MSN Groups, Retrieved from the Web, July 29, 2005.

38. Suzanne Goldenberg (June 20, 2002), Behind the suicide bombers, *The Age* (newspaper, Melbourne, Australia), Retrieved from www.Theage.com.au.

39. Ellis Schuman (2001), What makes suicide bombers tick? Retrieved from the Web: israelinsider, June 4.

40. James Bennet (May 28, 2003), From student to suicide bomber: The conflicted story of an Islamic woman, *New York Times*.

41. Ibid.

42. For example, a father of one of the youngest suicide bombers, a 16-year-old boy said after his son's death: "He was just a little boy and those who sent him should have left him alone." The *New York Times* report commented that the father's critical remarks against the Al Aksa Martyrs Brigade were unusual for Palestinians who "traditionally praise family members who carry out attacks," and by implication their sponsoring terrorist group. From: *International Herald Tribune* (2003), Palestinians and Israelis talk secretly about peace, November 4, 2003, with no author given but attributed to the *New York Times*.

43. Vered Levy-Barzilai (2003), Ticking bomb, ibid., quotation on p. 10.

44. Ibid., quotations on p. 13.

45. Habib Malik (2003), Can Christians and Muslims relate in peace? Ibid.

46. Alan Cowell (May 2, 2003), British suspects in Tel Aviv bombing defy image of militants, *International Herald Tribune*, with attribution to the *New York Times*.

47. Sarah Lyall (May 12, 2003), Beneath the surface, empathy for U.K. bombing suspect, *International Herald Tribune*, p. 7.

48. *New York Times* Editorial: Homegrown terrorists (July 18, 2005).

49. Roger Cohen (July 20, 2005), Globalist: A deadly idea defies any simple doctrines, *International Herald Tribune Europe,* Retrieved from the Web.

50. Lizette Alvarez (July 14, 2005), 2 youths, British to core: But suspects took turn toward Muslim piety, *International Herald Tribune* (with attribution to the *New York Times),* pp. 1, 4 (quotation p. 4). See also Elaine Sciolino and Don Van Natta, Jr. (July 15, 2005), A new danger born in Britain, *International Herald Tribune Europe* (with attribution to the *New York Times*), Retrieved from the Web.

51. Ibid.

52. Lizette Alvarez (July 19, 2005), New Muslim at 15, a bombing suspect at 19, *International Herald Tribune* (with attribution to the *New York Times*), p. 2.

53. Sandra Lowdl, David Ward, and Ian Cobin (July 14, 2005), Shock in Leeds after police raids in the homes of the terrorists: The families of the suicide bombers find it hard to digest: "All our world is shattered." The *Guardian* as presented in Hebrew translation in *Haaretz*, p. 7a, retranslated from the Hebrew.

54. From *Al-Hayat Al-Jadida* (Palestinian Authority), July 8, 2005, Cited in Middle East Media Research Institute (MEMRI) (2005), Arab Media Reactions to the London Bombing: "A Chapter in World War III," Special Report—Jihad & Terrorism, No. 36, July 8.

55. Abd Al-Bari: 'Atwan, Editor-in-Chief of London Arabic-language daily, *Al Quds Al-Arabi* (London), July 8, Cited in ibid.

56. Ibid.

57. Ali Sa'd-Al-Moussa in Saudi daily, *Al-Watan* (Saudi Arabia), July 8, Cited in ibid.

58. *Al-Madina* (Saudia Arabia), July 7, Cited in Middle East Media Research Institute (MEMRI) (2005), Arab and Iranian Media Reactions to the London Bombing—Part II: "The attacks were anticipated due to British leniency to extremists acting in Britain"—"Expel extremism today". Special Report—Jihad & Terrorism, No. 37, July 12.

59. Friday sermon in Tehran, July 8, 2005, www.memritv.org/Transcript.asp?P1= 747, Cited in MEMRI, ibid.

60. Zvi Bar'el (September 1, 2003), Twenty hours on the road with a fan of bin Laden. *Haaretz* (English Edition), p. 4.

61. Arnaud de Borchgrave (August 18, 2003), Clerics OK suicide-bombers, United Press International, Retrieved from washingtontimes.com. Arnaud de Borchgrave is the editor-in-chief of UPI. See also the report of the conference in the reference to Sheikh al-Qaradhawi in the report of the Middle East Media Research Institute (2004), July 8, ibid.

62. Thomas L. Friedman (September 12, 2003), Deaths grip in the Middle East, *International Herald Tribune.*

63. See in the final chapter inspiring case incidents, one of a woman who at the last minute had a change of heart based on her realization of the holiness of human life, and another a case of a man who decided he could not explode himself after he saw Jewish children playing.

Another case of a suicide bomber who experienced a change of heart involved a Palestinian woman who was ordered to dress sexily, in a Western mode, in order to gain entry to an Israeli area to blow herself up in a crowd of people. Her first misgivings had to do with her concern that she was being instructed to violate her normal religious precepts to dress unprovocatively, not exactly a profound spiritual reawakening to the value of life and its sacredness. Here she was going to commit the ultimate act of faith in loyalty to her religion, and in the process she was being ordered to go against what she believed in.

"They wanted me to have my hair loose, wear sunglasses and make-up and tight clothes. I said no, because it's against my religion," the newspaper *Maariv* quoted Thauriya Hamamreh as telling reporters. Still, one wonders if at least unconsciously she didn't catch on to the fact that her genuine religious identity and values were quite unimportant to her handlers who were out to exploit her devotion and sacrificial idealism simply to get themselves another "soldier" in their army of suicide bombers. In any case, what happened next is that her mind went to the genuine core issue. "I started thinking that I would be killing babies, women and sick people and imagined what it would be like if my family were sitting in a restaurant and someone bombed them," she said. She changed her mind. See Megan Goldin (2002), The suicide bomber who had a change of heart. A Palestinian woman has told how she came to question her motives in taking on a suicide mission, Retrieved from the Web: The *Sydney Morning Herald*: smh.com.au, with attribution to the *Washington Post* and agencies, June 1, 2002.

64. See the proposal to create a *"Worldwide Campaign for Life"* in the last chapter.

65. See I.W. Charny (2006), *Fascism and Democracy in the Human Mind*.

66. One psychoanalytic-psychiatric pioneer who effectively and touchingly continued the exploration of man's basic choices of life versus death was Karl Menninger (1938), *Man Against Himself*. Two other scholars in mental health who have made seminal contributions to the subject are Ernest Becker, a philosopher of psychology, on the acknowledgment or denial of death (Ernest Becker (1973), *The Denial of Death*); and Robert Jay Lifton on the psychology of immortality (Robert Jay Lifton (1979), *The Broken Connection: On Death and the Continuity of Life*), and on the psychology of genocidal mind (Robert Jay Lifton, and Eric Markusen (1990), *The Genocidal Mentality: Nazi Holocaust and Nuclear Threat*).

67. Zvi Bar'el (January 29, 2004), Women's work, Haaretz.com, (English).

68. O'Sullivan (January 20, 2004), Ya'alon: Yassin is in our sights, *Jerusalem Post*.

69. Abraham Rabinovich (January 20, 2004), Bomber died to atone for infidelity, *The Australian*. See also another story by the same newspaper reporter on the same date in another newspaper: Abraham Rabinovich (January 20, 2004), Atoning for adultery with 'martyrdom'; 'Purifies' self with suicide attack, *Washington Times*.

70. See Barbara Victor (2003), *Army of Roses: Inside the World of Palestinian Women Suicide Bombers*. The author looks at the first five Palestinian women suicide bombers who blew themselves up as well as other women who intended to but did not, and identifies, variously, poverty, religious zealotry, but also, according to her publisher's summary, "a startling emotional component to their death wishes: their broken dreams and blighted inner loves." From the book jacket. Text available from Blackwell North America on Internet.

71. Ehud Yaari (January 20, 2004), Israel TV Channel Two News.

72. It is of interest that Sheikh Yassin's assassination by Israel two months later may have been decided at this time of his sending the woman suicide bomber and his announced change of policy about allowing women to be suicide bombers. Of course, Yassin had been authorizing male suicide bombers for some time, and Israel had a huge score to settle with him.

According to a story in the far-away *Japan Times* attributed to the *Los Angeles Times*, Sheikh Ahmed Yassin was at the forefront of suicide bombings against Israelis. "With grim regularity," members of the Izzedine al-Qassem Brigades, Hamas' military wing, said their final prayers, and detonated their explosive belts in crowded cafes and buses. "The frail and ailing Yassin, although himself the picture of physical powerlessness, probably did more than any other single figure to sear into the consciousness of these young Palestinians the notion that death deliberately sought in order to inflict a bloody blow upon a hated enemy was a glorious one."

The newspaper story continues almost poetically.

For Hamas and its followers, "martyrdom" was the constant watchword—shouted over and over again at mass rallies that flowed like unruly rivers through the streets of the Gaza Strip, ceaselessly invoked in the carefully scripted videotapes that assailants left behind, seamlessly incorporated into the rote lessons taught to Palestinian schoolchildren.

A "shahid"—a martyr—was a hero of the highest order, someone not only to be admired and praised, but perhaps, when the time came, emulated ... Hamas made suicide bombings its weapon of choice—and the other Palestinian militant groups, alarmed by the stature and popularity Hamas was afforded as a result, scrambled to follow suit, in what evolved into a grisly competition. See *Japan Times* (English) (2004). Yassin dreamed of becoming martyr 'all my life,' March 23.

73. Amnesty International (2002), *Israel and the Occupied Territories and the Palestinian Authority. Without Distinction: Attacks on Civilians by Palestinian Armed Groups.* See also Avishai Margalit (2003), The suicide bombers.

74. Human Rights Watch (2002), *Erased in a Moment: Suicide Bombing Attacks on Israeli Civilians.* See also Sundre Bangstad (2002), Palestinian Islamist movements: An annotated bibliography, Bergen, Norway: Chr. Michelsen Institute [e-mail: cmi@cmi.no], Retrieved from Google September 21, 2003, quotation on p. 30.

75. Itamar Marcus (2003), Palestinian Authority music video promising "Maidens of Paradise" to *shahids*—2 days before suicide bombing, *Palestinian Media Watch Multimedia Bulletin*, August 12, 2003, Retrieved from the Web: http://www.pmw.org.il. The above bulletin gives an icon to access a video of the Palestinian Authority "advertising" the reward of "maidens of paradise" for suicide bombers.

76. Robert Melson is a Professor of Political Science at Purdue University. Personal communication, October 18, 2003.

Chapter 4

1. Zbigniew Brzezinski (October 14, 2005), George W. Bush's suicidal statecraft, *International Herald Tribune*, p. 6. Zbigniew Brzezinski was national security adviser to President Jimmy Carter. This Global Viewpoint article was distributed by Tribune Media Services International.

2. Munjed Farid al-Qutob (November 15, 2005) [a resident of London], Letter to the Editor, *International Herald Tribune,* (after suicide bombings by al-Qaeda of three hotels in Amman, Jordan).

3. Jim Yardley (October 11, 2001), A shy child's journey to fiery mass murder: His anger at America grew over the years, *International Herald Tribune*, p. 2. From an article in the *New York Times* "based on reporting by Jim Yardley, Neil MacFarquhar and Paul Zielbauer," October 4.

4. Elizabeth Neuffer (September 26, 2001), How did a polite student turn into a terrorist? *Haaretz*, p. A8, From an article in the *Boston Globe*, translated into Hebrew.

5. James Bennet (January 31, 2002), Filling in the blanks on Palestinian bomber: 'Independent' woman made secret decision, *International Herald Tribune*, p. 2. From the *New York Times Service*.

6. A newsletter of the Islamic Jihad movement in Palestine reproduced the following quotation from a woman described as the "spiritual mother" of girls aged 16–24 who expressed a willingness to be suicide bombers and who were in training at a camp in Gaza:

> "Darin, Wafa, Ayat and Andalib [the first four women suicide bombers of the intifada in Israel] were not ugly or unlucky, as the Zionist slanderers try to say. They were top university students who had a good living. They were planning to start families that would join in jihad [holy war]. They embarked on jihad to support the men who are fighting the enemy who has stricken all convention off his lexicon, the enemy who targets children and adults, men and women. These warriors are home-makers and they are just as good at fighting and carrying explosives as they are at moving furniture around the house ... The new suicide culture has stunned the Zionists because of its chances of success, and these are greater for women since it is easier for them to hide explosives and get them past the road blocks ... They have no answer to women suicide bombers." Arnon Regular (May 26, 2003), Suicide bomber training is almost feminist, *Haaretz* (English Edition), p. 1.

7. See later the information about numerous women suicide bombers in Sri Lanka and Chechnya, among others. A 2003 report to the U.S. Congress noted, "The use of women as suicide bombers is not historically unprecedented, but its frequency in many groups such as the Sri Lankan Tamil Tigers (or LTTE), the Turkish Kurdistan Workers' Party (PKK) and now the Palestinian Fatah-affiliated al-Aqsa Martyrs' Brigades and the Chechens, may indicate a social broadening of the phenomenon." See Audrey Kurth Cronin (2003), Terrorists and suicide attacks, Congressional Research Service, Library of Congress, Retrieved from the Web, quotation from page of Summary.

It was curious how much of a fuss was made in the media (including the *New York Times*) over the first Palestinian woman suicide bomber, and there was little to no mention of the fact that women have been notorious suicide bombers elsewhere. Of course, the first Palestinian female suicide bomber was not an insignificant movement across a cultural boundary line in the Palestinian-Israeli conflict.

My basic impression is that some of the news people were caught unawares of previous women suicide bombers because, in general, only slowly is awareness developing that various terrorist movements in so many different countries *everywhere* have much in common, and especially now that a worldwide web of Islamic terrorist movements is growing and literally sprouting new terror groups and movements all the time.

8. Alan Cowell (July 26, 2005), Bombings in London: The suspects, Police name 2 of 4 men linked to bomb attempts, *New York Times*.

9. Sheikh Yousef al Qaradhawi speaking to the Qatari newspaper *Al Raya* in April 2001, From Middle East Media Research Institute (MEMRI) (2001), *Inquiry and Analysis, No. 74—Jihad and Terrorism Struggle,* October 30.

10. Sheikh Abd Al-Salam, "Chief Mufti of the Palestinian Authority Police Force," Reported by Al-Hayjat Al-Jadida (Palestinian Authority), September 17, 1999, From Middle East Media Research Institute (MEMRI), ibid.

11. Bob Woodward (September 29–30, 2001), In highjacker's bag, a call for death: FBI agents find prayers and a checklist of practical terrorism, *International Herald Tribune*, pp. 1, 4.

12. Thomas L. Friedman (2002), Terror's most fearful weapons must be locked up, *New York Times*, Reprinted in the *International Herald Tribune*, March 25 (italics added by me to the words, "they are enemies of civilization").

13. Thomas L. Friedman (2001), Why the Ashcrofts have a point, *New York Times*, Reprinted in the *International Herald Tribune,* December 3.

14. In response to the agony of a ceaseless wave of suicide-killer attacks, a respected Jewish religious leader in Israel and former member of Knesset observed that the suicide bombers confer on their actions "an unequivocal terrifying image of the sanctification of death per se," while the Judeo-Christian code since Mount Sinai elevates in "life, tradition and legal code . . . life's sacred character." Avner Hai Shaki (March 17, 2002), Sanctify life, not death, *Haaretz* (English Edition), p. 5.

15. Ellis Schuman (June 4, 2001), What makes suicide bombers tick? Retrieved from the Web: israelinsider. The article attributes the sociological data to an Israeli newspaper poll.

16. Ibid. The above article also reports this public opinion poll by a Palestinian Center for Public Opinion among Palestinian adults on the Gaza Strip and the West Bank including East Jerusalem at the end of May 2001.

17. Nasra Hassan (November 19, 2001), The arsenal of believers: Talking to the "human bombs." *New Yorker*, Available at www.newyorker.com/fact/content/?011119fa_FACT1.

The same overall findings that the suicide bombers are *not* poor and *not* uneducated and *not* sociologically lost souls have been reported from a variety of sources. According to one commentator, this is also because of the *strategic advantages* of using the better educated. "It was, and is everywhere, a weapon of the relatively educated: Tamil Hindu women who were able to mix well at Buddhist electoral meetings in Sri Lanka; Palestinian high school and university students posing as Israelis; and it was Western-educated Islamists who trained to murder thousands in America on 9/11, hundreds in Bali, many in Casablanca and Riyadh." See Michael Radu (2003), Radical Islam and suicide bombers, E-Notes, Foreign Policy Research Institute, Philadelphia, PA, October 21, Retrieved from the Web.

An article in the *Chronicle of Higher Education* summarized the findings we have about Islamic suicide bombers in Israel but also added, fairly and helpfully, I believe, cases of murderous Jewish terrorism in which from 1980 to 1984, 23 Palestinians were killed by members of the Jewish underground and 191 injured. Although overall suicide killings as such by Jews have been rare—the most notable exception being what was to come later in February 1994 in the disgraceful shootings of Arab worshippers in Hebron by physician, Baruch Goldstein—the comparable information about Jewish terrorists, obviously including Goldstein, is that they were very well educated and well employed. See Alan B. Krueger and Jitka Maleckova (June 6, 2003), Seeking the roots of terrorism, *Chronicle of Higher Education.*

Other observers have picked up on the presence both of the well to do and the poor among suicide bombers. "In an overview of the relationship between poverty and terrorism, Karin von Hippel of King's College London noted that there are evidences both that many terrorists are well off, and that others are poor and are seeking the financial rewards of their terrorist activities. Von Hippel observes that many Palestinian and al-Qaeda terrorists 'enjoy a living standard above the poverty line [and] they normally had at least a secondary education.' At the same time there is also evidence that there are many volunteers for suicide bombings, especially in certain cultures such as Kashmir, who come from poor families." See Karin von Hippel (2002), September 11 & the war on terrorism: The roots of religious extremist terrorism, King's College London, Department of War Studies, September 13, Retrieved from the Web February 2, 2004.

The observations that the suicide bombers generally are not down-and-out people also ties in with a general psychological observation that the propensity for violence is greatest not among people with low self-esteem but more among those with a threatened sense of high self-esteem. See Roy F. Baumeister and W.K. Campbell (1999),The intrinsic appeal of evil: Sadism, sensation thrills, and threatened egotism; and Roy F. Baumeister, L. Smart, and J.M. Boden (1996), Relation of threatened egotism to violence and aggression: The dark side of high self-esteem.

18. Suzanne Goldenberg (June 20, 2002), Behind the suicide bombers, *The Age* (newspaper, Melbourne, Australia), Retrieved from www.Theage.com.au.

19. One American reporter summed up the promised reward thus: "They also are promised something more risqué: unlimited sex with 72 virgins in heaven. The Koran, the sacred book of Islam, describes the women as 'beautiful like rubies, with complexions like diamonds and pearls.' In one of the passages of the Koran, it is said the martyrs and virgins shall 'delight themselves, lying on green cushions and beautiful carpets.' Since the time of Mohammed, martyrs have always been considered those willing to die defending Islam. For some young Muslims, that offer is too much to turn down." See Jack Kelley (June 26, 2001), Devotion, desire drive youths to 'martyrdom,' Palestinians in pursuit of paradise turn their own bodies into weapons, *USA Today*.

20. The same reporter describes how in return for martyrdom, "Hamas tells the youths that their families will be financially compensated, their pictures will be posted in schools and mosques, and they will earn a special place in heaven." Ibid.

21. Muzamil Jaleel (no date ?2002), Suicide militancy-II. Martyrdom, the prize for taking one's life. Retrieved from the Web: expressIndia. KashmirLIVE, ibid.

22. Nasra Hassan (2001), ibid.

See also an article by Roger Griffin in which he quotes the above from Nasra Hassan in the course of his own poetic psychological discussion of how acts of political violence often derive from a deep-seated attempt to escape existential emptiness and futility. See Roger Griffin (2003), Shattering crystals: The role of "dream time" in extreme right-wing political violence.

23. Jack Kelley (2001), ibid.

24. Marianne Bray (2003), Why young Muslims line up to die, Retrieved from the Web: CNN.com, August 18.

25. Ibid.

26. Cited by Kaja Perina (2002), Suicide terrorism: Seeking motives beyond mental illness, *Psychology Today*, September–October.

27. Jason Burke (March 25, 2004), What does al-Qaeda really want? *Japan Times*. Credited to the *Observer*, Jason Burke is identified as author of *Al-Qaeda: Casting a Shadow of Terror*. The same writer adds a very hopeful observation and recommendation that will be important to us later when we address possible ways of reducing suicide bombing:

The most powerful weapon in countering the radicals' violence is the good will and moderation of 95 percent of the world's 1.3 billion Muslims. We must fight to keep it, and to use it, if we are one day, to be free of fear and violence.

28. The DSM is the standard-setting manual for psychiatric diagnosis by the American Psychiatric Association, and because of the authority and prestige of American psychiatry,

for much of the rest of the world. The prevailing edition of the DSM in recent years has been American Psychiatric Association (1994), *DSM-IV: Diagnostic and Statistical Manual of Mental Disorders,* fourth edition. A new edition is to be expected in the near future.

29. Larry Morton Gernsbacher (1985), *The Suicide Syndrome.*

30. Ibid., quotation on p. 187.

31. Durkheim's classic work has been reprinted several times and is the subject of many essays in the social sciences. See Emile Durkheim (1979), *Suicide: A Study in Sociology*; and see, among others: Robert Alun Jones (1986), *Emile Durkheim: An Introduction to Four Major Works*; Kenneth Thompson (1982), *Emile Durkheim;* Edwin S. Schneidman (1996), *The Suicidal Mind;* and Steve Taylor (1982), *Durkheim and the Study of Suicide.*

32. About Jonestown, see Ken Levi (Ed.) (1982), *Violence and Religious Commitment: Implications of Jim Jones's People's Temple Movement.*

33. Film (1999), *The Terrorist,* Review by Nicholas Frayn, Retrieved from the Web: www.culturewars.org.uk/2001-7/terrorist.htm.

34. Michael Radu (2003), Radical Islam and suicide bombers, ibid.

35. Source: 'Civilized Slaughter' vs 'Suicide bombers'(no date), Retrieved from the Web, January 12, 2004: www.guidedones.com/issues/regions/meast/suicide.htm. Note that although the first person is used in some places in the article, a concluding line gives authorship credit as follows: Elijah Wald and M. Shahid Alam who is professor of economics at Northeastern University, Boston.

36. Ibid., where the text as quoted is in the first person although the credit line gives the two people as stated in previous note.

37. D. John Spencer (2002), The suicide bomber—is it a psychiatric phenomenon? *Psychiatric Bulletin, 26*(11), 436. (Correspondence in response to Harvey, Gordon, The 'suicide' bomber: Is it a psychiatric phenomenon?)

38. Robert S. Robins and Jerrold M. Post (1997), *Political Paranoia: The Psychopolitics of Hatred,* quotation on p. 97.

39. Ibid.

40. Christopher R. Browning (1992), *Ordinary Men: Reserve Battalion 101 and the Final Solution in Poland.*

41. Lisa Keys (June 30, 2004), The making of martyrs: A documentary by a British filmmaker and an Israeli producer probes the minds of suicide bombers, *Haaretz* (English Edition), p. 9. See Film (2003), *Inside the Mind of a Suicide Bomber.*

42. Cited in CBS NEWS.com (May 25, 2003), Mind of the suicide bomber, Retrieved from the Web, August 2004.

43. Amira Hass (July 16, 2002), The suicide-bomber, says the doctoral student, is a happy person who loves life. *Haaretz,* B4 (Hebrew). The paragraph-long sub-headline of the story says at greater length, "In the Palestinian community, the opinion generally held is that the suicide bombers operate out of despair, poverty and a loss of life; but in the Hamas they insist that the motivation is patriotic and even a love of life. Under the surface there is controversy in the Gaza Strip about suicide bombings, but the opponents are afraid to come out publicly 'No one will convince me that religion allows a person to kill a child who is eating ice cream,' says one Islamic activist who now has doubts about suicide bombings, but he won't be quoted."

44. Amira Hass (April 4, 2003), Suicidal tendencies: How can anyone make sense of the mass phenomenon of young Palestinians who blow themselves up for the cause while also taking the lives of innocent people, including children? Interviews that veteran prisoner

Walid Dakah conducted with fellow inmates provide some insight into these acts, *Haaretz Magazine* (English Edition), pp. 12–15 (quotations on p. 15). [The cover for this issue of the magazine reads: Confessions of a dangerous mind: Three would-be suicide bombers share their motives with a cellmate.]

45. Steven Lee Myers (August 8, 2003), Young, female and carrying a bomb: Chechnya's unlikely terrorists, *International Herald Tribune,* p. 2, with attribution to the *New York Times.*

46. Roy J. Eidelson and Judy I. Eidelson (2003), Dangerous ideas: Five beliefs that propel groups toward conflict, quotation on p. 189.

47. Habib Malik has strong things to say about the naivite of so many liberal thinkers who want to preserve a picture of man as good and human society as more decent than not:

> The generally sorry state in which Islamic moderation finds itself renders it for all practical purposes an illusive mirage in the quest for international dialogue between the West and the Islamic world . . . Lone liberal Muslims here and there, especially at dialogue conferences, or among exile emigre communities in the West will speak of the need to reinterpret doctrines . . . The Islamic establishment on the whole, however, remains conservative and unyielding, unmoved by such overtures and refusing to entertain seriously these reformist outlooks. Habib Malik (2003), Can Christians and Muslims relate in peace? Ibid., pp. 2, 3 of Internet document.

48. Charles L. Ruby (2002), Are terrorists mentally deranged, quotation on p. 15 (italics in author's abstract).

49. Ghassan Hage (2003), "Comes a time we are all enthusiasm": Understanding Palestinian suicide bombers in times of exighophobia, quotation on p. 10 of printout on Internet. The article is identified as having been published in *Public Culture, 15* (1), 65–89, published by Duke University Press. The author, who is identified as teaching at the University of Sydney, explains exighophobia as "fear of the other's human sameness." The author also discusses what he calls a "logic of necessity" which means that for the Palestinians "suicide bombings are . . . a marriage between the necessity of resistance and the quantitative and qualitative deprivation of military hardware" (p. 5 of printout), and refers to a piece widely circulated on the Internet by Michael Neumann, "a professor of philosophy at Trent University in Ontario" in which "he contends that he sees no moral problem in the Palestinians' deliberate killing of civilians as such" (ibid.). To which I say: *What big Western words and sentences you gentlemen of academia use to justify killing!*

50. Charles L. Ruby (2002), ibid.

51. T. Strentz (1981), The terrorist organizational profile: A psychological role model.

Chapter 5

1. The audio recording was posted on various Islamic forums on August 3, 2005. The transcript appeared August 9 at www.minbar-islam.com/forum/viewtopic.php?t=81, Cited in Middle East Media Research Institute (MEMRI) (2005), Al-Qaeda in Iraq: The drafters of the Iraq constitution and those who support them are infidels who must be killed, Special Dispatch—Iraq/Jihad & Terrorism, No. 962, August 19.

2. Adel Sadeq (2002). Dr. Sadeq appeared on Iqra' Television (Saudi Arabia and Egypt), 24 April (Arabic). See MEMRI 373, 30 April 2002. In Israeli, Raphael (2005), The

new Muslim anti-semitism: Exploring novel avenues of hatred, *Jewish Political Studies Review 17,* quotation on p. 4 of e-mail printout, October 11.

3. President George W. Bush speaking on October 6, 2005 to the National Endowment for Democracy. United States of America: National Security: The White House, President George W. Bush (2005). Fighting a global war on terror, Retrieved from the Web, October 8.

4. CNN (2005), Politics: Iraq: Transition of Power: Bush: Iraq crucial in war on terror, Retrieved from the Web, October 8, CNN.com

5. Prime Minister Tony Blair (September 13, 2001), BBC-TV.

6. Donald Rumsfeld, U.S. Secretary of Defense, warned chillingly that terrorist organizations were likely to use "nonconventional" weapons of mass destruction, which they will receive from countries like Iran, Iraq, Syria, Libya, and North Korea and "they will not hesitate to use them." FBI chief Robert Mueller warned that suicide bombings in the United States were not preventable, *Haaretz,* May 22, 2002 (Hebrew).

7. Samuel P. Huntington (1996), *The Clash of Civilizations and the Remaking of World Order,* ibid.

8. Associated Press, October 10, 2003.

9. Phyllis Chesler, a psychoanalyst and feminist, refers to "Islamofascist terrorism." Phyllis Chesler (May 3, 2004), The psychoanalytic roots of Islamic terrorism, FrontPageMagazine.com. Robert Wistrich, a professor of Modern European and Jewish History at the Hebrew University of Jerusalem and director of the Vidal Sassoon Center for the Study of Antisemitism, refers to "clerical Islamofascism." Manfred Gerstenfeld (2004), Something is rotten in the State of Europe: Anti-Semitism as a civilizational pathology, An interview with Robert Wistrich, *Post-Holocaust and Anti-Semitism, 25* (whole issue), 1 October, Jerusalem Center for Public Affairs.

Chesler also asks an excellent question not about the psychological status of the suicide bomber but about the culture that produces them. "A crucial question must be asked: from a psychological and anthropological point of view, what kind of culture produces human bombs, glorifies mass murderers, and supports humiliation-based revenge?" I am not crazy about that part of her answer that emphasizes a culture in which "the debasement of women is paramount" and where there is "widespread sexual abuse [which] leads to paranoid, highly traumatized and revenge-seeking adults." But I think she is right in her observations of the crucial roles shame and honor play in the culture, and that only the evolution of democracy can put an end to the constant legitimation of violences.

10. Charles L. Ruby (2002), Are terrorists mentally deranged? ibid., quotation on p. 15 (in italics in author's abstract).

11. Kaplan has similarly pointed out that terrorists have a pathological need to pursue absolute ends, and that this is their psychopathology. Abraham Kaplan (1981), The psychodynamics of terrorism.

12. See Israel W. Charny (1999), The psychology of sacrificing.

13. As a footnote, I think the above commonsense conclusions can also be phrased in traditional classical psychoanalytic terms about the id, superego and ego thus:

- Experientially, suicide bomber terrorists do not experience the privilege of human existence. *'Id-wise,' they are missing the biggest joy of all, and the main point of it all—being alive and celebrating life.*
- Ethically, suicide bombers gloss over and deny the inalienable rights of human beings to live. *'Super-ego-wise,' they are definitely immoral and display a severely damaged basic conscience.*

- Behaviorally, suicide bombers obviously make a decision to be overwhelmingly violent and carry out their decision with terrible consequences to their own lives and to others. *'Ego-wise,' suicide bombers display the worst possible decision making that ends once and for all any possibilities for revising and correcting their thinking.*

14. The sarin gas attack that took place during morning rush hour on March 20, 1995 killed 12 people and sickened more than 5,000, some of whom remain ill to this day. Aum himself was sentenced to death by a Japanese court for the attack. *Daily Yomiuri* (Tokyo) (English), March 20, 2004.

15. Roger Cohen (July 20, 2005), A deadly idea defies any simple doctrines, *International Herald Tribune* (with attribution to the *Globalist*), p. 2.

16. Fareed Zakaria (March 22, 2004), Cruelty is all they have left, *Newsweek*, p. 15. Unfortunately, I do not agree with the further message of the author in this same column that "violence is a sign of weakness," and the comfort he seems to take in the fact that al-Qaeda operatives are not a large group. I see al-Qaeda as a beginning manifestation of a pan-Islamic thrust to power that is likely to grow more and more serious including the fact that, as Zakaria also acknowledges, "Technology means that small numbers can still do great harm. Given al-Qaeda's demonstrated genius for organizing damaging coordinated multiple attacks on a large scale, and in my opinion the likelihood of their use of WMD, I foresee the grave possibility of a worldwide conflict and its hell of human suffering in the coming years.

17. James Bennet (June 21, 2002), Rash of new suicide bombers showing no pattern or ties, *New York Times,* pp. A1, 10.

18. See the last chapter of the book for the fuller report of this inspiring case. The reference given is to Greg Myre (December 3, 2003), In mock peace plan, real friction, *International Herald Tribune,* pp. 1,4, quotation on p. 4.

19. Marc Pilisuk and Lyn Ober (1976), Torture and genocide as public health problems.

20. Israel W. Charny (1986), Genocide and mass destruction: Doing harm to others as a missing dimension in psychopathology; Israel W. Charny (1996), Evil in human personality: Disorders of doing harm to others in family relationships; Israel W. Charny (1997), A personality disorder of excessive power strivings.

21. See I.W. Charny (2006), *Fascism and Democracy in the Human Mind.*

22. Abdallah Al-Ash'al (2005), As quoted on www.islamonline.net/Arabic/politics/2004/10/article07.shtml, Cited in Middle East Media Research Institute (MEMRI) (2004), Conspiracy theories in the Egyptian media concerning the terrorist attacks in Sinai, Special Dispatch—Egypt/Jihad and terrorism studies project, No. 801, October 15.

23. Nahdat Misr (Egypt), October 9, 2004, Cited in MEMRI, No. 801, ibid.

24. Halib Malik, ibid., quotation on p. 4 of internet text.

25. Mamoun Fandy (October 10, 2004), *Al-Sharq Al-Awsat* (London), Cited in MEMRI, No. 801,ibid.

26. Amy Walman (2002), From boredom to jihad—lure of radical Islam in England: The tortuous journey of the 'Tipton Taliban,' The *New York Times*, Reprinted in the *International Herald Tribune*, April 25.

27. Richard Bernstein (October 1, 2003), News analysis: Fertile soil for Sept. 11 theories, *International Herald Tribune*, with attribution to the *New York Times.*

28. BBC reported that on the second anniversary of September 11, a sympathetic "conference" was called in North London in honor of the nineteen suicide bombers. A

leader of the fundamentalist group launching the conference referred to them as "the great 19," and explained that the conference would discuss the reason that prompted the "heroes" to undertake their action. The conference carried as its theme a verse from the Koran, "They were youths who believed in their Lord and we advance them in guidance." BBC reported further that there is no shortage of books, Internet publications and satellite TV promotions honoring the attackers. One book is entitled, *Bin-Laden: The Rejuvenator of Time and Conqueror of the American*. See British Broadcasting Corporation (September 11, 2003), UK Islamic organization leaders discuss "Bin-Laden's absence" on anniversary, Source: *Al-Sharq Al-Awsat*, London, in Arabic 11 September 03, Retrieved from the Web: lexisnexis@prod.lexisnexis.com.

29. Jonathan Eric Lewis (September 29, 2003), The dangers of Arab Holocaust denial, *Pakistan Today*, Retrieved from http://www.paktoday.com/lewis19.htm.

30. On May 1, 2004, terrorists identified with bin Laden burst shooting into the offices of an oil contractor in Saudi Arabia and killed seven people including two Americans. Granted this incident of suicidal killing does not involve a suicide bomber, but the way in which higher ups of the Saudi regime promptly proceeded to charge Zionists with the attack provides a clear and dramatic example of the perversity of crazy conspiratorial type of thinking, and how it is drawn on with immediacy. Saudi Crown Prince Abdallah ibn Abd Al-'Aziz told Saudi dignitaries including top Muslim clerics that Zionists were to blame. Similarly, the Crown Prince told the London Arabic-language daily, *Al-Hayat*, "Be assured that the Zionists are behind everything. This is certain," even as he added with a slight touch of empiricism, "I don't say this with 100%, but with 95%." He also expressed himself in the same way on Saudi television. A Saudi daily, *Okaz*, published, variously, the Crown Prince's accusation and also commentaries by several experts including an Egyptian military expert, a Jordanian specialist on Israel, and a lecturer on political science at the American University in Beirut, all of whom stated that it was most probable Israel was behind the attacks in Saudi Arabia, because it—along with the United States—had the most to gain. A third of the experts somehow acknowledged that it was Saudi youth who were in fact the terrorists, but just as Israel incited the United States to invade Iraq, so had the terrorist youths been misled into carrying out "the Zionist plan." Even in the year 2004, a spiderweb of fiction with touches of as-if reality is spun and has no relationship to objective reality. See Middle East Media Research Institute (MEMRI) (2004), Saudi Crown Prince: Zionism is behind terrorist actions in the kingdom, Special Dispatch No. 700, May 3.

31. Steve Lohr (September 29, 2003), Microsoft E.R. races to kill software bugs, *International Herald Tribune*.

32. The reference, of course, is to the outstandingly brilliant classical experiment of Stanley Milgram in which he demonstrated that two thirds of people will administer dangerous and possibly even lethal electric shocks to a subject in a scientific study just because the experimenter-professor tells them to do so. See Stanley Milgram (1974), *Obedience to Authority: An Experimental View*; Thomas Blass (Ed.) (2000), *Obedience to Authority: Current Perspectives on the Milgram Paradigm*.

33. Adrian Mirvish (2001), Suicide bombers, authoritarian minds, and the denial of others, quotation on pp. 7 and 5 of Internet reprinting. Mirvish is described as a Professor of Philosophy at California State University at Chico, who writes on Sartre and existential psychoanalysis.

34. Ellis Schuman (2001), What makes suicide bombers tick? Ibid.

35. Linda Skitka and Elizabeth Mullen (2002), The dark side of moral conviction, quotation on p. 35.

36. Robert S. Robins and Jerrold M. Post (1997), ibid., quotation on pp. 94–95.

37. Gustave Le Bon (1896), *The Crowd.*

38. An intriguing idea has been developed by David Mandel of the University of Victoria in Canada that although there are ongoing efforts to understand the psychology of perpetrators, there has been almost no work on the psychology of the people he calls the "instigators," among whom he includes a figure such as Osama bin Laden. While it can be argued that bin Laden is, like Hitler and Stalin and others, very much the leader and very much the perpetrator, the roles of these monstrous influencers of others to go and do major destructive mayhem is very much deserving of more powerful magnifying attention, including to the many lesser leaders who are instigators. In the cases of the suicide bombers, there certainly is a dramatic opportunity to look at the special "professional role" of people who keep themselves safe but send others to their fiery roles. See David R. Mandel (2002), Evil and the instigation of collective violence.

39. See Michael Radu (October 21, 2003), Radical Islam and suicide bombers, E-Notes, Foreign Policy Research Institute, Philadelphia, PA, Retrieved from the Web.

40. The story of Barko's research is told by an *Haaretz* reporter: Dalia Shechori (June 15, 2003), In his private life he is human, when it comes to Israelis he is not. *Haaretz* (Hebrew).

41. Ibid.

42. Lisa Keys (2004), The making of martyrs,

43. Reference is to a female suicide bomber in Israel in Janury 2002 reported earlier.

44. The article was entitled, "Class Isn't Over Yet, Stupid!" It appeared in the Egyptian newspaper *Hadith Al-Madina* in the form of an open letter to President Bush. Excerpted from interviews in *Hadith Al-Madina* (Egypt), April 23, 2002, Cited in *Al-Quds Al-Arabi* (London), April 23, 2002, and *Iqraa TV* (Saudi Arabia/Egypt), April 24, 2002, Published by the Middle East Media Research Institute (MEMRI) (2002), No. 373, April 30.

The statement of the Egyptian psychiatrist is striking in that an identity of a professor of psychiatry is used to create a rhetoric of glorification and legitimation of the combination of suicide and murder. It is, of course, metaphorically relevant to our concern with the mental health meaning of suicide bombing. In all fairness, however, it should be pointed out that the basic conception of suicide bombing as giving loyal service to one's people did not originate with Palestinian suicide bombers. See again, for example, the Japanese *kamikaze* fighters who gave their lives in WW II by diving their planes into American ships; their conception was that they were *serving* their god-like Emperor. Similarly, in Sri Lanka, where a battle raged for thirty years between the ruling Buddhist Sunhalese and the Muslim Tamil Tigers, the Tamil developed suicide bombing to a very extensive extent, and they used the same language of sublime self-sacrifice. As a specialist of the mind and speaking as if its language, the Egyptian psychiatrist gives us a further understanding of how concepts of loyalty and self-sacrifice can take over human experience to a point where the suicide bomber becomes a willing and even proud actor of his or her role at deep levels of their mind. Nonetheless, I argue that the inner mind knows the ultimate facts which are, plain and simple, that the suicide bomber is permanently killing both himself or herself and many others.

45. Lyman H. Legter (1984), The Soviet gulag: Is it genocide? In Charny, Israel W. (Ed.), *Toward the Understanding and Prevention of Genocide,* pp. 60–66.

46. R.J. Rummel (1999), The Soviet gulag state.

See also R.J. Rummel (1992), *Lethal Politics: Soviet Genocide and Mass Murder since 1917,* New Brunswick, NJ: Transaction Publishers.

47. See the discussion of a culture of death in Christoph Reuter (2004), *My Life Is A Weapon: A Modern History of Suicide Bombing*, Princeton, NJ: Princeton University Press.

Chapter 6

1. Egyptian researcher, Zaynab Abd Al-'Aziz, interviewed on Iqra TV, May 25, 2005, Cited in Middle East Media Research Institute (MEMRI) (2005), MEMRI TV special report 9/11 conspiracy theories on Arab and Iranian TV channels 2004–2005, Special Report—Jihad & Terrorism, No. 38, September 8. To view this clip, visit: www.memritv.org/search.asp?ACT=S9&P1=844.

2. Excerpts from a speech by then leader of Al-Qaeda in Iraq, Abu Mus'ab Al-Zarqawi, published in audio form on the Internet and from the Web site of Al-Qaeda's Jihad Media Battalion (www.k-j-i.tk) on September 14, 2005, Cited in Middle East Media Research Institute (MEMRI) (2005), Leader of Al-Qaeda in Iraq Al-Zarqawi declares "total war" on Shi'ites, states that the Sunni women of Tel'afar had "their wombs filled with the sperm of the Crusaders," Special Dispatch—Iraq/Jihad & Terrorism, No. 987, September 16.

3. Retrieved from news24.com, 'I understand suicide bombers,' January 22, 2004 (SA). The news report concludes, "Her comments came hours after 19 Israelis died and more than 40 were injured in a suicide bomb attack on a bus in Jerusalem."

4. Suicide bombers: Dignity, despair, and the need for hope, an interview with Eyad Sarraj, *Journal of Palestine Studies*, *124*, Summer 2002. The review on the Web was as follows: Arjan El Fassed (November 19, 2002), Shock: The mind of a suicide bomber, *The Electronic Intifada*.

5. Some have argued, and I am inclined to agree with them in part, that saturation bombings of civilian centers such as in Dresden were excessive and therefore even qualify as genocidal crimes against humanity. See Eric Markusen and David Kopf (1995), *The Holocaust and Strategic Bombing: Genocide and Total War in the Twentieth Century*.

6. Eric H. Boehm (1999), The fates of non-Jewish Germans under the Nazis.

7. The conference, "Stockholm International Forum: Genocide Threats and Prevention" took place in Stockholm, in January 2004.

8. Bret Stephens, then editor of the *Jerusalem Post*, has written of "the tendency among self-styled progressives and human rights activists to willfully ignore, or tacitly acquiesce in, some of the worst human rights abuses of their era." He cites, for example, liberals like Noam Chomsky and Edward Herman who denied that the Khmer Rouge in Cambodia were vicious killers. And he asks:

Why?
Among the oft-made arguments of people like Chomsky and Herman is that western policy makers focus only on the human rights abuses committed by their enemies, not their friends. Why, for example, was so much western attention and outrage devoted to goings-on in Communist Cambodia, instead of East Timor, which was then under the thumb of US-allied Indonesia? Why obsess about the sins of the Sandinistas in Nicaragua, but not those of the Pinochet regime in Chile?
It's a legitimate point. But what has been true of some quarters of the Right has been at least as true of parts of the Left. In their 1977 review, Chomsky and Herman did not merely point out hypocrisy in western attitudes; they systematically attempted

to shred the evidence that the Khmer Rouge was guilty of "autogenocide" (the killing of their own people). Furthermore, they repeatedly argued that most of Cambodia's suffering was either the direct or the indirect consequence of American actions.Thus, in discussing photographs of Cambodian civilians pulling plows in a field, they first alleged the photos were faked, then suggested that if people rather than oxen were in fact pulling plows, it was because "the savage American assault on Cambodia did not spare the animal population."

See Bret Stephens (April 16, 2004), On the denial of genocide: Why 'never again' has proved the most hollow slogan of our age, *Jerusalem Post Up Front (Magazine)*, pp. 7–9, quotation on p. 8.

9. Nicholas A. Robins (2002), *Genocide and Millenialism in Upper Peru: The Great Rebellion of 1780–1782*.

10. Margot Dudkevitch (May 3, 2004), Mother, 4 daughters killed en route to referendum protest, *Jerusalem Post*. See also the Web site of "Horsefeathers: Fighting folly, ignorance and cant," dated May 3, 2004 for a more detailed report, as well as a critical analysis of the reporting of the event by various news media.

11. Islam Awareness Homepage, 'Why the suicide bombers are heroes,' Retrieved from the Web, January, 25, 2004: www.thisisthenortheast.co.uk/thenorth_east/archive 2002/07/01/A6v32o.re.ht.

12. Subhash Kapila (2002), India's payback time to Israel, South Asia Analysis Group, Paper no. 442, April 10, Retrieved from the Web. Dr. Subhash Kapila is described as an international relations and strategic affairs analyst who can be reached at esdecom@vsnl.com.

13. The classic legal ruling that came out of the trials of Israeli soldiers who massacred Arab civilians in 1956 at Kfar Kassem established the standard that manifestly illegal military orders to harm and kill civilians are not to be obeyed, and if obeyed are subject to punishment without the possibility of a defense of following orders. See Israel W. Charny and Daphna Fromer (1992), A study of attitudes of viewers of the film "Shoah" toward an incident of mass murder by Israeli soldiers (Kfar Kassem, 1956).

14. Kay S. Hymowitz and Harry Stein (November 5, 2001), Earth to ivory tower: Get real! *Wall Street Journal*.

15. Human Rights Watch (2002), *Erased in a Moment: Suicide Bombing Attacks on Israeli Civilians*, ibid. See also Israel/PA: Suicide bombers commit crimes against humanity (November 1, 2002), Retrieved from the Web: hrw.org/defending human rights worldwide.

16. Associated Press (March 22, 2005), Qaeda suspects admit plans to attack Western targets, Retrieved from http://www.iht.com/articles/2005/03/21/news/suspects.html.

17. *Washington Post* (November 23, 2001), Fleeing Taliban leaves trail of revealing documents.

18. Brian Knowlton (December 4–5, 2004), Al Qaeda's next target? Europe seems vulnerable in ways U.S. is not, *New York Times*. The book referred to by Michael Scheuer was actually published under the name, Anonymous (2004), *Imperial Hubris: Why the West is Losing the War on Terror*. Only afterwards was the author's name revealed. According to one newspaper story, the author said the reason for his anonymity was that he "feared for his job at the CIA, not for his life at the hands of Al-Qaeda." See: Jason Veat (2004),The secret history of Anonymous, *The Boston Phoenix*, July 2–8, 2004, Retrieved from the Web.

19. *Spiegel Online* (July 15, 2005), More Shocks for Britain from terror investigation, Spiegel's Daily Take.

20. Committee for the Scientific Investigation of Claims of the Paranormal (CSI-COP), CSICOP Hoax Watch. Tracking hoaxes, "prophecies" and scams in the wake of the September 11, 2001 terrorist attacks in the United States. New items May 24, 2002, Retrieved from the Web, April 7, 2004.

21. *Response* (Winter 2003/2004), Unending trail of hateful lies, Simon Wiesenthal Center in Los Angeles.

22. Regine Mehl (2003), Non-violent civil alternatives to war on terrorism, Report of a talk at a conference sponsored by the Hiroshima Peace Institute, *Hiroshima Research News*, 5(3), March, p. 6. Note how this is the same kind of thinking we saw earlier that if Israel had much to gain from the destabilizing of Saudi Arabia, this in itself gives credence if not actually confirms the claim by the Crown Prince of Saudi Arabia that the Zionists were behind the terrorist attack.

23. A respected, impressive former ambassador from a small country (not Israel) to a major world power told me with absolute certainty that "everyone knows" already for a century the members of a certain worldwide fellowship (this time it's not the Jews but the Masons) are behind many of the major political events and especially the killings in the world, and that their members included the Turkish leaders who organized the genocide of the Armenians in 1915, U.S. Presidents Clinton and Bush (the father), and perhaps—a rare note of less certainty here—current leaders of Israel.

I had been so impressed by this bright forceful man up until I heard this garbage pouring out from his mouth. But then I also found myself wondering obsessively, "What if it's true? Could it be true?" I realized I was experiencing the first stages of possibly being inducted into the conspiracy thinking that would relieve me of so many of my worries about understanding the evils of our world, and that I had to shake off the seductive induction.

No, dear reader, it isn't true, and couldn't be true.

24. Steven Stalinsky (2004), Anti-American and anti-Semitic cartoons in leading Egypt government weekly *Al-Ahram*: 1998–2004, Middle East Media Research Institute (MEMRI), April 2.

25. Youssef M. Ibrahim (October 30–31, 2004), Shackles on the mind: The fear that chokes the Arab world, *International Herald Tribune*, p. 6.

26. The information appears in the magazine of the Simon Wiesenthal Center in Los Angeles which concludes the report with a disbelieving exclamation mark. See *Response* (Winter2003/2004), One-third of young Germans: U.S. behind 9/11, Simon Wiesenthal Center in Los Angeles.

27. Europe Terrorism Update: Britain-Al-Qaeda scouting Jewish targets. *Response*, ibid.

28. Committee for the Scientific Investigation of Claims of the Paranormal (CSICOP), ibid.

29. For a film on the development of suicide bombings as a weapon that once applied to military and political targets and now is intended to slaughter civilians, see Film (2002), *Human Weapon*.

30. Don Van Natta, Jr. and Desmond Butler (November 3, 2003), Hundreds of militants head to Iraq for jihad, *International Herald Tribune*; Michael R. Gordon (December 16, 2003), Iraq struggle doesn't stop here, Insurgents threats and citizens distrust go beyond Saddam, *International Herald Tribune*, p. 5.

31. Yair Sheleg (December 12, 2003), Catholics and Jews against radical Islam: Time is pressing, says Professor Yehuda Bauer, one of the outstanding Holocaust scholars in the

world. Radical Islam is still a priority but its concepts are penetrating the moderate Muslim majority, *Haaretz*, p. B7 (Hebrew).

32. Douglas Jehl (December 31, 2003–January 2, 2004), Pattern suspected in Saudi attacks: Qaeda tries to shake up state, U.S. thinks, *International Herald Tribune*, p. 1, with attribution to the *New York Times*.

33. Peter Bergen (2004), Al-Qaeda morphs from group to movement, *Los Angeles Times*. Peter Bergen is identified as the author of *Holy War, Inc.: Inside the Secret World of Osama bin Laden*, New York: Free Press, 2001.

34. Neil MacFarquhar (November 11, 2003), News analysis: Strike on Saudi complex sours Qaeda supporters, *International Herald Tribune*, with attribution to the *New York Times*.

35. *The Age* (Melbourne, Australia) (November 17, 2003), Associated Press, Newspapers given al-Qaeda statements.

36. John J. Cushman (December 22, 2003), U.S. raises terror alert: Risks 'perhaps greater now than at any point' since 9/11, *International Herald Tribune*, pp.1, 6 (quotations on p. 6).

37. *Christian Science Monitor* (August 11, 1998), The Monitor's view, Not an age of terror.

38. Scott Atran (March 17, 2004), Al Qaeda's web: The upgraded networks of global terrorism, *Kum Baya International Herald Tribune*.

The imagination of science fiction writers and satirists also are windows into the possibilities of our futures. A novel about suicide bombers that is touted as "a serious manual of mass instruction [and] a major warning for everyone everywhere" by Burt Keimach tells the story of a member of a Hamas terrorist cell. The reader is left with the disturbing question of where he or she will be *when—not if—*the next 'martyr' strikes hard. See Burt Keimach (2003), *Suicide String*, New York: Baltimore: Publish America.

39. *International Herald Tribune* (April 21, 2004), Jordan kills 3 in shootout, p. 3. Another report in *The Australian* said the plan involved a cocktail of chemicals planned to include acetone, nitric acid and sulphuric acid with 20 tons of explosives, and that the chemicals "would have caused toxic gas emissions capable of harming thousands of people." "Australia's foreign minister, Alexander Downer, is reported as saying the plot showed the huge risk of terrorists getting hold of WMD, and that "anyone who doubts the terrorists' desire to obtain and use these weapons only needs to look at this example." Source: Patrick Walters, John Kerrin, and agencies (April 28, 2004), Chemical terrorist attack foiled, *The Australian*, Retrieved from the Web.

40. Steven Emerson (1998), Foreign terrorists in America: Five years after the World Trade Center bombing, ibid., p. 7 of 31 pages of a printout from Internet.

41. Judy Keen (February 12, 2004), Bush targets nuclear market, *USA Today*.

42. *International Herald Tribune* (May 5 2004), What if? Europe tests a Qaeda hit, From news reports.

43. Peter Waldman (February 3, 2004), A historian's take on Islam—steers U.S. in terrorism fight: Bernard Lewis's blueprint—sowing Arab democracy—is facing a test in Iraq, *Wall Street Journal*.

Actually, personally I am not a great fan of Bernard Lewis. In fact, in 1995 I even testified as an expert witness against him in a Paris court where Lewis was being sued for denying the Armenian Genocide. This was a trial under criminal law. The judges ruled that the law under which Lewis would be liable only dated from World War II and the

Holocaust, and therefore Lewis could not be convicted. But the same judges strongly and purposefully went out of their way to characterize Lewis as a "negationist" or denier of the unquestionable historical record of the Armenian Genocide. Subsequently, Lewis was again sued in Paris under civil law, and now the French court did convict him. Peter Waldman also gives a brief account of the latter trial. For a full-scale report and analysis of the significance of Lewis' conviction, see Rouben Adalian (1997), The ramifications in the United States of the 1995 French Court decision on the denial of the Armenian Genocide and Princeton University, *Review du Monde Arménien Moderne et Contemporain*, 3, 99–122 (published in Paris, but this article is in English).

I have also content-analyzed some of Bernard Lewis' writing in which he denies the Armenian Genocide, and I compared the "mind mechanisms" or logical structures of his denials to another eminent academic, this one Professor Ernst Nolte in Germany, who denies the Holocaust. The content analyses show how the two quite respected professors are similar to each other and to other deniers of the two genocides. They "yes-but" obfuscate and create a virtual reality in which they in effect deny the enormous crimes, the one of the genocide of a million to a million-and-a-half Armenians by the Turks, and the other of close to 6 million Jews by the Nazis.

To this day, I know of no one who has figured out what Bernard Lewis' motivation may be for such a violation of history. But he remains otherwise a preeminent historian of the Middle East. The French civil court that convicted Lewis actually decided that— unlike the earlier criminal court—it did not have to rule on the historical authenticity of the Armenian Genocide, but that it was convicting Lewis for his abject failures to conduct himself properly as an academician so far as he had literally ignored the evidences and judgments of many others.

Given that Lewis has retained his position as both a beloved and prominent scholar of Islam and the Middle East, I have accepted that it is my responsibility to follow his other work respectfully. Lewis' work following September 11, *What Went Wrong*? has been a runaway best-seller in the West. Peter Waldman also points out that, remarkably, Lewis over and over again has been a charismatic guest-adviser of presidents, prime ministers, and countless senior political leaders and officials, especially in the United States and Israel. See Bernard Lewis (2002), *What Went Wrong? The Clash Between Islam and Modernity in the Middle East; also* Bernard Lewis (2003), *The Crisis of Islam: Holy War and Unholy Terror.*

44. Peter Waldman, ibid.

45. Bernard Lewis (November 19, 2001), The revolt of Islam, *New Yorker*, Retrieved from the Web: Watch-Selected articles and opinion—November 2001.

46. Thomas L. Friedman (January 9, 2004), The war of ideas, *International Herald Tribune*.

47. Ibid.

48. *Pakistan Daily Times* (no date but refers to month after the suicide bombing in Bali on October 12, 2002), Asia suicide bombers mark new terror phase, With attribution to Reuters, Retrieved from the Web, January 25, 2004.

49. Steven Emerson (1998), Foreign terrorists in America: Five years after the World Trade Center bombing, ibid., quotation is on p. 3 of 31 pages of a printout from Internet.

50. Daniel Pipes (2001), The danger within: Militant Islam in America, *Commentary*, November, Retrieved from the Web: Watch-Selected articles and opinion—November.

51. Daniel Pipes (2001), Fighting militant Islam without bias, *City Journal, 11* (4), Autumn, Retrieved from the Web: Watch-Selected articles and opinion—November.

52. Daniel Kahneman (2003), Psychology of large errors and of important decision, Seventh Oscar Van Leer Annual Lecture.

53. Ibid. The quotations are from my own recording of his lecture at which I was present. The full lecture is available on the Web site of the Van Leer Institute.

54. Thomas L. Friedman (December 1, 2003), *International Herald Tribune*, with attribution to the *New York Times*.

55. Eric Lipton (March 17, 2005), A grim list of terror scenarios: Document describes likely targets in U.S., *New York Times*, Retrieved from the Web http://www.iht.com/articles/2005/03/16/news/terror.html.

56. Israel W. Charny (1999), An International Peace Army: A proposal for the long-range future.

57. My reader has a right to know that I personally did support the war on Iraq to eliminate the weapons of mass destruction we believed were there (I know from my own small range of life experience that scuds did fall on Tel Aviv in 1991!), and to topple the genocider, Saddam—about whose mass murders of many thousands more of Iraqis we have learned more and more since the invasion. But I opposed, and retrospectively am still very much against, America's entry into Iraq against the will of the United Nations, thus seriously insulting and weakening our not very strong international system of governance.

58. Flora Lewis (October 12, 2001), It's sad, yes, but going to war is again necessary, *International Herald Tribune*.

59. Flora Lewis (October 28, 2001), A geopolitical new deal: Realism means helping the world, *International Herald Tribune*.

60. See William Pfaff (November 1–2, 2003), A fiction shattered by America's aggression. *International Herald Tribune*, 4.

61. David E. Sanger (November 1–2, 2003), Rice faults past terrorism policy, *International Herald Tribune*.

Chapter 7

1. The article by Dr. Shaker Al-Nabulsi, a Jordanian intellectual who resides in the United States was published in *Al-Siyasa* (Kuwait), August 7, Cited in Middle East Media Research Institute (MEMRI) (2005), Arab intellectual: Why has there been no fatwa against bin Laden? Special Dispatch-Reform Project, No. 965, August 22.

2. The Al-Manar channel that broadcast this episode is run by Hezbollah. Episode after episode portrays how the Jews have brought death and destruction to the world, Cited in Küntzel, Matthias (2005), National socialism and anti-Semitism in the Arab world, *Jewish Political Studies Review 17* (1–2), Spring 2005. Dr. Küntzel, an associate researcher of the Vidal Sassoon International Center for the Study of Antisemitism at the Hebrew University of Jerusalem, is a political scientist and author and lives in Hamburg. He is the author of *Dijhad und Judenhass. Über den neuen antijüdischen Krieg (Jihad and Jew-Hatred: About the New Anti-Jewish War)*, Freiburg: Ca ira-Verlag (German).

3. A letter to the editor in the *Bangkok Post* concludes that Israel "will remain a pariah to the civilized world (and quite frankly deserves to reap the whirlwind it has sowed)." D. Snowdon (March 28, 2004), Sharon's normal face, Letter to the Editor, *Bangkok Post*. See the note in the next chapter referring to another letter to the same *Bangkok Post* that explains the Holocaust as a rational event, as were also the nuclear bombings of Hiroshima

and Nagasaki. Needless to say, I confess to a deep anger at those who would explain holocausts of all sorts with ostensible sang-froid or "cool" as rational events that simply should be understood like all other war events in human history.

4. Jonathan Yardley (2005), Review of Terry McDermott (2005), *Perfect Soldiers: The Hijackers: Who they Were, Why They Did I*, New York: HarperCollins, Retrieved from the Web: Washingtonpost.com.The 9/11 hijackers, May 1.

5. See in the previous chapter reference to an article by Bret Stephens, former editor of the *Jerusalem* Post, about denials by liberals of human rights abuses. The article was no less than in a Holocaust Memorial Day edition of the *Jerusalem Post Magazine*. It focused intently on denials of the Cambodian genocide in the mid-late 1970s, including by the liberal publication, *The Nation*, and including by Noam Chomsky of MIT and Edward Herman of the University of Pennsylvania who were mentioned in the quotation in the previous chapter, as well as by Ben Kiernan of Yale University—who has since corrected his position and emerged as a prime scholar of the Cambodian genocide (for example, Kiernan wrote the entry on the Cambodian genocide for the *Encyclopedia of Genocide*). As noted in the earlier discussion of what I called the liberal fallacy of the underdog, Stephens observed a chronic tendency of extreme liberals to ignore, cover up, explain away, or even approve by some other name some of the worst human rights abuses when committed by the opponents of the big powers. See in the previous chapter: Bret Stephens (2004), On the denial of genocide: Why 'never again' has proved the most hollow slogan of our age.

6. Source: 'Civilized Slaughter' vs. 'Suicide bombers,' ibid.

7. Arnon Regular (March 16, 2004), Soldiers find bomb in 10-year-old's cart, *Haaretz* (English Edition). See also Hilary Leila Krieger (March 26, 2004), Use of children by terrorists condemned, *Jerusalem Post*.

8. Khaled Abu Toameh (March 26, 2004), Teenage bomber's family outraged, *Jerusalem Post*.

9. Hilary Leila Krieger (March 27, 2004), Sharansky slams BBC report on boy bomber, *Jerusalem Post*.

10. Imad Saada (April 1, 2004), Boy lured to suicide mission with promise of paradise, *Gold Coast Bulletin* (Australia).

11. Matthew Gutman and Khaled Abu Toameh (March 31, 2004), Islamic jihad promised heaven to teen recruit, *Jerusalem Post*.

12. Ibid.

13. Elaine Sciolino (March 12, 2004), Train blasts kill more than 196 in Madrid. 10 bombs at rush hour wounded 1200, *International Herald Tribune*.

14. Doreen Carvajal (March 15, 2004), In Madrid, a claim for Al Qaeda, *International Herald Tribune*.

15. From an al-Qaeda document as cited by Flora Lewis (2001), A geopolitical new deal: Realism means helping the world, ibid.

16. Associated Press (March 19, 2004), Cairo, Islamic group warns other nations. Japan, Italy, Australia and Britain listed, *International Herald Tribune*.

17. Dominique Möisi (March 19, 2004), After Madrid. Returning to old Europe and old America, *International Herald Tribune*.

18. Thomas L. Friedman (March 19, 2004), Axis of appeasement, *International Herald Tribune*.

19. John Vinocur (November 3, 2004), Now it's pay back time for Bush's staunch allies, *International Herald Tribune*.

20. Fareed Zakaria (2004), Cruelty is all they have left, ibid.

21. Islamic Human Rights Commission (November 11, 2003), Media Monitoring UK: Channel 4, 'Witness inside the mind of a suicide bomber,' 10 November 2003, Retrieved from the Web September 3 2005. *My own bibliographic reference to this video by UK Channel 4 does not include the word "Witness," but the description of the film of 5 failed suicide bombers (described by the present human rights site as "alleged suicide bombers") leaves no doubt it is the same film.*

22. Vatsala Vedantam (January 16, 2002), Front lines of terrorism: The view from India—attack on Indian Parliament. *Christian Century*, Retrieved from the Web: looksmart, January 31, 2004.

23. *International Herald Tribune* (2004), "From news reports": Qaeda plan: preemptive strategy? Tape urges Muslim youths to take initiative and strike West, October 2–3, pp. 1, 4.

24. Don Van Natta, Jr. and Raymond Bonne (February 8, 2004), Regional terrorist groups pose threat experts warn, *New York Times*. ["Raymond Bonner reported from Jakarta for this article and Don Van Natta, Jr. from London. Desmond Butler contributed reporting from Germany."]

25. Ibid.

26. Stanley Kurtz (November 19, 2001), The scandal of Middle East studies, *Weekly Standard*, Retrieved from the Web: Watch-Selected articles and opinion, November 2001.

27. Ibid.

28. "Touba, Senegal-Sacred Sites-Martin Gray," Retrieved from the list of Web sites given in the entry "Amadou Bamba," which is identified as updated 20 October 2002 and "managed by Aminta." I went to these Web sites in response to the information I first received on Amadou Bamba from the UCLA Center for Jewish Studies. See further in the text and the next note.

29. The title of the exhibition at the Center for Jewish Studies at UCLA on June 4, 2003 was "A Saint in the City: Sufi Arts of Urban Senegal," Received by e-mail from cjs@humnet.ucla.edu.

As I have been emphasizing, clearly there are meaningful trends in Islamic thought against violence that hopefully may build up some day to constitute the prevailing worldview of Islam. But these should not be allowed to be taken naively and romantically in denial of the prevailing power of a warring, destructive jihad philosophy in too many quarters of Islam today. The well-intended UCLA Jewish Studies flyer projected its fine program as if it were a correction of mistaken perception of Islam in general as a major source of terror. Bin Laden is *not* an anomaly in Islam, but one of the two poles of Islamic thought that prevails in many Muslim communities and certainly marshals an enormous amount of murderous fire-power that is killing many thousands of people in many places in the world.

30. There are many fascinating discussions pro and con of this thesis as rendered in the intellectual world by Bernard Lewis and Samuel Huntington and in the intelligence and journalistic communities by a large number of investigators, reporters, and commentators such as cited throughout this book. It is hard to "prove" the future, but it is a major responsibility of all of us to attempt to identify as early as possible real threats to human life. I suggest that the rate and number of Islamic suicide killings and other terror in so many locations in the world today qualifies this trend as a threat to world peace.

For a reading guide to discussions of Huntington, in journalistic sources, see Josh Burek (2005), Clash of civilizations: a reading guide. Online resources and expert commentary on Samuel P. Huntington's essay, "The Clash of Civilizations," Retrieved from the *Christian Science Monitor* on the Web: csmonitor.com. A changed world combating terrorism, Retrieved August 9, 2005.

It should be clear that there have been many critical reactions to Huntington's thesis. Many of them are, simply, that he is provoking more of a war than will be the case without Huntington, and that his thesis becomes the more dangerous if adopted by policymakers. Others object to the severity of his critique of Islam's aggressiveness—and for some this is coupled with his being indifferent to the West's own many violations of the peace of the world. Another criticism is that Huntington overemphasizes culture, and does not pay sufficient attention to nationalism. For critiques of Huntington, see: John Ikenberry (1997), *The West: Precious, not unique: Civilizations make for a poor paradigam just like the rest, Foreign Affairs*; Stephen M. Walt (1997), Building up new bogeyman, *Foreign Policy*.

31. Rudolph Peters (1996), *Jihad in Classical and Modern Islam,* Princeton, NJ: Markus Wiener, Retrieved from *Apologetics Index:* Islamic Suicide Bombers, January 7, 2004.

32. Statement rejecting terrorism, September 11, 2002, Retrieved from the Web: www.anis-online.de/pages/_21-ebene/palaestinainfo2.htm.

33. The compilation of statements against violence is given by Sheila Musaji (2002), Muslim reactions to September 11th, 'The American Muslim' e-zine, www. theamericanmuslim.org, Published in the September issue of *Islamic Reflections 2002*.

34. Ibid., with citation given to the *New York Times*, September 28, 2001.

35. Ibid., with citation given to the *Middle East Times*, September 28, 2001.

36. Ibid., with citation given to Islamic Republic News Agency, September 16, 2001.

37. Ibid., with citation given to Agence France Presse, September 14, 2001.

38. *International Herald Tribune* (April 21, 2004), Shiite cleric defends Hamas, p. 3.

39. Muzamil Jaleel (no date ?2002), Suicide militancy-II. Martyrdom, the prize for taking one's life, Retrieved from the Web: expressindia. KashmirLIVE, ibid.

40. Associated Press (April 2, 2004), Mosque council's call against terrorism: Response by European Muslims to effort in Britain is mixed, *International Herald Tribune*.

41. Ibid.

42. Charles Krauthammer (November 23, 2001), The silent imams, *Washington Post*.

43. Salman Rushdie (November 2, 2001), Yes, this is about Islam, *New York Times*.

44. Daniel Pipes (2001), Fighting militant Islam without bias, ibid.

45. See Arab American Institute (August 14, 2003), AAI statement on recess appointment of Daniel Pipes, Retrieved from the Web: March 10, 2004: Inside AAI: Press Releases.

46. See Michael Scherer (May 26, 2003), Daniel Pipes, peacemaker? MotherJones.com, Retrieved February 12, 2004.

47. Daniel Pipes (July 30, 2001), The jihad menace, *Jerusalem Post*. Daniel Pipes is described by the *Jerusalem Post* as director of the Philadelphia-based *Middle East Forum*, Retrieved from *Apologetics Index:* Islamic Suicide Bombers, January 7, 2004. *Apologetics Index (apologeticsindex.org, countercult.com, cultfaq.org)* is described as providing "research resources on religious cults, sects, new religious movements, alternative religions, apologetics, anticult, and countercult organizations, doctrines, religious practices and world views reflecting a variety of theological and/or sociological perspectives." The site is further defined as providing information to "help equip Christians to logically present and defend the Christian faith."

48. Aviezer Ravitzky (April 11, 2004), Clinging to the middle ground, *Haaretz* (English Edition), p. B4. The Hebrew version of this article is entitled more explicitly: Aviezer Ravitzky (April 11, 2004), The clash of civilizations is not our battle: The welfare and safety of the Jewish people require us to keep our distance from the "clash of civilizations" as distant as east from west, *Haaretz* (Hebrew), Bet 11. Ravitzky still hopes the "clash of

civilizations" can be avoided, but if not at least that Jews will stay out of it. "There can be no doubt about what the good of the historical Jew says of this 'clash': to preserve and protect himself, he will remain as remote from it as east is from west."

49. Robert S. Wistrich (November 16, 2001), The new Islamic fascism, *Jerusalem Post*.

50. Alan Phillips (September 13, 2001), New assassins queue eagerly for martyrdom, *Daily Telegraph* (London).

51. The same writer noted that some analysts have warned that violence looming in the Muslim world against Shi'ites could incite Shi'ite-Sunni violence throughout the regions of Islam "in a broad swath of Asia from Pakistan to Lebanon."

> Anti-Shiism is embedded in the ideology of Sunni militancy that has risen to prominence across the region in the last decade. Wahabi Sunnis, who dominate Saudi Arabia's religious affairs and export their philosophy to its neighbors, have led the charge, declaring Shiites "infidels" and hence justifying ... massacres of Shiite civilians. Even with the fall of the Taliban, widespread killings of Shiites and bombings of Shiite mosques and community centers in both Afghanistan and Pakistan have continued.

See Vali Nasr (March 10, 2004), Anti-Shiism in Iraq and beyond: Beyond the spread of Sunni anger, *International Herald Tribune*. Nasr is identified as "a professor of national security affairs at the Naval Postgraduate School."

52. Associated Press (March 20, 2004), Iskandariyah, Iraq. At least 660 killed in 24 suicide bombings, *Daily Yomiuri* (Tokyo) (English).

53. Rajiv Chandrasekaran (March 20, 2004), U.S. military leaders blame Iraq attacks on Islamic extremists. Officials say Hussein loyalists have declined, *Washington Post*; *International Herald Tribune* (April 7, 2004), From news reports. Fighting in Iraq boils on 2 fronts: While U.S. troops battle Sunnis, backers of a Shi'ite cleric attack coalition forces.

54. In one of those endless pieces of humor at all intellectual levels that circulate on Internet, I was sent by a very fine colleague who has been doing outstanding work on anti-Semitism—Manfred Gerstenfeld, Chair of the Steering Committee of the Jerusalem Center for Public Affairs—a piece entitled "LARK Program." LARK is an acronym for "Liberals Accept Responsibility for Killers." In this spoof, a person receives a letter from the White House thanking him or her for their "complaining about the treatment of a captive insurgent (terrorist)" who is being held by the United States. The citizen who has complained is told, "We have decided to place one terrorist under your personal care," and the spoof then continues with a vivid description of the psychopathic violence of the detainee who is due to arrive at the citizen's house shortly under heavy armed guard. "Perhaps you are correct in describing these problems as mere cultural differences," the letter continues. "We truly appreciate it when folks like you who know so much, keep us informed of the proper way to do our job . . . respecting his culture and his religious beliefs'—wasn't that how you put it? . . . You take good care of Ahmed—and remember . . . we'll be watching. Good luck!"

The text has been widely reproduced on the Internet, e.g., the following source that also gives some of the history of this modern "legend": Snopes.com (2005). LARK spurred. Urban Legends Reference Pages: Politics, Retrieved from the Web: www.snopes.com/politics/war/lark.asp.

55. Irshad Manji (August 10, 2005), Why tolerate the hate? *International Herald Tribune*; See Irshad Manji (2004), *The Trouble with Islam*.

Chapter 8

1. Thomas L. Friedman (July 9–10, 2005), Muslims in danger, *International Herald Tribune*, p. 6.

2. Mark Danner (September 9, 2005), U.S. fighting the war the terrorists sought, *International Herald Tribune* online. From an article in the *New York Times Magazine*. Mark Danner is the author of *Torture and Truth: America, Abu Ghraib and the War on Terror*.

3. The commission called for the creation of a national counterterrorism center that would both unify strategic intelligence gathering against Islamic terrorists and operational planning against them. David Stout (July 23, 2004), A 'failure' to protect U.S.: Scathing 9/11 report predicts even greater terror attacks. *International Herald Tribune*, pp. 1, 4, with attribution to the *New York Times*.

4. Brian Knowlton (June 17, 2004), Panel details a wider Qaeda plot that took aim at Congress and CIA: 10 hijackings would've hit both coasts, *International Herald Tribune*, pp. 1, 4.

5. Associated Press (June 17, 2004), 9/11 plan once included Asia attacks, Retrieved from the International Herald Tribune online.

6. News of new inventions are pouring out as mankind reorganizes to meet the new scourge: e.g., a system to be attached to civilian aircraft to deflect oncoming hand-fired missiles during the vulnerable proximity of the airplane during takeoffs and landings, or a laser-beam explosive-detection system that screens people approaching an area such as passengers boarding a bus—which is then tied to automatic closing of the bus doors, the theory being that an explosion outside the bus would cause fewer casualties than if detonated inside the enclosed space of the bus. Watching the creative processes at work in response to the new threats is almost fun, were it not for the horror of the dangers being addressed.

7. Marc Sageman (2004), *Understanding Terror Networks*. Foreign Policy Research Institute: Talk on October 6, 2004, Retrieved from the Web June 17, 1005: www.fpri.org/ enotes/20041101.middleeast.sageman.understandingterrornetworks.html. See also the book by this author: Marc Sageman (2004), *Understanding Terror Networks*.

8. Ibid.

9. Robert A. Pape (May 19, 2005), The suicide bombers: Blowing up an assumption, *International Herald Tribune*.

10. Michael Rubin (May 6, 2005), Soothing rhetoric—scary reality, *Haaretz* (English Edition). The speech by al-Zarqawi is reported by Rubin to have appeared in April 29, 2005 on "an Islamist Web site."

11. Alan Cowell (August 6, 2005), Blair is seeking to curb radicals who preach hate. *New York Times*.

12. Ibid.

13. Ibid. "This is not in any way whatever aimed at the decent law-abiding Muslim community of Britain. We know that this fringe of extremists does not truly represent Islam."

14. Irshad Manji (August 10, 2005), Why tolerate the hate? *International Herald Tribune*. See, Irshad Manji (2004), *The Trouble with Islam*.

15. Middle East Media Research Institute (MEMRI) (2001), 'I want to start a kindergarten for extremism.' Special Dispatch No. 298, November 8, Retrieved from the Web: Watch-Selected articles and opinion, November.

16. See the discussion of the pandering of violence in American mass media in I.W. Charny (2006), *Fascism and Democracy in the Human Mind.*

17. Jack Kelley (June 26, 2001), Devotion, desire drive youths to 'martyrdom'. Palestinians in pursuit of paradise turn their own bodies into weapons, *USA Today.*

18. *Response* (Winter 2003/2004), MVP of trading cards: Osama bin Laden, Simon Wiesenthal Center in Los Angeles.

19. Erik Schechter (August 6, 2004), Conversations with my killer: Erik Schechter meets suicide bombers (title on magazine cover); Where have all the bombers gone? (title on the article), *Up Front, Jerusalem Post Magazine*, pp. 11–13, quotations on p. 13.

20. *Response* (Winter 2003/2004), Arafat's PA: Corruption and terrorism continue, Simon Wiesenthal Center in Los Angeles.

21. Ibid.

22. Julia Magnet (November 16, 2001), His grasp of spin is chilling, *London Daily Telegraph.*

23. *Simon Wiesenthal Center* (2005), News Alert: Simon Wiesenthal Center calls on PA president to dismiss TV chief after live broadcast of anti-Semitic sermon, Retrieved from the Web, May 18, 2005. The sermon was delivered on May 13 in Gaza and broadcast live on Palestinian TV.

24. Middle East Media Research Institute (MEMRI) (2005), Special Dispatch—PA/Anti-Semitism Documentation Project, No. 908, May 17. This Week's Palestinian Authority Sermon: We (Muslims) will rule America; Israel is a cancer; Jews are a virus resembling AIDS; Muslims will finish them off.

25. Marc Sageman (2004), ibid.

26. *Response* (Winter 2003/2004), Education PA style—Hamas wins university elections, Simon Wiesenthal Center in Los Angeles.

27. Jihad Watch (March 18, 2004), 900 Saudi imams suspended, Retrieved from the Web.

28. Craig S. Smith (April 30, 2004), France wrestles with radical Islam, *New York Times*, Retrieved from International Herald Tribune online, April 30. See also: Associated Press (May 12, 2004), France cites extremist sermons in tailing imam. Internet *International Herald Tribune.* See also in Chapter 7 on regulatory responses to imams in the United Kingdom and Germany, and earlier in this chapter new far-reaching proposals by the British government.

29. Charis Dunn-Chann (April 30, 2001), China's Islamic concerns, BBC News, Retrieved from the Web, May 15, 2004.

30. *Response* (Winter 2003/2004), Another Ramadan miniseries of hate, Simon Wiesenthal Center in Los Angeles.

31. Jonathan Frankel (1997), *The Damascus Affair: 'Ritual Murder,' Politics and the Jews in 1840.*

32. Shlomo Avineri (November 21, 2003), Still raising its bloody head. Review of Jonathan Frankel (1997*), The Damascus Affair: 'Ritual Murder,' Politics and the Jews in 1840,* Cambridge: Cambridge University Press [the reviewer also reviews a recent Hebrew edition of book], *Haaretz (English Edition)*, p. B9.

33. Toby Harnden (November 18, 2003), Palestinians reprint schoolbooks praising jihad 'martyrs,' *London Daily Telegraph.*

34. *Response* (Winter 2003/2004), Unending trail of hateful lies, Simon Wiesenthal Center in Los Angeles.

35. The rationalization of evil—attributing thinkable, discussable, indeed justifiable reason and cause to the most heinous evil—knows no limit. Evil is allowed into print in some

public places as if it is a legitimate and honorable part of the most noble of all—democratic discourse, debate and controversy. In a letter to the editor to a major English-language newspaper in Bangkok, a writer proposed that Auschwitz was justified, that it was after all a perfectly understandable project for "liberating Europe from Jews, Roma, Communists, etc ... for the protection of the Aryan race, protection of Western values and individuals while practically serving the pursuit of power." Thus spoken, unbelievably, in March of the year 2004. See "Observer" (no name given) (March 28, 2004), Parallel rationalisations? Letter to the Editor, *Bangkok Post.*

The author of this letter actually was busy linking the Holocaust with the U.S. nuclear annihilations of Hiroshima and Nagasaki. His argument was that the Holocaust is no different from the nuclear strikes that are often defended in Western discourse as "less heinous and more rationaliseable" because of the ongoing U.S. military battle with Japan, and that "both crimes are rationaliseable within the context of the ideological and practical expediencies of their respective perpetrators." A nice guy this one, and at least he referred to both the Holocaust and the nuclear bombings as "crimes," but I have serious question whether any responsible newspaper should print a letter like his.

36. *Al-Yawm* (Saudi Arabia) (May 12, 2005), Cited in Middle East Media Research Institute (MEMRI) (2005), Bahraini author and journalist: The proponents of the suicide ideology have taken advantage of global communications, Special Dispatch—Reform, No. 909, May 17.

37. Dalia Schechori (June 15, 2003), In his private life he is human, when it comes to Israelis he is not. *Haaretz* (Hebrew).

38. Fareed Zakaria (August 25, 2003), Suicide bombers can be stopped: We sometimes treat suicide bombers as delusional figures, brainwashed by imams. But they are also products of political reality, *Newsweek.*

39. Winnifred R. Louis and Donald M. Taylor (2002), Understanding the September 11 terrorist attack on America: The role of intergroup theories of normative influence, quotation on p. 96.

At a meeting in Kyoto, Japan years ago of a Peace Commission for the Middle East of the International Peace Research Association, I presented a vision of a State of Israel which would be genuinely devoted to multiculturalism and adopt diligently a panoramic culture of respect, appreciation and celebration of its three constituent religious cultures of Judaism, Christianity and Islam. See Israel W. Charny (1994), "One very simple idea": A possible Israeli contribution to a lasting Middle East peace (and also a model for other ethnic hubs on Planet Earth). As an Israeli I note regularly with great regret that my vision was hardly ever undertaken systematically (although there are sputters of respect) especially with regard to Islam and the Muslim population living in Israel.

40. Cited by Middle East Media Research Institute (MEMRI) (2004), Satirist Ali Salem to Arab League: There's light at the end of the tunnel, *Al-Hayat* (London), May 4, 2004. MEMRI Special Dispatch—Egypt/Reform Project, No. 728, June 8.

41. Cheryl Benard (2003), *Civil Democratic Islam: Partners, Resources and Strategies,* Santa Monica, CA: Rand Corporation. Available on Internet. Quotation in printout of computer document is on pp. 8–9.

Chapter 9

1. Assaf Moghadam (November 22, 2005), Suicide bombers go global, *International Herald Tribune*, p. 8. This article first appeared in the *Boston Globe.* Assaf Moghadam is identified as a research fellow at the Belfer Center for Science and International Affairs at

Harvard University's JFK School of Government and author of the forthcoming book *The Roots of Terrorism.*

2. Khatibs, imams urged to highlight teaching of Islam against suicide bombing, *The Independent,* Bangladesh, December 9, 2005, Retrieved from the Web: independent-bangladesh.com/news/dec/09/09122005mt.htm#A5, December 20, 2005.

3. Source: al-athariyyah.com. ("About Us: We are a group of Salafees located in the London area.") The correct Islamic position on terrorism & suicide bombing: It is upon you to openly free yourselves ...! Recorded 11/06/2004, Retrieved December 20, 2005.

4. General Assembly of the Christian Church (Disciples of Christ) 2005, Portland Oregon, July 23–27, 2005, Retrieved from the Web: www.disciplines.org/ga05/ResolutionsPostGA/0533.htm.

5. Ian Fisher (December 14, 2005), Benedict condemns torture and terrorism, *International Herald Tribune,* p. 3.

6. A news report describes the concerns of the British Muslim community, but also notes that a crisis of belief also fell on the British population as a whole which was being forced to assimilate the truth that British-born Muslims were capable of violence against their British community. "Britons who learned just 13 months ago [the London suicide bombings in the Underground in July 2005] that Muslims born and raised here were capable of suicide bombings have been stunned once more." Souad McKhennet and Allson Smale (August 12–13, 2006). In Britain, a blow to Muslims. *International Herald Tribune,* pp. 1, 3.

7. Herb Keinon (January 22, 2002), Religious parley in Egypt decries killing of innocents, *Jerusalem Post Internet Edition.*

8. Joseph Algozi (January 22, 2002), The Chief Rabbi, religious leaders from the Palestinian Authority and the Roman Patriarch call for an end to violence. The murder of innocents is a desecration of God, declare the representatives of the three religions assembled in Alexandria, *Haaretz* (Hebrew).

Other sources about the Alexandria conference include the following, all retrieved from the Web:

James A. Diamond (February 14, 2002), The Alexandria Declaration: An Introduction, Retrieved from the Web. Interfaith education initiative, a joint project of Episcopal relief and development and the office of ecumenical and interfaith relations. James Diamond is identified as the Dean of Christ Church Cathedral, Cincinnati, and President of the Community of the Cross of Nails in the United States.

World Watch/Catholic World Report (March 2002), Religious leaders unite for peace: Wide backing for "Alexandria Declaration".

State of Israel, Ministry of Foreign Affairs (2002), The First Alexandria Declaration of the Religious Leaders of the Holy Land, January 21.

9. My source material in this case was a report on internet from an Indian news source, expressindia (no date ?2002), Suicide militancy-II. Martyrdom, the prize for taking one's life, ibid.

10. Islamic religious leaders are not the only religious leaders who sanction suicide bombings. Take, for example, the case of Attallah Hana, "a leading Greek Orthodox priest" in Jerusalem who says of suicide bombings for the Palestinian cause, "Whether it's martyrdom or any other means, we are part of it." However, one should also note that Hana spoke from the context where he lives among Palestinians in the Old City of Jerusalem and chose to put his lot with them. On the other hand, other Christians living in the Old City of Jerusalem have not sanctioned suicide bombings. Moreover, the Christianity Today Web

site on which the story appeared commented that one should expect heavy protests of the priest's remarks from others in the Greek Orthodox Church.

Christianity Today.com (2002), Weblog: We support suicide bombing, says Greek Orthodox 'spokesman.' Christianity Today Web site, Retrieved from the Web December 4, 2004.

11. Robert Spencer (April 23, 2002), Sheikh Tantawi grows in office. Free Congress Foundation, Retrieved from the Web: www.FreeCongress.org

12. Ibid.

13. Frank Gardner (2001), Grand Sheikh condemns suicide bombings, BBC News, December 4. Retrieved from the Web.

14. Reuven Paz (February 1, 2002), Religion and politics in Alexandria, Washington Institute for Near East Policy: *Policywatch*, Number 599, Retrieved from the Web.

15. Robert Spencer (2002), ibid.

16. The text concludes: "Web site associated with Al Azhar University, April 4, 2002." Source: ADL-Anti-Defamation League (2002), Arab leaders glorify suicide terrorism, Retrieved from the Web: The path to a suicide attack, April 17.

17. C.T. Rossi (April 22, 2002), Reports of moderate Islam's existence have been greatly exaggerated, CNSNews.com, Retrieved from the Web. The site is identified as maintained by FreeRepublic.com "A Conservative News Forum."

18. Israel Intelligence and Terrorism Information Center at the Center for Special Studies (2003), "Hate industry" in Egypt under official patronage. Attachment A: The al-Azhar Sheikh authorizes suicide attacks carried out by women, Retrieved from the Web.

19. C.T. Rossi, ibid.

20. See, for example: Middle East Media Research Institute (MEMRI) (2003), Arab Press: Jihad against the U.S.: Al-Azhar's conflicting fatwas, March 16, Retrieved from the Web from: Our Jerusalem; see also Al Ahram Weekly Online (2003), A confusing fatwa, 4–10 September, Issue No. 654.

21. BBC News (July 11, 2003), U.K. Edition, Retrieved from the Web. This beautiful text of peace and spiritual movement forward was already in place in this manuscript when I learned that its author, Grand Sheikh Tantawi of the Al-Azhar mosque of Cairo, the institution which is considered the highest authority in Sunni Islam, was the imam who had participated earlier in the Alexandria Conference in January 2002 and then withdrew his participation in the group of clerics who were supposed to continue developing "The Alexandria process." I then learned further that the author of the previous heartwarming statement had gone on no less than to approve suicide bombings against Israeli soldiers. Surely I then should have removed the seriously compromised piece of rhetoric quoted here! It would have made the text 'simpler,' meaning more consistent and less complex. But for a number of reasons, I decided to leave this text. For one thing, it gives me a way to express my anger and to retaliate. I can even imagine myself saying: "See Sheikh, and all the celebrants of your blessings of murderous violence, how much and how eloquently you were against violence. I hope you get into a big horrible mess with your new terrorist mates for how much you contributed earlier to the cause of peace!" For another thing, there couldn't be a clearer illustration of how difficult a process it is going to be to recruit many religious leaders to a campaign for peace. But, mainly, I think I retained this text because I really like its message to the earth and sky of our planet, and it was too painful for me to throw it away.

22. In 2002, a senior Palestinian official, Abdel Razak-Yehiyeh, denounced suicide attacks as "murders for no reason." Yehiyeh said: "Stop the suicide bombings, stop the murders for no reason. Return to the legitimate struggle against the occupation without

violence and following international norms and legitimacy." See Serge Schmemann (August 31, 2002), Stop attacks, Arafat aid tells factions, *New York Times*. Another news account added:

> Yehiyeh ... called on his countrymen to end all acts of violence against Israelis and switch to civil resistance ... "All forms of Palestinian violence have to stop," Yehiyeh said ... "All resistance acts that are characterized by violence, such as using arms or even stones ... are harmful. I call for civil resistance within the framework of the political struggle"...
>
> "Let's admit it ... we have lost a lot," he said of the suicide attacks ... The Palestinian leadership condemns every suicide attack. Shall we stop at condemnation? Is condemnation our only job? I say the whole concept has to change." See *Haaretz*, September 3, 2002 (Hebrew), with attribution to Reuters.

Yehiyeh, who was then slated to be Interior Minister in a Palestinian government, was promptly pushed out of his political position by Yasser Arafat.

23. Religious Information Service of Ukraine, September 24, 2003, Retrieved from the Web.

24. WorldNetDaily, September 30, 2003: A call for 'United Nations of Religions'.

25. The Muslim News, a U.K. organization, September 23, 2003, Retrieved from the Web.

26. Retrieved from a variety of sources on the Web in addition to The Muslim News just cited, including: OpenHere Arts & Entertainment, September 28, 2003; Kazinform National Information Agency, November 16, 2003; and Caspian World News, November 2003.

The story in The Muslim News emphasizes that the gathering took place "amid fears of a deepening rift between Islam and Western countries"; and quoted President Nazarbayev, "It would be a big error in humanity to assert that terrorism emerged from Islamic countries." The same source also credited Pope John Paul II, who had urged dialogue with Islam ever since September 11, with bringing about the conference.

27. Daniel Ben-Simon (January 9, 2005), Rabbis and imams unite against religious extremism, *Haaretz* (English Edition), pp. 1, 6. All quotations that follow are from the same source.

28. Shlomo Shamir (March 21, 2006), Spiritual leaders turn the other cheek for peace, *Haaretz* (English Edition); The smiles on the faces of the rabbis and imams disappeared when they began to speak of the occupation: "Imams and Rabbis for Peace"—140 Muslim and Jewish religious leaders are participating in a conference in Spain, *Haaretz*, March 21 (Hebrew).

29. Ibid.

30. Ibid.

31. The cooperation between faiths can also be extended to other sectors of society. A surprising story of ecumenical cooperation between a Jewish religious leader and a Palestinian military leader was reported in the Israeli press. General Nasser Yussef arrived in the Gaza Strip from Tunis with other members of the PLO following the signing of the Oslo Accords. Rabbi Menachem Froman of a nearby Israeli settlement introduced himself, and the two evidently became friends.

The settler rabbi says that the belief in peace through respect and freedom for both peoples living in the Holy Land . . . burns in Yussef. He is convinced that this belief will guide Yussef's efforts to put the demon of national extremism firmly . . . in its bottle.

"Abu Yussef is a very religious man in his world outlook," says Froman. "The inference here is not in the usual sense of someone who keeps the tradition, but a man for whom the godly interest touches his soul and who perseveres in his study of the roots of Islam. These meeting points enable us to hold a dialogue, not between an Israeli and a PLO member, but between one religious man and another religious man and here we have an almost identical outlook."

. . . The rabbi and the general . . . have set up an executive committee of rabbis and imams, spiritual leaders, writers and artists which will carry out an inter-religious and inter-cultural dialogue alongside the peace talks in better times. Akiva Eldar (October 1, 2003), The general, the rabbi and the Holy Spirit, *Haaretz* (English Edition), p. 3. The story is illustrated by delightful cartoon drawings of a long-flowing bearded Froman wearing his skullcap alongside of a military-bereted and uniformed Yussef.

32. I was fascinated by one newspaper account of how the knees of one then-powerful ruler of a European country shook when he had an audience with the Pope.

33. Sarah Bronson (August 20, 2004), 'When an Orthodox Jew and a Muslim invite you to a peace festival, you don't say no': Peace promoters from all countries and religions gather at the Sulha Way festival, which aims to 'heal the children of Abraham,' *Haaretz* (English Edition), p. A8.

34. The signators included: Dr. Akbar Ahmed, Ibn Khaldun Chair of Islamic Studies, American University; Merve Kavakci, Lecturer on Culture and International Affairs, George Washington University; Amina Khan, Executive Board, American Organization of Pakistani Professionals; Imam Mohammed Majid, All Dulles Area Muslim Society and Executive Council Member, Islamic Society North America; Sabir Rahman, Former President, Muslim Community Center, Maryland; Dr. Sulayman Nyang, Professor of African Studies, Howard University; Dr. Islam Siddiqui, Former Undersecretary, U.S. Department of Agriculture; Professor Jamshed Uppal, Catholic University; "and many others." The text of this announcement was forwarded to me by the Chief Administrative Officer of the U.S. Holocaust Memorial Museum in Washington, DC, William P. Parsons.

35. See Rachid Benzine (2004); Rachid Benzine and Christian Delorme (1997); and Rachid Benzine and Christian Delorme (1998).

36. John Kifner (September 9, 2004), In wake of Beslan, scrutiny in Arab world: Many express shame that terrorists in siege were Muslim, *International Herald Tribune* (with original attribution to *New York Times*), p. 4.

37. Alan M. Dershowitz (May 21, 2004), Does oppression cause suicide bombing?: Some overprivileged Muslims support a culture of death, while impoverished Tibetans celebrate life, *Jerusalem Post Magazine,* p. 17.

38. Alan Cowell (July 11, 2005), Day of contrasts in London: 3 arrested after bombings, while end of WWII is marked, *International Herald Tribune,* pp. 1, 6.

39. Yoav Stern (July 25, 2005), Egypt arrests 90 suspects in the Sharm terror attacks, *Haaretz* (Hebrew).

40. Pam Belluck (October 30–31, 2004), After the ecstasy, the angst of victory for Red Sox fans, *International Herald Tribune*, p. 22, with attribution to the *New York Times*.

41. Rabbi Samuel Karff of Houston, Texas, a former President of the Central Conference of American Rabbis, personal communication, December 2003. A beautiful inspirational book by this rabbi for people of all faiths, as well as those who question religious faith, is Samuel E. Karff (2005), *Permission to Believe: Finding Faith in Troubled Times.*

42. International Crisis Group (December 1, 2003), To Israelis and Palestinians: A statement of support, *International Herald Tribune*, p. 8.

43. Fareed Zakaria (March 22, 2004), Cruelty is all they have left, *Newsweek*, p. 15.

44. John J. Lumpkin (December 5, 2003), Associated Press, U.S. intelligence services take a crack at predicting 2020, *Philadelphia Inquirer*, Retrieved from the Web: philly@com.

45. National Intelligence Council (2003), Project, 06 November. Inaugural Workshop on the NIC 2020 Conference. Gordon, Theodore (2003), Frontiers of the Future: Madmen, Methods and Massive Change, A discussion paper of the 2020 Conference, Retrieved from the Web, December 28.

46. Habib Malik (2003), Can Christians and Muslims relate in peace? Ibid.

47. Mansour Al-Nogaidan (November 29–30, 2003), Telling the truth, facing the whip: Religious extremism will be difficult to defeat. I know because I once espoused it. *International Herald Tribune*, p. 8.

48. Greg Myre (December 3, 2003), In mock peace plan, real friction, *International Herald Tribune*, pp. 1, 4, quotation on p. 4.

49. It is not irrelevant to note also that she had not gone through a prolonged period of indoctrination, and previously had no connection to the militant Islamic groups. She had volunteered her services only five days before—in grief and revenge at the death of her fiancé at the hands of Israelis (though Israeli intelligence said he had accidentally blown himself up).

50. James Bennet (2002), Rash of new suicide bombers showing no pattern or ties, ibid. See also the case reported earlier where a Palestinian woman first was offended by being ordered to violate her religious dress code in order to carry out her suicide bombing, and the upset of her being betrayed in her beliefs apparently broke the spell of her completing her mission, and now she suddenly realized that she would be killing "babies, women and sick people" and turned back! See Megan Golding (2002), The suicide bomber who had a change of heart, ibid.

51. Film (2004), *Inside the Mind of a Suicide Bomber.*

52. Yoav Stern (2003), Nasrallah: Without freeing Kuntar there will be no hostage swap, ibid. At this writing, Kuntar is still the subject of discussions about a possible prisoner swap between Israel and Hizbolla. If Kuntar is released, it will be very interesting to see if, once returned to Lebanon, he remains true to the change of heart about violence that he described.

53. Habib Malik (2003), ibid., quotations on pp. 3–5 of text from Internet.

54. Yassin Musharbash (August 12, 2005), What al-Qaeda really wants, *Der Speigel*. Quotations taken from citation by "Watch-Covering the war on terror," August 12, 2005, Retrieved from the Web, September 3, 2005.

55. Woody Hochswender (March 29, 2002), I'm a Buddhist, but not a pacifist in war on terror, *Wall Street Journal*, p. A11.

56. See earlier in Chapter 2, Petition to United Nations and government leaders.

57. Simon Wiesenthal Center (2004), Press release (from Paris office): In Wake of Today's School Carnage [in Beslan, Russia] and Latest Surge of Suicide Bombings,

Wiesenthal Center Calls on Putin to Urge United Nations to Declare Suicide Bombing a "Crime Against Humanity," September 3.

58. I.W. Charny (2006), *Fascism and Democracy in the Human Mind.*

59. Remarks by I.J. Ellen, M.D., New York, personal communication.

60. "People who witness others expressing nonprejudiced attitudes (such as the calls for unity that were frequently made after September 11) are less likely to show bias themselves." Phyllis B. Gerstenfeld (2002), A time to hate: Situational antecedents of intergroup bias, quotation on p. 65. See also F.A Blanchard, T. Lilly, and L.A. Vaughn (1991), Reducing the expression of racial prejudice.

61. Simon Wiesenthal Center (2004), Simon Wiesenthal Center presents digital terrorism and hate 2004 to U.S. Congress, Retrieved from the Web, December 4; Simon Wiesenthal Center (2005), *Digital Terrorism and Hate 2005 CD-ROM.*

62. Audrey Kurth Cronin (2003), Terrorists and suicide attacks, Congressional Research Service, Library of Congress, ibid., quotation from pp. 2, 27, 73 from chapter, "How to counter the threat."

63. Yehuda Bauer (April 5, 2004), A threat to take seriously: For the first time since the Holocaust the Jewish people have an existential threat, *Haaretz* (English Edition*)*, Pesach Magazine Supplement, "The State of the Jews," p. 38.

64. Manfred Gerstenfeld (2004), Something is rotten in the State of Europe: Anti-Semitism as a civilizational pathology: An interview with Robert Wistrich, *Post-Holocaust and Anti-Semitism, 25* (whole issue), October 1, Jerusalem: Jerusalem Center for Public Affairs (quotations on pp. 3 and 5).

65. Middle East Media Research Institute (MEMRI) (2004), Ever since the murder of 'Uthman [The Third Caliph]'—Arab literary scholar on the evil spirit of murder and violence in early Islam re-appearing today. Special Dispatch—Reform Project, No. 704, April 30.

Afterword: Inshallah

1. *Al-Ayyam* (PA), March 25, 2004, Cited by Middle East Media Research Institute (MEMRI) (2004), Nonviolence and the fate of the peace process in the Palestinian media, Special Dispatch Series No. 698, April 21.

2. Middle East Media Research Institute (MEMRI) (2004), A Cairo conference for reform raises the use of the Egyptian religious establishment. Inquiry and Analysis—Egypt/Reform Project, October 22. Leading this wonderful initiative was Dr. Sa'ad Al-Din Ibrahim, Chair of the Ibn Khaldun Center for Development Studies in Cairo, a courageous man who also holds American citizenship, who previously was held for an extended period in an Egyptian jail on charges of violating state security, and who was released following major protests including from the United States.

3. www.elaph.com/elaphweb/Politics/2004/10/17789.htm, October 24, 2004. www.metransparent.com/texts/arab_liberals_appeal_to_un_for_int_court_against_terror_fatwas.htm, October 24, 2004. See Middle East Media Research Institute (MEMRI) (2004), Arab liberals petition the U.N. to establish tribunal for prosecuting terrorists, Special Dispatch—Reform Project, No. 812, November 8.

4. Ibid. (MEMRI document above)

Bibliography

Abboud, Loula (2003). The woman as soldier-martyr and suicide bomber. In Davis, Joyce, *Martyrs' Innocence, Vengeance and Despair in the Middle East*. New York: Palgrave.

Abuza, Zachary (2003). *Militant Islam in Southeast Asia: Crucible of Terror*. Boulder, CO: Lynne Rienner Publishers.

Adorno, T.W., Frenkel-Brunswik, Else, Levinson, Daniel J., and Sanford, R. Nevitt (1950). *The Authoritarian Personality*. New York: Harper.

Allam, Khaled Fouad (2004). *Lettera a un kamikaze* [Letter to a Suicide Bomber]. Milan, Italy: Rizzoli (Italian).

Altemeyer, Bob (1981). *Right-Wing Authoritarianism*. [Winnipeg]: University of Manitoba Press.

——— (1988). *Enemies of Freedom: Understanding Right-Wing Authoritarianism*. London: Jossey Bass.

——— (1996). *The Authoritarian Specter*. Cambridge, MA: Harvard University Press.

Alvarez, Alex (2001). *Governments, Citizens, and Genocide: A Comparative and Interdisciplinary Approach*. Bloomington: Indiana University Press.

American Psychiatric Association (1994). *DSM-IV: Diagnostic and Statistical Manual of Mental Disorders*. Fourth Edition. Washington, DC: American Psychiatric Association.

Amnesty International (2002). *Israel and the Occupied Territories and the Palestinian Authority. Without Distinction: Attacks on Civilians by Palestinian Armed Groups*. London: Amnesty International.

Anonymous (Michael Scheuer) (2004). *Imperial Hubris: Why the West Is Losing the War on Terror*. Dulles, VA: Brassey's.

Arendt, Hannah (1969). *Eichmann in Jerusalem: A Report on the Banality of Evil*. New York: Viking Press. (Original edition 1963)

Aron, Raymond (2002). *The Dawn of Universal History: Selected Essays from a Witness to the Twentieth Century.* New York: Basic Books. (Edited by Yair Reiner, translated by Barbara Bray.)

Ashton, E.B. (pseudonym for Ernst Basch) (1937). *The Fascist: His State and His Mind.* New York: William Morrow. (Reprinted by AMS Press, New York, 1972.)

Bandura, Albert (1990). Mechanisms of moral disengagement. In Reich, Walter (Ed.), *Origins of Terrorism: Psychologies, Ideologies, Theologies, States of Mind.* Washington, DC: Woodrow Wilson International Center for Scholars, and New York: Cambridge University Press, pp. 161–191.

Bangstad, Sundre (2002). Palestinian Islamist movements: An annotated bibliography. Bergen, Norway: Chr Michelsen Institute. [e-mail:cmi@cmi.no] Retrieved from Google September 21, 2003.

Barkan, Elazar (2000). *The Guilt of Nations: Restitution and Negotiating Historical Injustices.* New York: Norton.

Barltrop, Richard (Ed.) (2003). *Muslims in Europe Post 9/11: Understanding and Responding to the Islamic World.* St. Anthony's College and Princeton University, 25–26 April. Conference Report, Oxford-Princeton Conference Available at www.sant.ox.ac.UK/princeton/Report.pdf.

Bar-Tal, Daniel (2000). *Shared Beliefs in a Society: Social Psychological Analysis.* Thousand Oaks, CA: Sage.

Bat Ye'or (1996). *The Decline of Eastern Christianity Under Islam: From Jihad to Dhimmitude—Seventh-Twentieth Century.* Foreword by Jacques Ellul. Translated from the French by Miriam Kochan and David Littman. Madison and Teaneck, NJ: Fairleigh Dickinson University Press.

Baumeister, Roy F. (1997). *Evil: Inside Human Cruelty and Violence.* New York: Freeman.

Baumeister, Roy F., and Campbell, W.K. (1999). The intrinsic appeal of evil: Sadism, sensation thrills, and threatened egotism. *Personality and Social Psychology Review*, 3(3), 210–221.

Baumeister, Roy F., Smart, Laura, and Boden, Joseph M. (1996). Relation of threatened egotism to violence and aggression: The dark side of high self-esteem. *Psychological Review*, 103(1), 5–33.

Beck, Aaron T. (1999). *The Prisoners of Hate: The Cognitive Basis of Anger, Hostility, and Violence.* New York: HarperCollins.

Becker, Ernest (1973). *The Denial of Death.* New York: Free Press.

Benard, Cheryl (2003). *Civil Democratic Islam: Partners, Resources, and Strategies.* Santa Monica, CA: Rand Corporation.

Benzine, Rachid (2004). *The New Islamic Thinkers.* Paris: Albin Michel.

Benzine, Rachid, and Delorme, Christian (1997). *We—Christians and Muslims—Have So Many Things to Tell Each Other.* Paris: Albin Michel.

Benzine, Rachid, and Delorme, Christian (1998). *The Suburbs of God.* Paris: Bayard.

Berke, Joseph H., Pierides, Stella, Sabbadini, Andrea, and Schneider, Stanley (Eds.) (1998). *Even Paranoids Have Enemies: New Perspectives on Paranoia and Persecution.* London: Routledge.

bin Laden, Osama (February 23, 1998). *Jihad against Jews and Crusaders: World Islamic Front statement.* Cited by Federation of American Scientists (2001). Available from http://www.fas.org/irp/world/para/docs/980223-fatwa.htm [Original Arabic text version available at http://www.library.cornell.edu/colldev/mideast/fatwa2.htm].

Blanchard, Fletcher A., Lilly, Teri, and Vaughn, Leigh A. (1991). Reducing the expression of racial prejudice. *Psychological Science 2*(2), 101–105.

Blass, Thomas (Ed.) (2000). *Obedience to Authority: Current Perspectives on the Milgram Paradigm.* Mahwah, NJ: Erlbaum.

Bloom, Mia (2005). *Dying to Kill: The Allure of Suicide Terror.* New York: Columbia University Press.

Boehm, Eric H. (1999). The fates of non-Jewish Germans under the Nazis. In *Encyclopedia of Genocide.* Santa Barbara, CA: ABC-CLIO Publishers, p. 298.

Bourke, Joanna (1999). *An Intimate History of Killing: Face-to-Face Killing in Twentieth-Century Warfare.* New York: Basic Books.

Browning, Christopher R. (1992). *Ordinary Men: Reserve Battalion 101 and the Final Solution in Poland.* New York: HarperCollins.

Burdman, Daphne (2003). Education, indoctrination, and incitement: Palestinian children on their way to martyrdom. *Terrorism and Political Violence, 15*(1), 96–123.

Burke, Jason (2004). *Al-Qaeda: The True Story of Radical Islam.* London: Penguin Books.

Calhoun, Craig, Price, Paul, and Timmer, Ashley (Eds.) (2002). *Understanding September 11.* New York: Social Science Research Council and New Press.

Calley, William L. (1972). Lieutenant Calley: His own story. In Baird, Jay W. (Ed.), *From Nuremberg to My Lai.* Lexington, MA: Heath, pp. 213–234.

Camus, Albert (1980). *Neither Victims nor Executioners.* Translated by Dwight MacDonald. New York: Continuum. (First appeared serially in the Fall 1946 issues of *Combat*; translation first published in the July–August 1947 issue of *Politics.*)

Charny, Israel W. (1971). Normal man as genocider: We need a psychology of *normal* man as genocider, accomplice or indifferent bystander to mass killing of man. *Voices: The Art and Science of Psychotherapy, 7*(2), 68–79.

———— (1973). And Abraham went to slay Isaac: A parable of killer, victim and bystander in the family of man. *Journal of Ecumenical Studies, 10*(2), 304–318.

———— (1982). *How Can We Commit the Unthinkable? Genocide: The Human Cancer.* In collaboration with Chanan Rapaport. Introduction by Elie Wiesel. Boulder, CO: Westview Press. (Republished in paperback under the title, *Genocide, the Human Cancer: How Can We Commit the Unthinkable?* New York: Hearst Professional Books [William Morrow], 1983. Translation into Portuguese, with new Introduction to this edition by the author and updated Bibliography: *Anatomia do Genocídio: Uma Psicologia da Agressão Humana.* Rio de Janeiro: Editora Rosa dos Tempos, 1998. Translated by Roy Jungmann.)

———— (1982). The tragic illusion of self-defense. In *How Can We Commit the Unthinkable? Genocide: The Human Cancer,* pp. 167–182.

———— (1986). Genocide and mass destruction: Doing harm to others as a missing dimension in psychopathology. *Psychiatry, 49*(2), 144–157. (Originally presented in 1984 as Genocide and mass destruction: The missing dimension in psychopathology. In Charny, Israel W. (Ed.), *Toward the Understanding and Prevention of Genocide.* Boulder, CO: Westview Press, pp. 154–174.

———— (1994). "One very simple idea": A possible Israeli contribution to a lasting Middle East peace (and also a model for other ethnic hubs on Planet Earth). In Boulding, Elise (Ed.), *Peace and Justice in the Midle East* [Report of the International Peace Research Association Commission on Termination of War in the Middle East]. Boulder, CO: Lynne Rienner Publishers, pp. 287–294.

―――― (1996). Evil in human personality: Disorders of doing harm to others in family relationships. In Kaslow, Florence W. (Ed.), *Handbook of Relational Diagnosis and Dysfunctional Family Patterns.* New York: Wiley, pp. 477–495.

―――― (1997). A personality disorder of excessive power strivings. *Israel Journal of Psychiatry, 34*(1), 3–17.

―――― (1999). An International Peace Army: A proposal for the long-range future. In *Encyclopedia of Genocide.* Santa Barbara, CA: ABC-CLIO Publishers, pp. 649–653.

―――― (1999). The psychology of sacrificing. In *Encyclopedia of Genocide.* Santa Barbara, CA: ABC-CLIO Publishers, pp. 485–487.

―――― (2006). *Fascism and Democracy in the Human Mind: A New Bridge between Mind and Society.* Lincoln, NE: University of Nebraska Press.

Charny, Israel W., and Fromer, Daphna (1992). A study of attitudes of viewers of the film "Shoah" towards an incident of mass murder by Israeli soldiers (Kfar Kassem, 1956). *Journal of Traumatic Stress, 5*(2), 303–318.

Chirot, Daniel, and Seligman, Martin E.P. (Eds.) (2001). *Ethnopolitical Warfare: Causes, Consequences, and Possible Solutions.* Washington, DC: American Psychological Association.

Churchill, Ward (1997). *A Little Matter of Genocide: Holocaust and Denial in the Americas, 1492 to the Present.* San Francisco: City Lights Books.

Cohn, Norman (1975). *Europe's Inner Demons: An Enquiry Inspired by the Great Witch-Hunt.* New York: Basic Books.

Connor, John W. (1989). From ghost dance to death camps: Nazi Germany as a crisis cult. *Ethos, 17*(3), 259–288.

Connor, Robert J. (2002). The prolific use of suicide bombers by the LLTE. In *Defeating the Modern Asymmetric Threat.* Monterey, CA: Naval Postgraduate School, pp. 97–107.

Cronin, Audrey Kurth (2003). Terrorists and suicide attacks. Congressional Research Service, Library of Congress. Washington, DC: Congressional Research Service, Library of Congress [order code RL32058], 22 pages. Retrieved from the Web: www.fas.org/irp/crs/RL32058.pdf.

Darley, John M., and Batson, C. Daniel (1979). "From Jerusalem to Jericho": A study of situational and dispositional variables in helping behavior. In Pines, Ayala, and Maslach, Christina (Eds.), *Experiencing Social Psychology: Readings and Projects.* New York: Knopf, pp. 149–156. (First appeared in *Journal of Personality and Social Psychology* (1973), *27,* 100–108.)

Davis, Joyce M. (2003). *Martyrs: Innocence, Vengeance and Despair in the Middle East.* New York: Palgrave.

Dingley, James (2003). Suicide terrorism: A global threat. In Griset, Pamala L., and Mahan, Sue (Eds.) (2003). *Terrorism in Perspective.* Thousand Oaks, CA: Sage.

Dolnik, Adam (2003). Die and let die: Exploring links between suicide terrorism and terrorist use of chemical, biological, radiological, and nuclear weapons. *Studies in Conflict and Terrorism, 26*(1), 17–35.

Dolnik, Adam, and Bhattacharjee, Anjali (2002). Hamas: Suicide bombings, rockets, or WMD? *Terrorism and Political Violence, 14*(3), 109–128.

Durkheim, Emile (1979). *Suicide: A Study in Sociology.* New York: Free Press.

Eidelson, Roy J., and Eidelson, Judy I. (2003). Dangerous ideas: Five beliefs that propel groups toward conflict. *American Psychologist, 58*(3), 182–192.

El Sarraj, Eyad (2002). Suicide bombers: Dignity, despair and the need for hope: An interview with Eyad El Sarraj. *Journal of Palestine Studies, 31*(4), 71–76.

Ellens, J. Harold (Ed.) (2004). *The Destructive Power of Religion: Violence in Judaism, Christianity, and Islam.* Westport, CT: Praeger.

Elliot, Gil (1972). *Twentieth-Century Book of the Dead.* New York: Scribner.

Emerson, Steven (1994). *Jihad in America.* Documentary film. Aired by PBS on November 21.

—— (February 24,1998). Foreign terrorists in America: Five years after the World Trade Center bombing. Prepared statement of Steven Emerson before the Senate Judiciary Committee Subcommittee on Terrorism, Technology, and Government Information. Available at www.geocities.com/collegepark/6453/emerson.html.

—— (2002). *American Jihad: The Terrorists Living Among Us.* New York: Free Press.

Encyclopedia of Genocide (1999). Israel W. Charny, Editor-in-Chief. Associate Editors: Rouben Paul Adalian, Steven Jacobs, Eric Markusen, and Samuel Totten. Bibliographic Editor: Marc I. Sherman. Santa Barbara, CA, and Denver, CO (December 1999); Oxford, U.K. (February 2000): ABC-CLIO Publishers. A partial edition was published in French in 2001. Beginning in 2003, an e-book or electronic edition of the *Encyclopedia of Genocide* has been available on Internet from ABC-CLIO.

Encyclopedia of World Problems and Human Potential (1986). 2nd ed. Munich: K.G. Saur. "Orchestrator" [Editor], Anthony Judge. Published by the Union of International Associations [40 rue Washington, B-1050 Brussels, Belgium].

Esman, Milton J. (1994). *Ethnic Politics.* Ithaca, NY: Cornell University Press.

Fabick, Stephen D. (2002). Us & Them: Reducing the risk of terrorism (2002). In Stout, Chris E. (Ed.), *The Psychology of Terrorism, Vol. II: Clinical Aspects and Responses.* Series: *Psychological Dimensions to War and Peace.* Westport, CT: Praeger, pp. 225–242.

Fields, Rona M., Elbedour, Salman, and Hein, Fadel-Abu (2002). The Palestinian suicide bomber. In Stout, Chris E. (Ed.), *The Psychology of Terrorism, Vol. II: Clinical Aspects and Responses.* Series: *Psychological Dimensions to War and Peace.* Westport, CT: Praeger, pp. 193–224.

Film (1999). *The Terrorist.* Director: Santosh Sivan. Producers: Shree Passed, Jit Sashi. Produced in India. Language: Hindi. Available with English subtitles, 96 minutes.

Film (2002). *Human Weapon.* Director: Ilan Ziv. Producers: Ilan Ziv and Serge Gordey. Writers (in English, Arabic, Farsi, Hebrew, and Tamil, with English subtitles): Ilan Ziv and Nancy Peckenham. Filmed in Iran, Lebanon, Sri Lanka, Israel, Palestine, Europe, and the United States, 55 minutes/color. Released by First Run/Icarus Films. Screened on Channel 8, Israel TV on July 30, 2005.

Film (2003). *Inside the Mind of a Suicide Bomber.* TV documentary produced by UK Channel 4. Screened in United States by PBS on July 1, 2004, and on Israel TV Channel 8 on September 10, 2004. Writer and director: Tom Roberts. Producer: Israel Goldvitch. Israel Goldvitch and October Films Production, 48 minutes.

Film (2004). *Der Untergang* [Downfall]. Screenplay: Bernd Eichinger. Programme: Viacom Galas. Director: Oliver Hirschbiegel. Producer: Bernd Eichinger. Production Company: Constatin Film/ARD Degato/EOS Production. Produced in Germany in German, 150 minutes.

Film (2005). *Paradise Now*. Director: Abu-Assad, Hany. Language: Arabic, 90 minutes. Distributed by International Film Distributors.

Frankel, Jonathan (1997). *The Damascus Affair: "Ritual Murder," Politics and the Jews in 1840*. Cambridge: Cambridge University Press.

Frankl, Viktor E. (1959). *From Death Camp to Existentialism: A Psychiatrist's Path to a New Therapy*. Boston: Beacon Press.

Fromm, Erich (1973). *The Anatomy of Human Destructiveness*. New York: Holt, Rinehart and Winston.

Gernsbacher, Larry Morton (1985). *The Suicide Syndrome: Origins, Manifestations and Alleviation of Human Self-Destructiveness*. New York: Human Sciences Press.

Gerstenfeld, Phyllis B. (2002). A time to hate: Situational antecedents of intergroup bias. *Analyses of Social Issues and Public Policy*, 2(1), 61–67.

Girard, René (1977). *Violence and the Sacred*. Baltimore: Johns Hopkins University Press. (Originally published in Paris in 1972 by Editions Bernard Grasser, La violence et le sacré.)

Glover, Jonathan (2000). *Humanity: A Moral History of the Twentieth Century*. New Haven, CT: Yale University Press.

Goldney, Robert D. (2003). Altruistic suicide: Precedence in usage [Correspondence]. *Psychiatric Bulletin*, 27(3), 115.

Gordon, Harvey (2002). The "suicide" bomber: Is it a psychiatric phenomenon? *Psychiatric Bulletin*, 26(8), 285–287.

Greenwald, Anthony G. (1980). The totalitarian ego: Fabrication and revision of personal history. *American Psychologist*, 35(7), 603–618.

Griffin, Roger (2003). Shattering crystals: The role of "dream time" in extreme right-wing political violence. *Terrorism and Political Violence*, 15(1), 57–95.

Griset, Pamala L., and Mahan, Sue (Eds.) (2003). *Terrorism in Perspective*. Thousand Oaks, CA: Sage.

Gurr, Ted Robert (1993). *Minorities at Risk: A Global View of Ethnopolitical Conflicts*. Washington, DC: United States Institute of Peace Press.

Hafez, Mohammed M. (2003). *Why Muslims Rebel: Repression and Resistance in the Islamic World*. Boulder, CO: Lynne Rienner Publishers.

Hage, Ghassan (2003). Comes a time we are all enthusiasm: Understanding Palestinian suicide bombers in times of exighophobia. *Public Culture*, 15 (1), 65–89.

Hamden, Raymond H. (2002). The retributional terrorist: Type 4. In Stout, Chris E. (Ed.), *The Psychology of Terrorism, Vol. II: Clinical Aspects and Responses*. Series: *Psychological Dimensions to War and Peace*. Westport, CT: Praeger, pp. 165–192.

Hassan, Nasra (November 19, 2001). An arsenal of believers: Talking to the "human bombs." *New Yorker*, 36–41. Available at: www.newyorker.com/fact/content/ ?011119fa_FACT1.

Herschberg, Eric, and Moore, Kevin W. (Eds.) (2002). *Critical Views of September 11: Analyses from Around the World*. New York: Social Science Research Council and New Press.

Hinton, Alexander Laban (1999). Comrade Ox did not object when this family was killed. In *Encyclopedia of Genocide*. Santa Barbara, CA: ABC-CLIO Publishers, p. 135.

Hoffer, Eric (1951). *The True Believer: Thoughts on the Nature of Mass Movements*. New York: Harper.

Horowitz, Donald L. (1985). *Ethnic Groups in Conflict*. Berkeley, CA: University of California Press.

Human Rights Watch (October 2002). *Erased in a Moment: Suicide Bombing Attacks on Israeli Civilians*, Stork, Joe (Ed.). New York, Washington, London and Brussels: Human Rights Watch.

Huntington, Samuel P. (1996). *The Clash of Civilizations and the Remaking of World Order*. New York: Simon & Schuster.

Ikenberry, G. John (1997). The West: Precious, not unique: Civilizations make for a poor paradigm just like the rest. *Foreign Affairs*, *76*(2), 162–163.

International Policy Institute for Counter-Terrorism and the Anti-Defamation League (2002). *Countering Suicide Terrorism*. New York: Anti-Defamation League.

Jones, Robert Alun (1986). *Emile Durkheim: An Introduction to Four Major Works*. Beverly Hills, CA: Sage.

Jones, Ron (1979). The third wave. In Pines, Ayala, and Maslach, Christina (Eds.), *Experiencing Social Psychology: Readings and Projects*. New York: Knopf, pp. 203–211.

Juergensmeyer, Mark (2003). *Terror in the Mind of God: The Global Rise of Religious Violence*. 3rd ed. Rev. and updated. Berkeley, CA: University of California Press.

Kahneman, Daniel (September 9, 2003). Psychology of large errors and of important decision. Seventh Oscar Van Leer Annual Lecture, Van Leer Institute, Jerusalem, Israel.

Kaplan, Abraham (1981). The psychodynamics of terrorism. In Alexander, Yonah, and Gleason, J. (Eds.), *Behavioral and Quantitative Perspectives on Terrorism*. New York: Pergamon, pp. 35–50.

Karff, Samuel E. (2005). *Permission to Believe: Finding Faith in Troubled Times*. Nashville: Abington Press.

Katz, Steven T. (1987). The technocrat as murderer: The murderer as technocrat. In Institute for Research of the Holocaust Period. Haifa University and the Ghetto Fighters' House. *Studies on the Holocaust Period*, *5*, 43–60 (Hebrew), English Summary vi–vii.

Kepel, Gilles (2004). *The War for Muslim Minds: Islam and the West*. Cambridge, MA: Belknap Press of Harvard University Press.

Kiernan, Ben (1999). The Cambodia Genocide and its leaders. In *Encyclopedia of Genocide*. Santa Barbara, CA: ABC-CLIO Publishers, pp. 132–134.

King, Martin Luther (1991). *A Testament of Hope: The Essential Writings and Speeches of Martin Luther King, Jr.*, Washington, James Melvin (Ed.). Copyright by Coretta Scott King. San Francisco: HarperCollins.

Kotek, Joël, and Kotek, Dan (2003). *Au nom de l'antisionisme: L'image des Juifs et d'Israël dans la caricature depuis la seconde Intifada* [French]. [English translation of title: *In the Name of Anti-Semitism: The Image of the Jews and Israel in Cartoons since the Second Intifada*]. Brussels: Éditions Complexe.

Kramer, Martin (1990). The moral logic of Hizballah. In Reich, Walter (Ed.), *Origins of Terrorism: Psychologies, Ideologies, Theologies, States of Mind*. Cambridge: Cambridge University Press, pp. 131–157.

Kramer, Roderick M., and Messick, David M. (1998). Getting by with a little help from our enemies: Collective paranoia and its role in intergroup relations. In Sedikides, Constantine, Schopler, John, and Insko, Chester A. (Eds.), *Intergroup Cognition and Intergroup Behavior*, Mahwah, NJ: Erlbaum, pp. 233–255.

Kuper, Leo (1981). *Genocide: Its Political Use in the Twentieth Century.* London: Penguin Books; New Haven, CT: Yale University Press, 1982.

Kushner, Harvey W. (Ed.) (2002). *Essential Readings on Political Terrorism: Analyses of Problems and Prospects for the 21st Century.* Lincoln, NE: University of Nebraska Press.

——— (2002). Suicide bombers: Business as usual. In Kushner, Harvey W. (Ed.), *Essential Readings on Political Terrorism: Analyses of Problems and Prospects for the 21st Century.* Lincoln, NE: University of Nebraska Press, pp. 35–45.

Lachkar, Joan (2002). The psychological make-up of a suicide bomber. *Journal of Psychology, 29*(4), 349–367.

Lake, David A., and Rothchild, Donald S. (1998). Spreading fear: The genesis of transnational ethnic conflict. In Lake, David A., and Rothchild, Donald S. (Eds.), *The International Spread of Ethnic Conflict: Fear Diffusion, and Escalation,* Princeton, NJ: Princeton University Press, pp. 3–32.

Le Bon, Gustave (1896). *The Crowd. A Study of the Popular Mind.* London: Ernest Benn (Republished: Mineola, NY: Dover, 2001).

Leiby, Richard (December 31, 1999). The enemy is us. Why do we hate? For the same reason we love. Because we are human: Born to hate. Born to kill. *Washington Post,* MO9.

Lerner, Melvin J. (1980). *The Belief in a Just World: A Fundamental Delusion.* New York: Plenum.

Levi, Ken (Ed.). (1982). *Violence and Religious Commitment: Implications of Jim Jones's People's Temple Movement.* University Park: Pennsylvania State University Press.

Lewis, Bernard (2002). *The Assassins: A Radical Sect in Islam.* New York: Basic Books. (Originally published in 1968 in London by Weidenfeld and Nicolson.)

——— (2002). *What Went Wrong?: The Clash Between Islam and Modernity in the Middle East.* New York: Perennial [HarperCollins].

——— (2003). *The Crisis of Islam: Holy War and Unholy Terror.* New York: Modern Library.

Lewis, Sinclair (1935). *It Can't Happen Here: A Novel.* Garden City, New York: The Sun Dial Press.

Lifton, Robert Jay (1979). *The Broken Connection: On Death and the Continuity of Life.* New York: Simon & Schuster.

Lifton, Robert Jay, and Markusen, Eric (1990). *The Genocidal Mentality: Nazi Holocaust and Nuclear Threat.* New York: Basic Books.

Linz, Juan J. (2000). *Totalitarian and Authoritarian Regimes.* Boulder, CO: Lynne Rienner Publishers.

Louis, Winnifred R., and Taylor, Donald M. (2002). Understanding the September 11 terrorist attack on America: The role of intergroup theories of normative influence. *Analyses of Social Issues and Public Policy, 2*(1), 87–100.

Mamdani, Mahmood (2004). *Good Muslim, Bad Muslim: America, the Cold War, and the Roots of Terror.* New York: Pantheon.

Mandel, David R. (2002). Evil and the instigation of collective violence. *Analyses of Social Issues and Public Policy, 2*(1), 101–108.

Manji, Irshad (2004). *The Trouble with Islam: A Muslim's Call for Reform in her Faith.* New York: St. Martin's Press.

Marais, Hamar (October 12, 2003). Palestinian Authority music video promising "Maidens of Paradise" to *shahids*—2 days before suicide bombing. Palestinian Media Watch. Retrieved from www.pmw.org.il.

Margalit, Avishai (January 16, 2003). The suicide bombers. *New York Review of Books*, *50*(1).

Margalit, Gilad (November 18, 2004). A good uncle to bad nephews Hitler. A review of the film, "Downfall" by Bernd Eichinger. *Haaretz*, Heh 4.

Markusen, Eric, and Kopf, David (1995). *The Holocaust and Strategic Bombing: Genocide and Total War in the Twentieth Century*. Boulder, CO: Westview Press.

McDermott, Terry (2005). *Perfect Soldiers: The Hijackers: Who They Were, Why They Did It*. New York: HarperCollins.

Menninger, Karl A. (1938). *Man Against Himself*. New York: Harcourt, Brace & World.

Merton, Thomas (1962). Chant to be used in processions around a site with furnaces. In McDonnell, Thomas P. (Ed.), *A Thomas Merton Reader*. New York: Harcourt, Brace & World, pp. 404–406. (Reprinted from *The Catholic Worker*—date of original publication not given.)

Merton, Thomas N. (1967). A devout meditation in memory of Adolf Eichmann. Reprinted in *Reflections* (Merck, Sharp and Dohme), *2*(3), 21–23.

Milgram, Stanley (1965). Some conditions of obedience and disobedience to authority. *Human Relations*, *18*, 57–76.

———— (1965). *Obedience* (A Film). University Park, PA: Penn State Audio-Visual Services [distributor].

———— (1974). *Obedience to Authority: An Experimental View*. New York: Harper & Row.

Mirvish, Adrian (2001). Suicide bombers, authoritarian minds, and the denial of others. *Judaism*, *50*(4), Issue 200, 387–397.

Moghaddam, Fathali M., and Marsella, Anthony J. (Eds.) (2004). *Understanding Terrorism: Psychosocial Roots, Consequences and Interventions*. Washington, DC: American Psychological Association.

Nathan, Peter (1943). *The Psychology of Fascism*. London: Faber & Faber.

Oliver, Anne Marie, and Steinberg, Paul F. (2005). *The Road to Martyrs' Square: A Journey into the World of the Suicide Bomber*. New York: Oxford University Press.

Pape, Robert A. (2005). *Dying to Win*: *The Strategic Logic of Suicide Terrorism*. New York: Random House.

Peters, Rudolph (1996). *Jihad in Classical and Modern Islam: A Reader*. Princeton, NJ: Markus.

Pilisuk, Marc, and Ober, Lyn (1976). Torture and genocide as public health problems. *American Journal of Orthopsychiatry*, *46*(3), 388–392.

Pilisuk, Marc, and Wong, Angela (2002). State terrorism: When the perpetrator is a government. In Stout, Chris E. (Ed.), *The Psychology of Terrorism, Vol. II: Clinical Aspects and Responses*. Series: *Psychological Dimensions to War and Peace*. Westport, CT: Praeger, pp. 105–132.

Post, Jerrold M. (Ed.) (2003). *The Psychological Assessment of Political Leaders: With Profiles of Saddam Hussein and Bill Clinton*. Ann Arbor: University of Michigan Press.

Post, Jerrold M., Sprinzak, Ehud, and Denny, Laurita M. (2003). The terrorists in their own words: Interviews with 35 incarcerated Middle Eastern terrorists. *Terrorism and Political Violence*, *15*(1), 171–184.

Power, Samantha (2002). *"A Problem from Hell" : America and the Age of Genocide*. New York: Basic Books.

Pyszczynski, Tom, Solomon, Sheldon, and Greenberg, Jeff (2003). *In the Wake of 9/11: The Psychology of Terror*. Washington, DC: American Psychological Association.

Resnik, H.L.P. (Ed.) (1968). *Suicidal Behaviors: Diagnosis and Management*. Boston: Little Brown & Co.

Reuter, Christoph (2004). *My Life Is a Weapon: A Modern History of Suicide Bombing*. Princeton, NJ: Princeton University Press. Translated from the German by Helena Ragg-Kirkby.

Robins, Nicholas A. (2002). *Genocide and Millenialism in Upper Peru: The Great Rebellion of 1780–1782*. Westport, CT: Praeger.

Robins, Robert S., and Post, Jerrold M. (1997). *Political Paranoia: The Psychopolitics of Hatred*. New Haven, CT: Yale University Press.

Rosenbaum, Alan S. (Ed.) (1996). *Is the Holocaust Unique? Perspectives on Comparative Genocide*. Boulder, CO: Westview Press.

Rosenthal, A.M. (1999), *Thirty-Eight Witnesses: The Kitty Genovese Case*. Berkeley, CA: University of California Press. (Originally published in New York in 1964 by McGraw Hill.)

Ruby, Charles L. (2002). Are terrorists mentally deranged? *Analyses of Social Issues and Public Policy, 2*(1), 15–26.

Rummel, R.J. (1997). *Power Kills: Democracy as a Method of Nonviolence*. New Brunswick, NJ: Transaction Publishers.

——— (1999). China, Genocide in. *The Chinese Community Anthill*. In *Encyclopedia of Genocide*. Santa Barbara, CA: ABC-CLIO Publishers, pp. 149–151.

——— (1999). Khmer Rouge and Cambodia. In *Encyclopedia of Genocide*. Santa Barbara, CA: ABC-CLIO Publishers, pp. 132–136.

——— (1999). Power kills, absolute power kills absolutely. In *Encyclopedia of Genocide*. Santa Barbara, CA: ABC-CLIO Publishers, pp. 23–34.

——— (1999). The Soviet gulag state. In *Encyclopedia of Genocide*. Santa Barbara, CA: ABC-CLIO Publishers, pp. 520–521.

Sageman, Marc (2004). *Understanding Terror Networks*. Philadelphia: University of Pennsylvania Press.

Schechter, Erik (August 6, 2004). Conversations with my killer: Erik Schechter meets suicide bombers (title on magazine cover); Where have all the bombers gone? (title on the article). *Up Front, Jerusalem Post Magazine*, 11–13.

Schneider, Stanley (2002). Fundamentalism and paranoia in groups and society. *Group, 26*(1), 17–27.

Schneidman, Edwin S. (1996). *The Suicidal Mind*. New York: Oxford University Press.

Schweitzer, Yoram, and Shai, Shaul (2003). *The Globalization of Terror: The Challenge of Al-Qaeda and the Response of the International Community*. New Brunswick, NJ: Transaction Publishers.

Selzer, Michael I. (1983). Compliance or self-fulfillment? The case of Albert Speer. In Rosenbaum, Max (Ed.), *Compliant Behavior: Beyond Obedience to Authority*. New York: Human Sciences Press, pp. 213–228.

Sereny, Gitta (1983). *Into That Darkness: An Examination of Conscience*. New York: Vintage Books.

Shai, Saul (2004). *The Shahids: Islam and Suicide Attacks*. New Brunswick, NJ: Transaction Publishers.

Skitka, Linda J., and Mullen, Elizabeth (2002). The dark side of moral conviction. *Analyses of Social Issues and Public Policy*, 2(1), 35–41.

Society for the Psychological Study of Social Issues (2003). *Terrorism and Its Consequences*. Special Feature (major section of issue). *Analyses of Social Issues and Public Policy*, 2(1), 1–150.

Somerville, John, and Shibata, Shingo (1982). Ecocide and omnicide, the new faces of genocide. Presented at the *International Conference on the Holocaust and Genocide*. See Charny, Israel W., and Davidson, Shamai (Eds.) (1983). *The Book of the International Conference on the Holocaust and Genocide: Book One, The Conference Program and Crisis*. Tel Aviv: Institute on the International Conference on the Holocaust and Genocide, p. 43, also pp. 27, 46, and 244.

Spencer, D. John (2002). The "suicide" bomber: Is it a psychiatric phenomenon? [Correspondence]. *Psychiatric Bulletin*, 26(11), 436.

Staub, Ervin (1989). *The Roots of Evil: The Origins of Genocide and Other Group Violence*. Cambridge: Cambridge University Press.

Stein, Ruth (2003). Evil as love and as liberation: The mind of a suicidal religious terrorist. In Moss, Donald (Ed.), *Hating in the First Person Plural: Psychoanalytic Essays on Racism, Homophobia, Misogyny, and Terror*. New York: Other Press, pp. 281–310.

Stern, Jessica (1999). *The Ultimate Terrorists*. Cambridge, MA: Harvard University Press.

——— (2003). *Terror in the Name of God: Why Religious Militants Kill*. New York: HarperCollins.

Stout, Chris E. (Ed.) (2002). *The Psychology of Terrorism, Vol. II: Clinical Aspects and Responses*. Series: *Psychological Dimensions to War and Peace*. Westport, CT: Praeger.

Strentz, Thomas (1981). The terrorist organizational profile: A psychological role model. In Alexander, Yonah, and Gleason, John M. (Eds.), *Behavioral and Quantitative Perspectives on Terrorism*. New York: Pergamon, pp. 86–104.

Taylor, Steve (1982). *Durkheim and the Study of Suicide*. New York: St. Martin's Press.

Thompson, Kenneth (1982). *Emile Durkheim*. London: Tavistock Publications.

Totten, Samuel, and Jacobs, Steven Leonard (Eds.) (2002). *Pioneers of Genocide Studies*. New Brunswick, NJ: Transaction Publishers.

Totten, Samuel, Parsons, William S., and Charny, Israel W. (Eds.) (1997). *Century of Genocide: Eyewitness Accounts and Critical Views*. New York: Garland Publishing. (Originally published in 1995 by Garland Publishing under the title *Genocide in the Twentieth Century. Critical Essays and Eyewitness Accounts*)

Tucker, Robert C. (1965). The dictator and totalitarianism. *World Politics*, 17, 555–583.

Victor, Barbara (2003). *Army of Roses: Inside the World of Palestinian Women Suicide Bombers*. Emmaus, PA: Rodale.

Waller, James (2002). *Becoming Evil: How Ordinary People Commit Genocide and Mass Killing*. New York: Oxford University Press.

Walt, Stephen M. (1997). Building up new bogeyman. *Foreign Policy*, 106, 177–189.

Walzer, Michael (1977). *Wars: Just and Unjust. A Moral Argument with Historical Illustrations*. New York: Basic Books.

Weinberg, Leonard, Pedahzur, Ami, and Canetti-Nisim, Daphna (2003). The social and religious characteristics of suicide bombers and their victims. *Terrorism and Political Violence*, 15(3), 139–153.

Wiesenthal, Simon (1967). *The Murderers among Us: The Simon Wiesenthal Memoirs*, Wechsberg, Joseph (Ed.). New York: McGraw-Hill.

Simon Wiesenthal Center (2005). *Digital Terrorism and Hate 2005 CD-ROM*. Product Code AL20. Los Angeles: Simon Wiesenthal Center.

Zimbardo, Philip G. (1973). On the ethics of intervention in human psychological research: With special reference to the Stanford Prison Experiment. *Cognition*, 2, 243–256.

——— (1989). *Quiet Rage. The Stanford Prison Experiment Video*. Stanford, CA: Stanford University.

Zimbardo, Philip G., and Funt, Allen (1992). *Candid Camera Classics in Social Psychology: Viewer's Guide and Instructor's Manual*. New York: McGraw-Hill.

Zimbardo, Philip G., Haney, Craig, Banks, W. Curtis, and Jaffe, David (1974). The psychology of imprisonment: Privation, power, and pathology. In Rubin, Zick (Ed.), *Doing Unto Others: Joining, Molding, Conforming, Helping, Loving*. Englewood Cliffs, NJ: Prentice-Hall, pp. 61–73.

Zimbardo, Philip G.; Haney, Craig; Banks, W. Curtis; and Jaffe, David——— (April 8, 1973). The mind is a formidable jailer: A Pirandellian prison. *New York Times Magazine*.

Zimbardo, Philip G.; Haney, Craig; Banks, W. Curtis; and Jaffe, David (1975). The psychology of imprisonment, privation, power and pathology. In Rosenhan, David, and London, Perry (Eds.), *Theory and Research in Abnormal Psychology*, 2nd ed..New York: Holt, Rinehart & Winston, pp. 270–287.

Zimbardo, Philip G., Maslach, Christina, and Haney, Craig (2000). Reflections on the Stanford Prison Experiment: Genesis, transformations, consequences. In Blass, Thomas (Ed.), *Obedience to Authority: Current Perspectives on the Milgram Paradigm*, Mahwah, NJ: Erlbaum, pp. 193–237.

Index

About the Author

I. W. CHARNY is a renowned psychologist, and the editor of the *Encyclopedia of Genocide*. He is the executive director of the Institute on the Holocaust and Genocide in Jerusalem, and professor of psychology and family therapy at Hebrew University in Jerusalem. Charny is a past president of the International Family Therapy Association and the current president of the International Association of Genocide Scholars.